The Oneironauts

Using dreams to engineer our future

Paul Kalas

NEW TERRA PRESS

Copyright © 2018 by Paul Kalas

ALL RIGHTS RESERVED

For information about permission to reproduce selections from this book, write to
metamindnet@gmail.com

Visit the book's website at
www.oneironauts.org

COVER DESIGN BY ASPASIA GKIKA

All figure and image credits: Paul Kalas

Without limiting the rights under copyright reserved above, no part of this publication may be reproduced, stored in or introduced into a retrieval system or transmitted, in any form, or by any means (electronic, mechanical, photocopying, recording, or otherwise), without the prior written permission of both the copyright owner and publisher.

The scanning, uploading, and distribution of this book via the Internet or via any other means without the permission of the publisher is illegal. Please purchase only authorized editions and do not participate in or encourage electronic piracy of copyrightable materials. Your support of the author's rights is appreciated.

While the author has made every effort to provide accurate attributions and Internet addresses at the time of publication, neither the publisher nor the author assumes any responsibility for errors, or for changes that occur after publication. Further, publisher does not have any control over and does not assume any responsibility for author or third-party Web sites or their content.

ISBN 978-1-732-4631-3-4 pbk.

New Terra Press
Berkeley, CA 94720
USA

*For my father, who always seemed to know

how to connect the dots.*

CONTENTS

Preface: The Socratic Gamble i

1. Twin Towers Falling **1**

2. Destiny, Hope and the Trifid Nebula **5**
   Trifid Poster Falling 5
   The Paradox of Many Universes and Precognition 16
   The Janus in Us 20

3. The Heidelberg Dome **27**
   The Irrational Path to a Bargain Universe 28
   Expanding the Physical Basis of Instinct and Intuition 34
   Predetermined Destiny vs. Hyperactive Free Will 40

4. Fomalhaut **43**
   Fomal.... what? 45
   Road to Discovery 48
   Dreaming the Discovery 54
   House of Cards? 57
   Is it Jesus Toast? 62
   Fomalhaut vs. the Twin Towers 63
   Is it Science? 65
   The Janusian Mind: Two Times Meeting in One Brain 70
   Fate Revisited—The Question of Self 79
   Experiencing Many Worlds 87
   Pseudodivine Knowledge—What's at Stake? 89

5. Dissect the Oneironaut! **97**
   The Medical Interview 97
   Release the Oneironaut 100
   Dissect the Déjà Vu 101
   Summary 149

6. The Physics of Time Using Nature's Swiss Army Knife **151**
   The Big Knife: Speed of Light 153

The Magnifying Glass: Warps in Spacetime 157
  The Screwdriver and the Corkscrew: Particle and Wave 163
  The Swiss Cross: Entanglement 173
  The Little Scissors: Light Influences Biology 176

7. Hippocampus **179**
  The Gatekeeper 182
  Spacetime in the Mind 186
  The Gatekeeper's Tango 203
  Janus, the Glitch 210
  Ratman's Angels 212

8. The Oneironauts **215**
  The Dreamnet 216
  The Oneironauts of Today 225
  IAPO—The Oneironauts of Tomorrow 229
  The Local Oneironauts 230
  Research, Education and Funding for the Oneironauts 237
  The Global Oneironauts 247
  The Machine Oneironauts 263
  Law and Ethics: The LEO Branch 270
  Synthetic God 281
  What Dreams May Come 284

Appendix I: Characters in The Oneironauts 287

Appendix II: Glossary 293

Appendix III: Captions for Chapter Heading Images 307

Appendix IV: Videos 315
  "How luggage is lost" 315

About the Author 325

NOTES 327

INDEX 345

Preface: The Socratic Gamble

The Greek philosopher Socrates famously said: "ὁ δὲ ἀνεξέταστος βίος οὐ βιωτὸς ἀνθρώπω," which is ancient Greek for: "An unexamined life is not worth living." He was promptly executed.

I hope that doesn't happen to me, because I am about to examine the part of my life where I dream about future experiences, and this topic could get me fired from my day job, which is being a scientist. Actually, it's also a night job because I am an astronomer. My job is to look at objects in the universe, record their observable properties and further humanity's knowledge using the scientific method. This method is a remarkable set of procedures and standards that guide my day-plus-night job. What a scientist says is believed not only because the scientific method is sound, but also because scientists build up their scientific reputation through the course of their education, training and subsequent professional leadership. Writing about a fringe phenomenon falls squarely in the category of ventures that can mar a scientist's credentials—permanently.

But I can't help thinking that a hallmark of being a scientist is to be curious about things currently unknown or unmeasured. The hallmark of becoming a groundbreaking scientist is a tolerance for taking risks. These risks mean that if the efforts of a scientist are successful, then a new scientific discipline is born. But if the efforts are unsuccessful, that same scientist loses everything.

In Chapter 4, I will describe my major discovery in astrophysics, and you will see that my story is punctuated by persistence on a risky project. I have a high tolerance for risks; I will jump off the scientific cliff without knowing how high it is, barely able to tell if the decision is well calculated or foolhardy. Thus, I am going to claim that my discovery in astrophysics is *also* an important observation of how the mind works in relation to time and space. I am gambling that the facts I describe and the interpretations that I have are compelling enough to open up a new cottage industry in science. At the same time, this initial foray must be met with skepticism if it is to be distilled into useful, high-impact ideas. I welcome this learning process, but I do not look forward to the inevitable: many readers, including top scientists, will be harshly skeptical before they thoroughly read my story, and then simply focus on the evidence that *confirms* the skepticism they embraced from the start.

Fortunately, there are other core principles driving someone like me to write such a book, other than a strange attraction to re-enact a Socratic execution in the present day.

One vital reason is that the scientific method is based on honest and open communication with the goal of increasing knowledge and helping others. If I have a recorded observation of a phenomenon in nature, no matter how puzzling it may be, I believe in an obligation to communicate it the best I can. Einstein famously echoed these modern principles with the words, "Those who have the privilege to know have the duty to act," where the actions of a scientist are to think, experiment and communicate. Communication is necessary for improving knowledge, something Socrates identified as a virtue. Communication allows others to weigh in on the possible interpretations, or even point out the errors in the experiment. As long as a scientist does not fabricate or falsify what they communicate, the scientific method tolerates the subsequent findings of mistakes or misinterpretations. In principle, this is a more forgiving system than what Socrates faced 2,500 years ago, yet I am well aware that even today there are unkind consequences to expressing thoughts out of the mainstream.

Nevertheless, I am going to take the Socratic gamble, feel the Socratic pain, and give you a book that may not be in my best interests to write.

1. Twin Towers Falling

It all began one bright cold morning. Waking up in my sunlit bedroom, I slipped quickly to the bathroom across the hallway on the top floor of my home. My thoughts were those of pure puzzlement. In my dream just before waking, someone told me that they were injured by jumping from a "haycart to a sixteen-wheeler." "What could that mean?" I thought repeatedly to myself. My ability to answer the question was at that time quite limited—I was a shorter, younger person, an eighth grader in a Michigan middle school.

A few months later, at the beginning of gym class in the spring of 1981, a boy sat next to me during roll call. We were all required to sit in a row along one of the lines imprinted on the lacquered gym floor. His knee was injured with many scabs and scratches. Another kid asked him, "How did you get that?" He answered: "Jumping from a haycart to a sixteen-wheeler." I was instantly startled. My memory of the same unique sentence during that morning dream months ago was crystal clear.

Was this precognition?

Flash forward to a different sunny morning, over a quarter century later. I am sleeping in a different bed. Next to me is my wife, and quite possibly on top of me is the Siamese cat we brought to California from the island of Crete in the Mediterranean Sea. In the intervening 30 years, my life's journey has carried me across our beautiful planet to live in England, Japan, Germany, Hawaii, and even Baltimore, Maryland. But now I am in sunny California, and the phone rings unexpectedly just before 7:00 a.m. My wife picks it up to find one of our best friends is calling from Crete.

"Hi, how are you?" she asks with her eyes half-closed, grasping at the sleep stolen from the morning.

"How am I? How are you? America is being attacked!"

Not knowing what that means, she gets me out of bed, and we turn on the television. We discover images of a sunny day in New York City with fine blue skies—except that the World Trade Center towers are billowing black smoke huge distances downwind. The United States is indeed under attack. A dependable early warning system, family and friends in Europe, rustled up thousands of Californians like us with morning phone calls of the evolving disaster on the East Coast.

I watched the TV, perplexed. Presumably the fires would be put out eventually. Only certain sections of the buildings were on fire and I expected that the fires would eventually get smaller, not larger, as many hundreds of firefighters came to bear on the problem. Suddenly, one of the towers collapsed downward into an immense cloud of dusty debris, soon followed by the collapse of the second tower. Why did this happen? How many lives were lost?

This visual experience was perplexing and surprising, but *never* figured in one of the many precognitive dreams that I had over the years from middle school onward.

So what's up with my supposed precognitive dreams? And what about your precognitive dreams, if you've ever had them? One modern survey found that a whopping 95% of college students had at least one déjà rêvé experience, or "previously dreamed" experience like my "Haycart" dream.[1] A more commonly known term is *déjà vu*, which means, "previously seen." I'll be using the term déjà vu throughout this book, though all of the experiences I describe are "previously dreamed."

Certainly the World Trade Center events were as startling as hearing someone in eighth grade say "jumping from a haycart to a sixteen-wheeler." Where was my supposed precognition when it could have had considerable value? In the survey mentioned above, 74% of 442 respondents reported dreaming at least two future experiences in their lives, *per year*. Applying this to a population of approximately 1.4 million people in New York City that shares the 20–29 year-old age demographic represented in the survey, we find that one million New Yorkers had at least two dreams of events that they would personally witness in 2001.

Is the apparent absence of déjà vu for the events of September 11, 2001, a clear refutation of precognitive phenomena? *Is precognition an illusion of the mind?*

The test for precognition is surely becoming more and more stringent in today's society. You can boil down precognition to a grand exercise of recording information and comparing it to future events. If someone out there is able to see future events, it takes two minutes to post their thoughts on a blog or something like Facebook. Whatever they write is date-stamped, stored for a very long time, and accessible through sophisticated search algorithms such as those developed by Google. Precognition should therefore trend in one direction: either toward increasing skepticism or increasing validation. Which is it?

My story is going to advocate for increasing validation. However, I may as well tell you now that I do not know much about psychic phenomena, or religion, philosophy, mythology, witchcraft, spirituality, sorcery, black magic or angels.[2] Instead, my narrative will embrace ideas from astronomy, physics, psychology, biology, ethology, neuroscience and a portion of a professional astronomer's autobiography.

I am a type of astronomer called an observational astronomer. Spurred by curiosity about the universe, I formulate scientific questions and I consider the capabilities of telescopes to see if they are suitable tools to answer my questions. If so, I use these telescopes to observe our universe. Often what I actually find is not what I expected at all. At this point I take a deep breath and calmly ask, "What did I see, and what does it mean?"

Confronting the puzzling aspects of my precognitive experiences, I also keep asking myself: "Is the absence of precognition for the September 11 tragedy telling me that my apparent precognition is truly an illusion of the mind? Or, is it a real phenomenon, but its absence in this particular case gives me fundamental information about the qualities of the phenomenon?"

I should now add a bit more information about my scientific thought process. The answers to "What did I see and what does it mean?" are never crystal clear, even for the most rigorous of scientific experiments. Ironically, a successful discovery or scientific insight actually causes more questions to be asked, and they may be different from the questions asked at the beginning of the experiment. So the next question is, "What do I do next?"

I am writing this book to tell you about precognition:

(a) what I saw,
(b) what I think it means, and
(c) what I would do next.

In these pages you will witness the design of a scientific experiment. It's really a draft design, since the only way to make it an interesting and useful experiment is to add in the ideas of many others after they read what I have to say.

Unfortunately, the words "scientific experiment" may have conjured some light yawns among my audience. The reader's eyes may be glazing over at memories of high school chemistry class. Is reading this book going to be about as humdrum as memorizing the periodic table of elements?

So please allow me to rephrase my introduction: *An extraordinary story about time travel will unfold in this book.* I will define the *oneironauts* (oh-NEAR-oh-nauts)—the humans who have memories of dreams (*oneira* in Greek) that are future experiences. I am one of the oneironauts.

With this book I hope to share with you my *current* understanding of the *oneironaut phenomenon.* I will consider how this could be an illusion of the mind, but I will also consider the opposite possibility: it's precognition. You will see the scope and depth of my evidence, and you can make your own judgment on which explanation is valid for my story, and possibly your own. My story will deliver an unprecedented revelation: *One of the most important discoveries made with the Hubble Space Telescope was previously dreamed nine years earlier.*

The stakes are high if this book convinces you that the oneironaut phenomenon is real. If you sleep eight hours a night with two hours of dreaming, where 0.1% of dreaming represents experiences of the future, this means that every 24 hours you experience 7.2 seconds of a future time. Over your lifetime, you will have experienced over 50 hours living in the future.

The consequences could extend far beyond individual experiences. I will explain how the oneironauts may have a role in future societies because of incredible progress in physics, biotechnology and information processing. I will share with you why the terrible, highly visible events such as the attack on the World Trade Center were not seen by the oneironauts, but could be detectable in the future. This means that there is a future world where the most unexpected events in your personal life and in human history will be predictable and therefore changeable.

2. Destiny, Hope and the Trifid Nebula

Let's just get to the high-stakes question right away: If you could see the future, could you change it? Or, is there a law of the universe that forbids meddling with destiny? In ancient Greek plays written by Aeschylus and Sophocles, a guy called Mr. Oedipus got some fairly precise information about an unpleasant future ahead, he took it very seriously, but his fate remained tragically unchanged. If changing the future is forbidden, then do you, Mr. Oedipus, or I have free will? Should we hope for a future that we can control, or are we merely observers of a life predestined? It turns out that everything I currently know about the big questions in life concerning destiny and hope started with the Trifid Nebula.

Trifid Poster Falling

IN CASE THERE ARE QUESTIONS about my mental condition, let me assure the reader that I have not been to the Trifid Nebula, nor have aliens from there visited me. The Trifid Nebula is simply something you can look at with a telescope if you point it toward the constellation Sagittarius. It is incredibly photogenic, with hundreds of stars veiled by luminescent clouds of red and blue, where one of the clouds seems divided into three-ish parts, and hence the name. In 1981–1982, when I was 14 years old, I had a dream about a poster of the Trifid Nebula that goes something like this:

> I'm in a room with a lot of people who are sitting at tables. Above the tables on the wall to the right there are some posters of the Trifid Nebula and other astronomical wonders, but the top edges have fallen down. I try to tape one of the posters back up, and then I see that it is ripped near one corner. To my surprise, the four guys sitting around the table next to the wall accuse me of ripping the poster, teasing me, but I know they know I didn't do it.

This isn't a terribly hard dream to analyze. You could convince me that I was problem-solving an anxiety related to my peers in ninth grade. In the dream my mind invents a scenario to test what I would think and feel if I were to do something helpful in the class. This *dreamwork* tells me that I could be the victim of teasing, and I would feel horrible. OK, simple enough—no good deed goes unpunished—and this was a dream that I remembered very well after waking.

A few months after the dream, I was in a new ninth-grade science class. Today I still recall doing some experiments related to the nature of light—the fact that its intensity diminishes as the square of distance. However, on one particular day I had finished my work in class quite early. I was idle in my seat, and looking around the room, I realized that the posters on the wall to the right of me had appeared in my dream. Looking more closely, I saw that the top corner of the Trifid Nebula poster was both peeling downward and ripped. A table surrounded by four boys was right below the poster. I remembered the unpleasant events of my dream at that instant.

The instantaneous recall of past dreams while events are occurring I call *real-time déjà vu*. Such an experience potentially allows you to change your actions so that events occur in a different way than in the dream. Amazingly, among many such real-time déjà vu experiences, the Trifid Nebula event is the only instance so far when a choice was available for avoiding an unpleasant experience. The Haycart dream in Chapter 1, on the other hand, is a typical example of a situation where no choices were available for changing the outcome.

Returning to the real-life classroom, I certainly did not want to be teased for a good deed, so I decided to refrain from fixing the corner of the poster. The decision was based on the explicit memory of the dream. It was not based on anticipating at that moment what could happen if I put up the poster. It was not a feeling of nervousness, nor was it a vague notion of having been there before. It was not a gut instinct, an intuition or a fear. It was simple memory recall of the dream.

So what happened next?

Nothing. I was never teased. I just sat in my seat.

You would think that the moment someone willfully changes the future, something special would happen. Maybe the clouds should part so that rays of sunshine pierce the school from above, while a chorus of orchestral strings fills the air with dramatic movie music. You might think that this must have been a deep spiritual experience, or an affirmation that miracles are possible in this world. At the very least I should have perceived time slowing down, the space around me appearing distorted, dazzling lights interfering with my vision.

But if you had been there, you would have seen a boy doing nothing at a desk in total silence. I had no notion that a miracle had happened, or that the experience was spiritual in any way. I did not feel disoriented, or that I was watching myself from the outside. I perceived time and space to be completely normal. The awesomeness of the event was in the non-event. Lao-Tzu would have approved, silently.

This non-event, the creation of nothing, still qualified as a quiet and plain observation of how our universe works—a possibly very complex architecture expressing itself in a simple phenomenon that humans could experience. It was as if a person is given a split second to look at an iceberg for the first time, just barely comprehending what was visible, and requiring a lifetime of thought to deduce what might lay beneath the surface. The non-event was doubly awesome because in a small way it involved the fates of those four kids too. Wherever they are right now in the world, they were supposed to have a memory of making fun of another kid putting up a poster that was ripped. It never happened.

"Whoa!" you say. "Hold your horses for just one minute, Nostradaomus. Let's take a skeptical look. Is there a paradox here?"

In my dream I observed a situation with a certain progression of events. When the time came for the poster incident to occur, I decided not to do anything, which then begs the question of what happened to that apparent reality when I was ridiculed for taping the poster back on the wall. If it did not happen because I stopped it from happening, then how did I dream about it in the first place? What was the nature of what I experienced in the dream?

Below, I will take a look at three different explanations, starting from the most skeptical.

#1. It was *all* an illusion

Taken out of context, the best explanation is that several factors conspired to give me the illusion of foretelling the future. In general, illusions can arise from a mixture of physical and cognitive elements. Physical elements could include epileptic seizures (i.e., neurons in the brain misfiring), pharmacology (taking drugs), lack of oxygen (near passing out), or some other episodic physical effect. In Chapter 5, I will consider more closely the effects of epilepsy, but for now let me just state that I have no history of epilepsy, taking drugs, passing out or other related medical problems. A more likely source of illusion for myself and for most people is a cognitive blunder related to flawed memories, perceptions and thoughts.

For example, the great American physicist Richard Feynman encountered an amazing event during his life. During World War II he was working on creating the first nuclear bomb at a secret facility in Los Alamos, New Mexico. His wife, Arline, lived nearby in Albuquerque, but was seriously ill with tuberculosis. When she died, the death certificate recorded the time as 9:22, and the young Feynman discovered that a clock he had given Arline also stopped at 9:22. The clock was right near her bed. He remarks that this indeed has the illusion of a supernatural phenomenon, yet a little more thought reveals the cognitive blunder.

In the past, the clock often stopped and had to be fixed—this wasn't a very rugged clock. The nurse, to record the time of death, may have picked up the clock in order to check the time, and by doing so also broke the clock at that instant.[3] Though there was no proof that this is what happened, an explanation that involves a few normal events is more desirable than an explanation that requires a supernatural agency.

For my Trifid Nebula experience, consider the following hypothesis for a cognitive illusion. Those posters must have been on the wall from the first day of class. Subconsciously, I may have noticed them and the problem that one was both peeling off the wall and ripped along the edge. I would not assign explicitly attention to the problem during class. Instead, the posters, the thought of fixing them, and the concern of being publicly teased would come to my attention in a dream. However, even though I entered the classroom the very next day after the dream, I failed to remember the dream and connect it to the posters on the wall. Instead, I focused my attention on the posters many months later, when I was idle and looking around the room, and that was when I finally recollected the dream. In this scenario, the dream did not foretell the future.

To recap the timeline, I saw the problem with the poster before I had the dream, but I simply was not aware of that fact. The entire episode has the illusion of precognition because I believe the dream was the first time I saw the poster falling and ripped.

The broader version of the phenomenon is called *cryptomnesia* (hidden memory). For example, you might have a brilliant idea that seems original and new, yet your friend will remind you that he or she gave you the idea last year.

I have to admit, the illusion or cryptomnesia scenario could conceivably happen to anyone, and we should all be on our guard. On the other hand, this hypothesis is based on one assumption that is also very hypothetical. I am basically assuming that the poster could have been peeling off the wall before I had the dream, but it is equally likely that the poster started peeling off the wall after I had the dream. There are no data to inform us either way.

More importantly, notice that I qualified the beginning of this section with the phrase, "taken out of context." That is to say, I might strongly favor the illusion scenario if this were the *only* dream I've ever had involving apparent precognition. Instead, the Trifid Nebula dream belongs to a class of experiences that includes, for example, the Haycart dream, where the illusion hypothesis does not stand.

In the Haycart dream, there were no pre-existing conditions to enter my subconscious before having the dream. My classmate hurt himself and spoke those puzzling words *after* the dream occurred. And even though anyone can imagine and dream about a classmate being hurt, the words spoken were simply too unique to be guessed or anticipated.

Just to be sure, I Googled "jumping from a haycart to a sixteen-wheeler" and I found nothing like it. In my opinion, the chances of dreaming a unique phrase like this from some subconscious reservoir of bizarre thoughts, and then subsequently experiencing an illusion of precognition, are similar to the chances of correctly guessing a high-quality computer password composed of lower- and upper-case letters, plus numbers and symbols.

The only other possibility is that in 1981 the other boy and I heard this odd phrase from a common source, yet this phrase does not exist in the record currently digitized by Google. Perhaps it was a teacher we had in common, or something on TV or the radio. In fact, one purpose of publishing this book is to reach a wider audience who may know of such a source. However, I have yet to find such a source and strongly believe that the boy's words originated from his creative mind.

Therefore, the context of the Trifid Nebula poster is that it belongs to a class of dreams and déjà vu experiences that have been occurring for a lifetime, and many of these dreams have unique imprints, like passwords. The skeptical hypothesis of a cognitive blunder does not receive any additional validation when the sum total of experiences is taken into account.

#2. It was precognitive, but power over fate was an illusion

Suppose that a dream can be a mixture of a future reality stimulus and present-day thought and imagination. Therefore, my dream begins with the sight of a poster falling off the wall sometime in the future. This part is precognitive, like the unique words spoken in the Haycart dream. However, in my dreaming brain, while I am lying there in bed, I continue my dream by imagining the consequences of fixing the poster in front of other people. Though the dream appears to be a continuous sequence of events, only the first part is a real future experience. The second part is how my mind in the present time reacts to that future experience. When all is said and done, I reach the conclusion that I changed my fate just because I believe that an imagined part of my dream was supposed to happen in the future.

This scenario is based on the well-known phenomenon that external stimuli can be perceived while you are asleep, which then actively influence your dream content. Salvador Dali's 1944 oil-on-wood painting *Dream Caused by the Flight of a Bee Around a Pomegranate a Second Before Awakening* presents a complex dream scene involving an elephant with flamingo legs, and a tiger jumping out of another tiger jumping out of a fish jumping out of a pomegranate. The external stimulus to the person sleeping is the sound of a bee, and everything else is manufactured by the mind. Scientific inquiry into this phenomenon began more than seventy years before Dali's painting. The Marquis d'Hervey de Saint Denys in the late 19th century conducted an experiment in which he placed lavender under a sleeping person's nose, then woke them up and found that their dreams included being in a field of lavender while on vacation.[4]

Therefore, in the case of the Trifid Nebula poster, one could postulate that the *only* future stimulus perceived in my sleeping brain was a vision of the peeling poster and its ripped edge. The rest of the story, being made fun of by the kids at the table, is manufactured by my imagination while dreaming.

I am fascinated as I think through this because it illustrates *The Great Ambiguity* that exists in reality and our perception of it. What we know about the world and ourselves is *always* a mixture of external stimulus and thought, whether you are dreaming or awake. You may think you saw something that you take as reality, but as many studies have shown, what you think was real is partially manufactured in your brain. These problems of perception and memory recall are a very real challenge with high stakes in our judicial system, which relies on witnesses reconstructing past events.

Though I cannot entirely exclude The Great Ambiguity with respect to the Trifid Nebula dream, I can weigh in with a reasonable opinion based on two arguments. First, I believe that being teased after taping up a poster is so entirely unexpected, I don't think that I could have imagined it. There are many cases where reality is stranger than fiction, and the progression of events in this déjà vu experience seems to me as a reality that is stranger than I would be able to imagine at the time. To be ridiculed for fixing the poster, given the environment and conditions, would really have "come out of the blue," as the saying goes. This is what made the dream so memorable in the first place.

Let me tell you a story to clarify what I mean. I recall hearing a local news report of a Good Samaritan in San Francisco who raced into a burning building to save someone's pet. Later, as he was sitting outside, relatively uninjured, the San Francisco Fire Department came over to see if he would like to breathe in some oxygen. He agreed.

Now, pretend that this is your dream of something that happens to you in the future. You risked your life to save someone's pet from a fire and the firemen are giving you oxygen. What would you imagine happens next in your dream? Think about it. Wouldn't you be recognized as a hero and perhaps collect a handsome reward that allows you to buy the car you always wanted? Or maybe this turns into a nightmare where the breathing mask doesn't work, and you start suffocating anyway? There are many possibilities given the context of the story involving heroism.

But what *actually* happened after the Good Samaritan took the oxygen mask? The San Francisco Fire Department billed him approximately $350 to cover their services to him. Well, he sure didn't see that one coming! San Francisco is one of the most expensive cities in the world, but who knew they charge premiums for oxygen too? In the shoes of the Good Samaritan, I certainly wouldn't have thought to worry about it. I wouldn't have imagined it, and I don't think that if I had a precognitive dream of the first part of the story, it would have ended that way. The bill for $350 just comes too far "out of the blue."

The insight is that the Good Samaritan had a new learning experience, and so did I when I heard the story. It seems like a strange new fact of life that if I were to interact in any way with emergency medical response, they could bill me too. Further research shows that having an ambulance transport me to a hospital may cost around $2,000, and it may not be covered by my medical insurance. Since I have never been in an ambulance as a patient, I would have to hear this story about the Good Samaritan to learn these facts.

So too, being teased for ripping a poster that I did not rip seems to me equally out of the blue given the circumstances that surrounded me all those years ago in that ninth-grade science class. I don't recall being bullied as a kid, and I simply would not grasp that good deeds risk punishment. This social phenomenon, the *tall poppy syndrome*, is very counterintuitive to me, even now. A planet where lobsters evolve to play classical guitar seems more likely to me than a planet where humans evolve to dislike their best citizens, but the latter is our absurd reality. The very first lesson on this topic was delivered to me in the form of the Trifid Nebula dream. I found a way to avoid this particular reality, but nevertheless it represents new knowledge gained through experience.

Therefore, my opinion based on this first argument is that the entire Trifid Nebula dream was precognition, but in a rare moment of realization I changed my fate that day in school. It's as if the Good Samaritan, while sitting down in a moment of quiet, recognizes events as experiences from a dream. He also remembers taking the oxygen from a fireman, but in the dream it cost him a lot of money and he felt severely disappointed. So when the fireman in real life approaches to offer him oxygen, he declines and never receives the $350 oxygen bill. The non-event saves him $350.

My second argument invokes the "context" of the Trifid Nebula dream, just as I argued in the previous section. The context is that I have had other déjà vu experiences where dream recall happens immediately as events are unfolding in real life. Whenever real-time déjà vu is happening, I see no obvious obstacle to my changing the course of events, if a decision could be made. For example, the Haycart dream was real-time déjà vu, but there was no decision point in the dream or the events surrounding the beginning of gym class. Nevertheless, I feel that if, once I heard the Haycart phrase from the boy, something else were to happen afterward, the dream content would have allowed me to change the course of these events.

Let me illustrate this with a more recent example. In 2009 I was traveling a lot due to a scientific discovery I had made the previous year. As a result, I would end up receiving access to airport lounges that I didn't even know existed. One of them, at Heathrow Airport, had a secluded section with several half-beds where travelers could rest lying down. One of these beds was available, and much to my delight I found that I could look out the window at a passenger aircraft just 50 meters away (**Figure 2-1**).

I instantly recalled that private space and the scene before me as a memory of a dream. Yet there was no continuing story in the lounge, or in my dream. There was no one else that I would interact with. There was nothing to decide. In fact, you could say the déjà vu dream was quite accurate or "clean" because it lacked imagined events appended to this visual information from the future. Nevertheless, if something had happened during my stay in the lounge, something where a decision could have influenced events, then I strongly believe that I could have acted just as in the Trifid poster story.

Figure 2-1: View out the terminal window as I rest on a bed in a lounge at Heathrow Airport.

This experience in the airport lounge is incredibly interesting because it so clearly illustrates more of The Great Ambiguity: how waking experiences, imagination and dreams are so easily mixed. If I had told a psychiatrist that I had a dream of lying in a comfy bed looking at a passenger jet parked out the window at 50 meters distance, the interpretation would be obvious. No such thing exists. There is no way someone could lie in bed and look at passenger jets 50 meters away. Instead, I am clearly wishing to have a comfortable flight, and I could achieve this if I only had an imaginary bed outside the plane to rest on. Maybe mother can tuck me in for good measure. Or, I have an unconscious fear of flying that I am able to keep in check by denying that I am on the plane and putting myself instead in a safe place.

Well, these psychological interpretations of this particular dream would all be hogwash.[5] I would not know it until it happened, but that lounge actually exists, and I would lie on a real bed and look at a real plane 50 meters away. Reality in the future can potentially be equal to any apparent fiction in our minds. *The Great Ambiguity strikes again.*

To sum up, I do *not* believe that power over fate was an illusion in the Trifid Nebula poster dream. The events in the poster dream were too "out of the blue" to be imagined, and in all other real-time déjà vu experiences I felt that I *could* make decisions that would alter the progression of events.

#3. It was precognitive, and two lifepaths in two universes were experienced

Here is the hypothesis that I favor, and I think it has the potential to be experimentally tested by the oneironauts. My entire dream was pure precognition, without any significant additional dream elements imagined by the mind. The paradox of dreaming about a future event that would not take place is consistent with controversial concepts proposed in physics that suggest our universe continuously splits into many universes, representing all of the possibilities of a new action. The basic idea is that there are an infinite number of universes, or *many worlds*, that contain all possible changes through time. In my case, I have knowledge of a lifepath in a universe where I fixed the poster and was teased. However, since I acted differently, the universe I currently inhabit has a history where I never fixed the poster and was never teased.

So what happened to the Paul who fixed the poster? He's OK, I would think. There is a universe among an infinite number of universes where that Paul exists and has a memory of fixing the poster and being teased. There are four men in that universe who might recall teasing the boy who fixed the poster that day in school. But then a different one of these universes contains the Paul who refrained from carrying out that action, and who is now writing about it in this book. You, the reader, happen to be reading it, but there are other universes where no such book has appeared. In the present waking moment, you and I can only experience one of these universes, but when receiving future information through the oneironaut phenomenon, you may be seeing one of the universes that could exist for you.

The notion that you might experience other universes has a wide range of implications. First and foremost, you earn a full scholarship to the college of the insane. This is because even though the two concepts of infinity and multiple universes are the subjects of scholarly inquiry, the human ability to experience through dreaming more than one of the infinite multiple universes is not. This would imply that dreams in which you have detailed and unique discussions with people you don't know in your reality are actual experiences in some other universe, a timeline where you made different friends and ended up in different places. This is such a leap in interpreting something that would normally be called "imagination," that your scholarship to the college is well earned.

The second major implication of experiencing other universes is that I'm telling you about another universe. If you pause for a moment, you might appreciate that it's not every day such information is available. A different universe exists where I put that poster up and was teased, I have knowledge of these events in the current universe, and that means *communication can occur between the two*. To paint this more starkly, imagine what I see with my eyes is a continuous video recording with a physical existence on a hard drive. What I have now revealed is the existence of a second recording of a world that did not exist, but there is a video of its existence. On one hard drive there is physical information about two different worlds.

Sorry to drag you into this business, but the current situation is that you and I are now experiencing a universe where we know about an event that happened in a different timeline. The event is insignificant in and of itself, but if this book convinces you the oneironaut phenomenon is real, then you are accepting the possibility that an unobservable universe is known to you because I communicated my observation to you.

So now the potential significance of the Trifid poster experience is greatly amplified. I started out saying that I had a precognitive dream. The fact that humans can experience the future through dreams is awesome. But if you can then change the future experience based on this knowledge, a paradox is born because the original dreaming brain could not have had the experience that is later deleted from your universe. I propose that there are in fact a nearly infinite number of possible lifepaths, residing within an infinite number of universes, which can communicate between them.

Proving through empirical observation that a separate parallel universe exists seems out of reach, but I think we had a chance in my ninth-grade classroom. What I needed was one other oneironaut in the room, one of the boys that was to tease me, and he too should have dreamt about teasing me about the rip in the poster. After it did not happen in that reality, we would have compared notes. If he, independently from me, also described a dream where he saw me put up the poster, then we can more or less conclude that there is a different universe where these things happened.

The purpose of this book and the final chapter is to argue that a group of oneironauts can indeed be brought together to conduct this experiment. I think it's possible to test for the existence of many worlds. It may even be possible without using the oneironauts. What we need is an experimental test particle or a simple organism that has a measurable property at the present time based on something that could happen to it in the future. I'll circle around to explain this more thoroughly later.

The Paradox of Many Universes and Precognition

IF ANY POSSIBLE UNIVERSE is allowed at any point of time when a decision needs to be made, how would you possibly be able to have an accurate dream about it now when the number of future scenarios in your life is huge?

To illustrate my concern, let's take a look at a single neuron (i.e., a nerve cell) in your brain. A single neuron is connected to many other neurons, but say there are just five connections, and each connecting neuron has five more. This means that for a single nerve signal to travel a single path from the first neuron to a tenth neuron, there are almost two million possibilities. So let's say before the signal is sent outward, the first neuron has an accurate dream of where the signal will be some time in the future at the tenth neuron. For this to succeed, the first neuron would have to have two million dreams. Or, put another way, if the starting neuron has one dream of where the signal will be in the future, and it turns out to be true, then the odds of that happening is one in 2,000,000.

In the case of people who possibly experience a future universe out of all the possible universes, how likely is it that they would ever have a correct match? If you live for 70 years and on average remember two dreams every night, then you might have a grand total of 51,100 dreams under your belt. If there were truly an infinite number of universes, you would be very lucky indeed if just one of those 51,100 dreams ended up corresponding to something you will experience.

The paradox seems to indicate that the two million possibilities are not equal possibilities. Indeed, one should consider that our hypothetical neuron may have a purpose or goal, and therefore it will send a signal to a smaller selection of pathways instead of two million.

Perhaps a better example for a life path that has free will, purpose and very many decision points is the Rubik's Cube. There are 43 quintillion possible arrangements of the cube, but this doesn't mean that you have a one in 43 quintillion chance of ever arriving at the specified goal of having like-colored cube faces. It doesn't mean you will be randomly trying out all 43 quintillion positions, where by chance you'll get to the solution at some point. No, it takes less than 100 moves to solve a Rubik's cube, because you can make rational decisions along the way to arrive at your goal, if you wish. Your goal is known in advance and your purpose is clear.

The analogy with the Rubik's Cube illustrates that it should be possible to match a limited number of dreams to a limited number of future circumstances. However, the goal of solving the Rubik's Cube is like a self-fulfilling prophecy. If you were to predict that you would solve the Rubik's Cube, then that will come true if you try hard enough. In contrast, the oneironaut phenomenon usually contains random events that are not necessarily in your control, and therefore you cannot have the goal of a self-fulfilling prophecy.

Pretend that you have a childhood dream of perfect bliss sailing a boat. Would you think that the dream is precognitive if 25 years later you were sailing a boat happily? Clearly you can dream about things that you want to happen in the future and act in ways that would realize these dreams. This is a self-fulfilling experience based on the memory of a pleasant dream, but it's not precognitive. In the oneironaut phenomenon, what the end state looks like is mostly out of your control, or largely controlled by other people or nature. There is no way for me to wish and act in a way that would force someone next to me to say "sixteen-wheeler" and "haycart" in the same sentence.

In the next chapter, I will tell you how I used dream information to find a group of people. This resembles a self-fulfilling prophecy, but the crucial distinction is that the dream gave unique pieces of information about how to find them. And in a later chapter you will see that even though my goal is to make major astronomical discoveries, there is specific information in dreams and in actual discoveries that match in a way that is not under my control. I cannot force nature to look like what I dream about.

At this point I have danced around the paradox of many universes and precognition without really solving the paradox. The obvious solution is to propose that fate exists. A limited number of dreams sample tiny bits of this future fate, and somehow a few of these bits can be changed. In my opinion this is unsatisfactory because it requires the existence of a mysterious force or architecture to reality that resembles some mastermind that is purposefully rotating the sides of the Rubik's Cube—i.e., your life. It doesn't seem that an external agent manipulates us in every decision every day. Is this really the only possible explanation for how you would be able to see something about a random future state clearly? Let me give a different explanation below that is equally mysterious, but seems simpler overall.

Are you changing yesterday instead of tomorrow?

Is the Trifid dream an example of changing the future, or changing the past? The former concept is what I have assumed so far and which gave rise to the paradox. But why wasn't the latter phrase given equal consideration? It's probably because one of the most unassailable experiences of humans across time and space is that you cannot change the past. It's done.

But let's bury this assumption for a moment and assume that the reference frames are equivalent. In this chapter I have chosen language such that the present-Paul in his dream state time travels to a future-Paul in his waking state, so that present-Paul can then act and change future events. Why not give equal credence to the model where future-Paul communicates backward in time in order to change an outcome that has just been discovered?

Consider that you are experiencing an unpleasant event, and right afterward you wish you could change this recent past. What would you do? A "time-machine" for the future is useless—the event happened and now it's too late. What you really want is a method to send information—the oneironaut signal or *osignal*—to your past self. So, what you are effectively doing is attempting to modify an experience in the very recent past by sending information further back in time to yourself.

Is there a difference between the two reference frames—the first frame is future-looking, the second frame is past-looking? Yes, it specifies who is acting and this will help define the questions we ask concerning the reasons and the mechanisms underlying the oneironaut phenomenon. For example, I recall a newspaper story from 1988 or so. The Americans and Russians were adversaries then, and the piece reported two of their submarines colliding. The pro-American journalists used the following language: "Russian sub smashes into U.S. sub," whereas the pro-Russian journalists wrote, "U.S. sub rams Russian sub." They are referring to the same event, but the exact description of the event specifies who caused the event to happen.

So, what is more likely, that the present brain is sensing a near infinite number of future universes and by chance will have a dream concerning the lifeline that will occur a few years down the road? Or is it that the waking brain initiates the osignal in order to better inform the past? As long as we're OK with the concept of information traveling through time, the latter explanation makes more sense to me and solves the paradox.

Let's revisit the neuron with five connections that could send a signal to two million other neurons in the future along a single path. When it is looking forward to identify the tenth neuron that will receive the signal, this tenth neuron is embedded in a vast cloud of other candidates for the signal. But if you take one of the two million future neurons that actually receives the signal, it can easily specify the path that the signal already took and uniquely identify that first neuron.

This neuron example is abstract and hypothetical so let's illustrate the point with an example that involves a common decision-making activity. Say there is an experiment where you are browsing the Internet, and every 30 seconds you must click on a new link. Is it easy to predict the final webpage that you will be viewing 60 minutes into the future? You probably won't be clicking links randomly, but based on your interests and/or your goals. Nevertheless, you do not know what choices will become available to you along the way.

Of course, you can see that it's much easier at the 60-minute stage to exactly define the history of your web browsing decisions than to predict the future path of your web browsing decisions before the experiment begins. I don't believe in fate because it means that the seven billion different people on this planet are getting to seven billion final webpages only because a mysterious power is in control—none of the nearly one trillion clicks of the mouse would be real choices.

In summary, the solution to our paradox does not require the existence of a predetermined destiny. Instead, the hypothesis of infinite multiple universes and timelines is still compatible with the oneironaut phenomenon if the direction of information travel is reversed. *Information is sent backward in time.* In middle school, when the fully awake Paul learned through an embarrassing experience that good deeds are punished, he was the person who initiated the signal that would cross time. If true, then we have a major insight.

The oneironaut phenomenon seems to concern dreaming during the sleeping state, but equally important is the study of learning during the waking state. It's as if the biology of learning occurring in the brain has developed a timeless property. The dreaming brain in the sleep state picks up fragments of a future learning process, as if two minds have spontaneously found a fleeting way to collaborate.

The Janus in Us

THIS TOPIC OCCURS TO ME because the memories of that other universe where I fixed the Trifid Nebula poster continue to have a physical existence in my brain. When my brain activity during sleep witnessed a future universe, the synaptic connections between neurons in my brain were modified so that the memory would be stored. A *synapse* is a connection between two neurons, but the relative strength of this connection can be changed. Learning physically changes the brain. By making a decision later not to fix the poster, I am now living in a timeline that never included those events, yet my timeline contains those changed neurons. I have learned something from a universe in which I did not live.

The study of the oneironauts has to contend with this question of multiple universes physically interacting in the brain. It's as if the Roman god Janus could be present in every one of us. Sculptures of the god show one head with two faces looking in opposite directions, but they are joined in the middle. One face is looking to the past and the other is looking to the future. Thus, the first month of the new year is called January, because this is the month when we mortals look back in time and contemplate the year that just finished, and forward in time to the year that is ahead of us. In recent years neuroscientists have discovered that Janus is not merely a mythical god. It turns out that hypothetical thinking about the future activates the same areas of the brain as thinking about the past.[6] We have Janus in us.

The oneironaut phenomenon gives our minds this Janusian property of multiple faces in one person, where different versions of the future and the past are physically connected in the same biological place, and must interact. I have to wonder if there are limits to this interaction, and to what extent we would be able to manipulate it. These questions were brought to an interesting focus by one of my Berkeley colleagues in astronomy, Professor Marc Davis.

Marc is best known for his groundbreaking efforts to understand the architecture of our universe as it evolved from the big bang to the first generations of stars and galaxies. Though his field of study is very different from mine, he has broader interests and I greatly enjoy our conversations together. Moreover, he is one of those rare people like Richard Feynman who has a twinkle in their eye; when talking to him I would always admire this Santa Clausian twinkle phenomenon.

Unfortunately, he suffered a stroke in 2003 and was partially paralyzed on the right side, though the twinkle in his eye is still very healthy.

One evening over dinner in 2012 we started talking about his stroke, and it was a remarkable conversation. His first sentence was quite a sound bite: "I had a stroke because I flossed my teeth." I'm sure that dentists everywhere will strongly protest, but what Marc told me is that when you engage in any type of dental work, bacteria can enter the bloodstream, and there is a risk of infecting the heart, which can slowly create a buildup of plaque. If the plaque dislodges and starts flowing through your circulatory system, it may find its way to the brain, block the blood flow and cause a stroke.[7] So if billions of people floss their teeth today, maybe that was a bad idea for one person. I should at this point tell you that Marc is quite a healthy-appearing, healthy-behaving person. There is no other obvious explanation such as, "Yeah, flossing could be risky, but you eat too much and should have quit smoking." Nope, Marc had a stroke, but was healthy otherwise.

At that point I said, "Well, if you believe in multiple universes, then there is another universe where your left side is paralyzed instead of your right side." Hearing that comment, Marc's eyes went from light twinkling to supernova twinkling. He became very animated and he told me about a dream he had in the hospital after his stroke. In his dream he knew that there were alternate universes and he finds the universe where he is paralyzed on the left side of the body instead of the right. His mind—like a god of its own making—figures that if he can unite these two Marc Davises, then the two good halves would come together to recover a fully functional body. However, to accomplish this, he has to get into the closet in his hospital room. At this point he wakes up, and starts pulling out the various tubes connected to his body. The hospital nurse rushes in and puts him back into the bed, and he thus never makes it to the closet.

In the *classical* interpretation, Marc's dream is a memorable example of how dreams are an imaginative, problem-solving activity, among other things. As an astrophysicist, he summons his vast knowledge to problem-solve his way out of a half-paralyzed body. He is well aware that in physics we have the theoretical concept of many worlds. Ergo, if he could move between these universes, or mix them to his liking, he could find a way to heal himself.

In the *oneironaut* interpretation, Marc observed a future world in his dream where his right side is healthy, just as I experienced the consequences of putting up the ripped Trifid poster. *After* this experience occurs, Marc realizes that it could contain a solution. In other words, he did not imagine or anticipate the alternate universe based on prior knowledge. Instead, he got the idea after witnessing the other universe for himself while dreaming.

In this particular case, I don't think the oneironaut interpretation is better than the classical one because his prior knowledge of physics is adequate. Little comes "out of the blue" or constitutes a learning experience in the way that I have argued for the Trifid poster dream.

Nevertheless, Marc's story could be used to exemplify a more general oneironaut interpretation of health and healing. Since the college of the insane has given me a full scholarship, I really should own up to the consequences of what I think the Trifid dream teaches about reality. I stated that certain neurons in my brain must have changed because they perceived an alternate universe where events occurred differently. Therefore, if the brain were to perceive itself in a future universe where currently unhealthy neurons are healthy, is it possible for those neurons to change more quickly in the direction of a healthy state? Stated differently: If the dysfunctioning brain during periods of dreaming were able to experience the functioning brain, would brain function improve afterward?

It sounds crazy, and of course you might worry that the opposite could occur. I'm lucky to be healthy in this universe, but that darn brain in my other universe is disturbing my health here. Can I hold the door closed when the unhealthy timelines come knocking? How would we control the issue in our favor?

I do not know the answer, but I wonder if nature lets this happen naturally in our favor. Positive feedback is perceived because we seek it, but negative feedback is ignored because we don't want it. Positive feedback is selected by the species, whereas negative feedback is deselected. Over millions of years of natural selection, animal brains naturally take the route of exploiting the positive feedback.

For individual humans, the biological roots of fast healing vs. slow healing, and even optimism vs. pessimism, could originate in a person's agency to focus attention on positive vs. negative future timelines, respectively. The fundamental principle is that the brain changes—for better or for worse—as a consequence of perceiving information. Since the oneironaut phenomenon happens in the brain, information from the future must have an effect.

To illustrate the point, consider a paralysis where most of the brain is fully functioning and certain motor neurons can send signals to move the legs. Let's call these the A neurons. But the synapses have been damaged and the signal does not cross over to the B neurons. The synapses to the next line of neurons, C, D and E, are just fine, but all signals have stopped coming down the line from B, the person cannot walk and ultimately these neurons will weaken their synaptic connections as a result. But for the oneironaut during dreaming, some portion of this web of connections perceives physical activity in different future universes where paralysis has not happened. The C, D and E neurons in their dreaming brain may sense a signal from B as if the A-B connection is working. Therefore, the functional decay or reassignment of these neurons may be halted or slowed. Perhaps this explains why recovery from brain injury has a random, unpredictable side to it. Maybe this is one reason that sleep and dreaming are so important for health in general, but also for recovering from physical trauma. I think my speculation is testable. Experiments could specifically test for correlations between the indicators of brain injury recovery and the quality of sleep and dreaming.

To summarize, the brains of mammals are naturally selected by how well they manipulate information to provide an advantage. My guess is that if it's possible in nature, this includes sending that information to the past. Thus, our brains possess information and its neural correlates from the past, present and possible futures. The most successful mammals will be those that can attend to the information that improves, maintains or repairs their physical fitness.

The illusion of fate and the physical basis of hope

My hypothetical paradigm that new experiences and learning literally have a timeless quality accounts for the sense of fate that is so common across human history. As events unfold and our mammalian brains process sensory information, it may seem that the new things we experience were supposed to happen because we somehow knew that they were going to happen. Our species would try to explain this experience by creating the concept of fate, as in the famous phrase, "Que sera, sera." This is partly an expression of the oneironaut phenomenon, the tenuous memories of precognitive dreams. However, the Trifid poster story taught me, "Que sera, depende." What will be depends on quite a few things that can dictate if it goes into or stays out of your life history. If choices are available, then there is no force that demands a specific outcome. Fate seems to exist, but it's an illusion.

Thus, we can also glimpse the physical basis of hope. The oneironaut phenomenon provides an awareness of events that were supposed to happen, but then you vaguely perceive that the actual events were changed. The concept of hope then gains substance. The perception of *real* future life paths by way of the oneironaut phenomenon makes hope *real*. It is not necessarily a desire, a wish or pure imagination. Thus when

I read that Aristotle defined hope as "a waking dream,"[8] I take the word "dream" to signify the perception of real future timelines.

Hope is expressed in so many ways in human languages, cultures, religions and arts. I'll just pick out a more modern example that resonated with me—a poem by Miklos Radnoti. As a Hungarian of Jewish origin, he found himself close to death in 1944 while being marched across Eastern Europe. He was killed and buried in a mass grave, but later a collection of poems that he wrote while in captivity was found in his coat pocket.

So here is a young man whose life path was altered by the choices of others to wage war and to destroy entire groups of people such as Jews. In the personal histories of countless people during World War II, some would make it out alive, and others would not. Here is an English translation of what Radnoti wrote while he was still alive, marching near death, not knowing if he would be among those who would make it or not:

> Collapsed exhausted, only a fool would rise again
> to drag his knees and ankles once more like marching pain
> yet press on as though wings were to lift him on his way,
> invited by the ditch but in vain, he'd dare not stay...
> Ask him, why not? maintaining his pace, he might reply:
> he longs to meet the wife and a gentler death. That's why.
> But he's insane, that poor man, because above the homes,
> since we have left them, only a scorching whirlwind roams.
> The walls are laid. The plum tree is broken. And the night
> lurks bristling as a frightened, abandoned mongrel might.
> Oh, if I could believe that all things for which I yearn
> exist beyond my heart, that there's still home and return...
> return! the old veranda, the peaceful hum of bees
> attracted by the cooling fresh plum jam in the breeze,
> the still, late summer sunshine, the garden drowsing mute,
> among the leaves the swaying voluptuous naked fruit,
> and Fanni waiting for me, blonde by the russet hedge,
> while languidly the morning re-draws the shadow's edge...
> It may come true again—the moon shines so round—be wise!
> Don't leave me, friend, shout at me, shout! and I will arise![9]

I don't think Radnoti believed in his heart that he would necessarily have to die in this brutal march. The power of this belief gave him strength to lift himself off the ground. It seemed like he was bravely surviving this ordeal. His mind, through dreaming and the oneironaut phenomenon, perceived a future world that was similar to what he remembered, and this world could possibly still be lived in one of his timelines. Like Marc Davis, who hoped that there was a way to reconnect two fully functioning sides of his body, Radnoti hoped to reconnect his life path back to this future world, if he could only affirm this Janusian feeling that it would exist for him. Yet no person is an island, entirely in control of everything around them. Many actors make decisions that change the lives of others, and in 1944 Radnoti was shot to death by his captors.

Hope is the all-important reason to write this book. With the Haycart dream I learned that the future could be detected. With the Trifid Nebula dream I learned that the future could be changed. If I had discovered the first part and proved that the second is impossible, there wouldn't be much point in writing the book. What good is it to demonstrate that a major disaster such as the collapse of the World Trade Center could be foreseen, but nothing could be done about it? Instead, my experience with the Trifid Nebula poster and several more dreams introduced later suggest that through introspective decision making, there is hope to have a future that is the most desirable one.

Paul Kalas

3. The Heidelberg Dome

The Trifid poster dream taught me that I could learn from dreams of future events, and act to avoid an undesirable outcome. Have I subsequently accomplished amazing feats of avoiding imminent danger and winning fortune? No, sadly, this type of learning method, the oneironaut method, is mostly useless in its current form.

I was useless for 9/11 and other undesirable world events. Given two choices in career paths, I would never become explicitly conscious of a dream that would tell me what to do. When I was but a wee student giving my first presentation to a room packed with astronomers, the most famous living astronomer on the planet, Carl Sagan, interrupted my talk, asked me a simple question, and in my panic I could not answer it. Where were my oneironaut skills when I needed them most, when stress and defeat were standing at my doorstep?

I really wish I had an oneironaut story that involved outwitting Carl Sagan, but instead I have to accept that the oneironauts only have stories with quiet victories. In the Trifid poster story, a dream guided my behavior in order to *avoid* a future universe that I did not like. This was a silent and subtle victory in deleting future events from my timeline. But the opposite is also possible. A dream can influence my behaviors so that I can *affirm* future events that otherwise would not materialize in my timeline.

The example I am going to give was not real-time déjà vu like the Trifid poster experience. Instead, I encountered real-life obstacles that interfered with a *desirable* outcome that I recalled from a dream. I then used clues from dream recall to follow a course of action that would lead me to experience what occurred in the dream. You will have to read the details of my story first, and then you can decide if this is a self-fulfilling prophecy or a genuine consequence of the oneironaut phenomenon.

Fortunately, the event did not happen in ninth grade, but in 2013. This means that I can give you more specific and tangible evidence than in the Trifid dream. I will also take my story a step further and conjecture about the nature of instinct and intuition. And like a moth compelled to circle a light, I will revisit the ideas of destiny and free will.

The Irrational Path to a Bargain Universe

THE SETTING is yet another sunny summer day in the majestic university town of Heidelberg, Germany. Heidelberg is an old city in the southwest region of Germany split by the Neckar River. The green hills on either side of the river make the whole place fairly cute, and thus the theme song of the city is: "I lost my heart in Heidelberg (*Ich hab' mein Herz in Heidelberg verloren*)." My first postdoctoral appointment was with the director of the Max Planck Institute for Astronomy in the hills just above the Renaissance-era *Schloss*, or the castle. My wife and I lived in Heidelberg from 1996 to 1998, but then a decade would pass until I was invited in 2009 to speak at the Physikalisches Institut on the street called "Philosophers Path." Heidelberg, you see, is for lovers and for philosophers, possibly both at the same time.

I experienced some interesting déjà vu during my 2009 visit, but the focus of my story here is my third visit in 2013. The scientists of Heidelberg and their collaborators organized a huge conference concerning the formation of stars and planetary systems. These large scientific meetings are excellent opportunities for smaller scientific teams to meet face-to-face. For this particular trip, I planned to have dinner with a science team that specialized in discovering planetary systems in our galaxy using the Herschel Space Observatory. This was a space telescope larger than the Hubble Space Telescope, but Herschel only observed the places in the universe that glowed due to warmth.

As I was preparing for the trip, I recalled a vague dream of having dinner outdoors near the Neckar. I could not recall any faces, but the place seemed to have a wood deck with an open view to the sky. My only existing knowledge of such a place would be an establishment called Hemingway's, which was not exactly on the Neckar, but across the street from the road that goes along the river. I could not know for sure if this trip was going to include the experience that I vaguely recalled. Nevertheless, I reflected on these memories of a dream as I embarked on this third trip to Heidelberg.

Unfortunately, the Herschel team dinner time was set for just 80 minutes after I would be landing at Frankfurt's international airport, which is about a 60-minute drive from Heidelberg. Moreover, no dinner location had been specified in advance. Instead, at 7:30 p.m. the team would meet outside the conference hall, and then go someplace by foot for dinner. To compound my difficulty even further, no one on the team had a cell phone that worked in Germany. So, there was no way for me to join the dinner if I missed the 7:30 meeting. Of course, given that a group of ten or so people had to get together and then start moving, I thought that maybe 7:45 was the latest that I might catch them.

Time was of the essence, decisions had to be made, and I am a cheapskate.

My flight landed on time at 6:10, so I had to decide whether or not to take a taxi at a cost of $230 or take a train at a cost of $30. In one universe I would spend a lot of money and most likely make the dinner that I had dreamt. In a different universe, I would save $200 and greatly reduce the chances of being included in the dinner.

Of course, when in Germany you can rely on the trains to arrive and depart on time. They are globally famous for this. It is a fact of this universe, and this is true across nearly all universes. Unfortunately, I would end up living in that one universe where the train was late by 20 minutes. *Es tut mir leid, meine Leser.* You too live with me in the universe where the German trains are not up to the standards of the other universes. This 20-minute delay meant that I missed a connection in Mannheim on the way to Heidelberg. Thus, the trip to make it on time to dinner using the $30 option was a total disaster.

I arrived into Heidelberg around 8:00 p.m. When I checked my email upon arriving at the hotel, I found no message concerning the dinner location. I then spent a few minutes trying to decide if I really wanted to go in search of the restaurant from my dream. I could even say that fate was dead set against it. The easier course of action was to give up on the dinner, relax, and walk across the street to find a place to eat.

On the other hand, oneironauts can be a stubborn bunch. They do not like to see events such as late trains interfere with something they were looking forward to. We quietly hold as a prize the willful, self-fulfilling prophecy. We are seduced by a belief that we have the ability to make things happen that could not happen. So, quite begrudgingly, I forced myself to put my shoes back on and ventured outside to look for this dinner at some outdoor place with a wood deck on the banks of the Neckar River.

My first stop would be Hemingway's, since this was the only place to eat outdoors near the Neckar River that I remembered from my previous residence in Heidelberg. But my teammates were not there. The outdoor space also looked too small and claustrophobic compared to my dream. The area was cramped with tables and red chairs, a huge tree and a giant blue umbrella covered the space, and the floor consisted of square stone tiles. It wasn't right, so I decided that I had to keep walking along the Neckar (**Figure 3-1**).

This decision would have been completely wrong and irrational if it were not for the dream recall steering my behavior in a rational way. Except for Hemingway's, all the restaurants that I knew about were on the main street that runs through old Heidelberg called the Hauptstrasse. To reach it I should have walked uphill several short blocks away from the river. Instead I stayed the course along the riverbank.

Things weren't looking good as I walked because, as I just explained, there were no restaurants or bars overlooking the Neckar, and, needless to say, there were no wood decks. However, I was confident that I would find this place, almost as if its existence were a fact. In hindsight, I wonder if I should have asked the hotel reception or a pedestrian for a hint. I suppose that I did not want to ask the external world for directions because it would have ruined the adventure taking place in my mind. More importantly, a conversation with an oneironaut can get awkward very rapidly:

Me: "*Entschuldigen Sie*, do you know of a restaurant on the Neckar with a wood floor deck and an open view to the sky."

German person: "Hmmm, what kind of food does it serve?"

Me: "I don't know. I just remember that it has a wood deck and an open view to the sky."

German person: "So you have been there before, but you do not know where it is, or what food it serves?"

Polizei: "*Ist alles in Ordnung?*"

German person: *"Nein, diese Touristen muss gehen das Krankenhaus, schnell."*

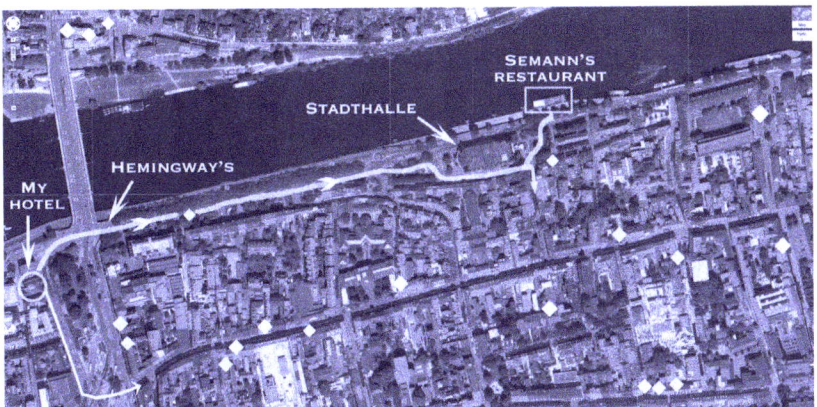

Figure 3-1: This satellite map from Google shows my hotel location, circled in the far left. Based on what I knew of the city, I should have turned *right* out of the hotel (path away from river), and walked to the Hauptstrasse, which is the long road crossing from the lower left to the upper right and has many stores, cafes and restaurants. Diamonds mark the restaurants identified by conference organizers. Instead, I turned left out of the hotel and walked along the river. At many junctions I should have taken a road to the right to go back up to the Hauptstrasse, but in the end I stayed left. After going around the large Stadthalle near the river, again I should have turned right (arrow), but turned left again and found the restaurant on a boat (rectangle). The satellite resolution is high enough to show tables at outdoor locations, yet this satellite image gives no such evidence that this object is a restaurant.

Ja, so I was on my own. The quest was to be a private affair if I were to avoid a night's stay in the local *Krankenhaus*. I checked two more restaurants that I saw along the way, but these were both indoor locations. Finally, the pedestrian road entered a small park, and before me was the Stadthalle—the conference venue itself. It was nearly deserted—I was positively too late to make this dinner a part of my autobiographical history. Fate, as dictated by a late German train, was against me.

Maybe now was the time to turn right, walk uphill to the Hauptstrasse, which was filled with people and places to eat, and search for different dinner colleagues. The crossroad in my life was fairly simple. There was no reason to go downhill to the left toward the Neckar

River, where apparently no restaurants existed. It would be totally irrational to go left.

I turned left.

After a few paces, I realized that hidden behind some large green trees a fairly large boat was anchored on the riverbank. As I walked closer and more of the boat became visible, I could see that it had tables and people sitting on the top level. It was indeed a restaurant I had never seen before called Semann's. As I approached a few steps closer, a hand rose over the crowd and waved to me.

My group! They were having dinner on the wood deck of a boat on the Neckar. It was open to the sky and spacious.

I ascended the stairs to the top level, and the team leader, the brilliant Canadian astrophysicist Brenda Matthews, immediately exclaimed in a high-pitched voice of disbelief:

"How did you find us?"

The sound of her voice saying these words is perfectly recorded in my memory—it is the oneironaut's prize. It's a bit of a masochistic prize because I took some risks and made some efforts that were not the simplest or easiest one could take for the day. I will discuss this later in the book when I define the psychological characteristics of the oneironauts.

I answered her question plainly and told them I had a dream that I would find them there. The literal meaning of my statement would not be detected. Yet Brenda and the others had a good reason to be surprised. They had chosen to dine at a restaurant that should not have been found by anyone going to this conference. In fact, out of the hundreds of scientists attending the conference, not a single other conference attendee was at the restaurant. All others had gone to restaurants located along or near the Hauptstrasse.

The reason is that the conference booklet distributed to the attendees has a map of 56 recommended restaurants (**Figure 3-2**). I would not receive the conference maps until I registered at the Stadthalle the next day. All of the restaurants except Hemingway's are inland, yet my group decided to do something completely different and find a place that was not on the conference map. My chances of finding them were highly improbable. For all practical purposes they were hiding from me (unintentionally, I hope). As I noted before, I did not attempt using Google maps, or some type of tourist information, or simply ask a local person for restaurants on the Neckar. I had a chance at the hotel when I realized how late I was in my arrival, but I just went out the door without searching on the Internet. In some sense the result would have been the same if I had found Semann's on the Internet and walked straight to it. Brenda Matthews still would have been shocked to see me because the Internet could not tell me that I would find them at this specific restaurant.

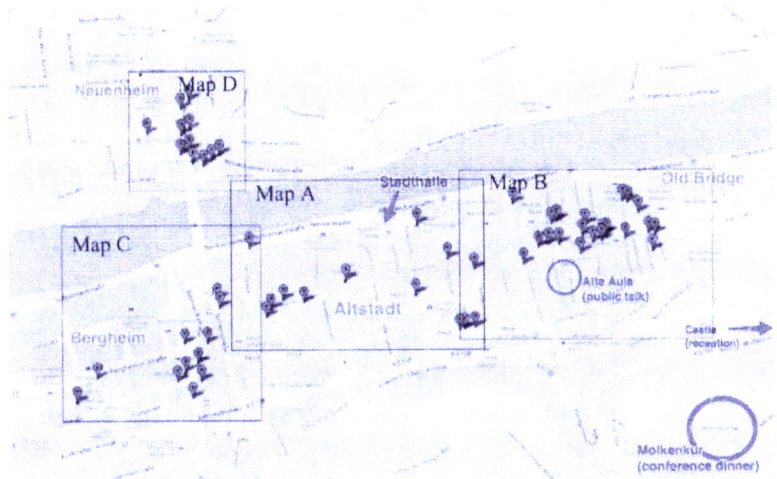

Figure 3-2: This map was provided to conference attendees. Each pin shows the location of a restaurant. Old town Heidelberg is the Altstadt. Stadthalle is the location of the conference hall. It is clear that the highest concentration of restaurants is away from the Neckar River. My science team decided to eat at a restaurant that is *not* marked with a pin, located roughly below the letter "d" in Stadthalle.

In fact, not only did I find them, but I wasn't extremely late either. My dinner order arrived on the table a short time after theirs. The universe that I experienced would thus be the one where I had dinner with the science team, but it was the Bargain Universe—I saved $200 by not taking the taxi from Frankfurt.

The Bargain Universe very broadly represents the evolutionary path that defines success for most organisms—we strive to minimize our costs while increasing our benefits. If we find ways to eat and avoid being eaten, using the minimum effort, then that is the Bargain Universe.

However, despite the bull's-eye in finding my group, I cannot say this experience was déjà vu in the way I usually talk about it. In all other stories of déjà vu, the recall of the dream occurs at the time of the event, or afterward. In the Heidelberg case, I recalled a dream before the event so that the content of the dream became synonymous with my working memory of where to find my group. Once I got there, stepping onto the deck of the restaurant, looking around at the other tables, the open sky, and the hills of Heidelberg, I did not feel a distinct déjà vu. I had remembered the dream long before I arrived in Germany. The Heidelberg experience might be called precognitive thinking.

Expanding the Physical Basis of Instinct and Intuition

WAS MY STORY really another example of changing fate through precognition, or just the regular, everyday application of your gut instincts to follow a path? Let's pretend that we can put everything in the Heidelberg Dome. Heidelberg is now an artificial place covered by a big dome, as in the films *The Truman Show* or *The Hunger Games*. You are the scientist, the Heidelberg Dome is your experiment, and your objective is to study me, ratman. There are cameras everywhere recording events 24/7. You made a maze of streets and alleys in the Heidelberg Dome, with food sources located only along one street going through the center called the Hauptstrasse. You have put me in the maze many times before, and I have learned where to go for food rewards. We have a pretty good relationship, I've started calling you ET, and my mind has an excellent cognitive map of the Heidelberg Dome.

In this trial, however, you set me loose at one end of Heidelberg, and you have one new condition: food will be given to me only if my ratfriends are also eating there. I suppose you are investigating the interplay between food rewards and social rewards among ratpeople, and the relative plasticity of my cognitive map. You put the food in all the usual places, but it will not be given to me because my friends are not located there. Instead, you constructed a brand new, out-of-the-way restaurant that I do not know about, and that is where my ratfriends are dining. I could *not* have learned to find it from previous trials. It's not in my cognitive map.

Hemingway's is the closest place to eat, it is very comfortable, but no food is given to me because my ratfriends are not there. You predict that my walking path should go up to the Hauptstrasse where I have learned from many previous trials to find a multitude of good places to eat, and many other ratpeople eat there too. Yet you notice that my walking path stays away from the Hauptstrasse and meanders along a route least likely to result in success given everything that ratman could possibly know about the maze and this particular trial.

Amazingly, ratman takes the shortest path through the maze to find the reward. The experimenter has to conclude that ratman's actions were not the result of learning in the Heidelberg Dome. Instead, ratman had an *instinct* of where to go.

Instinct is the adaptive behavior related to the survival of a population that cannot be causally associated to prior learning in any single individual during their lifetime.[10] Releasing millions of ratpeople into the Heidelberg Dome over 10 million years would mean that those with instincts best suited for the environment would more likely receive the rewards needed to succeed, and genetically pass on the trait for these successful instincts to future generations. At the end of 10 million years, all the inhabitants of the Heidelberg Dome possess a particular instinct because it was a tiny advantage for survival over many generations. The instinct to find social connections would be particularly strong. For example, since baby mammals are extremely helpless at first, the instinct to rejoin the group when separated from it has to be of utmost importance. The instinct to create a Bargain Universe is a natural quality for us ratpeople after 10 million years of natural selection.

So if you look at my behavior in Heidelberg, you would conclude that I had a strong intuition of what to do, like the instincts that are evident in the animal kingdom. However, when I look at my behavior in Heidelberg, what I see is that I learned what I should do from experiencing a future universe.

When you look at my behavior, you might conclude that instinctual choices are irrational because they do not follow the *cognitive map*. When I look at my behavior, my choices were entirely rational, because I had a *precognitive map*.

When you planned the Heidelberg Dome experiment, you wanted me to explore the environment, *seeking* a reward. But then the experiment shows that my path was direct, and you do not know how to reconcile the fact that a path of exploration should display a variety of choices in ratman's navigational turns. When I look at my behavior, the explanation to your paradox is crystal clear. My dear ET, what you were witnessing was not exploration or foraging for food. Instead, I was *returning* to my food via the shortest route. There is a universe where the train was not late, and I experienced the dinner by the Neckar. But the universe in my current timeline that contains the late train required that I use the oneironaut phenomenon to *return* to the desired timeline where I dine on that boat with my ratfriends.

When you look at my behavior from outside the Heidelberg Dome, you hypothesize that instinct is genetically hardwired in my brain. Nature meticulously selected the neuronal connections in my brain and other aspects of physiology that manifest as the observed behavior. More specifically in this experiment, you surmise that neuronal hardwiring attends to location cues. The organism therefore makes decisions in travel that rejects paths that are not correct because they will not be useful, and chooses paths that will lead to the locations containing useful things like food and the social group.

When I look at my behavior, I see that I learned the location cues from dream recall. Nurture or learning from the future created the neuronal connections used for the behavior—I was not born with these connections. What I was born with was the hardwiring that perceives the future. Overall, I would say that the mechanism is quite elegant. I would not need to recall whom I would meet or what I would eat. Instead the minimum amount of information needed was provided—the location. Egocentric knowledge of place, the self-centered viewpoint of the world, is fundamental to survival.

There are many consequences to my arguments that in terms of cognition and behavior, animals and humans are in fact much closer to each other than expected by a human observer. For example, Aristotle in Book III of his work "On the Soul" (a.k.a. Περὶ Ψυχῆς or *De Anima*) made a distinction between the senses and imagination:

> Sense is either a faculty or an activity, e.g., sight or seeing; imagination takes place in the absence of both, as e.g. in dreams. Again, sense is always present [among living things], imagination not. If actual imagination and actual sensation were the same, imagination would be found in all the brutes; this is held not to be the case; e.g., it is not found in the ants or bees or grubs.

Importantly, because only humans had rational imagination, only humans were held to be rational beings capable of "thinking." Aristotle accepted that some animals can possess "sensory imagination," related to retrieving memories of sensations, but this was not the same as using rational processing, which only humans can do, supposedly. For millennia afterward the distinction between rational and non-rational beings was central in arguing that Western ethical values apply only to humans and not to animals.

The lessons from the Heidelberg Dome weaken Aristotle's claims on at least two accounts. First of all, I am proposing that when we see something in a dream, we may be really seeing an "activity" at a future date. Dreams are not always virtual worlds—they can be the perception of real future worlds. Therefore the senses and imagination cannot be cleanly separated—*The Great Ambiguity* strikes again. Second, this sense can produce what appears to be irrational instinctual behavior to an outside observer, but to the organism it is a rational behavior derived from learning.

We can now consider the same argument for animals. What appears to be instinctual behavior by animals is the perception and rational processing (learning) of sensory information from dreaming. Aristotle was too bold in presuming that animals do not function rationally like humans. Not only can animals act rationally, but also some experiments reveal that animals appear to enjoy learning.[11] If animals are in fact rational creatures that enjoy learning, then a portion of our ethical values must include them as stakeholders.

While my arguments give animals a bit of an upgrade, they also suggest that human intelligence is overrated. Sorry to disappoint you ET. Note that when I was looking for my companions in Heidelberg I was not using any of the intelligence that distinguishes humans from animals. I did not talk to anyone or ask for directions—that would have required language. I did not use electronics or a map to search for this place—that would have required abstract reasoning to translate a map into physical space, mathematics to interpret distances, and, of course, language to figure out the meaning of words.

The map I had in my mind was very basic. It was knowledge of an environment from my point of view (egocentric), which is quite universal among living things. You could reflect on the hubris we have as humans that we are using immense intelligence most of the time, but the reality could be that the majority of the time we are merely engaging in very basic behavior and decision-making. My behavior in the Heidelberg Dome could be regarded as very old, before language, map-making and mathematics were mastered by humans.

This leads me to another insight: the oneironaut phenomenon is hard to believe, understand, and utilize because primitive information does not easily translate to higher-level information required for complex functioning. Primitive information is what we have moment-to-moment as we perceive the world from our point of view. This was called *egocentric* because the organism perceives the world in relation to itself. When you start viewing an element of the world in relation to another element, and not necessarily in relation to yourself, this can be called *allocentric* (centered on others). If I'm looking around the room, I'm processing *egocentric* information, but if I'm going to multiply 9 x 7, then this is *allocentric*, involving abstract relationships existing outside of myself, and quite a bit more complex than stating the sofa next to me is the color white.

To effectively utilize precognition, we need dates and times, which are mostly allocentric. A modern human calendar system requires information from astronomy and mathematics, and the primitive, egocentric oneironaut experience simply does not provide this type of information. Accurate calendars of this type do not exist in animals, and therefore we are unable to take the oneironaut phenomenon and combine it with the higher-level functions that humans have developed. The challenge is creating a Rosetta stone that can accurately translate primitive time to higher-functioning time.

For example, when I lived in Hawaii the weather had relatively minor differences between seasons, but you could characterize the winter very distinctly by seeing whales off the coast. The egocentric sight of whales is a proxy for an allocentric calendar that gives you the words February or March. A primitive experience of seeing a type of animal gives you a translation to the higher-level calendar we use as humans. Later I will propose other ways of creating such a Rosetta stone. The stakes are high, though. If no Rosetta stone can be made, the oneironaut experience will continue to be useless.

I can't resist pointing out another great irony in the whole story of the Heidelberg Dome. The outside observer, while investigating the properties of instinctual behavior, has botched the interpretation by not recognizing that the experimenter has instincts too. The experimenter's instinct is to hold time as solely linear in the direction past to future. Therefore, he or she would never consider the possibility that future information could be responsible for nurture or learning.

The lesson learned from the Heidelberg Dome is that the physical basis of some apparently instinctual behavior is knowledge gained from the behavior or environment that the organism is going to do or encounter in the future. I must then posit that one function or consequence of sleep, which is universal in the animal kingdom, is to nurture this apparent instinct. My guess is that building instinct was not the original function of sleep. Instead, I think that sleep was originally needed as a rest state in the energy cycle of biological activity, and the emergence of instinct was a side effect that became ever more dominant through the natural selection of efficient and useful traits. We still need rest, of course.

Note that I would not deny the proposition that most instinct is genetically based. Genes create the common brains of a species, and complex behaviors that are necessary for the species to survive are mapped to neurons in the species' brains. In other words, most instinctual behavior is inherited.

The type of instinct I'm talking about *expands* on the definition above. This instinct is an episodic, rare, but decisive behavior that is needed to give an individual in the species a survival advantage. This type of instinctual behavior is not inherited. What is inherited is the oneironaut mechanism. For example, the instinct to successfully find a mate exists in our brain wiring, but when the organism must make a choice among different possible mates, the oneironaut phenomenon could come to the fore—so too for the decisions related to avoiding danger, or finding food and water.

Imagine a time in the past when a pioneer is leading her family across a wilderness, stopping at a fork in the path forward. Turning right, the path goes downhill to a lake, which probably has fertile ground and abundant fish. Turning left, the path is a difficult uphill climb to rockier ground that is more exposed to the elements. Turning right is the rational choice. But in a moment of silence, the pioneer knows that the rocky, high altitude location to the left is correct, a place where she'll see the birth of grandkids and great grandkids. Going to the right, she seems to hear the sad words spoken as she buries her children, and the sight of their father's grave.

Three thousand years later a physical anthropologist discovers that a mosquito-borne disease devastated all the settlements started near the lake, but the settlements at a higher altitude were safe. There was less to eat, but the lack of mosquitos saved them.

An evolutionary biologist, on the other hand, might hypothesize that the settler had a gene mutation that permitted survival and reproduction at high altitude. Indeed, the oneironaut phenomenon twists evolutionary biology into a pretzel. In the classical interpretation, many different settlers attempt to survive and reproduce at high altitude, but only the babies with the gene mutations profitable for high altitude would survive to become a population of adults naturally adapted to high altitude.[12] In the oneironaut interpretation, the first settler would select the mountain environment because he or she already possesses the gene mutation and perceives the fact that he or she would survive and reproduce in the future. The genes for the oneironaut phenomenon therefore drive evolution like a charioteer, whereas the gene mutations for high-altitude survival are the horses that can win the struggle for survival, as long as they are guided correctly.

Whatever the case, the humans who first chose the best location did not need to know why it was the best, but they would survive and pass on the oneironaut trait. The humans who could not select correctly would die. Nature would select the oneironaut trait for humans and many other organisms.

In the present time, note that in Heidelberg I managed to live the "Bargain Universe" because I saved money. But notice also how the maps of Heidelberg show that I took a direct path to food and companions. Simple information from the future guided me as if my instinct was as efficient as the technologically complex GPS systems of the modern era. Of course, I wasn't going to die if I took the wrong path, in this case. But consider the possibility that the path is a long trek across a hot desert with little water. If I take the shortest path, I will survive. If my path is one day longer, I am dead.

Or consider a future time, where the first human expedition on Mars meets with misfortune, so that the team must split up to follow several possible paths in order to find a critical portion of the supplies needed to survive. If one person is the oneironaut, they might use this ability to find the supplies, they will survive, and the first humans living on Mars will have the oneironaut trait passed on through successive generations.

The overarching themes in this book concerns improving the skills and utility of the oneironauts so that humans can make decisions that give advantage. The Heidelberg Dome suggests that an outside observer would regard such decisions as instinctual behavior. What I will suggest is that we should use technology to create an augmented human instinct unlike anything seen before in the animal kingdom. *It will be the instinct of a technological civilization.*

Predetermined Destiny vs. Hyperactive Free Will

AFTER EVERY ONEIRONAUT EXPERIENCE I have to grasp again at the big picture questions that tease the mind with hints that big answers are within reach. In the last chapter, I contemplated how the oneironaut phenomenon repaints our concepts of fate and hope. I'm going to circle around again and ask if destiny and free will exist.

Are we active participants who define our own destiny, or merely observers of a life predestined? Earlier I pointed out that you only have about 50,000 dreams that you could possibly remember in your life, yet there are trillions of possible daily events to dream about, given the large number of life choices that are possible. Thus the chances of experiencing a precognitive event are miniscule, and you might then conclude that life is predestined. Destiny is exactly what you need to match a dream to a future event.

However, a predetermined destiny does not sit well with me because it means that we have to give up the notion of free will. My actions in a middle-school classroom and more recently in Heidelberg demonstrate a series of choices. Predestiny demands that these choices were illusions, yet I was confident that the choices could go either way depending on my will. In scholarly lingo, I had a strong "sense of agency"—that I control most of my actions. Or, as Hans Solo said in *Star Wars*, "There's no mystical energy field [that] controls my destiny!"

Predestiny demands that none of my actions—not one—are under my control, and this must also apply to everything around me. All the associated events, such as the late train at Frankfurt Airport, imply that everyone around me made a thousand more predestined choices to make that train late that day, which was a key event in my subsequent predestined choices. If it were a mechanical failure in the train that caused the delay, then human choices were barely involved. It could have been the warm temperatures that day causing something to fail on that train. Thus predestiny invokes a magical mechanism that specifies the exact choice every organism will make in its lifetime, and exactly describes every feature of the universe for all time, including the weather.

You might think that if you took a snapshot of every element involving the weather right now, and if in that snapshot you had perfect information about every quantity, then you could predict the weather for billions of years into the future, until the Sun goes through its red giant phase and wipes away our atmosphere.[13] However, it is impossible to exactly define both the location and momentum (mass multiplied by velocity) of the fundamental particles that make up the universe. This is called Heisenberg's uncertainty principle, and it is quite real. This law of the universe says that if you were to measure your location perfectly, your velocity would *not* be perfectly knowable. If you were to then measure your velocity to increasing accuracy, your location would become increasingly unknowable. You would need perfect information of both to predict the weather, but this is simply not possible. Predestiny seems to me as fundamentally impossible.

A second reason to disfavor predetermined destiny is that I have an alternative explanation, as mentioned in the previous chapter. As we exercise our free will, we occasionally believe that something has occurred which we knew about beforehand, as if destiny or fate could be the only explanation. But this is simply an illusion created by a tenuous perception of the oneironaut phenomenon. When you send experiences backward in time, these experiences, whatever they may be, were always the outcome of free will as you interacted with your unpredictable environment.

To sum up, I think we are active participants in what we call destiny. On top of this, I am claiming that we haven't even realized the full extent of how this works to date, and how it could work in the future. We are actually "hyperactive" in choosing our future experiences because the brain and the mind can imprint information in a way that persists backward in time. New memories from the *future* then become added elements for making choices in the *present* that either result in the future event, or avoid it. *Free will is hyperactive.*

Paul Kalas

4. Fomalhaut

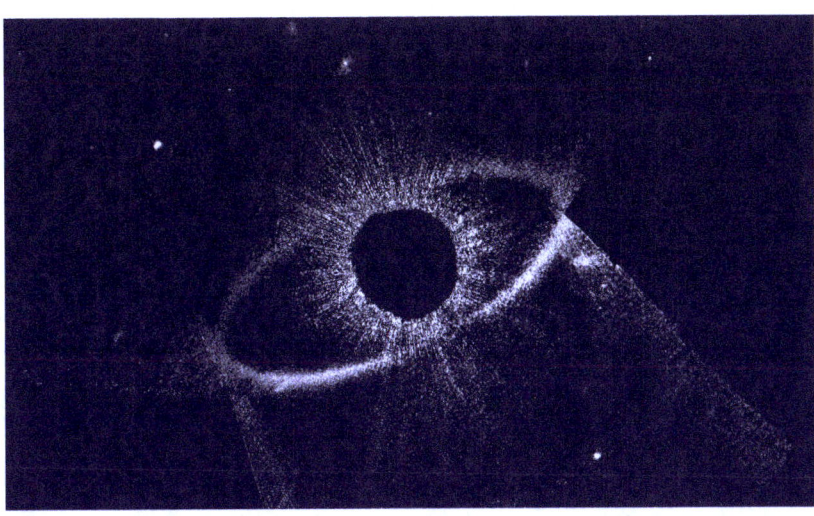

The previous chapters identified some fairly major consequences if the oneironaut phenomenon were real. We might have a scientific path to test for the existence of infinite multiple universes, recovery from brain injuries could be advanced, we could understand some critical instinctual behaviors in the animal kingdom, and in the meantime, causality gets twisted into a pretzel.

With the stakes so high, it is very unsatisfying that these concepts sprout from a ninth grader in science class and a cheapskate astronomy professor lost in Germany. You, *meine Leser*, would have to assume that I have a good memory and that I'm not intentionally making stuff up. Even if you happily accept my stories, all it means is that I believe these things happened and that I have accurately told them to you, yet they could be grossly misinterpreted or fabricated in my mind.

Are you a collector of fancy words? Then *pareidolia* should be in your collection. This word describes a fairly common human trait whereby we mistakenly perceive patterns in random or incomplete information. Instead of an unconscious memory glitch such as cryptomnesia, pareidolia involves a conscious comparison between our senses and our pre-existing models of the world—we tend to seek out matches between new experiences and the patterns already defined in our mind. Thus the fluffy white cloud drifting across the sky may look exactly like Bubbles, your childhood goldfish.

Consider the following path to such a thought blunder that could happen to just about anyone. Assume that in eighth grade I clearly remembered a dream in which a boy with an injured knee says the startling phrase about jumping from a haycart to a sixteen-wheeler. A belief in the possibility of precognition through dreams would be instilled in my mind thenceforth, and I would be searching for more evidence of it the rest of my life.[14] A hypothetical parallel example is if in eighth grade I discovered a resemblance of the face of Jesus in burnt toast. The belief in the possibility that Jesus is communicating with me through toast could take hold, and thenceforth I would be looking for and selecting evidence to support this early experience. By the year 2017 I have created an album of 100 Jesus toast images, I show these to you, and then, very politely, you tell me to look up the word *pareidolia*.

Let's take a look at yet another path to a thought blunder called *confirmation bias*. Decisions and actions based on gut instinct, such as the events of the Heidelberg Dome, could lead to success half the time and failure the other half. When blind chance successfully leads me to my goal, such as that dinner boat in Heidelberg, I chalk it up to a confirmation of my deeply instilled belief in precognition. In fact, the stakes are so high, the idea of time travel so seductive, that I am quite satisfied if I am successful only one time in 100 in this game of chance. The 99 failures need to be ignored because the one success is a game changer. Yet all that has really happened is that I have built a *house of cards* out of a few experiences. As a scientist I can describe many interesting qualities of these cards and how I put the structure together, but it's all flimsy, ready to collapse and to be forgotten. As the Athenian leader Demosthenes said over two thousand years ago: "Nothing is easier than self-deceit."

This chapter on Fomalhaut will relate events that have convinced me, and may convince you, that the story of the oneironauts is *not* a house of cards. This chapter has a very special quality about it. In all of the other stories about dreams that come true in the future, you, the reader, were not with me. You were not in my eighth-grade gym class when the injured kid said he jumped from a haycart to a sixteen-wheeler. And you were not in my ninth-grade class when a poster of the Trifid Nebula was peeling off the wall. But in this chapter you are going to look at a record of one of my dreams, and then compare it to a real event that occurred nine years later. You can be the judge of what happened.

I can be the judge too. That's because so much time passed between the dream and the reality that I totally forgot about the dream. So when I look at my dream notes, it's as if I'm reading someone else's scribbling, and then I have to compare this to the record of historical events. It's as if I'm now outside the Heidelberg Dome looking in. Some might call it the Archimedean Point. Even though I am the subject of what I'm looking at, so much time has passed that I have lost a subjective notion of the experience and can weigh in as an objective observer.

In the end I decided the evidence shown here is good enough to present the déjà vu phenomena as a time-travel experience that has implications for the physical universe, as opposed to just my own psyche. But don't get me wrong—the evidence you will see here isn't amazing, rock-solid proof. Nevertheless, given the nature of the dream, what you read here may be the best evidence ever recorded for déjà vu as time travel.

Fomal.... what?

THE EVIDENCE IS FOMALHAUT. I pronounce the letter "t" at the end, whereas others make a "ho" sound for the end of the word. To understand what Fomalhaut is, we begin with a short astronomy lesson. When you look up in the sky, you see parts of our solar system, such as the Sun during the day and, at night, other planets that orbit the Sun. These other planets within the solar system look like stars to the naked eye, but with a telescope you can often discover for yourself the rings of Saturn, or the moons of Jupiter, surrounding what you previously thought was a star. All of the other stars that you see in the night sky are actual stars that exist in our galaxy, the Milky Way. The difference between stars and planets is that stars are massive balls of hydrogen and helium that create energy through nuclear fusion. Planets can be rocky or gassy or watery or whatever, but they do not create significant energy of their own. The Sun is just one star out of billions that together form the Milky Way Galaxy. If you know where to look, and you are in a dark location, you can see with the naked eye another galaxy not too far from the Milky Way—it's called the Andromeda Galaxy. With a telescope you can take pictures of many galaxies, and as you upgrade to larger telescopes, you eventually find that our universe is filled with billions of galaxies, everywhere you look.

If you already know everything in the paragraph above, then you are a fifth-grader in elementary school. If you do not know everything above, then you are most likely an adult, and should commit the paragraph above to memory. It's just basic knowledge of what is around us. According to a 2014 report by the National Science Foundation, one out of four adults did not know that the Earth orbits the Sun.[15] In Europe, one out of three got this fact wrong. So, let me repeat that the Earth is a planet that orbits the Sun, the Sun is a star that orbits within the Milky Way Galaxy, and the Milky Way is just one of an infinite number of galaxies spread evenly throughout the infinite space called our universe.

However, everything we see is not everything there is. You see our solar system's planets because light from the Sun reflects off their surfaces or atmospheres. But what would happen if you flung the Earth very far from the Sun? It would still exist as a spherical chunk of matter, of course, but it would appear dark. Most of the universe is dark, and by most I mean 95%. So, what you see everywhere you look is just 5% of what there is.

One of the reasons we know that dark matter exists is because all objects with mass bend "spacetime," through a phenomenon we call gravity. Mass bends space, but time is also distorted, and therefore it is better to put the two words together. So even though our Earth removed from the solar system would be undetectable because no sunlight would be bouncing off it, it still could be detected because Earth's mass bends spacetime (i.e., has gravity) wherever it happens to be. The more massive the object, the more it bends spacetime. The Sun bends spacetime a lot more than the Earth does. If you have dark matter sitting somewhere out there in space, but you also have a star even farther away in the background, behind the dark matter, what you would notice is the light from the star bending around the invisible dark matter. Because you see the light bending from its regular path, you know that dark matter is in the way, and you can even estimate the mass of the dark matter by measuring how much the light is bending, thanks to equations developed by Albert Einstein.

If I have lost fifth-graders and adults alike, let me turn to a different example concerning a swimming pool. If nothing is swimming in the swimming pool, the surface will be relatively flat. However, when someone dives in, the mass and motion of that body distorts the surface of the water. If you were not able to see the swimmer, you would still know that they are there, and you could even estimate their mass and motion based on the properties of the changing pool water. So too, dark matter produces observable distortions in the visible things around us.

To summarize, you can find things in our universe when they give off light, when they reflect light, or when their mass influences spacetime and hence the motion of objects near them.

With that knowledge, let's now ask: What is the Trifid Nebula from Chapter 2? A nebula or nebulosity is a cloud of dust and gas in space that is easily seen and photographed because light from nearby stars reflects off the dust and/or makes the gas glow. If a star is not nearby, the dust and gas cloud would still exist, but we would have to find methods other than our eyes or visible light photography to map its location, size, and shape.

There is another nebulosity that I discovered with my colleagues using the Hubble Space Telescope (HST, or just "Hubble"), which orbits more than 500 km above Earth's surface. The nebulosity looks like a belt or ring circling a very bright star called Fomalhaut. I previously used the phrase "immense cloud of dusty debris" to describe the collapse of the World Trade Center tower. The nebulosities around Fomalhaut and other mature stars are also called "dusty debris" disks or belts because the source of dust is violent collisions between comets and asteroids that have already formed there.

Fomalhaut is located in the Milky Way, and if you could travel at the speed of light, you would get there quickly in a mere 25 years. That may not sound like a short time, but in astronomy this is considered super close to our solar system. Because it's so close, Fomalhaut is one of the brightest stars in the night sky, located in the southern constellation Piscis Austrinus, which means the Fish of the South. Fomalhaut is the Arabic designation for the "mouth of the fish." Even though it's far south, you can still see Fomalhaut with the naked eye from much of the northern hemisphere, and in fact it's been viewed by humans since time immemorial.

The surprising thing about really bright stars is that even though we can see them with the naked eye, they actually hide a significant part of the universe from our view. This is because when you look at these bright stars with telescopes they produce a significant glare, like looking straight into the Sun. I was interested in Fomalhaut ever since I started graduate school for astrophysics in 1990. At the time, other astronomers had found indirect evidence that Fomalhaut may be a star that hosts a planetary system. The hard part was getting a picture of the planetary system since the star was so bright. Fortunately, various clever scientists understood that we could block stars with a device called a *coronagraph* that was originally designed for blocking the Sun. The French astronomer Bernard Lyot had invented the coronagraph in the 1920s because scientists wanted to study the faint corona surrounding the Sun. The solar corona is the "atmosphere" of the Sun, but to see it you have to block the Sun in the same way that the Moon occasionally blocks the Sun during a total solar eclipse. If you attach a coronagraph behind a telescope, you get a similar eclipse of the Sun, and eventually we realized that you could artificially eclipse stars as well.

Paul Kalas

Road to Discovery

AS A DOCTORAL STUDENT in the early 1990s studying under the pioneering astronomer David Jewitt, I was a frequent visitor to the observatories atop a 4.2 km high volcano called Maunakea, on the Big Island of Hawai`i. Using the coronagraph at night, I was occulting or blocking various bright stars, searching for their planetary systems. Fomalhaut was one of them, but nothing could be found. The atmosphere of the Earth, even after you climb (i.e., drive comfortably in an SUV) to 4.2 km in altitude, has a frustrating turbulence that blurs light from celestial objects. Blurry light is bad. You want it focused, sharp and crisp. The sharper the image, the more starlight can be blocked by the coronagraph, and the easier it is to find these planets.

This problem with blurry pictures taken through Earth's atmosphere was one of the major reasons HST was built. Put a telescope in space, and the problem of blurred images would be gone. Hubble was a great way to look at stars like Fomalhaut, and every year astronomers had an opportunity to ask for telescope time. I first asked for time on HST in 1999 to look at Fomalhaut, but the request was not successful. Other scientists review the requests, and often you simply lose out to other programs—there are a fixed number of hours that the telescope is available. I tried again a year later; again no dice. I tried a third time in 2001—denied. My fourth attempt in 2003 finally met with success. One reason was that in 2002 astronauts had installed a new instrument called the Advanced Camera for Surveys (ACS). It was superior to other visible-light cameras aboard Hubble in several ways, but for me the icing on the cake was that it had a coronagraph.

As the first images of Fomalhaut were obtained with the ACS coronagraph, I discovered a faint elliptical belt around the star (**Figure 4-1**). On June 24, 2004, I sent an email to my two friends and collaborators on the project, Professor James Graham at UC Berkeley, and Dr. Mark Clampin at NASA's Goddard Space Flight Center: "I just got the following result!! Simply Spectacular!! This is Fomalhaut!"

I don't usually use exclamation points when writing, but there are only a few precious moments in a science career when new discoveries are made. A journalist once asked me if scientific discovery is like seeing your newborn baby for the first time. My answer was that having babies is an *expected* part of the natural universe. In fact, to make sure you don't suffer a heart attack and die from surprise, mother nature gives humans nine months to think about that day when Junior will eventually be born.

The marvel of scientific discovery is the experience of seeing something in the natural universe that has never been seen before by another human. You are *hoping*, not expecting, to find something, and when it is finally revealed to you, it can be a total shocker. Thus, feelings of happiness and satisfaction can be mixed in with thoughts of confusion, bewilderment and curiosity. Hopefully, those of you who have had babies weren't too confused when you saw Junior for the first time.

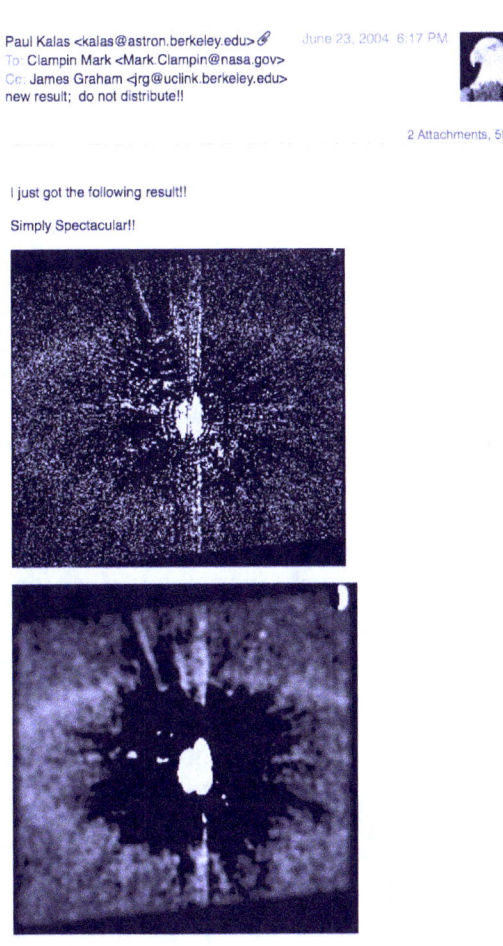

Figure 4-1: The initial discovery image of Fomalhaut's dust belt. The star is located at the center of each image, but the light is cancelled by the coronagraph. This allows a faint elliptical belt to be discerned for the very first time around the star with long axis oriented horizontally in the frame. The top image shows every individual pixel in the camera whereas in the bottom frame the pixels are merged in a way that emphasizes bright and dark features.

What was surprising with Fomalhaut is that I was hoping to find a planet, which would appear as a tiny speck of light near the star. Instead I found an elliptical nebulosity. Though Fomalhaut was known to be surrounded by dust from comets and asteroids that could create nebulosity, its predicted brightness was supposedly too faint for the HST cameras to detect. As a result, James, Mark and I began to work furiously to determine if the elliptical belt could be explained by reflections of starlight from one of the optics that comprise Hubble's sensitive cameras. This is what we call a "false positive"—a signal that has many qualities of a real signal, yet can be attributed to a problem with the experiment. This is why the email subject line says, "Do not distribute." More work needed to be done. Though we were fairly confident that the belt was not spurious, the nail in the coffin would have to be a more sensitive follow-up observation with Hubble.

By November 1, 2004, we had obtained the new Hubble images of Fomalhaut (**Figure 4-2**), and my email to James and Mark had the subject heading "wow." The word "wow" does not need an exclamation point—it is self-punctuating. "Hi James and Mark, Attached is the first result... The images are really amazing... The first robust science result is that the ring is not centered with respect to the star."

In the absence of any other objects around Fomalhaut, the dust ring should have been perfectly centered on the star. Going back to the swimming pool analogy, in the absence of any other forces, the surface of the water should be flat. But with Fomalhaut, my eyes had picked up the fact that the center of the dust ring was displaced away from the position of the star. It's as if the swimming pool water had a wave traveling across it and the challenge was to determine the source. We eventually theorized in a manuscript published in the journal *Nature* that the offset ring of Fomalhaut was due to a planet orbiting the star in an elliptical orbit.[16] Though the gravitational pull of the planet was minor compared to that of the central star, over time it was sufficient to modify the orbits of nearby dust particles, creating a vast dust ring that would not be centered on the star. Moreover, I measured the inner edge of the dust ring and determined that it has a knife-edge inner boundary. Such a sharp inner edge is not expected unless a planet is sweeping through the edge, pushing back the belt's dust like a snowplow making its way down a snowy street.

Since we had excellent indirect evidence for a planet orbiting Fomalhaut, and a spectacular picture of a dust belt around a nearby star, we were able to obtain even more sensitive Hubble data nearly two years later. Comparing the 2004 observations to those made in 2006, I noticed an extremely faint point of light just within the boundary of Fomalhaut's dust belt. All my tests showed that this was neither a faint star located in the distant background nor a false positive signal. Yet it moved slightly as if in orbit around Fomalhaut, and once again Fomalhaut yielded a second science shocker—an extrasolar planet called Fomalhaut b.

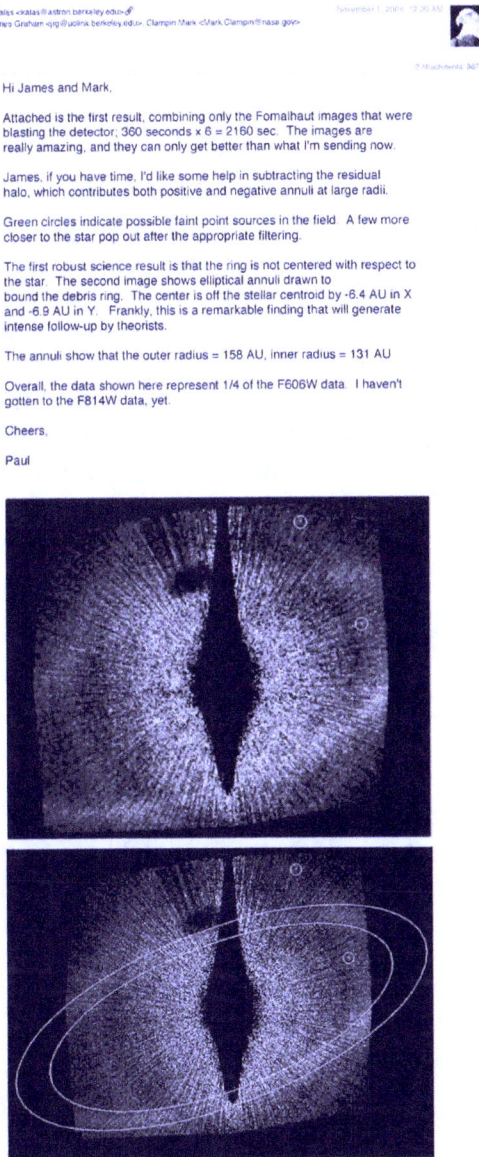

Figure 4-2: Follow-up images that reveal an offset between the star (located in the middle of the central black area), and the dust belt (outlined by two nested ellipses).

Though at that time extrasolar planets had been discovered around many stars based on indirect evidence, and a few had been imaged at near-infrared wavelengths, Fomalhaut b was the first nearby extrasolar planet directly observed in visible light seen moving around its star. After we published our discovery in the journal *Science*,[17] the planet would be heralded as one of the key scientific breakthroughs of 2008. From the great number of comments that I received and the international news coverage, I understood that many millions of people, quite literally everywhere on our planet, had seen my Hubble images of Fomalhaut b.

To give you an idea of its significance, I traveled to NASA Headquarters in Washington, D.C., to participate in a press briefing held in their auditorium. This was broadcast live on NASA TV, and I was accompanied on a stage with my co-investigator Mark Clampin, and two experts on exoplanets, Professor Sara Seager from MIT and Dr. Marc Kuchner from NASA's Goddard Space Flight Center. Sitting in the middle was NASA's Associate Administrator for the Science Mission Directorate, Dr. Ed Weiler. After I spoke to the cameras, I recall looking directly at Ed Weiler to my left, and noticed that he was teary-eyed. He seemed moved by what was happening. My best guess is that as we were speaking on that stage, Dr. Weiler was reflecting nostalgically about all of his years spent with Hubble. Many years later I would try to figure out if Hubble was really that significant to him. Indeed, he wrote the following passage in a popular book about Hubble:

> I could never have imagined that after being hired by NASA in 1978, I would become Hubble's chief scientist in 1979 and hold that job for twenty years. It was a constant battle for me to keep the project alive. I became a determined force for Hubble supporters and a formidable shield against opponents. Despite a multitude of challenges, I never gave up.[18]

The covenant with Hubble over all those years of work was that it would make groundbreaking discoveries, advancing science like no other observatory before it. Despite unexpected challenges and some superlative successes, the one thing that Hubble *had not* accomplished by 2008 was the discovery an extrasolar planet. Dr. Weiler must have felt a stirring surge of emotion when he joined me to tell people that the great telescope, his life's opus, had finally uncovered a new world orbiting a nearby star.

In a second example, the well-known neurologist Oliver Sacks was asked in 2005 what he wanted to accomplish or discover, if he were given a blank check. Dr. Sacks replied:

> I think basically I'm a sort of naturalist and an explorer, and I would just want to see more of the human and animal and plant and mineral diversity of the world. And why stop at this world? I would like to see Titan. I would like to see an extrasolar planet.[19]

He would have to wait three more years, but on November 10, 2008, the front page of the *New York Times* showed Fomalhaut b. I never had a chance to talk to Dr. Sacks, but since he worked in New York City, I believe that on that day I delivered the picture that he had asked to see.

Nevertheless, Fomalhaut b was as puzzling as a dream because using two enormous telescopes on the ground, both much larger than Hubble, we were unable to image Fomalhaut b at the infrared wavelengths where the planet's heat would be detected. Meanwhile, the camera aboard Hubble broke, and two years later journalists discovered that some scientists were skeptical that Fomalhaut b existed. The underlying source of skepticism was in fact a clear-cut case of the tall poppy syndrome. The most prominent skeptic came up to me during a coffee break at a science conference, and without mincing any words told me that he was jealous that my image of Fomalhaut had appeared in the most popular introductory textbook in astronomy. Personally, I thought he should have kept those thoughts to himself, but sometimes jealousy is too powerful to contain. It's practically a separate force of nature.

Tall poppies or not, if a science journalist can get one astronomer on the record to say that another astronomer is completely wrong, then the headline is too seductive to ignore—the science breakthrough of 2008 was pummeled by the press in late 2011. The science writers selectively published the opinion of one skeptic, this created more skeptics among the many astronomers who keep up with the field through news headlines, and finally the overwhelming consensus view was that Fomalhaut b does not exist. The absence of new evidence was new evidence for absence.

Fortunately, the Hubble data are always publicly available, and two independent groups replicated my results a year later. Evidence defeated any ideology born out of jealousy. Or, as John Adams said, "Facts are stubborn things; and whatever may be our wishes, our inclinations, or the dictates of our passions, they cannot alter the state of facts and evidence." Fomalhaut b was real. The absence of infrared light merely meant that Fomalhaut b was not as massive as Jupiter, but just like Saturn, reflected a lot of light by having dust rings orbiting the planet. With the existence of Fomalhaut b confirmed, it would become a part of NASA's history,[20] the National Air and Space Museum in Washington, D.C., would display my image in its exhibit halls, and in 2015 I was asked by the International Astronomical Union to propose a name for Fomalhaut b.

I reflected on the controversy over the previous years and understood that an overwhelming number of people, including my colleagues in astrophysics, had been telling me that I was dreaming. Fomalhaut b was a figment of my imagination. I got this message so often that I was compelled to periodically review my scientific notebooks and the images from Hubble. I could see Fomalhaut b was real every time I checked. There were no mistakes. And so, for a period of time, I had a special loneliness that I take as an honor to experience at least once as a human being. I had knowledge of a very real phenomenon in the universe that no one else had. To everyone else on our planet, Fomalhaut b was just a dream in the mind of an astronomer in California. Thus, for the naming of Fomalhaut b, I proposed the name *Phantasos*, one of the ancient Greek gods of dreams.[21]

As you read the next section, you will see that my Fomalhaut story is extraordinary in at least three ways. First, this little piece of astronomy is unexpectedly the large piece of evidence that the oneironaut phenomenon is real. Second, there is a genuine irony in what the world mistook for my dream was literally my dream. Third, the controversy over Fomalhaut taught me that I could present evidence that goes against the consensus view and survive. Fomalhaut taught me that the road to discovery is risky, that after a success there is a backlash that requires mental endurance, but that I can come out on top if I always employ skill and honesty to travel the road. Thus, Fomalhaut is not merely evidence for the oneironaut phenomenon, it is also the personal emotional and cognitive lesson needed before I would dare to present the oneironaut phenomenon to the world.

Dreaming the Discovery

DURING THIS TIME OF SCIENTIFIC DISCOVERY, I had a vague recollection of a dream many years ago where I was viewing or traveling past something like a ring of dust around a star. Searching through the dream logs that I had kept with me for many years, I was surprised to find a rare sketch of a dream image made on Thursday, November 16, 1995 (**Figure 4-3**). I had drawn an elliptical ring tilted relative to the lines on the page, and wrote:

> 11/16/95 dream of β [Greek letter beta] Pic seen in Dave's office. Surprised at the circular structure; the star seems displaced relative to the center of the material. At the same time, NE [Northeast] extension is concentrated near the equator while the SW [Southwest] opens from the region closer to the poles.

The text "the star seems displaced relative to the center of the material" matched the text of my discovery email to James Graham and Mark Clampin on November 1, 2004, nearly nine years later to the day. In addition to the text, there are at least four striking similarities between my drawing and the eventual scientific images contained in the November 1 email attachments (**Figure 4-4**):

1. Fomalhaut's belt in my email is tilted downward to the lower left by approximately 21° from horizontal. My drawing also has the ellipse tilted down to the lower left, by about 27°.

2. The star is "displaced" (offset) to the upper right relative to the geometric center of the belt. The dream drawing depicts this same displacement direction.

3. In the Hubble image, the ratio of the short side of the ellipse to the long side is 0.53. In my drawing it is approximately 0.5.

4. The Fomalhaut dust ellipse in the Hubble data is brighter in the lower half than the upper half. My drawing has a single line defining the lower boundary of the ellipse whereas the upper part is not defined.

However, the dream log has several items that appear to confuse the association with my future knowledge of the Fomalhaut system. In the dream, I call what I am seeing "beta Pic," the dusty debris disk that I was studying in great detail back in 1995.[22] The star "Fomalhaut" was well known to me at the time, so there is no reason I couldn't have described the system as Fomalhaut instead of beta Pic. Also, I am in "Dave's office." This would be David Jewitt. However, when I first discovered Fomalhaut's belt, I was in Berkeley, California, and had never met with

Dave Jewitt. Finally, I describe what I am seeing as having a "NE extension," which means the portion of the belt northeast of the star. Beta Pic has a "NE extension" but Fomalhaut's belt is oriented differently on the sky—the long axis of the belt runs from northwest to southeast.[23]

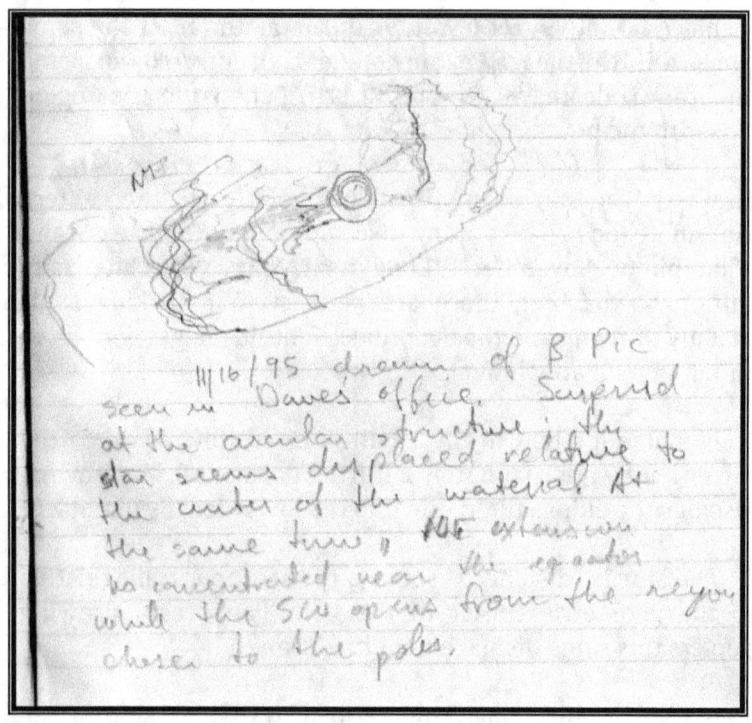

Figure 4-3: Scan of my dream log written November 16, 1995.

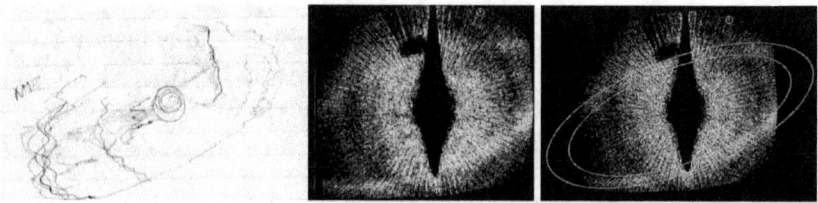

Figure 4-4: Side-by-side comparisons of the dream sketch (left) and the discovery images (middle and right; see **Figure 4-2**).

There is some additional text that is puzzling to me: "NE extension is concentrated near the equator while the SW opens from the region closer to the poles." I am not sure what this means, and the drawing doesn't help much. It's as if I drew something I had a picture of in my head, but there was additional, more abstract knowledge or interpretation that I wanted to also write down. Also, the edges of Fomalhaut's belt (to the left and to the right) are outside the field of view of the HST camera, whereas in the dream log I drew the belt from edge to edge. However, conceptually, you can see that in my email I digitally drew an elliptical annulus that fills in the missing information that lies outside the field to the left and to the right (**Figure 4-4**).

To sum up, there are aspects to the dream log that can be taken as evidence for foreknowledge, whereas other qualities weaken this conclusion. I think the resulting uncertainty is very curious, as if something can be learned from it. When observations have puzzling aspects, then these are exactly the places where new knowledge can be gained. More questions are raised, and one has to define new experiments that will tackle these questions. Given this glass-half-full attitude, I now have to more thoroughly evaluate my Fomalhaut "déjà vu" experience.

House of Cards?

BEFORE JUMPING TO A CONCLUSION that the Fomalhaut dream matches a future reality, do other explanations exist that are just as good as, or even much better, than the déjà vu interpretation? For instance, with confirmation bias we tend to find agreements (and ignore disagreements) between the outside world and our own internal models, expectations and wishes. Some sizeable fraction of the human population may naturally contemplate if they have some psychic ability, witnessed some miracle, or encountered a UFO. If they really "wish" to engage in something extraordinary and mysterious, then they may go to a lot of effort to create the experiences that will validate that wish. In my case, if I have always wished to prove the déjà vu phenomenon, then I will plan and take actions that will give me a match between a dream and a real future experience.

Consider two of the ways for me to build this house of cards:

1. The dream I describe above matches something else in the past or present time of the dreaming brain (in 1995 or earlier). It may seem to match Fomalhaut in the future, but the origin of the dream is traceable to the past or to a recent memory contained within that dreaming brain.

2. The dream matches a future Fomalhaut because I have recorded hundreds of dreams concerning possible future discoveries, and in the last ten years I have actually made very

many scientific discoveries. An apparent match will eventually be made, and it would have nothing to do with a déjà vu interpretation.

Let's consider the first very reasonable explanation that what I dreamt had something to do with a recent or past event with respect to the 1995 frame of reference. The most obvious culprit would be if I had seen such an image of a displaced ring around a star during my waking hours back in 1995 or earlier. Sigmund Freud gave this dream phenomenon the name "day residue."[24] An experience during the day would manifest as a dream at night. In other words, my dream could be work-related—I had seen another image of debris belt around a star that happens to match what Fomalhaut looks like nine years later. In the next chapter I will show that non-visual imagery can also be part of the déjà vu phenomenon. So all it takes is for me to read or hear about an offset debris belt and my mind would construct such an image. Or, perhaps this information about an offset ring came from a science fiction show or book.

In 1995, I was in fact intensely studying the debris disk surrounding the bright star beta Pic and discovered that the shape is not symmetric. However, the key difference between beta Pic and Fomalhaut is that the beta Pic dust disk is seen exactly edge-on from the point of view of Earth (**Figure 4-5**). The dust nebulosity looks like two flames shooting out from the star on either side, and these "flames" are unequal in their length. The most important fact about beta Pic is the following: *In 1995, beta Pic was the only image of a debris disk in existence.*

So, an offset dust belt around a star did not exist, but how about speculation or allusions to such a thing? This is a genuinely open-ended question because someone could have spoken to me about this and there would be no record of such a conversation. Fortunately, I have one handle on the problem, and that is email from 1995.

Yup, I saved my email from back then. These were the good old days when I had only three or four email messages a day. Apparently on November 10–15, 1995, I was communicating with a few friends and family, but most messages were professional. The astronomer Brad Smith, who co-discovered beta Pic with Rich Terrile, was replying to me about a different target, 51 Peg, that I had suggested for observations. On October 12, 1995, Swiss astronomers Michel Mayor and Didier Queloz announced that they had indirectly detected a planet around 51 Peg. This redefined the study of exoplanets as a discipline based on observations rather than just theory. Thus the context of the Fomalhaut dream is that it occurred a month after one of the most significant discoveries in astronomy was made. 51 Peg, however, does not have a belt of dust around it.

Figure 4-5: In the early 1990s I was studying the beta Pic debris disk, producing figures such as this one for manuscripts, presentations and my doctoral thesis. The star is behind the black mask. The colored regions encode light intensity, white representing the brightest parts of the nebulosity and blue the faintest. The nebulosity is not exactly symmetric from one side of the star to the other. Yet the shape of what we see resembles two flames shooting out from either side of the black mask, and is very different from the Fomalhaut image.

Perhaps the best contender for a day-residue stimulus is an email Dave Jewitt sent me on November 14, 1995, concerning new observations of beta Pic made by a different group. If this email record had mentioned something about a "circular structure" that was "displaced from the star" my dream would have been clearly attributed to day residue. However, there is no mention of words involving concepts such as "circular" or "displaced." Nevertheless, I'm glad that I have these records because they remind me that I was working very closely with Dave Jewitt on debris disks at that time. This could explain portions of the Fomalhaut dream— "beta Pic" appears thrice in Dave Jewitt's email. Moreover, I have other emails from astronomer Al Schultz concerning a press release on beta Pic from the Space Telescope Science Institute.

All of this convincingly highlights that "beta Pic" was simply the main target of study, worldwide, among all astronomers in the discipline.

I searched my emails further back (until 1990) and did not find evidence for ideas of the offset ring, though the word "ring" does come up in my work as an astronomer. For example, on October 9, 1995, I received an email about a press release involving James Graham at UC Berkeley with the title "Keck observations confirm Saturn has a blue ring." Saturn's rings clearly circle a planet, not a star, as specified in my dream. The press release concerns the color of a ring, not its geometry. Moreover, the observations occurred during the "ring plane crossing" of Saturn. That means that Saturn's rings as viewed from Earth are edge-on and look somewhat like beta Pic, in fact. They do not look circular or ring-like, as most commonly depicted. I would also be observing the ring plane crossing in those days with Dave Jewitt using a telescope on Maunakea.

It is notable that the person I would work closest with on Fomalhaut in the future, James Graham, was introduced to me by name about five weeks before the precognitive dream. Overall, there is a big mystery about why a precognitive dream should appear at a given time as opposed to some other time. I wonder if in this case the reading of an email concerning an astronomer named James Graham who studies a planetary ring triggered or primed the precognitive action to happen at this time rather than some other time. This is all quite speculative, yet worth keeping in mind.

Another e-mail on October 9, 1995, from the editor of *Astronomy* magazine asked me if I "knew of any images of Fomalhaut, Vega, or other stars that show a dust ring." The answer, as stated above, is that beta Pic was the only debris disk image in existence, and it does not look like a ring. Again, it occurs to me that such a message could trigger or prime the precognitive dream to occur in a specific time period. However, the text of this email has no content concerning an offset ring around a star.

How about a science fiction show, book illustration, or film? I have to admit that I've watched a lot of science fiction, but I do not recall any images of a displaced dust belt. I would argue that for artists to begin drawing dust belts displaced from their host stars, they would first have to see my Hubble images of Fomalhaut published in 2005 to obtain the notion that something like this actually exists in nature.

Just to double check, I looked at every page of several astronomy books I had as a child and teenager. For example, *New Worlds* by

Wernher von Braun and Frederick I. Ordway III was published in 1979 and has sat on my bookshelf since then. It's amazing to flip through astronomy books that preceded the Hubble Space Telescope. All the photos of planets, comets and nebulae seem so blurry, as if I started my life with poor vision, and didn't know it until I put on a remarkable pair of glasses orbiting our planet. In this book, ellipses are drawn that depict the orbits of comets and planets. The tilted orbit of Pluto relative to the Sun and other planets has some similarity to my dream drawing. Yet there are so many more differences, that looking at these illustrations only serves to reinforce my opinion that the dream drawing of 1995 is best matched to the discovery of 2004 rather than the old textbook illustrations of planetary orbits.

Thus I have no evidence that my dream and subsequent sketch was inspired by anything I saw in 1995 or earlier. The origin of the dream is NOT traceable to the past or recent present of my dreaming brain at the time. *Human knowledge simply did not contain a dust belt displaced from a bright star.* Nevertheless, by writing this book, I am enabling a search by a much wider audience for evidence that could have influenced me in 1995.

The second question asked in this section is: how many times have I drawn a picture of one of my science targets and how many scientific discoveries have I made? The concern here is that I could have page after page of dream logs from 1990 to 2004, every day drawing a different possibility of how a belt or disk of dust might appear around a familiar star. Some are edge-on like beta Pic, others five degrees from edge-on, 10 degrees, 15 degrees, etc. In the end I have covered all possible shapes, sizes and peculiarities with my drawings. Then in 2004, all I have to do is match the discovery in the physical universe with one drawing out of thousands, claiming a unique match.

This is what I would call wishful cheating instead of a confirmation bias. For example, if you wished to claim that you are a darts champion because you've hit the bull's-eye 100 times, you could make that a true statement by the end of the week by biasing the game accordingly. You could make the bull's-eye unusually large and with vague boundaries. Then you could add 10 more such bull's-eyes to the wall and throw the darts 10,000 times. Soon you will definitely succeed in your goal, but because of the biases, the result has a different meaning. Instead of demonstrating your talent in throwing darts, it really means that you cheated. Someone who is skeptical about your claim could ask you for further details and would quickly realize that you are no darts champion.

What similar circumstances could diminish the validity of precognition as an explanation for the Fomalhaut experience? First, I can tell you that my dream logs rarely have drawings. I have made just a few drawings over decades of time. For the most part, my dream logs are almost entirely written narratives. So my illustration of 1995 is in fact a rare example of when I sketched something. Moreover, when you read my dream logs, they are rarely (if ever) describing the qualities of a science object.

The converse scenario is that even though I rarely dream and sketch objects in the universe, I ended up making hundreds of scientific discoveries in the future. Now my task is simply to match a large database of later events to a singular remarkable dream of 1995. Again, this is not the case. My discovery of Fomalhaut's belt would be a singular highlight of my professional career. I have discovered a few other debris belts, but none have the belt-like shape and offset from the star that Fomalhaut has. For example, in some of my discoveries the dust patterns resemble a "fan," a "needle" or have a "striated morphology."

To conclude, I have searched for evidence that the Fomalhaut dream could be more simply explained as a memory or reaction to events up to that point of my life in 1995. As far as I know, this is not true. An offset belt around a star was not part of the existing scientific landscape in 1995. Moreover, I considered the possibility that I made thousands of drawings where one would eventually match a future reality, yet this is simply not the case. I have to conclude that my match of the 1995 dream to the 2004 Hubble discovery is not a house of cards.

Is it Jesus Toast?

IS THE FOMALHAUT SKETCH, and my interpretation of it, a clear case of Jesus toast? For Jesus toast, I could in fact make quantitative measurements of features on the surface of the toast. I could demonstrate that the apparent eyes are exactly in proportion to the apparent nose and mouth of a human face. Anyone else could validate the numbers, and they would see they were not made up. Yet, Jesus toast is unlikely to gain a broad consensus that it is a real phenomenon. The simpler and quite common human cognitive phenomenon of pareidolia would be a better explanation, and thus the preferred explanation. Why should we then favor precognition over pareidolia or chance as an explanation for the match between the Fomalhaut dream sketch and the Hubble images?

As the previous section argued, the simpler explanations, such as day residue, can be ruled out for Fomalhaut. Yet, there should still be some lingering skepticism. Deep down, it just does not seem possible that anyone would really have a direct experience of events that have not happened yet.

My response appeals to three more arguments. First, I know from my scientific training that the universe is non-intuitive. Later in this book I will review some properties of the universe that are well established and show that the nature of time and space is in fact very different from our typical day-to-day experiences.

Second, as with the Trifid Nebula dream, the context of my argument matters a lot. This context is my life history of experiencing this phenomenon. The Fomalhaut oneironaut experience really seems consistent with many of the other experiences that I am reporting in this book (more details are found Chapter 5). The Fomalhaut dream is not a quantum leap to a tipping point that convinced me the phenomenon is real. Instead, the evidence has been building up in a consistent way and continues to be experienced.

Third, the big difference between the Fomalhaut image and Jesus toast is the tiny nugget of information that mirrors the password-like phrase of the Haycart dream. The ring offset from the star is not a random detail; it is a unique feature. In contrast, Jesus toast features are relatively vague shapes. But imagine that you burn toast one day, and the burn marks say, "Hi, Jesus here." Well, then I would certainly be open to believing in Jesus toast. Three words on a piece of toast is the type of specific, non-random information that the Fomalhaut offset represents in my dream drawing. Of course, I would first have to look at your toaster, to make sure that it is not a selfie-toaster (this is a real toaster for sale that will burn images into toast).[25] Then I would also review how that bread was handled from start to finish.

Yet you might still say that this single dream of an offset ring matches future knowledge by chance. It was just dumb luck. This is when the context becomes important again. Dumb luck works as an explanation for any single oneironaut experience. But now you have to look at the entire history of my experiences. Were the Haycart dream, the Heidelberg Dome experience, the Trifid nebula dream AND the Fomalhaut dream ALL dumb luck? To me this is not the case and the summed weight of evidence compelled me to take the Socratic Gamble.

Fomalhaut vs. the Twin Towers

IF YOU LOOK AGAIN at the beginning of this book where I mentioned 9/11, and consider where we are now, it is supremely annoying that a relatively inconsequential astronomical discovery is presented as evidence for precognition instead of a tragic historical event. Yet I believe that my inconsequential discovery is actually *better* proof than a hypothetical dream about the destruction of the twin towers. A dream of the two towers crashing to the ground fails the test of day residue, on multiple accounts.

First, I visited the top of the World Trade Center in December 1982, and it is possible that I thought about the problem of aircraft hitting the towers, given that they were so much taller than other buildings. I took a few photos, one of which can be seen at the beginning of Chapter 1. In a different photo, I pointed my Nikon F3 toward the Brooklyn Bridge as a helicopter flew at roughly the same altitude as the top of the World Trade Center. I may have also learned from the publicly available information that attention had been directed toward the safety of the towers given possible aircraft collisions and severe weather conditions.

Second, in late October 1990, for the first time in my life, I would fly into Reagan National Airport, which is in Washington, D.C. I had a window seat, and as we were landing we passed right next to the Pentagon. It seemed so close, I distinctly remember questioning if it was really wise to have hundreds of planes flying next to it, given the possibility that one could crash into it.

Third, in late February 1993, the lower-level garages of the North Tower of the World Trade Center were severely damaged by a powerful truck bomb. I recall hearing, reading and viewing news reports about this, and came to understand that the terrorists' plan was to destroy the foundation so that the entire building would collapse.

Thus, a dream about the destruction of the World Trade Center in 2001 would be difficult to separate from day residue. Since the press material about the skyscrapers' safety features probably appeared during construction between 1966 and 1973, any oneironaut dream predicting the crime would have to appear before 1966. If such a dream appears after that time period, then to qualify as precognitive it would require a uniquely identifying correspondence to the actual events. Having dreams about these towers, or any skyscraper, on fire, collapsing, struck by planes, etc., is simply too general and already foreseen, e.g., by architects and engineers.

Thus, the inconsequential astronomical discovery has some advantages. As a new discipline of study, little had been predicted or foreseen by the few people working in the field. Comet belts around stars were not general knowledge, by 1995 the scientific literature on the topic was only 11 years old, and the specific offset of Fomalhaut's dust belt represents a unique identifying correspondence between the dream and the actual events. The events of 9/11, on the other hand, correspond to a huge body of prior human experience, least of which is our primitive cravings to fight and destroy.

Is it Science?

HOW WELL DOES THE FOMALHAUT STORY sum up as scientific evidence for the perception of future events during dreaming? The ingenious 18th-century French scholar Pierre-Simon Laplace is often quoted for saying, 'The weight of evidence for an extraordinary claim must be proportional to its strangeness." Or, take the shorter version from Carl Sagan: "Extraordinary claims require extraordinary evidence." So how does Fomalhaut stack up?

First of all, a critical reviewer has to consider whether or not the evidence is real. In more scientific terms, we should question whether or not the experimental, observational, or even the theoretical results that are presented by someone are *falsified* or *fabricated*. *Fabrication* means that a scientific result is invented out of thin air. It never happened. It's entirely made up. *Falsification* means that the experiment or observation did happen, but the results are distorted or misrepresented. This is not the same as a false positive, which is a real result, but known to be incorrect. For example, if your home fire alarm goes off because the electronics inside it fail one day, then that's a false positive with respect to detecting an actual fire. Falsification could involve a failure of the electronics, but a person records it as a real fire (e.g., to collect an insurance claim). Fabrication would be the case where the alarm is never triggered, but a person claims that it happened.

Falsification is a nuanced concept because scientists make many decisions about how to plan an experiment, execute it, and what portions to record and analyze. The key step in guarding against falsification is that significant decisions are *reported*. For example, a scientist could present a graph of data and use the phrase, "Figure 1 shows our result. For clarity, we omit the 2002 data." The reader may in fact disagree with the decision of not showing the 2002 data, but at least the decision was reported accurately, and is therefore open to further questioning. Falsification is when the scientist shows Figure 1 and intentionally hides the fact that the 2002 data are not shown. A possible motivation is that the 2002 data contradict other data in the figure, and therefore weaken the claimed result. If the scientist wishes to make an extraordinary claim, then the motivation is even stronger to massage the evidence so that it appears extraordinary, with no weaknesses whatsoever.

Let's return to the Fomalhaut story to illustrate fabrication and falsification. Fabrication would mean that I created a fake record of the Fomalhaut dream after the Fomalhaut discovery in 2004 (which was published in 2005). Falsification means that the dream log has this entry from 1995, but I am somehow manipulating the evidence. For example,

I reported above that I rarely sketched images from my dreams. This would be a falsification if in fact by 2005 I had drawn 1,000 sketches of possible scientific discoveries, and when something in my work as an astronomer resembles one of the sketches, I put this forth as a unique dream that foretells the scientific discovery.

To guard against an accusation of falsification or fabrication, I can offer my original dream log for a physical inspection, and give you reasonable arguments that falsification and fabrication are not likely. A key argument is that if I were to go about fabricating a dream entry *after* the Hubble image of Fomalhaut was published in 2005, the dream entry would have described the shape accurately, but the writing would not have included elements that contradict the claim of foreknowledge. As it stands, my dream entry calls the sketched image "beta Pic" instead of Fomalhaut, and parts of the text are vague and confusing. If I wanted to fabricate extraordinary evidence, then I would not have created elements that require additional explanation or invoke skepticism. The same token applies to falsification. If in this book I wanted to present definitive, unassailable proof of foreknowledge, I could have taken the dream entry from 1995 and digitally deleted the handwriting that detracts from identifying the sketch as the Fomalhaut discovery.

To sum up, I certainly would have an easier time arguing that the oneironaut phenomenon is real by showing you a dream entry that invokes less skepticism. It seems to me that "imperfect" and "puzzling" data are not what fabricated and falsified data aim to show. In fact, imperfect and puzzling are exactly the types of words that come to mind when real experiments reveal new phenomenon in the physical universe.

Does a sketch qualify as scientific data?

The second question a critical reviewer might ask is whether or not my dream should be considered scientific "data" or measurement. Just because I'm connecting it to astrophysical data that I obtained with the Hubble Space Telescope doesn't mean it should necessarily gain the status of "data" too. If the dream log is not considered data, then the arguments that there is something to learn about the way the universe works are significantly weakened.

My impression is that scientists in the behavioral human sciences would consider the self-reporting of dreams a data point. However, I'm going to take this a step further and say that a scientist who studies the physical universe should also take this dream log as data too. The reason is that the technology to directly record dreams in a modern scientific format did not exist in 1995. Yet I was using the best available technology for the problem at hand, i.e., recording an experience with pencil and paper. Scientists have used pencil and paper to record their observations until better techniques and standards were developed. Dream recording hasn't made it this far yet.

Let's take Leonardo da Vinci's scientific work as an example. In his body of scientific thought and illustration called the *Codex Leicester*, Leonardo writes down his observations of erosion:

> When a river flows out from among mountains it deposits a great quantity of large stones... And these stones still retain some part of their angles and sides; and as it proceeds on its course it carries with it the lesser stones with angles more worn away, and so the large stones become smaller; and farther on it deposits first course and then fine gravel... until at last the sand becomes so fine as to seem almost like water... and this is the white earth that is used for jugs.[26]

Millions of humans may have observed the same effect over many millennia prior to Leonardo, but what makes this scientific is that the observations are written down, and have important details concerning the sizes and shapes of stones as a function of their position along a river, which is also related to their time exposed to erosive forces.

Not only are da Vinci's observations written down, they are recorded in the best data format of the time—accurate sketches, drawings and paintings. Take for example his *Madonna of the Rocks* (**Figure 4-6**). The foreground is a holy playdate, but the background is his research record of rock erosion due to wind and water. In fact, I consider this painting (actually, there are two of them, one in London and one in Paris) as a terrestrial parallel to Fomalhaut's dust belt. Just as rocks are eroded into sand here on Earth, comets and asteroids orbiting stars such as Fomalhaut are eroded into fine dust, which is exactly the nebulosity you see when looking at my Fomalhaut images.

Leonardo could have been a better scientist by actually measuring the sizes of boulders and counting how many fall within different size ranges. Obviously, there was no technological barrier to measuring a length. If he had done so, he might have been one of the most cited scientists of all time, since the measurement is what we call the "size distribution of collisionally evolved objects." Size distributions are used in my field and in many other fields. This is the ultimate measurement needed to elevate a limited set of observations to a physical law or principle.

Figure 4-6: A portion of the *Madonna of the Rocks* (1483–1486) by Leonardo da Vinci as it appears to a viewer in the Louvre Museum in Paris. The scientific mind of da Vinci puts detail in the shapes of background rocks eroded by water and wind. The artistic mind of da Vinci adopts the sfumato technique in other areas of the painting.

I suppose we can forgive Leonardo, because he observed, thought, wrote and illustrated these insights in 1514, which is 128 years before the birth of Isaac Newton. Isaac Newton and his contemporaries would build the principles of science used today, such as making quantitative measurements with interpretations supported mathematically. As Lord Kelvin said in 1883: "To measure is to know." Maybe I have to wait 128 years before dream imagery can be recorded and measured more accurately than memory recall, pencil, and paper. Once it is better quantified, the physical laws could then be inferred.

The weight of four stories

If I have convinced you that my dream log represents acceptable data that are not fabricated or falsified, and in fact about as good a method of data collection as was available to me, then we should review whether or not the "weight of evidence" is sufficiently weighty for the extraordinary claim that the oneironaut phenomenon constitutes time travel. Scientific weight is provided when a result endures various elements of the scientific method. Since it takes time (i.e., years, decades and centuries) for the scientific method to establish a fact about the physical universe, we would not expect to have an airtight case for the oneironaut phenomenon instantaneously.

For experiments that explore new phenomena or test hypotheses, the results should be repeatable or reproducible by the first experimenter, and *then* by others not affiliated with the first experimenter. A key motivation for writing this book is to achieve the *then* part, where others weigh in with their unique and independent expertise. But have I established the first part of the scientific method, which is to repeat the results of the Fomalhaut dream experiment, and therefore validate my extraordinary claim?

In my opinion, that question incorrectly assumes that it is the Fomalhaut dream that requires confirmation. Instead, I believe the Fomalhaut dream *is* the reproduction of previous observations. My first observation of the oneironaut phenomenon was my story from a gym class in middle school. The second and third stories involve a ripped poster and a travel adventure in Germany. There have been many more examples of the phenomenon repeating, and the Fomalhaut dream is a very good confirmation because of the written record. Other observers now have the opportunity to disprove my data or interpretations or, alternately, validate them. In other words, the oneironaut experience appears to me as internally tested and validated, and now external tests and validation are needed. The very fact that the proposed oneironaut phenomenon has testable features and predictions, such as those explored in the remainder of the book, are consistent with the scientific method.

The skeptic can nevertheless persist with the power of deduction: "Time travel is unphysical—it does not exist. Cognitive blunders, on the other hand, are common and well documented. It is therefore reasonable to put little weight on the offset and elliptical ring sketch, which could be due to chance. We should instead put more weight on the mismatches between the dream sketch and future reality. These are clear evidence in support of the cognitive blunder hypothesis."

For the first objection concerning chance, I have to appeal again to the overall context. The Fomalhaut story is merely one of four stories presented so far in this book. Each story in isolation may carry little scientific weight because of the "chance" argument, but together the four stories add up to a much greater scientific weight. If I guessed one difficult password correctly, you could call that luck, but if I guessed four difficult passwords correctly, then you would suspect something other than luck was involved.

For the second objection concerning the mismatches in the dream sketch, I owe the reader a plausible explanation that fits within my theory of the oneironaut phenomenon as time travel. I will need to give you additional data and interpretation concerning the oneironaut phenomenon in the next few chapters. You would need to learn more about the phenomenon and me before you could decide if the weight of evidence is sufficient. For the time being, consider below my explanation of how the very nature of thinking and dreaming accounts for the mismatches in the Fomalhaut dream.

The Janusian Mind: Two Times Meeting in One Brain

ONCE AGAIN WE RETURN TO THE ROMAN GOD JANUS, whose head has two faces that represent the ability to simultaneously see the past and the future. What's going on in the mind of Janus when one set of eyes replays past stimuli, and a second set of eyes perceives future stimuli? A more comprehensive explanation for the elements in my Fomalhaut dream can be developed by contemplating such Janusian questions.

With the oneironaut phenomenon, a perception of a stimulus from the future becomes embedded in the dominant reference frame of my present. That future signal—the osignal—is torn from its native reference frame and sits within the mental activity of the present. My memory of the dream cannot distinguish between the part that is from the future and the part that is from the present. Memory conflates two times. When I am awake and looking at a picture of Fomalhaut's dust belt in 2004, I may not be concurrently thinking that this is Fomalhaut. Nor am I concurrently thinking, "This is 2004. I no longer work with Dave Jewitt." My mind is simply studying a shape around a star. Back in 1995 I had a memory of seeing this shape in a dream, and called it beta Pic, because in 1995 that was the only nearby star known to have a visible nebulosity around it. The fact that in the dream I have added the context of being in Dave Jewitt's office suggests that the future vision is not preserved as a mental picture that sits in isolation from all other mental activity, but instead becomes incorporated into my dreamwork.

The reader might notice a contradiction between the Trifid Poster dream, where I claimed that the dream elements are not manufactured (imagined) because they are too out of the blue, and the Fomalhaut dream, where some elements are taken as manufactured. The key is that in the Fomalhaut dream, the words beta Pic and David Jewitt do not come out of the blue—they can be expected to appear in my dreams. In the Trifid Poster dream, being ridiculed for a good deed is unexpected, out of the blue, and therefore deemed to be implausible as a manufactured element.

Below I will discuss four different but related models of why the Fomalhaut dream, and precognitive dreams in general, *should* contain a problematic mixture of information from the past, present and future.

1. The Beholder's Share

For those of you artistically inclined, you may recognize this phrase from the middle of E. H. Gombrich's 1960 book *Art and Illusion: A Study in the Psychology of Pictorial Representation*. Gombrich builds on the old notion that when you look at art, what you perceive must be a mixture of the external world and your internal world. In fact, he reviews pareidolia, referring to an ancient passage written by Philostratus, in which two men, Apollonius and Damis, discuss what clouds seem to imitate:

> ...these cloud shapes have no meaning in themselves, they arise by pure chance; it is we who by nature are prone to imitation and articulate these clouds. 'But does this not mean,' probes Apollonius, 'that the art of imitation is twofold? One aspect of it is the use of hands and mind in producing imitations, another aspect the producing of likenesses with the mind alone?' The mind of the beholder also has its share in the imitation.

Thus Gombrich emphasizes that art is not merely a construction of concrete information—lines, colors, shapes, surfaces, etc.—that is intended to purely imitate something else in the world. Art emerges only when the mind of the beholder has included its "share."

Nowadays, you might substitute the word "share" with the word "model"—the viewer's mind has internal cognitive models that are used to interpret external stimuli. Our perception of reality is model-dependent. Modern readers could also understand the beholder's share as the art version of *augmented reality*. When additional information enters into your visual field, what you perceive is a mixture of reality and something manufactured in addition to reality. If *everything* you perceive is manufactured, then that is called *virtual reality*. So if a cloud in the sky looks like a goldfish to me, that's my augmented reality. If I am dreaming about a cloud that looks like a goldfish, then that dream is virtual reality.

Gombrich goes further and demonstrates that artists intentionally leave out details so that the beholder must project their mental models to fill in the blanks. Importantly, the master artist does not randomly leave out information, but chooses to leave out those things that a beholder's expectations are more likely to fill in. Writers like Hemingway can do the same thing, describing a visible iceberg in just a few words because the reader can infer so much more that lies beneath the surface.

Gombrich adopts the following clever rule from information theory[27]: "...the greater the probability of a symbol's occurrence in any given situation, the smaller will be its information content." In other words, the artist may provide minimal information in the work of art at the places where the beholder's expectations are most likely to fill in the blanks. Gombrich gives the analogous example for speech—"Where we can anticipate we need not listen"—and also praises magicians for their remarkable art of manipulating the expectations of beholders.

Consider an example of anticipation and listening. Suppose that you pass someone in the hallway and they say, "S'up?" The next day, someone might take you to court, and under oath, you might swear with 100% certainty that the person said, "How are you?" Yet what happened is that your mind created its own reality. You would remember hearing "How are you?" but a much smaller amount of information was actually communicated to you. Interestingly, the person who spoke to you might testify that they actually said, "What's up?" but this would also be shown to be false if a recording objectively shows that "S'up?" was actually spoken. Thus, both the sender and the receiver have a beholder's share. *An oneironaut is simultaneously the sender and the receiver, thus amplifying the beholder's share effect.*

Gombrich extols Leonardo da Vinci as the first painter to take advantage of the beholder's share phenomenon: "...the greatest protagonist of naturalistic illusion in painting, Leonardo da Vinci, is also the inventor of the deliberately blurred image, the *sfumato*, or veiled form, that cuts down the information on the canvas and thereby stimulates the mechanism of projection."

If you return to the *Madonna of the Rocks* painting, you will notice that the landscape behind the playdate is NOT a blurred image. Leonardo could have used a sfumato style here, but he did not, because this was his research record of a phenomenon that needed accuracy and detail. Scientists do not intentionally leave out data so that others may fill in the blanks with expectations. Scientists want to create data that reproduce their observation accurately, and so too Leonardo does not want the viewer to reconstruct the scene based on their beholder's share.

Therefore, I stand by my own beholder's share that Leonardo injected a scientific record into his artwork.

If da Vinci paintings aren't your cup of tea, let me illustrate the same concept by taking you to Disneyland. There's a wonderful evening show where they project clips of Disney movies on a giant spray of water outdoors. The spray is a sheet of fine droplets launched upward to nearly 20 meters. Powerful digital projectors then display the film clips, using the water as the screen. So even if you haven't seen this yourself, you can tell that the picture is going to be fuzzy and shimmering. This is supposed to be the completely wrong way to project a picture, yet it is exactly the right way to do it.

The dreamlike magic that happens is the beholder's share. Because these Disney movies are so much a part of the viewers' background and expectations, our minds fill in the missing details with what those Disney movies mean to us. We don't have to see the images sharply—what matters is what we remember and feel when reminded about these clips. The ingenious artists and engineers who created this show understand Gombrich's rule: "The greater the probability that we know what those Disney clips are about, the less visual information is necessary." It is totally correct to project a well-known film on a giant, shimmering screen of water droplets. And I have to say, this show is perhaps the best imitation of dreaming that I have ever experienced as a fully awake person.

How does the beholder's share apply to the oneironauts? Very simply, the future world is witnessed in the present day during sleep and dreaming, but a person's past and present dominate the beholder's share. I could see Fomalhaut's dust belt in the dream, but it is my present-day mind (i.e., the mind that had the dream, and then had to remember it and draw it in 1995) that fills in most of the blanks with anticipation and expectation. The most important information that I needed to have from the future—the shape of the belt and the offset from the star—was the least probable, the hardest to anticipate, and was depicted in my dream clearly. The ancillary parts of my dream were filled in by what I expected to be contained in such a dream in 1995.

In the analogy to the Disneyland show, if several of these films are missing from my past experiences, I can certainly describe what I see, but I could be very wrong about the identification. "I see the Evil Queen from *Snow White*," I might recall, yet it's really the evil witch Maleficent from *Sleeping Beauty*. My full statement was wrong because I could not assign the correct label to what I saw, yet the basic element that I saw a witch is still true. So too, in my dream I saw something that is a dusty debris disk offset from a star, but I could not give it the correct name.

Or consider my court case involving what I heard in the hallway. The lawyers would declare that I am an unreliable witness because a recording reveals that the person said, "S'up?" and not, "What's up?" or "How are you?" So too you could take the discrepant information I'm reporting in the Fomalhaut dream as clear evidence that the phenomenon is false. Yet it's a reasonable argument that the beholder's share is responsible for creating discrepant information because there was missing information—it is a natural phenomenon whether asleep or awake. My recollection of Fomalhaut's shape, the minimum amount of information, was true to reality.

More specifically, if James Graham were seen in the dream, he is a person from my future and I would not recognize him in the dream. I do not know him and I cannot write "I see James Graham" next to the sketch of Fomalhaut. But even though I have this identification problem in the dream, I may still be aware that I am viewing this image with the person that I am very closely working with on research. Not only that, this research has to be on beta Pic, because there is no other star with a debris disk for us to study in such detail. My expectation in 1995 must be that I am talking to Dave Jewitt about beta Pic, and therefore the missing information is filled in with these names.

To sum up, in 1995, when I am dreaming of being in a work environment with my closest colleague, the expectation is that I am in Dave Jewitt's office speaking about the star beta Pic. This is how I would naturally think about it in the dream, and how I would write it from memory in my dream log. However, the dream contains a unique stimulus that is least contaminated by the beholder's share—the visual perception of a shape (Fomalhaut's dust belt) relative to a center point (the star).

2. Future Day Residue

As discussed earlier, day residue is when something happens during the day, your cognitive and emotional reaction includes thoughts linked to that stimulus, and more thoughts and emotions are further spawned from those initial thoughts. You may even be busy with something else, so that all of this sort of simmers beneath the surface of consciousness. Finally, when you are asleep, apparently out of the blue, you have a dream of your childhood goldfish leaping out of its fishbowl and dying. That is because the same day you heard someone talking about the Olympic Games, in your head you thought of swimming and track and field events, and then you thought about drowning and jumping, and later that night you would assimilate this cognitive and emotional reaction into a dream about your goldfish, poor little Bubbles.

Hearing someone mention "the Olympic Games" is the day residue responsible for a sequence of associations that ultimately produced the childhood goldfish dream. In my opinion, this makes a lot of sense for many of my dreams. Daytime events, not necessarily serious issues related to problem solving or anxiety, trigger a dream that is entirely beholder's share. The trigger may not necessarily appear in the dream explicitly, but it is a real event in your recent past.

The oneironauts could have future day residue. The trigger is a real future event that they will experience, and the sleeping brain will manufacture a dream in response to this. For me, the shape of Fomalhaut's belt, its orientation, and its offset, were new conscious visual experiences that triggered further construction of elements that make up the rest of the dream. The construction of these ancillary elements has to rely on the material available from my existing memories. Thus, I would have to call the star beta Pic and the person with me David Jewitt.

I speculated earlier that there may have even been a type of spark between past day residue and future day residue. I had received an email concerning Saturn's rings, and if I read it, then the name James Graham would be in my consciousness, perhaps for the first time in my life. Perhaps this day residue was the trigger that made the connection to viewing Fomalhaut's dust belt in the future.

Future day residue is similar to the beholder's share in the sense that viewing something triggers a response from the beholder. In the case of the beholder's share we're talking about a conscious, waking activity. In terms of future day residue we are talking about unconscious cognitive activity and sleep. Yet they are both very similar. To make the oneironaut phenomenon give more accurate information, we would want to find the organism or the human who contributes the least beholder's share. Or maybe a non-biological mechanism or switch would contribute the least beholder's share. For all we know, the beholder's share may be necessary in order to bring the osignal to a conscious, observable state. But these are all open questions.

3. Neurons as Computers

Yet still another way to conceptualize the explanation of the Fomalhaut dream is to reduce the scope of the problem to a single neuron in the brain that has a problem and must compute an answer. I used the verb "reduce" because there is in fact a scientific approach called "reductionism." This method presumes that if something is extraordinarily complex, you may begin understanding it by looking at a basic building block of the issue. So in this case, assume that my dream was the result of a single neuron in my brain that received some input signals, performed some type of computation with the information, and then output a sequence of images and thoughts that created a dream that was stored in memory.

As **Figure 4-7** illustrates, one evening during sleep, the neuron receives signals from the future. One is an astronomical image that looks like an offset ring. The other is a middle-aged man with a British accent that looks like James Graham. The other inputs are from the present and from existing memories. For example, my memories have "beta Pic" as the word associated with an image of a debris disk. An image of Dave Jewitt is in a catalog of faces I recognize and can put a name to. Dave Jewitt is also in the catalog of people I expect to hear speaking in a British accent (both James and Dave have British accents to my ears).

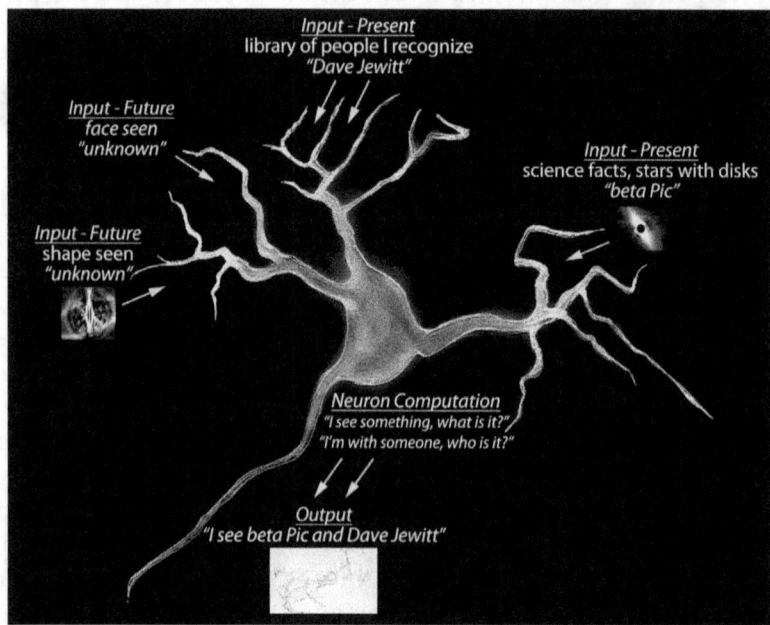

Figure 4-7: Sketch of a single neuron that receives input signals from its connections with other neurons in the upper half of the image, but must output a single narrative in the lower half of the image.

Let's suppose that the neuron is going to take this large variety of input data and bind a few of them together to output signals stronger or of higher quality than any of the inputs. Put another way, the neuron will receive bits of information, each of which has little individual significance, and must construct an output that is recognizable and meaningful. In this scenario, the image of Fomalhaut binds with the image of beta Pic and my recognition of "beta Pic." So when the neuron asks, "What is this toroidal debris disk that is seen offset from the star?" it computes an answer, "This is beta Pic." The experience of seeing Fomalhaut is also tied to the identity of James Graham. But when the neuron asks, "I am with someone, who is it?" the neuron does not recognize the face from a library of faces. Computing the most likely possibility (e.g., from the library of people that I work with on debris disks at the dream epoch), a match is made to Dave Jewitt.

Again, this is similar to the beholder's share, but we are trying to frame the problem in terms of neurobiology and computation instead of cognitive psychology. Instead of thinking about how your thoughts and emotions react to art, we are now considering how a hypothetical neuron reacts when it has to process a future signal in the presence of dream epoch libraries of information. The difference is that in the model of the beholder's share there are no "errors"—everyone is entitled to have their own reaction—whereas the "Neuron Model" points out that the beholder's share for the oneironauts is an error. The brain is not properly distinguishing between the different time frameworks.

Everyday language is a good way to clarify my point. Consider a personal narrative consisting of two sentences spoken in the following order: #1. Today I was in David Jewitt's office studying the dusty disk around the star beta Pic. #2. We saw that it is in the form of a ring not centered on the star. Assume that sentence #1 is my memory of what happened yesterday and #2 is a memory of the dream I had last night and I need to write it down. The problem is that sentence #2 has two pronouns, which are like variables in math or computer languages. In the logic underlying language, "we" must refer to Dave Jewitt and me, and "it" must refer to beta Pic. However, if sentence #2 is from the far future, I have made an error in identifying which nouns these pronouns refer to. "We" is actually James Graham and I; "it" is Fomalhaut.

Finally, I should mention that the Neuron Model is not exactly the same as a computer. If you type the wrong commands into a calculator, you might get a message like "Invalid Syntax." The computation cannot be made. The mind, on the other hand, is a different kind of computer that must always construct an answer, even if it is formally wrong or nonsensical. If a human brain is asked, "What's two plus apple?" the answer is clearly "platypus." At least that's what my brain came up with, probably because, "I was just thinking about a platypus when you asked the question, and it seemed like the best answer to that question." In the future I bet one way human consciousness will remain distinct from artificial intelligence is that humans will always be able to respond to nonsense in a weird yet logical way that other humans can relate to. Computers will probably not have an intrinsic ability to genuinely say something like, "Oh, I was just thinking about that." Of course, computer scientists are certainly determined to prove all of these points wrong.

4. Connecting Memories

The framework of memories is my fourth and final way to explain the disconnect between the drawing of Fomalhaut's dust belt in the dream, and what I actually wrote down about it. I'm going to study memories in greater detail later, but for now let me just tell you that when you recall a fact or knowledge, this is called *explicit memory*. This contrasts against memories of skills such as riding a bicycle, called *implicit memory*.[28] But an explicit memory requires that two other types of memory be joined together successfully. The first is a memory of events, as if you are video recorder, and this is called *episodic memory*. The second is remembering what things mean, how they are defined, how they work, what they are called, etc. This is called *semantic memory*. For example, you can replay in your mind what you saw a few pages ago in my emails. This is episodic memory. You recall a picture of roughly a square dimension which has an ellipse inside of it. Fortunately, I added information that gives you semantic memory. You recall that when you see this ellipse, this is something that surrounds a star, and for it to be bright, dust grains must be reflecting light from the star in the same way as a cloud in the sky is visible when sunlight or moonlight illuminates it. The episodic and semantic memory combine to form an explicit memory in your mind that you have seen and understood Fomalhaut's dust belt by reading this book.

I ran across a different example when reading Rudyard Kipling's *The Jungle Book* to my children. The panther Bagheera instructs the human boy Mogli, "Go thou down quickly to the men's huts in the valley, and take some of the Red Flower which they grow there...Get the red flower." Bagheera has seen something colored red that fans outward. When he thinks about this, Bagheera is using episodic memory. He remembers what he saw in form and color, where he saw it and when. From his library of words and concepts, this must be a red flower, and since it is only seen in the village, it seems to be grown by humans. Now he's making use of semantic memory. Of course, what he has really seen is a flame from a fire, but he categorizes it conceptually and in language as a flower. Those are the limits of his semantic knowledge made available to explicit memory, and I can sympathize. When I was seeing a future image of Fomalhaut in the present, it was as foreign to me in the dream as fire would be to Bagheera. But the neurons must compute. So the Fomalhaut image ended up as beta Pic in my explicit memory of the dream.

Oneironauts have the problem that episodic memories of future events are disconnected from the time-appropriate semantic associations. My dream as a whole, and my written-down memory of the dream, are both explicit memories. I have experienced something sensed in a future epoch, creating an episodic memory in the present-day sleep state. The episodic memory of what I saw will be most accurately reproduced as a drawing. However, for me to describe what I see in language and assign labels to the drawing, I have to use my semantic memory, which draws from the present-day epoch of sleep. Therefore, one can split oneironaut dreams into two parts: an episodic "as if a video" portion that will be most accurate, and the semantic, "personal" portion, that will be least accurate. According to this model, the Fomalhaut dream *should* be labeled just as incorrectly as Bagheera calling fire a flower.

These insights into why the Fomalhaut dream is confusing are also the keys to finding ways to make the oneironauts useful. These neurons are time machines, but the information from the future time is mixed with the semantic noise of the present and past. How do we get the signal to stand out more clearly from the noise? This is a central question that will be tackled in the final chapter.

Fate Revisited—The Question of Self

IF I AM BEGINNING TO CONVINCE YOU that the oneironaut phenomenon is real, then there is an implication for your identity. The things you are conscious of because of your dreams matter for who you are right now. But if some fraction of these conscious elements is from the future, then the definition of self is not complete if you only think of the self as emerging from the sum total of experiences that you've had up to the present day. The self emerging at any instant includes events that could be known to you from your possible futures. Each one of us resembles Janus. A major part of our identity comes from the face that looks to the past, and a minor part comes from the second face that sees into the future. A statement such as, "I knew I could do it because I knew I would do it" actually makes sense in the Janusian context.

The Fomalhaut dream in 1995 and the Fomalhaut discovery in 2004 have brought these issues of identity to my attention. First of all, after reading the segment on "The Janusian Mind: Two times meeting in one brain" you might entertain the very similar phrase: "The two selves meeting in one brain." The stark reality is that in the oneironaut dream, my present self is experiencing a future self, whereas the default is supposed to be that the present self should only draw on the memories of the past self.

To be even more dramatic, I am equating the oneironaut phenomenon to walking down the street and encountering yourself. This isn't the type of encounter where you get to chat—you only have a moment to share an experience with each other. The window to you is too short to entertain questions and answers. This future person is not an exact duplicate of you, but some other person that has evolved and is reacting to the world as it has evolved in the future. Yet, in what resembles a paradox, this person becomes you the moment you meet.

Just to be clear, I'm not talking about encountering yourself by viewing yourself from the outside, as if some *doppelganger*. Instead, I'm sticking to the logic in Shakespeare's play *Julius Caesar*, when Cassius asks Brutus: "Tell me, good Brutus, can you see your face?" Brutus replies: "No, Cassius; for the eye sees not itself, / But by reflection, by some other things."[29] So in fact the oneironaut phenomenon is not a case of becoming a disembodied observer who can watch itself from the outside. Rather, the experience is of watching the outside world *through the eyes* of that future self, which simultaneously becomes your present self. James Joyce hints at this concept when he wrote:

> In the intense instant of imagination, when the mind, Shelley says, is a fading coal, that which I was is that which I am and that which in possibility I may come to be. So in the future, the sister of the past, I may see myself as I sit here now by reflection from that which I then shall be.[30]

But what is the situation if that future self will not exist at all because of different choices and a different timeline of events? Is your self some combination of future selves who are not necessarily going to be part of your timeline? I already hinted in the Trifid Nebula chapter that if you take all the parts that make up my "self" today, I simultaneously have the selves that were and were not ridiculed by my classmates. But the Fomalhaut dream emphasizes this too.

To understand why, you have to know one more thing about me: In 1997 I quit astronomy. The Hubble discovery of Fomalhaut's belt would not take place in 2004, and as a result the planet Fomalhaut b would probably not have been discovered in 2008—perhaps not at all in human history. The fates of several million visitors to the National Air and Space Museum would not come to pass. They would not see the image of

Fomalhaut and its planet displayed in the museum's second-floor gallery.

The idea to quit astronomy started around 1994. As a doctoral student I realized that job prospects for the future were dismal, and it would make sense to have a backup plan. Put another way, it was irrational to continue with a career in astronomy when better options were available to me. You don't have to take my word on this one. Just consider that the American Association for the Advancement of Science would state the following in a policy alert: "Given the lack of tenure-track jobs in academia...graduate students should consider a broad range of career paths and not view a postdoc position as the default step after completion of a Ph.D."[31] Sadly, I'm quoting from a science policy alert written in 2014, not in 1994. Twenty years may have passed, but the situation was the same.

I wasn't the only student in 1994 that had such concerns. A fellow astronomy student would get his Ph.D. in astrophysics, but immediately go to medical school afterward. Others would go to work for Microsoft or Apple. For myself, I enjoyed topics in political science related to global affairs. So I applied to several master's degree programs, and was accepted at Georgetown's prestigious Walsh School of Foreign Service. In the U.S. a degree from Georgetown was a sure way to succeed in a multitude of great career paths involving business, government or non-profit service.

At the same time, as I was writing my doctoral dissertation in Hawaii, I was also offered a prestigious job as a postdoctoral researcher at the Max Planck Institute for Astronomy in Heidelberg. The offer came directly from the director himself, the highly regarded astronomer Steve Beckwith, and unexpectedly my backup plan had to contend with an "offer you can't refuse" situation. Fortunately for me, Georgetown was gracious and accepted my request for a year deferral, so that I could take one last look at astronomy as a career.

Would an astronomy career as a postdoc in Germany make me change my mind? Postdoctoral research can be a great part of a career when one has freedom, authority and a corresponding paycheck to conduct research at a high level. After a year in Heidelberg the career pendulum swung back toward astronomy, but got stuck in the middle. I couldn't decide. It seemed like a no-brainer to just go to Georgetown, get a prestigious degree, and have a secure future. But my gut instinct was telling me that my identity had become and could continue to be a professional astronomer, even though the chances of success were obscure to the rational mind.

Who am I now and who would I become in the future? The dream log of Fomalhaut that I presented in this chapter was made in a waking state, when I could write and sketch. Therefore, in 1995 I became conscious of a future in 2004 where my identity is an astronomer, a researcher, an explorer of the night sky. Thus, while living in Heidelberg in 1997 but possibly heading to Georgetown, a small part of my brain, a tiny portion of my identity, the intangible third man, was already the astronomer of 2004 who would see Fomalhaut's dust belt with his eyes.[32]

Did knowledge of a future self help me in making the decision to stay in astronomy? No, it made it harder. *Knowing the future does not provide answers—it provides choices.* If this future self had been absent from my conscious mind, the rational decision to pack my bags and go to Georgetown would have met few obstacles. And even with its existence in my conscious mind, I still had free will. I could reject this future self just as I rejected the taping up of that torn Trifid Nebula poster. There was nothing stopping me from doing so. And so a great battle would erupt between the rational mind that said, "Duh, go to Georgetown," and the irrational, gut instinct that said, "Hey, you could find something really amazing around a star that no one else has ever seen before."

So when people talk about "acting on gut instinct," that gut instinct may in fact be the part of your future self that you've experienced as an oneironaut. It doesn't cover every possible action that you need to decide upon. Maybe gut instinct is absent for most decisions. And even when it's present, you may decide the opposite of your gut instinct, and that future self will never materialize. When you encounter that future self in the street, you can always walk away and say: "Hey, dude, I'm not going to be you."

The three Steves

One of the founders of Apple, Steve Jobs, gave a speech at Stanford University on June 12, 2005, where he offered his perspective on these concepts:

> Again, you can't connect the dots looking forward; you can only connect them looking backwards [i.e., the skill of the rational mind]. So you have to trust that the dots will somehow connect in your future. You have to trust in something—your gut, destiny, life, karma, whatever. This approach has never let me down, and it has made all the difference in my life.

So for me, which side won the great internal struggle—mind or gut? Given enough time, the mind is persuasive and can trump the gut—a charioteer must ultimately control the horses, even if the horses know better—and so my decision was to leave astronomy. I did not go the way of Jobs. I contacted Steve Beckwith and told him that I would be leaving for Georgetown. My future self as an astronomer would be unrealized. Fomalhaut's dust belt and Fomalhaut b would not be discovered with the Hubble Space Telescope.

This is probably a true statement, at least for Fomalhaut b. As I noted earlier, Fomalhaut was not going to be observed by Hubble until I formally proposed, several years in a row, to be allowed a chance to observe it. Fomalhaut b cannot be detected with ground-based telescopes, and the camera aboard Hubble that I needed to make the discovery would fail in January 2007. Therefore, even a brief, one-year delay in the progress of my work could make all the difference. Moreover, phenomena in the universe are not static. The physical mechanisms that make Fomalhaut b optically bright may last a limited time. Therefore, an astronomer in 2026 may not be able to detect an astronomical object with a new generation of telescopes—the object may have changed in a way that makes it no longer detectable, including the possibility that it could have been destroyed as part of its evolution.

So now you might appreciate that the stakes are getting quite high. In 1997 I had rejected a career path that would put me in a position to target Fomalhaut with Hubble. Despite HST's prominence across astrophysics, the history of the observatory would simply not include the discovery of an exoplanet through direct imaging. I alone—a single human on our planet—would have a memory of it as a dream, it would be a small part of my self, but it would not materialize in the history of humanity. You, *meine Leser*, would never see it in on NASA's web page or in the National Air and Space Museum.

But the fact is, you cannot fully understand fate if you are only thinking about yourself. The minds and gut instincts of others react to what you do. Your self—past, present and future—is entangled with the fates and decisions of others. As it turns out, Steve Beckwith would accept my resignation, but noted that if I came back I would have a leading role in one of the major projects operated by the Max Planck Institute. This tipped the pendulum a tiny bit back in the direction of astronomy. After all, not only did I have my gut instinct pushing me back to astronomy, but Steve also gave me a rational reason to go back.

I should note that this offer was entirely his decision. I didn't expect or request a counteroffer—it was a surprise. So whatever Steve Beckwith was thinking about connecting dots in the future, it influenced my future and the history of scientific discovery with Hubble. I returned to the timeline of an astronomer.

Of course, he wasn't the only influence in my life. More generally, your parents, relatives, friends or even a random stranger might give you that nudge to connect a certain dot at a certain time. For example, I recall attending a lecture by Sir John B. Gurdon, the Nobel laureate who many years ago discovered the biological principles of cloning. Sir John happily started his lecture by showing the typed text on his school report card. Not only did it show that he failed biology, but the teacher added the following note:

> I believe Gurdon has ideas about becoming a scientist; on his present showing this is quite ridiculous; if he can't learn simple biological facts he would have no chance of doing the work of a specialist, and it would be a sheer waste of time, both on his part and of those who would have to teach him.[33]

Wow, talk about knocking a kid down to the ground and then kicking him hard for good measure! The young John Gurdon was ranked 250th in the program, out of 250 students.

So how did young Mr. John become Sir John, the great scientist, when all the science dots were ripped away? About an hour after he gave his lecture, we were both caught in the time warp of the evening dinner buffet, and I posed the following question: "If you received such a low grade, then wasn't it entirely irrational for you to become a scientist? How was it that you pursued the irrational path?"

His answer was that despite his performance in school, his parents recognized his keen interest in biology, and they were the ones that helped in rebuilding the bridge of dots that would become the path toward the Nobel Prize.

Thus, when you look at how you connect the dots for your future, there are all sorts of influences that can interfere with or nurture that path. The key ingredient was that he himself held an interest in biology. Recognizing this as a fundamental aspect of his identity, his parents pushed him over the hurdles that would have otherwise stopped him in his tracks.

Therefore I think that Steve Jobs missed a crucial insight in his Stanford speech. No matter how good his instinct was to connect dots into his future, he depended on yet another Steve, a man nicknamed "Woz" (Steve Wozniak), to also connect his own dots in a certain way. Steve Jobs' Stanford speech should have said, "So *we* have to trust that the dots will somehow connect in *our* future."

When answering the "self" questions about who you are, and who you will become, the question is more accurately phrased "who we are" and "who we will become." The poet John Donne expressed the same understanding in the following way:

> No man is an island, entire of itself; every man is a piece of the continent, a part of the main...Any man's death diminishes me because I am involved in mankind, and therefore never send to know for whom the bells tolls; it tolls for thee.[34]

It gets even more complicated: this future involves you, the reader. A chain of decisions led you to spending your time reading this book, and so reading about Fomalhaut was in your future self. But it didn't have to be this way. You too have a self who would never encounter the stories and knowledge presented here.

The Poultry Matrix

In a book about the brain and memories, the psychologist Sheri Mizumori writes the following:

> The experiences of our lives, whether good or bad, continually shape or modify the knowledge base that we call our memories. These memories define who we are and which purposeful behaviors become engaged in any given situation. Without these memories, we have no personal identity or purpose.[35]

Why did Professor Mizumori add "or purpose" to the sentence? Why not just leave it off—do you really need memories (acquired knowledge) to have a purpose? In this chapter describing parts of my life, are my identity and my purpose necessarily linked? If you had no knowledge or memories, would you still have an identity? If dreams that you remember contain experiences from your future, does that influence your purpose?

And how about this scenario: Does a newborn human with practically zero past experiences obtain identity and purpose from new memories gained through dreams? For example, if the oneironaut experience is real, doesn't this mean that a baby can fear dogs even though it has yet to interact with a dog? But if you accept this scenario for humans, and given that many other animals also dream during sleep, then isn't it possible for a bird to identify and fear its predators, and understand where to build its first nest, before it has witnessed any of these things?[36]

A major problem with the oneironaut phenomenon is that it spawns an abundance of speculation such as the above. Nevertheless, I can try to select the speculation that has a chance of being experimentally tested. The above questions seem out of reach, yet there's a very clever experiment involving newborn domestic chickens—*Gallus gallus domesticus*, an excellent animal name if you say it out loud in Latin. The key is that chicks imprint, or form a strong social attachment, to the first thing they see in life, and then follow it wherever they see it going. Unlike other experiments that require training the animal (i.e., changing the brain through experience), the chicks perform this behavior innately. One can therefore test the qualities of this behavior to see what are the limits of innate knowledge before an animal starts experiencing its future. Put another way, we can hope to disentangle the purpose and identity provided to an organism by the physiology it is born with, versus its subsequent modification through experience.

In a lab at the University of Southern California, psychologist Justin Wood takes 60 newborn chicks and puts each in a high-tech box that creates a virtual world for each chick, and then records everything that chick does in that world 24/7. Their world is extremely sparse (food and water are provided), except that two of the walls are computer screens that display whatever scene the experimenters choose for the chick. Three boxes can be stacked on top of each other, forming a wall, and the room can have many such walls of boxes within it. Thus the whole experiment has been called "The Poultry Matrix" by psychologist Alison Gopnik. This refers to the science fiction film *The Matrix*, where millions of humans are raised in a controlled environment and experience a virtual world designed by artificial intelligence. This in turn derives from Plato's diabolical thought experiment 2,500 years ago where humans chained to a wall can only observe shadows projected in front of them and interpret these virtual images as reality.

So what world do you, Poultry God, create for *Gallus gallus domesticus*? To keep things simple, the head of a rabbit could be shown, but only from a face-on viewpoint. Thus the chick will imprint on this image. You can tell it recognizes this image later because when it is displayed on the left wall, the chick will move left, and then it moves to the right if the image is projected on the right wall. The head of a rabbit has a distinct shape when seen face-on, and as far as the chick is concerned, its entire universe is the rabbit head viewed face-on. But what would happen if you rotate the image so that the head is viewed from the top down? This is a very different profile, an entirely different universe for the chick. It should not recognize this universe as the same one that it imprinted on. Yet the experiments show that the rabbit head can be rotated in every direction, and the chick recognizes it.[37] Thus without prior learning the chick brain has an innate ability to represent its simple knowledge of the universe from many different viewpoints.

Such experiments could test whether or not a bird or other animal could identify and fear its predators, or perform other vital functions, before it has witnessed any of these things. The oneironaut phenomenon seems so random and sparse that it may not account for the general behaviors necessary for survival. Nevertheless, as I stated in Chapter 3, the oneironaut phenomenon could play a role in rare decisions that are important. Using the Poultry Matrix, one could start playing around with some of these ideas. For example, since chicks are monitored 24/7, one could determine how the natural and experimentally modified sleep of each chick may correlate to its behaviors. If there was a novel visual stimulus to be presented in the future, does the recognition or reaction to this novel stimulus correlate to aspects of sleep? Or, take two groups of chicks that are destined to have a good or bad experience associated with an image of a cat. When the chicks see the cat for the first time, will those that are destined to have a bad experience further in the future show a different reaction than those that are destined to have a good experience?

In the Poultry Matrix, the past, present and future worlds of *Gallus gallus domesticus* can be predetermined, and therefore the Poultry Gods could test if information travels across time. However, animal models always suffer from the criticism that the results may not translate accurately to humans. Nevertheless, the principles of the animal experiments could be adapted to human subject experiments. The Heidelberg Dome was a type of experiment that involved a test between prior learning and apparently innate precognition. The human experiment has the huge advantage that the subjects can communicate how they know something. Thus I could tell you that my apparently innate knowledge of finding a novel location was really a memory of a future experience. One day the Heidelberg Dome could be constructed on a scale much larger than the chick boxes to determine what aspects of human identity and purpose arise from past experience, and what aspects stem from the oneironaut phenomenon.

Experiencing Many Worlds

WHAT DOES IT FEEL LIKE to have knowledge of a universe where the timeline is different than the one you are currently experiencing? I believe I can offer a portion of that experience to the readers who can make it to the Smithsonian National Air and Space Museum in Washington, D.C. First, as you enter from the main entrance on the National Mall, you can turn left and go to a large ground-level space where you will see a replica of the majestic Hubble Space Telescope. The ceiling is so high, they have the telescope more or less propped up vertically.

After that, you can go to the second floor, where you will find Gallery 207, which is called "Exploring the Planets." As you walk by a model of the Mars Exploration Rover, you encounter several displays under the heading "Mars: World of Change" and a multi-panel presentation called "Enduring Mysteries and New Challenges." In the lower right you will see my image of Fomalhaut's dust belt and planet under the heading "Looking Outward: Worlds Beyond Our Solar System." (**Figure 4-8**)

Figure 4-8: A man at the National Air and Space Museum looking over the display containing my Fomalhaut image. There are timelines where this person and millions of others visit the museum, but they do not experience my image in this room because the discovery in this form never came into existence in Earth's history.

After all the things that I've told you about myself so far, you would have to realize that there is a universe where you are standing there amidst all this science and technology, and when you look at that multi-panel presentation, you do NOT see an image of Fomalhaut. It is not there.

If you really can get to the museum before the display is changed, just pause for some moments in that space directly in front of my Fomalhaut image. If you can feel that that the image is not there, but somehow exists as if a wispy fragment of a dream, then that is a version of yourself who came to the museum in a timeline where I did not become an astronomer. The knowledge of Fomalhaut represented by this specific image never materialized. That's you experiencing the many worlds.

If you cannot travel to the museum, then consider that there are many versions of you in the many worlds representing all possible timelines, who will never read this book because I never wrote it. Remember, I chose to write the book because I decided that the Fomalhaut experience was just enough to make me take the Socratic Gamble. Without Fomalhaut, there is no book.

Pseudodivine Knowledge—What's at Stake?

IN THE LAST SECTION I reasoned that having experiences of the future must impact our existing knowledge, beliefs, identity and purpose. If it were possible to hone the abilities of the oneironauts such that they provide accurate and reliable knowledge from the future, then wouldn't it be possible to ascertain facts in the present day as if by divine knowledge? For example, suppose that in 1995 I had become an established oneironaut scientist with an excellent track record. This means that in 1995 I could have stated a series of scientific facts, such as the fact that the star Fomalhaut is surrounded by a dust belt oriented by 24 degrees away from edge-on and offset from the star. These facts are scientific in the sense that they are testable, but divine because there was no scientific method employed up to that epoch of time to directly establish the facts. The fact-finding would have to occur at a future epoch.

As far as I can tell, such pseudodivine knowledge is not forbidden. The result is that when distinct information is transmitted from the future to the present, the timelines can be changed and experienced differently. Just as in the Trifid Nebula poster example, I can experience a different future timeline that doesn't even involve the specific one that I dreamed about. For example, for the Fomalhaut dream, I could have used the knowledge gained in 1995 to target Fomalhaut's dust belt sooner, using another Hubble camera called STIS that was available back then. The Fomalhaut discovery would have been made in 1997 with STIS and not in 2004 with ACS. Thus the 2004 discovery of Fomalhaut's dust belt with Hubble would have been advanced by seven years using pseudodivine knowledge.

Big deal, right? The stakes are pretty low for the world if astrophysics is progressing a little bit slow or a little bit fast. For example, several students from the U.S. and Japan have come up to me to say that they were inspired to go into astronomy as a career because of the Fomalhaut discoveries, and so I know that the oneironaut experience has already had some small impact on this planet. But that's just a few people. Of course, who knows what they might end up doing, and whom they might influence in their lives? It could be important and derive from the influence of Fomalhaut, among many other influences, but maybe not.

I sometimes wonder what could have been at stake if I were instead a scientist attempting to eradicate a major human health problem on the planet, such as Jonas Salk and the polio vaccine. What would those seven years translate to in human terms when it comes to a medical advance? In the case of the 1952 polio epidemic in the United States, 3,145 people died and 21,269 were disabled. If the U.S. population was around 153 million, that is 0.002% of the population that died from polio. With today's population of 319 million, the deaths in one year would amount to 6,557, or 18 people per day. So in this case, if an oneironaut scientist could find a cure just one day earlier, then that translates to 18 lives saved within the United States.

This is quite a sobering notion. If the Fomalhaut discovery were instead the vaccine for such a virus, that head start of seven years would have amounted to over 45,000 people saved in the United States alone. The only consoling thought is that perhaps the oneironaut phenomenon is present in the scientists actually doing such work, but they don't know it. I would never know if Jonas Salk was in fact inspired by the dreams that he recalled every morning. Yet it's possible, and thus the fatalities would have been much greater in the end if the oneironaut phenomenon did not exist.

Hearts that beat together need a liquid tether

I have found one case in which a medical advance seems to be related to information from dreams. Back in the early 20th century, the nervous system had been anatomically described by master scientists such as a Spaniard named Santiago Ramon y Cajal.[38] You could see the structure of neurons just like you could see wiring in an electronic device. But nerves didn't connect together like twisting two wires together. Instead, a gap, called a synapse, was discovered between neurons. The neuroscientists were thus faced with a puzzle: how does an electrical impulse move across the gap? Is there a "spark" that jumps the gap, or could you move the signal by releasing and absorbing chemicals?

The neuroscientist who figured this out claims he got the idea from a dream. Actually, two dreams, because the first dream showed him how to do the experiment, which he couldn't quite remember the next day, so he had the same dream a second night just to make sure he got the details right.

Enter neuroscientist Otto Loewi, Nobel laureate and candidate oneironaut. Herr Doctor Professor Loewi was from Frankfurt, Germany, and passed away in 1961. But back in 1921 his dreams showed him that he could solve the question of nerve signal transport in the following way. Take two live frogs and remove their beating hearts (and with that thought I am so glad that my job is to look at the stars instead). These disembodied frog hearts will keep beating for a few hours, and you can attach a wire to the nerve that controls the heart rate, and thereby manipulate the heart rate electrically. This was no mystery at the time. Soon after the American Revolution in 1776, the Italian scientist Luigi Galvani discovered that frog legs twitch when electricity is applied to them. So electricity put into nerves could make muscles move, but what about those gaps between nerves? How did the signal cross the gaps?

Amazingly, Otto Loewi's dream showed him that the question could be answered with an experiment where he would take fluid from one beating heart and transfer it to a different beating heart. First, he electrically changed the heart rate of one disembodied frog heart using the wire. He then took a fluid sample from this heart and transferred it to the other frog heart, which had no wire attached to it. He found that the second heart also changed its rate, when the only connection between the two hearts was the fluid. What this showed is that the second beating heart was responding to a change in chemistry and not to a change of electricity. The nerve in the first heart was being electrically manipulated externally by Otto, and in response it must have been releasing chemicals to jump the nerve gaps, but these same chemicals then controlled the beating of the second heart.

This is called chemical neurotransmission. Your brain and nervous system command your heart muscle to beat by transmitting and absorbing chemicals at every connection that your nervous system has. One of the proteins that regulates neurotransmission is called "stargazin," which thus gives astronomers like myself full license to speak authoritatively about neurobiology. [39] More widely known neurotransmitters include melatonin, dopamine and adrenaline.

Otto Loewi achieved an incredible breakthrough with this experiment, but was the dream an example of pseudodivine knowledge?

I would claim that his dream more likely shows an example of thinking through a problem instead of obtaining unknowable information. According to his Nobel lecture of 1936, he had already heard ideas that the heart nerve could affect the heart by releasing the chemical potassium. So, a reasonable test of whether or not this is true would involve connecting two hearts by a chemical bridge only, and see if a change in activity of one heart induces a change in the activity of the second heart. Given this broad outline, thinking and dreamwork could provide a mental picture of how to set up this experiment in the lab.

Therefore, I don't think that Otto Loewi was an oneironaut. Earlier in the chapter I applied similar skepticism to myself and the Fomalhaut dream. I found that there was no idea presented to me, or even within the scope of human knowledge, that a ring of dust around a star would be offset. There is no such unique nugget of information in Loewi's dream and the resulting experiment that would distinguish it from creativity and problem-solving ability.

Nevertheless, if you think Loewi's dream was an oneironaut experience, then many millions of people have benefited from the medical advances that resulted from the early discovery of neurotransmitters. Another famous scientist central to saving millions of lives from disease is Louis Pasteur. He once said, "Where observation is concerned, chance favors only the prepared mind." It seems to me that in addition to my formal training, it was also my dream of Fomalhaut that prepared my mind to make the observation of Fomalhaut. So too it may be that the life-saving contributions of Loewi, Salk, Pasteur, and many others are due to the ability of the mind to advance discoveries because of how the perception of the future prepares the mind.

Woofing insane knowledge

How far in the future could we obtain useful knowledge, such as an experiment that gives us a critical, life-saving vaccine? Suppose that 25 years from now I am going to die and today I have a dream with the information my children are going to tell me 24 hours before I die. My children are oneironauts, so that this information is 25 years in their future. So right now I could tell you something from 50 years in the future. But my children's children do exactly the same thing in communicating knowledge from their future. So you can easily see that an unbroken chain of information can keep on going for a long time. Technically, it doesn't have to be my children. It can simply be "the oneironauts" in every generation of humans. It would be an interesting exercise to figure out at what point information becomes completely unintelligible to a given observer. Would an ancient Mesopotamian understand the words "cell phone" or "nuclear war"?

Of course not everyone gets to say that information from 5,000 years in the future is knowable—you'd have to be from the college of the insane to say that out loud. But those of us in the college understand that for most living things, it is equally insane to have knowledge from 5,000 years in the past. Such knowledge is available to humans only because we evolved a single skill that no other creature living on this planet seems to have acquired to the same degree.

Let's see how this works. Consider the hypothetical day when a weird mushroom grows in my backyard, our small Maltese dog, Bebe, eats it, comes back into the house, and says:

"S'up?"

Stunned, I reply: "Bebe, you can talk? Can—you—un—der—stand—me?"

"Most certainly. After eating that mushroom, I can talk, I know language now."

"Wow, amazing things happen when you mess with neurotransmitters. Bebe, you're going to be the most famous dog in history, more famous than Argos, the legendary dog that was faithful to his master Odysseus thousands of years ago."

Bebe becomes perplexed, cocks her head sideways, looks at me very suspiciously, and asks, "How do you know about a dog that lived thousands of years ago? You weren't actually there, were you?"

"No. It's just that when you have language, you can tell stories to your children, and they pass it on to their children, and this can go on for thousands of years. When a species acquires language, it can know facts from thousands of years in the past."

Bebe is amazed: "Woof! That is woofing insane!"

"Why is it woofing insane?" I ask.

"Because it's woofing impossible to know things from so long ago if you weren't there."

I pause and consider the dog's perspective, "Well, I suppose you learned to talk only 10 minutes ago, except for the curse words. Consider your keen sense of smell. Using scent, you can discover the history of a place, and create a mental story about what was there in the past, even if you weren't there to see it. Humans use language and their mind to discover the history of a place, going much further back than the history encoded in a scent, and in fact as far back as the beginning of time in our universe. You will find that language can make something that you thought was impossible very real and relevant to your everyday experiences."

But Bebe is a quick study: "Then how about famous dogs from 5,000 years in the future? Can I know who they are by using language?"

"Ah yes, language is indeed necessary for that, but not sufficient. We also need to boost a mysterious ability expressed during dreaming that is the Napoleon of our senses. Now let's go back in the yard and find more of those woofing mushrooms!"

The Icarus Gamble

Before embarking on any such search to know things from far in the future, I should address the brazen head in the room—doesn't pseudodivine knowledge have an ominous aspect to it? Should it be feared, because unexplained power cannot be wielded safely by fallible humans? Is knowledge of the future like the Ghost of Christmas Yet to Come, who made Scrooge tremble and declare: "Ghost of the Future…I fear you more than any spectre I have seen."[40]

In the long run, I really don't think so. Knowledge of the future is just a thing, not a ghost. Consider a parallel that I can make to human flight. On November 21, 1783, free flight became a new experience to humans. Jean-Francois Pilatre de Rozier and Marquis d'Arlandes floated off the Earth's surface in a hot air balloon, traveling to nearly a kilometer in altitude and for about 9 km distance over the outskirts of Paris, before landing safely. The early balloonists achieved a magical feat. You wouldn't expect a dog to learn how to speak, and yet humans weren't supposed to be able to fly either. There were indeed many things to fear with this new human ability. If you entered a cloud, would everyone on board get electrocuted? If you flew too high, would your proximity to the Sun roast you as in the legend of Icarus?

In the end they were not electrocuted or roasted, but they found that they could only make it to 9 km altitude without oxygen, and thus set a boundary to this type of human exploration. There were accidents and fatalities along the way, but the curiosity and ambition to go further than any human had done before could not be contained. Among the rewards for taking these risks was realizing that our beautiful Earth provides a mere 13 km layer of life-sustaining atmosphere near the surface, and that's it. There is no infinite supply of life-sustaining atmosphere and what we have should therefore not be ruined.

So too with the oneironauts we have barely explored the limits of these abilities. Are there fundamental rules that cannot be broken? How far can we really go in obtaining information from the future? What are the unintended consequences? What would we understand about our existence that would be extremely valuable to know? Like the balloonists who got to 9 km altitude and began to lose consciousness but made it back down safely, we should find ways to explore the limits of the oneironaut phenomenon without endangering ourselves, and reap the rewards of accelerated knowledge.

Paul Kalas

5. Dissect the Oneironaut!

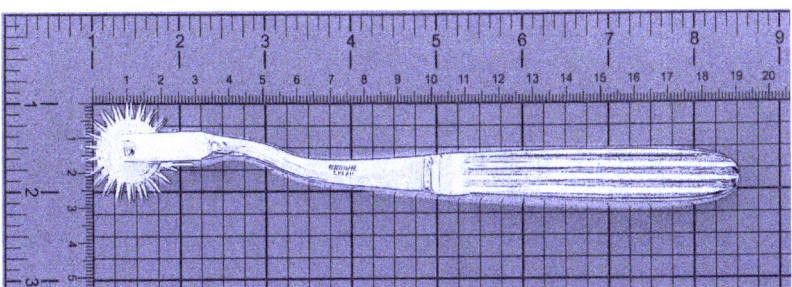

If we were able to prove the theory of multiple universes discussed in Chapter 2, I would be worried about the universe where harsh rulers govern the Earth and medical ethics never took hold. If I revealed myself to be an oneironaut, the authoritarian society would seek to harness the abilities of the mind in a very bad way. The Party rulers would command the military doctors in their Unit 731 to dissect my brain: "Find this mysterious brain part responsible for future knowledge so that we may defeat our enemies and vaporize those who have future thoughtcrimes. Muahaha!"

"Wait a minute," I plead in desperation. "My brain suits me just fine in its current undissected state, and I shall therefore promise to tell you everything I know, if you let me be." The evil doctors are somewhat unhappy at a missed opportunity to take blade to brain. But on that day I would escape vivisection in Room 101 by telling them everything I know. And so I embark on a series of exams, tests and stories that could hold rare clues of the when, where and what of the oneironaut phenomenon.

The Medical Interview

"HAVE YOU EVER HAD the *feeling* that a present-day experience is familiar, as if experienced in an undefined past time?"[41] If you were conducting a survey for the déjà vu phenomenon, this is a basic question defining the experience. In various surveys, approximately seven out of ten people have answered yes to this question.[42] But my answer is no. This is because two things in this question do not match my experience.

First, my déjà vu is not a feeling; it is a memory of a dream. For example, if you ask me to calculate 4 x 9, my answer is 36 because I immediately recall the answer from past experience. My déjà vu experience is as plain and simple as remembering multiplication tables. It has little or no feeling to go along with it.

The second discrepancy is related to the first, which is that the déjà vu memory is not "undefined." Instead, I *recognize* it very specifically as a dream and not as some other type of experience. For example, some respondents who have the déjà vu "feeling" have a vague sense that it arises from some past experience, but it is so vague they might entertain the notion that a past life is being recalled. For me, I have always had déjà vu linked to a dream memory. It is not a flashback to some other life that is disconnected from my autobiographical past. In fact, I used the word "recognize" above because of its clinical definition. Recognition is a cognitive event that has two parts: (1) understanding that an experience is familiar (e.g., I know you...), and (2) remembering exactly why the experience is familiar (...because we sat together two years ago on a flight from LAX to Heathrow).[43]

So now you know why the book title is "The Oneironauts" instead of something like "My Life with Déjà Vu." The oneironauts are the "dream travelers." The experience is not of an undefined feeling but of dream recall. Research has in fact shown that there is a large subset of respondents to the déjà vu question who describe déjà vu as a recollection of a dream (déjà rêvé).[44] Thus many others share my experience of the déjà vu phenomenon.

The evil doctors take careful notes, binding the pages from the interview with a paper clip, but they are skeptical about the precognitive aspects of my déjà vu. The medical literature clearly says that many people have reported déjà vu experiences, and these experiences are not precognitive because they are clearly associated with other factors, such as...

Pathology

"Do you hallucinate, hear voices, and/or lose consciousness? Have you ever been hospitalized for a head injury? How about migraines? Do you take drugs?" Medical practice and research are well aware of the reported experiences of déjà vu, and any medical exam to discover the origin would probably involve these questions. For me these would be quick questions to answer because the answers are all, "No."

But the next question the evil doctors ask me is: "Do you suffer from temporal lobe epilepsy?"

It turns out that temporal lobe epilepsy (TLE) is correlated to the déjà vu experience. Epilepsy involves episodes of aberrant brain function. The temporal lobes of the brain are on the sides of your head, above your ears. A TLE "attack" could create symptoms such as an altered consciousness, physical convulsions, and sensory distortions named "aura." The aura may be associated with migraines, dizziness, strange smells or tastes, and euphoria.

Of all the famous people throughout history that have suffered from epileptic seizures, the remarkable Russian author Dostoevsky probably had TLE.[45] We know this because of his personal diary and how he wrote about these seizures as experienced by some of his fictional characters, such as Prince Myshkin in *The Idiot*. Dostoevsky writes:

> He remembered among other things that he always had one minute just before the epileptic fit (if it came on while he was awake), when suddenly in the midst of sadness, spiritual darkness and oppression, there seemed at moments a flash of light in his brain, and with extraordinary impetus all his vital forces suddenly began working at their highest tension. The sense of life, the consciousness of self, were multiplied ten times at these moments which passed like a flash of lightning.[46]

It's fairly clear from my medical history that I am not epileptic, even though my family history has epilepsy in it. This revelation means what it says; yet what it says does not reveal the meaning. The hidden meaning is that my father earned a Ph.D. in neurology from New York Medical College in the 1960s (I used his Wartenberg Pinwheel for the chapter heading image), and his research topic was the characterization of epileptic seizures via electroencephalograms (EEGs). Epilepsy was part of his expertise as a physician.[47] He didn't actually have epilepsy, nor does my mother's side of the family. However, one book I distinctly remember seeing in the house while growing up had the most memorable of titles: *The Idiot*. I would not realize until I started writing my own book why Dostoevsky's novel was in my family's home. Any medical doctor interested in studying epilepsy would own this book. Childhood mystery solved! You might take a moment and reflect on some of the memorable objects in the home that you grew up in. Why were they really there? Who were they significant to?

Unfortunately, it is not entirely clear that I do not have TLE. It turns out that TLE attacks could also have *none* of the symptoms described above. Instead, the person could experience unusual sensations, including feelings of déjà vu and even *jamais vu*. Jamais vu is the feeling that the situation you are in is completely unfamiliar, even though it should not be the case (e.g., you just walked into your home). The presenting symptoms can be so mild that a person with TLE may never consider these episodes a medical problem, and hence never goes to a doctor.

With a definition more nebulous than either the Trifid Nebula or Fomalhaut, I have to think a little harder to see if I might suffer from TLE. After all, I am reporting déjà vu experiences, and people with clinically diagnosed TLE also report déjà vu experiences.

In the end my answer is still, "No, I do not have TLE." Like I said earlier, the déjà vu experience for me is not a vague feeling or sensation that seems characteristic of a TLE aura. My déjà vu is a specific recall of a memory, and Chapters 1–4 adequately demonstrate this experience as separate from clinical pathologies.

Release the Oneironaut

THE EVIL DOCTORS ARE NOT TERRIBLY HAPPY WITH MY CASE. The problem is that in their training to become doctors they learned to ask the questions above, but since my answers don't fit neatly into the general medical literature of the déjà vu experience, they really don't know what to do next. They decide to let me go and report that their medical interviews revealed that I clearly failed every known test for déjà vu—I *do not* have déjà vu experiences.

To my surprise, I actually feel slightly disappointed in their loss of interest in my déjà vu. Sure, their plan was to use it for evil, but it was nice to feel wanted. Then I realize that in this alternate universe the doctors have been selected to have certain traits. When a society is ruled by doctrine, those with creative sparks would be extinguished. Galileo Galilei on this alternate Earth was quickly quashed for his heretical ideas, and the subsequent totalitarian societies enforced paths for its citizens from childhood to adulthood that did not tolerate deviations from an established program.

Thus the doctors didn't have the type of creative thinking to ask me any further questions. If one of them did think creatively, he or she would not speak up because deviations from the group would limit their career prospects and livelihood. In fact, I finally figured out why they used paper clips to bind their notes—no one had dared to invent the stapler.

But I would be quite pleased because this insight should have consequences for technological civilizations that last 10,000 years or more. Those societies that encourage creativity would be the first to learn how to use the oneironaut phenomenon, and they would be the first to develop a technology that would allow visits to other planetary systems. Therefore the societies that spread first across the Galaxy will be those that value the freedom and the dignity of other beings.

Fortunately, you and I live in such a technological civilization that values these ideals. There's a bit of an anthropic principle to acknowledge—I wouldn't be able to write this book and you wouldn't be able to read it if totalitarian societies had become firmly rooted in Earth's timeline. Therefore, given that I've found myself living in this timeline that might be eager to hear my ideas for the ultimate good of the universe, let me give you additional details about the oneironaut phenomenon that will never be heard by those evil doctors in the evil universe.

Dissect the Déjà Vu

FIRST, WHY IS IT THAT A FUTURE WAKING EXPERIENCE should be perceived while asleep and dreaming? After all, many aspects of the dream/sleep state are attainable when awake. Any waking person can close their eyes and let thoughts flow into the mind. You could perceive non-visual imagery, or non-aural sounds. You are still awake, but the body could be relaxed in the same way as when sleeping. Thus, it seems to me that one avenue toward understanding the déjà vu experience is determining which elements of the brain and mind are different between the waking and sleeping states.

Second, what kinds of life experiences trigger déjà vu and why not certain other experiences? Do they involve all of the senses and cognitive functions, or a limited subset? If it's a subset, can we localize an area of the brain as nature's time machine? To answer these questions, I really have to collect a more thorough sample of déjà vu experiences.

Third, why do I have no control or will over the déjà vu experience? This means that I do not know how to make a specific night a déjà vu dream night. My déjà vu experience is distinctly different from others who would claim to conjure a vision of the future at a specific time and for a specific purpose.[48] I am unemployable in the soothsaying trade. If I have no control, does that mean déjà vu is a *reflex*, like sneezing, in which case I can investigate the triggers?

These are just some of the basic qualities and open questions. One day we might ascertain a few of the answers—the *why* and the *how* of the déjà vu phenomenon. But to determine the underlying mechanisms, I have to first produce as much information as possible about the *when, where and what* of my déjà vu. This requires observing and recording the déjà vu experiences, which started back in 1981. Though my experiences are continuing every month, at the present time I will analyze everything through the end of 2016.

My technique for recording information has become more methodical over time, and more rigorous ever since 2008 when I discovered the match between Fomalhaut and a dream diary entry from 1995. My records consist of two diaries: one for nightly dreams and one for déjà vu experiences. The dream diary is problematic in that I often have too many dreams to write down every day compared to my time available to write. The last section of this chapter addresses this issue in greater detail. In addition to text, the Fomalhaut experience taught me the value of including a sketch, so I'll draw something for a dream entry if text is inadequate for describing a geometry or appearance of something.

In the déjà vu diary I describe the experience as completely and as soon as possible. This includes the time the event happened and the time when I recognized the experience as a memory from a dream. I will then search through the dream diary for matches using several key phrases from the déjà vu entry. In the vast majority of cases I do not have a corresponding recording of the dream, though from memory I can occasionally estimate the approximate year that the dream occurred.

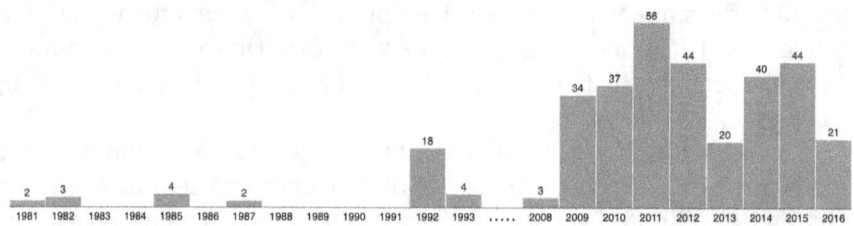

Figure 5-1: Annual distribution of recorded déjà vu experiences between 1981 and 2016. For example, in 2011 I recorded 56 déjà vu experiences.

For the purposes of writing this book, I revisited every déjà vu entry through 2016 and tagged it for various attributes. For example, if I enter a nearby house and I have déjà vu of a real estate agent who greets me with an unusual phrase, I would record this as a déjà vu event involving a person, indoors, listening, language, novelty, daytime, and problem solving, but it does not include travel away from home, outdoors, color, maps, geometry, etc. A moment later I may step into a room alone and have déjà vu of the space and a painting on the wall, which now counts as a separate event involving both a place and thing, indoors, novelty, daytime, and viewing, but not language, reading or listening. Note that I count these as two separate déjà vu events even though they occurred very close in time.

Figure 5-1 shows 332 déjà vu experiences between 1981 and 2016, with a large gap in the observations and records between 1993 and 2008. This gap does not mean that déjà vu was absent, but instead that I did not keep a record. Like many others who have déjà vu, I found it to be an interesting experience most of my life, I occasionally recorded the most memorable examples, and I still have these records in my possession as I started to write this book in 2008. For example, in 1992 I took a very interesting trip to Egypt and Israel where I kept a travel journal and recorded my déjà vu experiences. I traveled to amazing places in other years too, but I did not keep a journal. It was the discovery of the Fomalhaut dream record that motivated me to methodically study the phenomenon and keep better records. Thus between 2009 and 2016, I recorded 296 déjà vu experiences at an average rate of 37 per year.

So now that I've collected some data, let's think.

The *when*: Onset

The *when* questions refer to a time or time interval in the déjà vu phenomenon. The general question is: Why should a certain thing happen at a given time or time interval? What does it teach us?

So let's consider the first *when* question, and that is the time when the déjà vu phenomenon first appeared: Why did it first happen in the spring of 1981 during adolescence (my age was 13, going on 14)?

Is it possible that the answer has nothing to do with my development, but instead, say, I hit my head and that trauma triggered the mechanism? I don't recall anything like that, and there is no record of my going to the hospital for such a thing. Not only that, in some surveys of the déjà vu phenomenon, something like 70% to 80% of teenagers report having the experience about twice a year.[49] So unless we're all hitting our heads accidentally as teenagers, there must be some common feature of *normal* human development linked to the onset of the déjà vu phenomenon.

What does a teenage brain suddenly acquire or lose compared to the brain of a child? For the most part, the structure of the teenage brain resembles the structure of the adult brain, yet this time period includes a small increase in brain volume and the obvious onset of hormonal changes that impact function and behavior.[50] For example, there is a huge spike in sensation seeking that can have important consequences—the most likely time for you to be injured or killed is by your own behavior in your teenage years.[51] On a more positive note, puberty produces more hormones and neurotransmitters such as acetylcholine, which are correlated to memory and learning.[52]

Another notable change between children and teenagers is that more neurons in the frontal lobe become coated with a fatty sheath called myelin.[53] The frontal lobe governs executive function (planning, decisions, reasoning). Fatty myelin has a light color and it's called "white matter." The flip side of the coin is the brain's "gray matter," which decreases a bit in adolescence as its color converts to fatty white.[54]

The "myelination" of neurons increases the diameter of their structure, strengthens their connections, and thereby improves the speed of signal transmissions. Speed improvements allow parts of the brain that are spatially far from each other to communicate and integrate with each other more effectively. Thus, some parts of the brain can start exchanging more information, whereas previously they were more functionally isolated. The myelination of neurons can continue for your entire life, and recent findings show a causal link between myelination and learning.

How do we know? Medical researchers can genetically modify mice in a way that stops the creation of new myelin in their brains.[55] In other words, they can switch off a gene that is supposed to create a protein that is needed for myelin production. This type of mouse has a very difficult time learning how to use a modified running wheel compared to normal mice. This experimental finding is specific to motor learning, and one could reason that this causal mechanism is also true for other types of learning. For example, in humans, several diseases, as well as our natural cognitive decline with advancing age, are correlated to decreased myelin production.

These discoveries suggest to me that the déjà vu phenomenon may be enabled after the frontal lobe is well integrated with the rest of the brain during the myelination that occurs after childhood.[56] Myelination is causally linked to learning, and I generally believe that déjà vu is linked to biophysical phenomena taking place during learning. However, since children are "always learning" and later we have cognitive decline, the déjà vu phenomenon should be very strong earlier in my life rather than later. In fact, surveys of the déjà vu phenomenon suggest that there is a decline with age.[57] In my case, however, I have *not* detected an obvious decline in the déjà vu phenomenon with advancing age—I am something of an outlier.

In summary, I suspect that the key clue given by the age of onset is that improvements in overall brain connectivity are needed for the déjà vu phenomenon to start functioning. Once it gets going, the simplest forms of learning, such as walking into a store that you have never been to before, are enough for the déjà vu phenomenon to emerge.

Since nearly everyone in this pre-teen and teen age group undergoes the same brain development, I haven't quite pinpointed what might be unique or special about my development at this age. After all, don't you want to know what happened to the oneironaut that made him an oneironaut? For this I can only reflect on some of the skills and activities that became new parts of my life at that time.

In these early teen years, I would start becoming physically active by joining the middle-school swim team in eighth grade (1980–1981). The first swim practice was Monday, November 17, 1980 from 4:45 to 6:30 p.m. The Haycart dream would occur about four months later. Starting vigorous exercise such as swimming means that dopamine levels would have increased significantly in my brain. I wonder if one day someone will isolate a drug concoction that involves various teenage hormones blended with dopamine to jump-start the oneironaut mechanism in people who haven't had it before. When you start seeing 40-year-olds running, cycling or swimming incessantly, but with abundant acne on their faces, you'll know who is trying to become an oneironaut in your neighborhood.

It is worth noting that under experimental conditions, there is a possible link between increasing dopamine and pareidolia. Dopamine is a neurotransmitter that improves communication between neurons (it also dilates blood vessels). One effect is to produce euphoria, and thus exercise is correlated with increased dopamine levels in the brain, presumably to allow the individual to get through a stressful and painful activity. Too much dopamine, on the other hand, can produce hallucinations.

Researchers discovered that one could take a group of test subjects who were initially skeptical about paranormal beliefs, give them dopamine, and this would make them less skeptical.[58] The stimulus in the experiment was a vague and incomplete pattern, like burnt toast, and with the dopamine they were more likely to see Jesus than without the dopamine. A second group already had beliefs in the paranormal, they were more likely to see Jesus toast, and increasing the dopamine did not change that. So it's possible that for me the increase in exercise by swimming every day suddenly boosted my dopamine levels, and I would then become more susceptible to perceiving patterns where none existed. The main argument against this is that the Haycart dream was very concrete, specific, unambiguous and plain, as if the burnt toast had the letters "Hey, it's me Jesus" written in a Helvetica 16-point font.

Another aspect of the dopamine experiment is that it is unclear if the skeptical group should be taken as the "normal" group that is perturbed into an abnormal state by dopamine, or should the group that already believes in the paranormal be taken as normal, which means that dopamine is a cure or therapy for the skeptical group. It could be said that humans who can perceive patterns are also intelligent and insightful, maximizing the qualities needed for survival. Those who miss patterns are less likely to survive, but you could give them a dopamine shot to improve their chances.

Much more research is needed, including replication of the study cited above, before the role of dopamine is fully understood. Certainly the benefits of swimming (or exercise in general) could have provided a dopamine boost, but swimming has other effects too. Swimming greatly improves the duration and quality of my sleep because it exhausts the body and forces it to spend time resting. Swimming is also a sport that requires efficient and disciplined breathing, which may also factor into the quality of sleep. My overall aerobic fitness would start improving immensely in those years. To this day, I continue to swim athletically, and my resting heart rate can be as low as 45 beats per minute. Perhaps this helps explain why déjà vu in my case has not diminished with age.

This latter point may be important in the following way. Under certain circumstances while sleeping, I can hear my heartbeat via the pulse in my ears. As I'll describe later, there is a sleep stage called slow wave sleep that is known to be important for memory and learning. Slow wave sleep is defined by the brain's electrical activity dropping to 60 oscillations per minute. By improving my aerobic fitness with swimming, one can posit that my resting heart rate would have dropped so that the audible pulse in my ears would start to occasionally sync with the oscillations of slow wave sleep. Meanwhile, experiments have since shown that human subjects show a clear improvement in memory when a simple auditory stimulus is played through headphones while they are in slow wave sleep, and that auditory stimulus is synced with the slow wave rhythm.[59] Thus, it may be that a chain of events stimulated the oneironaut phenomenon somewhat accidentally: swimming improved my aerobic fitness, boosting dopamine and dropping my heart rate to around 60 beats per minute so that it would occasionally sync with slow wave sleep, enhancing memory and learning, and the combined cognitive effects nurtured the oneironaut phenomenon.

Competitive swimming would also change the cognitive fitness of my brain and mental state. Swimming workouts require a constant focus on technique and perseverance in effort while confronting ever increasing physical pain. In the Fomalhaut chapter I mentioned that I had the mental endurance required to weather criticism, and one way to develop mental endurance is by practicing sports like competitive swimming. Moreover, in competition, thinking about what you are about to do physically is an essential aspect of what will actually happen. Swimming, along with many other activities, is not just a race against the clock; it also involves creating and maintaining a mental picture of your future state. In general, gaining the ability to have such mental pictures, or priming for the future, defines the transition from childhood to adulthood.

The problem with pinpointing a causal factor in the oneironaut phenomenon is that swimming was only one of the activities that engaged my body and mind in those years. For example, in those middle-school years I would start amateur astronomy—I received my first telescope in June 1981—and ultimately photography. Both of these exercise the mind's spatial attention. When you are looking through the optics of either a telescope or a camera, you are deciding how to select a small piece of the world around you, and you summon all of your attention to this small piece. Not only is the mind focusing on it, but also the visual functions of the brain are asked to operate at full capacity, typically at the expense of the other senses.

In the words of the great modern scientist Jared Diamond: "Exercising body systems improves their function; not exercising them lets their function deteriorate."[60] This sounds obvious, but he is referring more specifically to medical research that proves the brain changes as you repeatedly practice something. Thus astronomy and photography were not merely a hobby, but also a repeated workout for the brain that matches what any 4,000-meter swim practice does for the body. I would begin these workouts in middle school.

Here is another example of an "attention workout." Sometimes amateur astronomers have to find intended targets such as faint galaxies by staring over a prolonged time through a telescope eyepiece while moving the telescope in various directions to scan the field. As you are staring at this pitch-black field, you have an expectation that something should happen, that the object you are trying to find would zip across the field as you move the telescope. Some objects, however, are so incredibly faint that they appear a little less black compared to the rest of the blackness around them. The event is therefore so subtle that most people would miss it unless their skills were honed through practice.

I practiced this skill when I was a teenager, and many years later in graduate school I would accompany a fellow student to the top of

Maunakea to use the smallest telescope on the mountain. While we were there, Dave Jewitt had asked us to also image a comet, but the pointing accuracy of the telescope failed, and we had to find the comet using a finder scope (a smaller telescope attached to the main telescope). I recall my friend searching for quite a while with no luck, and then it was my turn. A few seconds later I had the telescope pointed at the comet. You could say I was lucky, but I also had considerable experience over the years exercising my brain and vision to see such things. That comet was in fact an extremely faint patch of diffuse light in the blackness of the night.

In case you are about to get a telescope and start practicing because you think this is the key to becoming an oneironaut, let me just say these skills can be developed in many other ways. You can be in broad daylight looking down instead of looking up at a starry sky. The paleontologist Neil Shubin recalls that when he first started walking around with fossil experts in Arizona, all he saw were rocks on the ground, whereas the experts would immediately pick up fossils:

> But then one day, you know, it just kicked in. I start to see the distinction of bone from rock. And when it did, it was like I was wearing a whole new pair of glasses. You know, all of a sudden, I saw fossils everywhere, and then it hit me—my brain was trained![61]

For me, photography was a second exercise for the brain on top of amateur astronomy. Photographers have to consider the entire space surrounding them, and then choose the place and time to point the camera. In school, my skills would be finely honed with photojournalism, including sports photography. With this type of photography, instead of searching for something faint or imperceptible in a visual field, the mind is searching for an instant in time among a continuity of rapid events. The world captured with the press of a camera button is not merely a rapid selection of space, but also a selection of time.

Back in the Fomalhaut chapter when I introduced the "beholder's share," I bet some readers thought that photography is the one art form that involves pure imitation. This might be true when photography is used for certain purposes, such as maps. But in the majority of photography, even the ubiquitous selfie, a photographer has to choose how space will be depicted within the frame and must select a moment in time. Photography is not a mere imitation or recording of human experience, it also depicts a series of choices that are unique to the artist.

The important aspect of photojournalism and sports photography is that they both exercise the brain for predicting the future. The mind has to instantaneously understand what is happening in the present so that the camera lens is on its way to point where events will take place in the future, and the brain signal to press the shutter is sent to the finger before the event has taken place. In fast-paced action, you have to be slightly ahead of the present, selecting the most probable place that a future event will occur.

How do you know what these probabilities are? Your training has an automatic feedback and reward system. You know you missed a great photo as surely as missing a shot in basketball. Just as getting the ball in the basket improves with practice, photography is also a case where your control over motion and perception of future possibilities are honed by making mistakes and learning from them. This feedback process leads to a mental model of how the world should work across *time*. The better the model gets, the more successful you are at the task. The reason Neil Shubin could suddenly identify fossils across *space* is that his mental model had become sufficiently accurate through training. Through photography I would learn to build and exploit models of what should happen a few moments in the future. The famous quote from Louis Pasteur summarizes my point: "If your mind is prepared, you are more likely to succeed in an observation." For the oneironaut, the mind that is prepared to *model* events outside the present time is more likely to *observe* events outside the present time.

After telling you about my new hobbies in middle school, the things that shaped my unique identity, is it reasonable to conclude that swimming, astronomy and photography helped the oneironaut phenomenon emerge? Have I pinpointed a unique aspect of my development, or should we consider that all three pursuits are a consequence of a different root cause in brain function? My guess is that both options have merits. I would conjecture that my particular developing brain would have strengths in visual attention and anticipation that would sow the seeds for astronomy, photography and the oneironaut phenomenon. However, in middle school I was only beginning my hobbies of astronomy and photography, neither of these hobbies is particularly rare in the modern world, and therefore they don't seem to be the unique cause of the oneironaut phenomenon. Moreover, the Haycart dream and subsequent déjà vu was both a visual *and* auditory experience. The most unique signal in the Haycart dream was in fact a processing of language and meaning. Therefore the onset of the oneironaut phenomenon shows that many more parts of the brain were integrated into the experience than merely visual attention.

Whatever caused me to be an oneironaut is also the same thing that attracted me to photography and astronomy. With the beginning of vigorous physical exercise, perhaps the properties of my sleep also changed, and this would be important for dream recall.

Restating this more generally, suppose that most people have a few déjà vu experiences when they are children or adolescents, but these experiences do not naturally continue into adulthood. For me, the déjà vu experience begins in adolescence, persists through adulthood, and even crosses above a certain threshold where it is frequent enough that I can begin to study it. Perhaps the explanation for why the phenomenon continued into my adulthood is that I was exercising my brain in the right way by having certain reinforcing hobbies. Use it or lose it, which is what Jared Diamond was trying to say above. It's like saying that if all of us started learning a foreign language at age 10, then only those who keep practicing will be competent in that language at age 50.

The far-reaching consequence of my interpretation above is that *the oneironaut phenomenon can be learned and strengthened.* If my abilities were reinforced by certain repeated tasks and behaviors, then other people can also become oneironauts. The oneironaut phenomenon can be an acquired skill.

These arguments suggest an innate oneironaut ability emerging to prominence in the young brain, where some individuals stumble upon behaviors that reinforce and strengthen the skill over time. Let's call this the *reinforcing theory* of creating an oneironaut. The next steps would be to conduct empirical studies to test various facets of the theory, but this is somewhat boring in isolation. A more exciting scenario is when we have two or more theories, and then the experiments have a clear motivation to test which theory is the best one, if any.

So, let me propose a competing idea, which I'll call the *compensating theory* of creating an oneironaut. Why not consider the proposition that the oneironaut phenomenon is *not* a special power that some people nurture successfully, but rather a crutch to a learning disability that some people need in order to be successful?

In this alternate view, what happened was that in middle school my mind was having difficulty keeping up with the increasing demands of learning abstract knowledge and correctly interpreting situations in my new environment. Things like attention, working memory and social skills were problems for me. I struggled to understand what I heard and saw, and amid this struggle the oneironaut phenomenon emerged and remained permanently. My mind discovered a mechanism to send information to the past so I could have more time to study for the real-life tests that were hard for me to pass.

It may appear to be a superpower, but the oneironaut phenomenon is actually compensating for my weakness in processing and reacting to information in real time. Most people would quickly and correctly react to a new phrase involving a haycart, or to the unexpected sight of a ripped poster on the classroom wall. In my case, I need months to figure these things out, and the oneironaut phenomenon gives me the extra time that I need. I am compensating for my inadequate learning ability—I need repetition in both the sleep and waking states in order to learn.

I like the compensating theory for at least three reasons. First, it's humbler than presuming an oneironaut is someone who was born with an amazing mind that is destined to become even more amazing as they learn and develop.[62] The compensating theory aligns with the principle that all humans are equal, and no one is perfect or special. By extension, there can be no master race, and you might even say no master species.

Second, the theory is consistent with our natural ability to compensate for weaknesses in order to solve problems. For example, my secondary language is Modern Greek, but my vocabulary is probably one tenth of what it is in English. Very often I know exactly what I want to say in English, my mind does not know the correct word choice in Greek, but I can compensate by using synonyms or by constructing longer, explanatory sentences. I can even start waving my hands around, trying to mime the vocabulary words that I don't know. In this way, even though my weakness in vocabulary is a serious hurdle to communication, I can compensate by choosing these different paths. Did I learn these tricks in school or read about them in books? No, they occur naturally as a result of an innate problem-solving ability. So too it's possible that the oneironaut phenomenon emerges naturally as a physiological and cognitive trick that compensates for areas of weakness.

Third, the compensating theory allows various testable predictions. Over a large sample of children and teenagers, evidence for the oneironaut phenomenon should be correlated with subjects who have measurable forms of learning difficulties. To my knowledge, studies of the oneironaut phenomenon have not yet parsed test subjects in this way.

It is worth noting that both the reinforcing and compensating theories align with a cognitive process mentioned earlier called *priming*.[63] Priming means practicing a response to a cognitive stimulus so that the response becomes automatic, like a reflex, when the stimulus is experienced again in the future. With physical stimuli there can be repetitive exercises in order to optimize reflexes; e.g., if a blade is thrust at your face, then you must respond automatically by parrying or ducking, because all other conscious behaviors would be too slow. Without any training, your innate reflexes might make you duck, but a primed duck will be even faster. Childhood playing across the animal kingdom is in many ways the outcome of natural selection for primed reflexes that provide survival advantages. In terms of cognition and memory, priming the mind by stimulus repetition will make learning, recalling or classifying something easier, faster and more accurate. Thus, in a game where you have to identify wild cats (tiger, lion, jaguar, etc.) faster than someone else, you will improve accuracy and speed if you practice at least once.

Déjà vu is stimulus repetition that primes the organism for novelty, or for other future events. I may have learned to prime my mind after a single chance experience (reinforcing theory), or because as a poor learner I simply needed this skill (compensating theory), but in either case the déjà vu experience is similar to repetition priming. However, in psychology, priming begins as a willful exercise whereas the déjà vu phenomenon "emerges," which is why I include the concept of reflexes to denote that déjà vu is an instinctual or innate form of priming similar to childhood playing.

One additional perspective is that amnesic subjects who cannot form new memories are just as good at experiments involving priming as a normal control group.[64] They cannot consciously remember a prior learning experience, such as classifying wild cats, yet they exhibit the same performance improvements from a priming exercise as a control group. This has inspired various scientific insights into the characteristics of different types of memories. For me, this raises the possibility that a larger fraction of the population actually dreams about the future, it primes them to respond easier, faster and more accurately to upcoming events, but like amnesiacs they don't remember the dreams. The oneironauts are simply the minority who can remember why they have seen something before, yet the dreams serve both populations equally well.

To sum up, there are many factors that could explain the onset of the oneironaut phenomenon at a particular time in one's life. I presented some of my lifestyle changes that occurred in middle school, yet it's hard to say if one thing is far more important than the others, if they are all needed to work in unison to get the effect, or if at the end of the day they are all irrelevant and some other mechanism is the key. Certainly, the way to make progress is to study the personal characteristics and lifestyle changes that occur in many other individuals who experience the oneironaut phenomenon for the first time, and perhaps the common denominators will then become obvious.

The *when*: Event-to-awareness intervals

Another *when* of déjà vu is the interval between a waking event and recalling that the event happened in a dream. I break this down as (1) *real-time* déjà vu, (2) *24-hour* déjà *vu*, and (3) *impersonal* déjà *vu*. The most common is 24-hour déjà vu, followed by real-time déjà vu, and with only two instances of impersonal déjà vu.

Real-time déjà vu is exemplified by the Haycart and Trifid experiences. As the waking experience occurs in real time, I recall my dream instantly. I immediately try to recall the details of the dream so that I can determine and act on what will happen next. This is definitely the most exciting déjà vu. In those few minutes my attention and thoughts are focused on the events before me and a search through my memories. My records reveal that approximately one out of five experiences are real-time déjà vu (**Figure 5-2**).

Unfortunately, real-time déjà vu teaches a counterintuitive lesson. Even though we think that life is filled with important choices every day that we are alive, most of the time we have nothing of significance to really choose from. When real-time déjà vu happens, it becomes quite clear that there is no specific action we can personally take to change things over the next few moments.

For example, in the Trifid Nebula chapter I described the real-time déjà vu experience in the airport lounge, where I had no significant choices to make. Let me offer one more example. On October 15, 2010, I was in Torino, Italy, and entered the cathedral (Duomo di Torino) that hosts the Shroud of Turin. What I saw was a brilliant red cloth covering a long table, with thick glass protecting it from the viewers. I immediately recalled a morning dream in Berkeley of a brilliant red cloth on a long table, yet in real time there was nothing to act on at the Duomo. Even though the memory of this visit seems significant to me, there was no choice available to change the experience. I do feel that if something interesting had happened, I could have changed a sequence of events in exactly the same way as the Trifid Poster experience transpired. But in this case, all I could do was take a picture and leave, end of story.

If viewing the red cloth was such a clear memory from a dream, then could I have predicted what I would see in Torino? Unfortunately, the acts of viewing scenes are not continuously associated with thoughts that have the necessary semantic context. In other words, during my visit I was not continuously thinking, "Now I am viewing the Shroud of Turin display for the first time." The dream, therefore, did not have the information that I needed to make a prediction. My brain binds the episodic and semantic memories together now, when I recall the experience, but real-time awareness does not work this way. As I said in the Fomalhaut chapter: "...episodic memories of future events are disconnected from the time-appropriate semantic associations." Therefore, the experience of déjà vu had the perceptual elements, but lacked the thoughts needed to specify the place and time. I do believe that if another person in the Duomo had said something memorable that contained the words, "Shroud of Turin," I would have been able to make a prediction. But this was not the case. Fortunately, as I shall outline in the final chapter, we have emerging technologies that will assist us in making dreams an actionable precognitive experience.

More commonly, in roughly four out of five cases, I have *24-hour déjà vu* (**Figure 5-2**). In these cases, a waking experience occurs, and upon reflecting on the experience within the next 1–48 hours, I recall that this was in a dream. There is not much to do except write it down in a déjà vu logbook. As you can see, I use the term "24-hours" rather loosely. The interval is a perhaps an hour to a day or two. However, after a few days, there is no déjà vu experience; it's too late, except in the rare instances of impersonal déjà vu.

If I had to briefly speculate on why 24-hour déjà vu is the most common, I would invoke the timescales involved in the consolidation of memories and synaptogenesis. The 24-hour period includes one sleep cycle when short-term memories of new experiences are made more permanent as long-term memories. It may be that the brain must get these experiences into long-term memory before they can be connected to very subtle memories of dreams. At the same time, we know that synaptogenesis, which is the growth of new connections between nerve cells, takes from 30 minutes to over 15 hours. It may take even longer than this to stabilize the connection. In one amazing experiment involving the learning of a song by a songbird called the zebra finch, researchers found that the growth and stabilization of a neuron occurs within a 24-hour period. [65] Therefore, the physiology of creating memories by rewiring the brain is also consistent with the 24-hour déjà vu timescale. Once a new memory becomes permanent, it can be matched to a much older memory of a dream, and that's when the "Aha!" or déjà vu experience occurs. It's as if the memory comes to life, looks around, and discovers an identical twin.

Impersonal déjà vu refers to events that have the precognitive aspects of déjà vu but not the experience of dream recall when the event happens or soon thereafter. The first example of impersonal déjà vu is the Fomalhaut dream. My personal memory of the dream is mostly forgotten and therefore the feeling or sensation of déjà vu is not experienced. All I have is a record of the dream, plus a record of the future waking experience. The second example is the Heidelberg dream that was recalled *before* the experience occurred—the experience was in my short-term or working memory before the event happened. By the time I made it to the deck of that restaurant boat, I had been thinking of the dream too much to get that astonished realization that the dream is really taking place. Another way to look at it is if real-time and 24-hour déjà vu are both missed, there will be no sensation of the déjà vu experience.

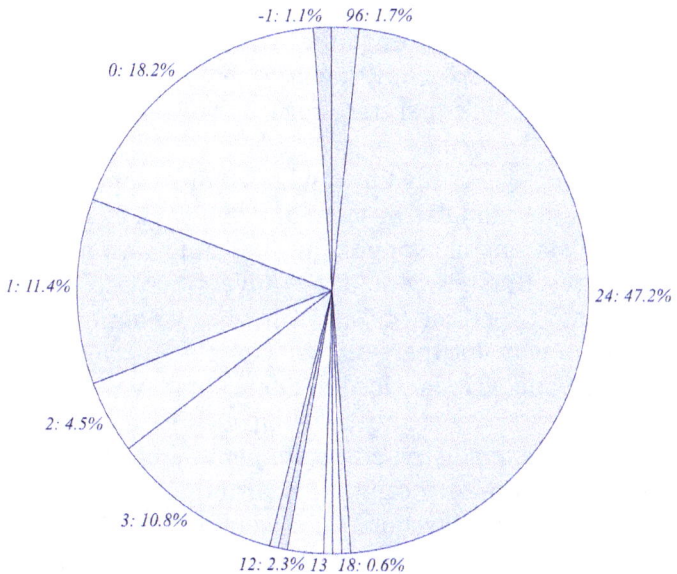

Figure 5-2: Out of 175 déjà vu events where I recorded the event-to-awareness interval, the vast majority of intervals are between 1 and 24 hours. The pie chart shows hours:percentage, where -1 refers to impersonal déjà vu, 0 refers to real-time déjà vu, and everything else qualifies as 24-hour déjà vu, with the longest recorded interval of 96 hours and the shortest interval of 1 hour.

What do these different types of déjà vu intervals teach us about the phenomenon? My answer derives from an extreme case of déjà vu that occurred *four days* after the events were experienced (the case of 96 hours in **Figure 5-2**). As I was driving my daughter to school at 7:30 on a Wednesday morning in 2015, I had strong déjà vu of events that occurred on Saturday.

On Saturday, October 10, we had gone to The Walt Disney Family Museum in the Presidio, a wooded naval base in San Francisco overlooking the Golden Gate Bridge. The distinct déjà vu I would have four days later on Wednesday concerned viewing the first exhibit, which was a World War I ambulance that Walt Disney drove in Europe when he was a teenager. There were two more instances of déjà vu involving the animation lab in the museum and viewing a very large model of Disneyland itself.

But Saturday was also a day of unprecedented emotional drama. On Friday BuzzFeed News reported that Dr. Geoff Marcy—a fellow faculty member in my department and one of the most well-known astronomers in the world—had sexually harassed four women over nearly a decade.[66] Over the last 20 years, Marcy and his collaborators had made pioneering discoveries about planets orbiting other stars using a hugely successful technique involving spectroscopy that was very different from my direct imaging approach. He was therefore regarded as a superstar professor at the University of California.

On Saturday no one really knew what would happen to Marcy due to this monumental scandal. I was one of a thousand or more scientists who signed a statement supporting the four women, implicitly condemning Marcy. But, how would the University react?

You might have seen me at The Walt Disney Family Museum that day, but my mind was not there—I was completely captivated by this disturbing drama and scandal close to home. Sunday was the same. On Monday, at our astronomy faculty meeting, we heard more facts about the case, and then we finally issued a statement that included the words, "We believe that Geoff Marcy cannot perform the functions of a faculty member." The postdoctoral scholars also condemned Marcy's behavior, and so did the astronomy graduate students and undergraduate students. Yet, by Tuesday night, there were no obvious consequences. Finally, on Wednesday morning, at 6:42, we received an email that Marcy was resigning.[67] Forty-five minutes after this watershed moment[68] I would experience the déjà vu of events at the Disney Museum that were four days in the past.

To me this shows that even though the déjà vu signal can be strong, an individual's ability to perceive it is influenced by the state of their attention. If it is focused on pressing and difficult matters of the present time and place, déjà vu does not occur. Instead, they have to be in a mentally relaxed mode that is open to random thoughts, much like window-shopping without any specific goal of buying anything.

Remember that the real-time déjà vu in my Haycart dream occurred *before* the gym class had started. My attention probably wasn't occupied by anything important, such as the gym teacher's instructions. So too the real-time déjà vu in the Trifid poster dream occurred *after* I had finished my work and had nothing else to do. So the distinction between real-time and other types of déjà vu probably does not have much to do with the mechanism of time travel itself. It merely reflects how memory recall is influenced by external factors.

On a related note, researchers have found contradictory relationships between déjà vu experiences and stress. In his 2004 book *The Déjà Vu Experience*, psychologist Alan Brown cites 43 studies that discuss how a déjà vu experience could be correlated to high stress levels and fatigue. However, his own research finds that 51% of déjà vu experiences involve recreational activities, and he speculates: "This may be because of the greater variety of visual and social stimulation during recreation."

I agree with Brown's findings but not entirely with his explanation. I evaluated my 332 déjà vu experiences with respect to their potential for fatigue. For example, if on the day of déjà vu I had woken up very early, or just arrived somewhere from an international flight, I would flag this déjà vu positive for fatigue. The result is that only 9% (30/322) of déjà vu experiences may have been experienced while I was fatigued. Thus, fatigue does not trigger or otherwise correlate with my déjà vu. My explanation for Brown's finding is that during periods of relaxation one is able to assign explicit attention to introspection. As your mind achieves a quieter state, you free up the natural ability to relate present-time experiences to older and extremely subtle memories of precognitive dreams. It is true that recreation takes a person out of their routine and can stimulate their senses in novel ways, as Brown says, but the critical factor is the opportunity to mind-wander and remember.

My hypothesis also indicates why disturbing images of death and destruction, such as the events of 9/11, can be completely missed by the millions of people who experienced these events. If an experience is emotionally charged, and this extreme mental state lasts for too many days, the window for having a déjà vu experience closes. Ironically, the most hurtful experiences are simultaneously what we would most like to foresee, and least likely to foresee. Instead, the oneironaut phenomenon thrives when both the internal and external worlds are quiet. I can now also see why the oneironaut phenomenon could not help me anticipate that simple question from Carl Sagan when I gave my first professional talk. It was indeed a simple question, but my mind was overwhelmed with stress before, during and after the event.

The *when*: Dream-to-event intervals

One more aspect of "when" is the time between the dream and the future event. For me, this interval is almost always greater than three months or so. Of course I would have no problem proving the déjà vu experience as time travel if I could tell you what might happen next week, but in fact the intervals are so long as to be mostly useless. Yet this is another clue that means something. The skeptics' answer is that three or more months is just enough time to create false memories; the déjà vu experience is a cognitive blunder. Yet by ruling out a cognitive blunder in many of my cases, studying the dream-to-event time interval could reveal an underlying process or element of the oneironaut phenomenon.

The most accurate interval that I have is for the Fomalhaut dream. The interval between the dream on November 16, 1995, and the email event on November 1, 2004 (**Figure 4-2**) is 3,273 days (8.97 years). However, the image you see in that email has a creation date on my computer of Sunday, October 31, 2004, 11:28 p.m. Therefore, the interval may be 3,272 days (8.96 years).

For a dream that I remember but was not written down, I can roughly estimate the year of the dream because I recall which home I lived in when I had the dream, and I know the years when I occupied each home. For example, I distinctly recall having the Shroud of Turin dream when I was sleeping in a Berkeley condo, and I moved into this condo in July 2002 and left it in June 2011. The Shroud of Turin déjà vu occurred in October 2010. Therefore I am certain the dream-to-event interval is less than eight years.

There are two tentative cases where I may have a match between my dream record and the event. The déjà vu events occurred in early 2018 and I present them as two exceptions to the rest of my analysis that uses only those déjà vu events that occur through 2016. I call them tentative because they do not stand up to the same scrutiny as Fomalhaut which had a unique identifying feature. On the night of January 14, 2013, I dreamed of "handgliding [sic] or equivalent on a beautiful island"—wishful thinking indeed! Then, on January 9, 2018 (1,821 days or 4.99 years later), a friend showed me a video clip from her vacation on a remote Pacific Island. The vibrant colors of the water, the island and the sky were staggering to behold. Very briefly the video was shot hovering above the island. This immediately raised a novel puzzle in my mind and I asked with astonishment: "Did you guys have drones with you?" The answer was yes and about an hour later I remembered these scenes were from a dream. The fascinating aspect is that in 2013 such drones were less commonplace, so what I saw in my dream was an experience provided by a future technology that I could only vaguely associate with hang gliding.

The second tentative case concerns a dream on January 1, 2013, involving the Boston Marathon bombing of April 15, 2013. However, a key dream image corresponds to the film "Patriots Day" that dramatized the bombing. I saw that film on January 14, 2018, which gives a dream-to-event interval of 1,838 days or 5.04 years.

Since a time interval may be associated with a separation in space, we might ask if there is some relationship between time and space. For example, is the time interval between the dream and the event proportional to the distance between the dreaming brain and the waking brain? The Fomalhaut dream occurred in Honolulu, Hawaii, and the Fomalhaut discovery occurred in Berkeley, California. If the space we are talking about is a distance across the Earth's surface, then that distance is 3,840 km. For the Shroud of Turin déjà vu, the distance between Berkeley and Turin is 9,613 km, and the time interval was <8 years. The Pacific Island and Boston Marathon dreams occurred in California, the waking events also occurred in California less than 20 km away, and the intervals were both five years. Therefore, I currently have no evidence that the dream-to-event interval depends on the physical separation between the sleeping brain and the waking brain.

There is some very good news in this apparent lack of correlation between the déjà vu intervals in time and space. For example, if we wanted an oneironaut to go on a Mars mission to anticipate potential problems on the surface of the red planet, then the oneironaut phenomenon should work just fine while the person is still dreaming on Earth, even though the distance to their future Mars location could range between 50 and 400 million kilometers.[69] The oneironaut phenomenon doesn't seem to care if huge distances separate a dream and a waking event.

A related question is if the information content is smaller and/or noisier for greater dream-to-event intervals? It doesn't seem like it. Your attention is transported to the past/future as if you are really there. It resembles digital information—either it's there or not there. The problem lies in the changes of semantic associations over time, as illustrated with the Pacific Island dream of hang gliding versus drone perspectives. A similar example is if in 1984 I had a dream that "my phone needs to be unlocked." I probably would not understand what that means, attribute the phrase to nonsensical dreams, and forget about it. It would take more than a decade before smartphones would become popular and have a feature where that statement makes sense.

The *when*: Dream-to-event order

Does the night-to-night order of dreams correspond to the order of events experienced in the future? This would be extremely helpful because I could always focus on a specific portion of my dream record to predict events that may be coming up. Or, could it be that my dream last night contained an experience two years in the future, my dream next week might be for one year in the future, and my dream two weeks from now contains something five years in the future? Charles Dickens imagined that the Ghost of Christmas Yet to Come moved Scrooge through his future events randomly, with "no order."

Unfortunately, my records do not provide a clear answer yet. The Fomalhaut dream occurred in 1995 and jumped to 2004. The tentative Boston Marathon and Pacific Island dreams occurred in 2013 and jumped to 2018. Studying the dates carefully, we see that the Boston Marathon dream should have occurred a few weeks later if dreams are experienced in the same order as future events. Thus, we have a tentative indication of the *Scrooge effect*—a jumbled order of dreams vs. future events—but I need more data to answer this question with greater confidence.

The *when*: Asleep

The final "when" characteristic of déjà vu is that the future signal is received and/or perceived only when asleep. This is quite a comical situation. If the oneironauts were ever drawn as superheroes, then I don't think the illustrators would be terribly challenged. All the action would involve some unremarkable humans, dressed in their pajamas, lying unconscious in beds. This is their superhero work.

But why should the phenomenon take place during sleep instead of a waking state? Is it that the sleep state is necessary for future information—the *osignal*—to travel through time? Or, is the osignal implanted in our minds at other times, but sleep and dreaming are needed to perceive it? By analogy, is sleep like the act of writing a book, or is it merely the act of reading a book and we have yet to understand how and when it was written?

Figuring out why animals sleep often involves measurements of what happens when they sleep normally, and what happens when sleep is diminished or altered. The basics are that memory and learning performance improve the more sleep we get, and we can barely function if sleep is taken away from us. One could generally reason that both the body and the mind need sleep for two different reasons related to energy and information.

The energy intensity of biological activity has peaks and valleys, and so this pattern may naturally sync to the diurnal patterns of a planet, such as day vs. night and hot vs. cold. If you do not allow a resting phase, then the peak of activity and all the necessary functions carried out during that time (e.g., finding food) cannot occur effectively. With respect to information, advanced nervous systems are limited in terms of how much experience they can process and preserve as memory. If there were a species of primates that only remembered and learned from the last few days of information, they would be wiped out by a competing species of primates that remembered and learned from many years of prior experience. It seems that brains need to be sleeping, with practically zero sensory information arriving, in order for recent short-term memories to become stable and connected to older memories, without overwriting the old memories.

Yet one wonders why staying still and resting is not the same thing as sleeping. Moreover, there are portions of our sleep where our brain is functioning at the same level as when we're awake. This is so paradoxical that it's actually termed "paradoxical sleep." Why not be awake at this stage with the capacity to respond to stimuli? Surely the more hours a day that you can preserve the capacity to respond to threats, the better your chances for survival.

One can come up with all sorts of interesting hypotheticals, yet the sure way to make progress is through measurements. Among the many ways to observe brain activity is measuring the level and form of its electrical output at the outer surface. This measurement is called an electroencephalogram, or EEG. Your brain's electrical activity oscillates up and down about 16 to 25 times a second (16–25 Hertz, or Hz) when awake, and the measured signal is 10 to 30 millionths of a Volt (microVolt). As you relax the oscillations will slow down to about 10 Hz, also called an alpha wave. If you fall asleep, these EEG measurements and other attributes distinguish four different stages.

Stage 1 sleep is the transition from awake to asleep, where the oscillations diminish to about 5 Hz. Stage 1 is the funny stage, and maybe that's what it should be called. Some random body part might twitch out of your control, and you might see bright lights or hear weird sounds. You might even think you're awake, but an expert will tell you that your brain is asleep because the brain's electrical activity has clearly slowed down and calmed down compared to any waking state. But please do not panic if you find yourself twitching or hallucinating—this is all normal for Stage 1, "funny sleep." Also somewhat funny is that since your brain stops sending and receiving most signals to the rest of your body, it's as if every day we transform ourselves into bubble brains no longer associated with arms, legs, etc.

Next, Stage 2 sleep continues the 5 Hz oscillations, but there are brief interruptions of 14 Hz activity called "spindles," and then occasional slow waves that will dominate the next stage. You can be woken fairly easily in Stage 2 sleep, which is called "light sleep."

When you get to Stage 3 sleep, you become the most boring person you will ever be each and every day. The brain oscillation slows down to about once a second (1 Hz) and this is the "slow-wave sleep" mentioned earlier (also called deep sleep). I dislike this term because "slow" doesn't give you a number to keep in mind. I prefer to call this "heartbeat sleep," because the oscillation is similar to a person's heart rate of one beat per second. In addition to the slowing of the brain's electrical oscillation, blood flow diminishes in many areas of the brain. It is very hard to wake a person from heartbeat sleep, and if you succeed they will be extremely boring. It's not worth the effort. Let them get to the next stage so they can tell you something interesting afterward.

After heartbeat sleep ends, the fireworks erupt. Your eyes start twitching back and forth, blood starts flowing more normally in the brain, and your mind starts dreaming. This is called REM sleep, where REM is an acronym for rapid eye movement. Everything else is called non-REM sleep. During REM, electrical oscillations in some parts of the brain can speed up to 40 Hz. Dreams may also occur in the non-REM stages (where they often resemble rational waking thoughts), but they are much more prominent in the REM stage (where the dreams are more dramatic). REM sleep is the paradoxical sleep phase mentioned earlier because brain activity can resemble that of a fully awake person. For most people, the eyes are probably scanning the virtual scenes in dreams just as they would a real scene when awake.[70] A *lucid dreamer* is someone who becomes aware they are dreaming and can then control their dreams, cognitively blurring the line between asleep and awake. For me the oneironaut dreams are *not* lucid dreams, and generally I am not a lucid dreamer. What I can say is that the Haycart dream occurred just before waking in the morning, which was most likely REM sleep.

The first complete sequence of stages from *funny* to *light* to *heartbeat* to *REM* sleep lasts 90–100 minutes. Humans then typically alternate between REM and non-REM sleep about five more times in a night. This is called an *ultradian* rhythm because it is a cycle that completes in less than 24 hours, whereas a *circadian* rhythm refers to a 24-hour cycle. For each successive sleep cycle, the REM stage takes a greater and greater fraction of time than the non-REM stages. Moreover, the mix of these stages and the time spent sleeping is different for different age groups. Babies famously sleep for something like 15 hours a day.[71]

OK, fine, but how does the oneironaut, *moi*, sleep? The answer is: "Like a fussy baby."

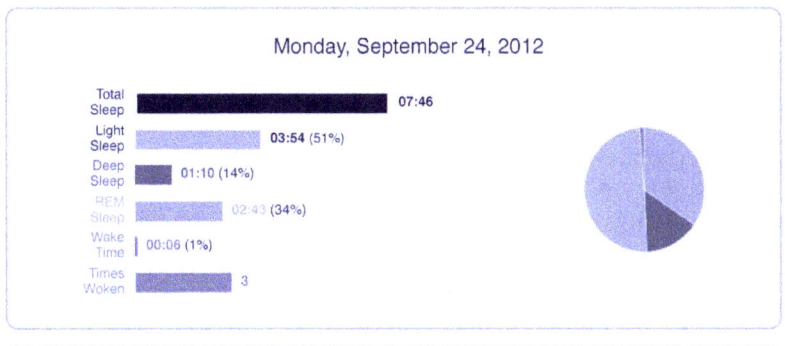

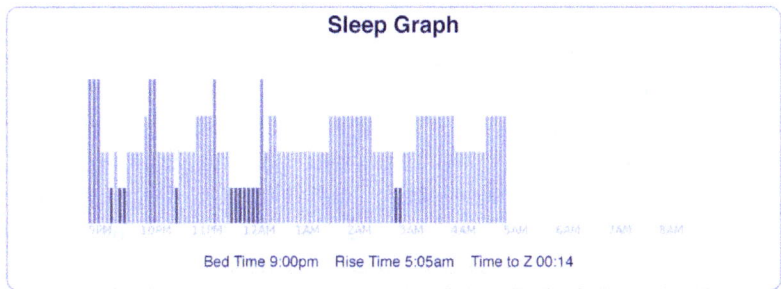

Figure 5-3: A sleep report produced for me by the Zeo device that shows the cycling from light, to deep (heartbeat) to REM. The increasing REM time throughout the night is fairly typical for most people, but the fraction of time I spend in the REM stage (34%) is rare for adults. In this particular night it took me 14 minutes to fall asleep ("Time to Z") and the tallest bars reveal that I woke up three times in the first half of the night. This is consistent with mild sleep apnea. Though the measurements are finely sampled in time, the bar graph on the bottom shows five-minute intervals that represent the dominant mode of sleep stage in that five-minute interval.

In 56 measurements of my own sleep phases at age 44 where I slept five hours or more at home (see **Figure 5-3** for an example), the REM stage has a median value of 36% of my total sleep (with one standard deviation of 6%).[72] Normal adults my age should be spending around 20% of their sleep in the REM stage. Instead, if all you knew about me is that I spend 36% of my sleep in the REM stage, then your best guess for my age would be that I am four months old.[73]

On the other hand, if I told you that my median total sleep time is 7.1 hours, then you would postulate that I'm over 30 years old. In this regard I'm "normal" for my age. However, note that these numbers suggest that I typically spend a total of two and a half hours dreaming every night. If you were to suppose that 1% of the time that I spend dreaming is in the "oneironaut phase," this means that every 24 hours I experience 90 seconds of a future time. Every 365 days, I perceive 9.1 hours of the future, and in 70 years more than 26 days of experience are outside the present time.

It is easy to scale these numbers. If you suppose that only 0.1% of my dreaming phase is in the oneironaut phase, then I spend 9 seconds per night, and 2.6 days of my life, experiencing the future. If the percentage is 10%, then I spend 900 seconds or 15 minutes in the future every day. My intuition tells me this number is too large—if I had 15 minutes of future experiences every night I would be able to draw you all sorts of diagrams about future events. I would have been a famous oneironaut by the time I got to high school, a teen wonder that predicted the Challenger Space Shuttle disaster, the crimes of 9/11 and the tsunami that hit Thailand.

Instead, nine seconds seems commensurate with the duration and information content of the déjà vu experience. It took about nine seconds to think about that kid's reference to a Haycart, to notice the ripped Trifid poster on the wall and to study the geometry of Fomalhaut. Nine seconds seems about the right time where something can be perceived, but the larger context of a precise time, date, location and the names of the people surrounding you is impossible to specify completely. The readers can try it for themselves. How much can you say out loud in nine seconds that would distinguish the features of your day today versus a different day in the past 365 days? If something unique were to be witnessed today, then those nine seconds is enough to distinguish today's event from other events in your year, but such unique events are rare during anyone's week.

Nine seconds is also in the ballpark of 2–3 second episodes of 10 Hz neurological activity during REM sleep called "alpha bursts." These are quite a mystery because they have qualities of the waking state at precisely the time where all other measurements say that you are asleep. Based on their detailed studies of alpha bursts, neuroscientists Jose Luis Cantero and Mercedes Atienza state: "Alpha bursts may also work as a micro-arousal in human REM sleep to facilitate a connection between the dreaming brain and the external world..."[74] Of course, they mean the present-day world, but I'm going to speculate that the alpha bursts may also represent the times when the brain is awake in a future world.

Paradoxical sleep (the REM stage) now doubles its paradoxicality. The measurements made by neurologists say your brain is awake, and speculation from the oneironaut, *moi*, says that your brain is in two places at once—sleeping in the present, awake in the future. This now begs the question of whether or not the REM stage is helpful for my memory and other restorative functions that I need daily. If I am awake in a future world, then there are parts of me that are not always sleeping every night. In fact, I have to tell you that I do not feel like I get a full night of sleep every night. The only time I feel rested is after a midday nap—I'm a pretty good napper, though not outstanding. These symptoms could be due to mild sleep apnea, but I often wonder if it's because the oneironaut phenomenon interferes with the normal restorative functions of sleep and dreaming.

Finally, you may remember that I used the words "fussy baby" to describe my sleep. I'm like a baby based on the fraction of time spent in the REM stage, but I'm also fussy because I wake up a median of four times a night. Basically, I have a mild sleep disorder, yet the "problem" of waking up may actually help me as an oneironaut. You could call it the *Goldilocks sleep disorder*. If I were to never wake up before morning, I would recall too few dreams. If I were to wake up too often during the night, I might not benefit from the quantity or quality of REM-stage sleep. But if I wake up just the right amount, then I'm maximizing my ability to remember dreams.

The *where*: Indoors vs. outdoors

The *where* of déjà vu is rather interesting. I never would have thought of asking, "Should there be a preferred place for déjà vu to occur?" Nevertheless, the where of déjà vu is preferentially indoors (74%). In the less common cases when déjà vu occurs outdoors (26%), it involves human structures and/or interpersonal interactions. Déjà vu never occurs with an outdoor scene or situation that only involves pristine nature.

Why should this be the case? If the déjà vu experience is highly visual, and there are many amazing things to discover outdoors, then why should outdoor scenes be underrepresented?

Consider, for example, my first visit to the Grand Tetons in the fall of 2011. The weather was somewhat unsettled, with periods of rain, but a brief partial clearing at sunset produced a spectacular visual display of distant mountain peaks painted in red light. None of this sparked déjà vu. Instead, an unusual arrangement of countertops and seats at the simple hotel cafeteria caused déjà vu (**Figure 5-4**). What do we learn when the mind of an oneironaut selects a cafeteria over the splendor of nature?

Here is my best guess: the oneironaut phenomenon relies on the recognition, description and memory of experiences, and indoor objects simply give modern humans more to talk about than outdoor experience.

If you show me eight different chairs, I can describe each one in a few words so that you would recognize which one I am talking about. If you show me eight pine trees, it might take me a lot longer to describe one in sufficient detail that you could uniquely identify it. In addition, a certain type of chair might have a lot of semantic meaning associated with it, whereas I don't have strong semantic associations with pine trees. The oneironaut phenomenon works best with a minimum of descriptive information and a maximum of semantic meaning—indoor locations have both of these qualities.

Figure 5-4: Which one of these scenes is more likely to be a déjà vu experience? Both are at the Jackson Lake Lodge in Wyoming. Looking outdoors to the west I see a spectacular sunset, but indoors looking into a room that I've never entered before, I see a cafeteria with many serving counters from the foreground to the background. It turns out that the latter is the déjà vu experience because it presents a cognitive puzzle that involves a maze-like geometry and one of my important goals in life, finding food.

The above may pertain to me and probably most people I know yet there could be others who are excellent at describing trees efficiently. For example, I recall a film called *Black Robe* set in 1634 in Canada. A European missionary gets completely lost in the forest, and when the Native Americans find him, they are pretty sure he's an idiot because to them a cathedral of trees gives exactly the information the European needs to find his way through the forest.

For the Native Americans in the forest, retaining a memory of the trees was important because it was needed—among the strongest memories are those that are useful and part of a reward system.[75] Humans and other animals pay attention to things that they need (to get, or to avoid), and even more so if what they need involves a cognitive challenge that can be solved only with focused attention. For me, the sight of the Grand Tetons at sunset was memorable, yet neither useful nor cognitively challenging. The cafeteria, on the other hand, is what I needed to find food, and I wasn't quite sure how the serving countertops were arranged throughout this room. In the end I would pay attention to it, and I would be able to describe it in greater detail than the sunset.

However, if I were Robinson Crusoe stranded on an island, and a view of a specific mountain peak warned me that I was walking straight toward a cannibal feast where I would be served for dinner, I bet that mountain peak would be the déjà vu scene instead of a useless thought about a cafeteria. Thus, my memories of indoor locations are stronger because of the needs and rewards in my specific lifestyle, but I believe I could be just as good an oneironaut with outdoor locations if they demanded my attention for problem solving and for survival.

Recall that my Heidelberg dream also involved food finding. My memory was that the space was open to the sky near a river, and, importantly, the floor was a wood deck. That deck was central to finding the right place in Heidelberg. That tiny nugget of information was the key to exclude 99% of the places that might have outdoor seating in Heidelberg but didn't have the right floor (such as Hemingway's). Finding the correct location rewarded me not only in terms of food, but also in joining my social group.

Finally, I think that indoor locations are more common in déjà vu for one more reason: the walls. Are you still collecting fancy words? Then *thigmotaxis* should be added to your repertoire. This describes a group of behaviors among plants and animals, one of which is wall hugging. Why should the oneironaut phenomenon be correlated to proximity to walls? Correlating time travel to thigmotaxis may be the most absurd combination of concepts ever invented, but later in the book I will speculate that the déjà vu phenomenon occurs because spatial memory and planning are the cornerstones of memory in general. Walls define the space of modern humans, they activate specific brain cells, and these cells may hold the mechanism for a signal to travel between time periods.

These ideas on the indoor/outdoor distinction offer some possible tests for the future. First, if I were to design an experiment to probe the déjà vu experience, I would want test subjects to be located in a small, simple space with just a few recognizable and distinct objects that are part of a reward system to focus attention. Second, given that various people have expertise in different aspects of experience, the strengths of their subjective memories will be different, and therefore a team of oneironauts is better than any single oneironaut. If I could team up with someone who recognizes trees and plants, and another person who recognizes faces, and a third person who recognizes architecture, and so

The *what:* Vision, hearing and location

How about the *what* of déjà vu? The two strongest sensory stimuli involved in déjà vu are vision and hearing. Among my 332 déjà vu experiences, 311 involved vision, and within the 21 that did not involve vision, 19 involved listening. Déjà vu experiences involving smell, taste and touch are rare and vague. This is consistent with an online survey of roughly 3,000 participants that found déjà vu is related to sight, hearing, touch, smell and taste, in order of decreasing frequency.[76] Nearly 100% of déjà vu reports involve sight, 85% involve hearing, but the other senses are involved in only about a third to half the cases of déjà vu.

Strangely, there are only six instances of déjà vu where I am speaking. I think this is because déjà vu is based on the accumulation of information through the senses, which in neurology is called an *afferent* pathway, whereas speaking activates the nervous system to broadcast information, the so-called *efferent* pathways. Thus, for the oneironauts, silence is demonstrably golden. This is a surprisingly valuable discovery from my déjà vu record because I often have too many dreams each night that I could write down, but if my dream involves me talking, I know it is most likely psychological, it will not be part of a future reality, and it has low priority for my record keeping.

In addition to the five senses, I would vote for a sixth sensory ability that is involved in 50% of my déjà vu: the sense of space, or the awareness of location. As **Figure 5-5** shows, when I classified each déjà vu event as pertaining to a person, place or thing, or any combination, the sense of location is involved in half of the experiences. One might argue that location is a stimulus perceived by other senses, such as vision and proprioception (knowledge of your own body). Location doesn't seem deserving of membership in the club of senses. For example, the other senses are off or neutral unless they are stimulated to be on, and once stimulated you can adjust their intensity in a variety of ways. The sense of location always seems to be turned on during our waking hours, and it would seem that you cannot increase or decrease the stimulus for "location."

Yet I don't think this is exactly true. You can increase the stimulus for location when you enter a new location, a place that you have never been to before. The stimulus shoots up to a peak in the first moments or minutes, and then decays at some rate, depending on factors such as how complicated or simple the location is, or how quickly you move through it. Just as with your awareness of your other senses, you can focus attention on the sense of location, to the exclusion of everything else.

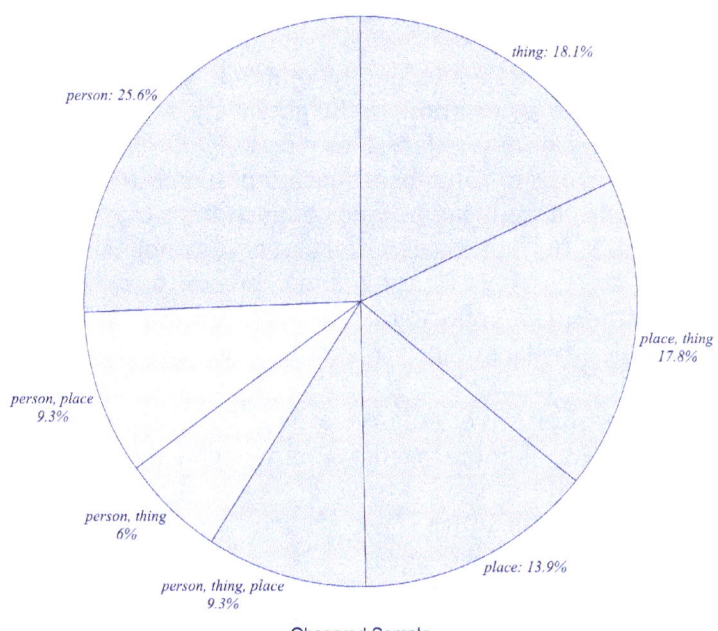

Observed Sample

Figure 5-5: Distribution of déjà vu when the elements involved a person, place and/or thing. A thing is déjà vu concerning an object, whereas place involves the sense of location.

One key example for my sense of location is going to my garden. This is hardly a "new location" to produce a strong stimulus, and if I proceed quickly to do some digging, planting and pruning, my sense of location has hardly been exercised. But if I stop and take a breath, then wait for one minute without focusing on anything in particular or guiding my thoughts in any way, I become aware of my location in the garden. I notice things that I had no awareness of previously, and I sense that I am there with these things, in that space. All of the senses are involved, not just vision. If I enter a new room instead of the garden, I do not need to stop and focus to have the same sense of space. This new space automatically triggers attention, almost like a reflex.

Thus, like some modern-day Nunez, I nominate "location" as a new member in the current club of five senses. Supporting my nomination, researchers have found that just as vision depends on special cells, and so too with touch, smell, taste and hearing, the sense of location also has special cells. What are these called? They are called "place cells." These are located in the hippocampus, a region of the brain that I will explore in Chapter 7. Of course, the cells that hold memory might be called time cells, and we'll also get to that later.

Ironically, even though one might think the sense of time could be promoted as the seventh sense after location, time is actually not an important sense for déjà vu. In my opinion, when I experience a heightened stimulus of location, or heighten my sense of location by pausing in a garden or other place, I have no tangible awareness of time. Time in those moments of sensing location seems to consist of the present only, and there is no specific connection to the past or future. One might think that the sense of current location should include awareness of the previous location, and a mental picture of how one entered into the present location. For me, anyway, this is not the experience. The present time is the only time. You might call it the *timeless present*.

A few years after I wrote these words I discovered the 1935 poem *Burnt Norton* by T.S. Eliot that seems to partly echo my sentiments:

> Time past and time future
> Allow but a little consciousness.
> To be conscious is not to be in time
> But only in time can the moment in the rose-garden,
> The moment in the arbour where the rain beat,
> The moment in the draughty church at smokefall
> Be remembered; involved with past and future.
> Only through time time is conquered.[77]

To recap, the majority of déjà vu experiences involves the three senses of sight, sound and location. Any one of these, or a combination, helps transmit future waking experiences to the sleeping experiences of the past.

The *what:* Novelty and surprise

Many people who have déjà vu describe it as a surprising experience. I would agree and like to refer to it as the "Aha!" or "Eureka!" experience. Déjà vu could be real time or delayed by hours and days, but the moment that it happens is a moment of recognition. One suddenly gains an insight that in the past you had the experience as a dream.

For my database I determine whether or not the source of the déjà vu is "novel, surprising." The Haycart and Fomalhaut dreams are clear examples of events in a timeline that were not anticipated and therefore surprising. Out of 332 déjà vu experiences in my log, 73% could be tagged as "novel, surprising." Some events can be ambiguous. For example, one day I met a new person who was wearing a burgundy sweatshirt. The sweatshirt was the object of déjà vu, not the person. After some thought, I decided that there are plenty of burgundy sweatshirts that I might encounter in a lifetime, and therefore tagged this déjà vu as "no" for novelty and surprise. A less ambiguous case concerned déjà vu when staring at a series of doorbells at the bottom of a German apartment building trying to find a friend's name. Looking at a series of names did *not* feel surprising or novel, but I did classify this as déjà vu related to "searching, lost."

What is happening in the brain as we face novel problems and experience insight? Interestingly, researchers have found that there is a burst of 40 Hz electrical activity in the temporal lobe of the brain.[78] You might recall that 40 Hz bursts also occur during REM sleep. Thus, at the superficial level of EEG recordings, the brain is electrically similar when dreaming and when creatively solving new problems while awake.

Recognizing that an experience was previously dreamed could be called "remembering" instead of "insight," though there is equivalence between the two. In laboratory testing of insight, subjects may be asked to solve a brief puzzle, such as finding a single word that could be attached to the words "pine" and "crab." The moment of insight is defined as when they remember that "apple" can be attached to both words. Déjà vu is also a moment of insight when a person transitions from a cue to a sudden recollection that the experience was previously dreamed. In laboratory tests, a night of sleep greatly improves performance on such insight tasks.[79] This helps explain the prevalence of 24-hour déjà vu. Sleep helps people solve problems and understand which short-term memories of recent experiences are related to long-term memories and semantic knowledge.

Aside from the moment of déjà vu, why should "novel, surprising" events trigger 73% of my déjà vu experiences? This is again mostly a bias concerning memorable events. I simply cannot have déjà vu if I do not remember the connection between everyday experiences and past dreams. The more distinct or unusual the event, so too with the dream itself, and the higher the probability that I will recall that dream. During everyday waking life, "flashbulb memories" are those very important, surprising and rare autobiographical events that are preserved in long-term memory.

In summary, it is difficult to know if there is something particularly special about novel events in terms of activating the mind, though in Chapter 7 I will offer some speculation. Certainly, novel events can be viewed as a broader class of brain function that involves learning. Novelty is a form of prediction error, and thus novelty becomes a punctuated learning experience in order to minimize future errors. Learning contains a spectrum of common and uncommon experiences, but it is the uncommon experiences that are more likely to be retrieved or recognized from memory. For example, I don't quite remember how I learned to ride a bicycle, but I do remember an error many years later that caused me to flip over the handlebars onto a sidewalk. I've never made that mistake again.

The *what:* Travel, maps, searches, colors, crying and even toilets

At this point the reader might ask why should we continue parsing the déjà vu experience into ever more detailed pieces? The answer is not just that we want to understand how the phenomenon works, but we also wish to make the phenomenon more manageable, both for study and for practice. For example, if I have a night filled with many dreams, and I can only write down a few things in my logs, which single dream do I focus on? If I parse my déjà vu log in terms of color, and discover that the color red is very common, from that point onward I know that if one dream among many has the color red in it, I should write it down. So too if I realize that my speaking almost never involves déjà vu, I can choose to ignore those dreams where I am speaking. Or, if I know that traveling stimulates déjà vu experiences, I know to keep a journal with me on trips and allocate some time to write.

In fact, 192/332 (57.8%) of déjà vu experiences involve what I call "real travel." This means that I am located away from a region where I am living long-term. So even though I might have déjà vu by going to a museum in San Francisco, I count this as a "daily activity" close to my home, and not as real travel. Travel is very general and does not specify the exact nature of the déjà vu. For example, I may have déjà vu of a person who is crying, but I may be near home or on a trip away from home. In Alan Brown's 2004 study of the déjà vu phenomenon, travel also appears to be positively correlated with déjà vu experiences.

I think there are several possible reasons why travel is correlated to déjà vu. First, travel creates more memorable experiences and hence biases these experiences toward inclusion in any study of déjà vu based on questionnaires that require quick memory recollection. Second, if the function of déjà vu is to prepare a person for unexpected events, or if the triggers for déjà vu are unexpected events, then travel offers a higher concentration of such events. Third, cause and effect could be reversed—

déjà vu produces more travel—something akin to a self-fulfilling prophecy. For example, if in school a déjà vu experience sparks your curiosity about science and medicine, then you might be more likely to go into these careers that allow for abundant travel, and hence when the déjà vu questionnaire appears, it seems that travel is correlated to the déjà vu phenomenon. On a related noted, Alan Brown shows that déjà vu is also positively correlated to education levels, which could be explained by the correlation of factors evident in the example above.

Of my experiences, 44/332 (13.2%) involve using a map or trying to understand a spatial geometry, such as the cafeteria in the Grand Tetons. Though by percentage this is small, it is important because its qualities are very specific, and this specificity increases the ratio of signal to noise, which I will discuss below. The category of "real travel" discussed above is fairly general—the déjà vu elements could be anything—whereas "looking at a map" is a specific activity that could translate to strong déjà vu.

A smaller fraction, 18/332 (5.4%), concerns a spatial search for something. Seventeen of these involve vision, four involve hearing, twelve involve real travel, and three involve food and drink. This category is similar to using a "map" or understanding "spatial geometry," but here the activity has the element of searching for something that is lost or is needed.

I have recorded 8/332 (2.4%) cases that involve a trip to toilets in public spaces such as restaurants. The déjà vu is usually about something else, but the place where I have the déjà vu is in the bathroom. At 2.4% it is not that common, but since it's kind of weird and curious, I'll talk more about this later.

Even less frequent, 6/332 (1.8%) of déjà vu experiences concern the color red, and overall only 22 experiences involve color. White, green and black are the second most popular colors at three occurrences each. No particular color is absent.

Finally, 5/332 (1.5%) involve watching or hearing someone crying.

The *what:* Food and drink

The Heidelberg chapter and my discussion about the hotel cafeteria versus the Grand Tetons suggest that food and drink are part of déjà vu because we need them—they are important. However, out of the 332 déjà vu events, only 47 (14%) have some connection to food and drink. This is relatively minor, but again we should consider the context of my current lifestyle, which has an uninterrupted supply of food and drink. Food and drink are important, but many other things seem even more important because my basic needs to eat and drink are routinely satisfied. On the other hand, the oneironaut phenomenon with respect to food in other organisms may have a more prominent role because most of nature engages in a daily life and death struggle.

Thus, I think the 14% value would have been higher earlier in human history (or at other locations in the present day where food is scarce), and in animals it may be significantly more prominent. Finding food is such a critical and universal task for all organisms that if the oneironaut phenomenon operates in other animals, you can bet it involves food.

The *what*: Factual vs. counterfactual déjà vu

This is a broad but important distinction—is the déjà vu in my logbook about something that happened, or is it about something that *would have* happened? The Trifid Poster dream is a key example. The déjà vu of my actions in putting up the poster and the four boys teasing me is counterfactual, real-time déjà vu.

The word counterfactual is not very common, and here it means "against the actual facts in my autobiographical past." With language one talks about a counterfactual conditional statement, such as, "If I had fixed the poster, then the boys *would have* teased me." In a branch of physics called quantum mechanics we have the term "counterfactual definiteness." This is when we know the consequences of a possible measurement even though the measurement is never made. There will be more about quantum mechanics in the next chapter.

Counterfactual déjà vu is rare (only three cases in my record of 332 déjà vu events), and there is a Great Ambiguity involving our natural tendency to *anticipate* pending events. For example, one afternoon I was supposed to take an astronomy class on a field trip to Lick Observatory in the mountains east of San Jose, California. However, I experienced some chest pain and ended up cancelling at the last minute in order to go to the hospital. I was trying to ignore the pain, yet going to an isolated mountaintop is probably a bad idea if you suspect a pending health problem. Even though I did not go I thought I had a dream about stopping with the group at a place to get sandwiches before proceeding to the summit of the mountain. This vague memory is a candidate for counterfactual déjà vu, yet I have to dismiss it because it's too easy for me to anticipate stopping for food and imagining the entire event. If I had gone on this field trip with the students, we would have stopped at a sandwich place, and this is too obvious.

A case that I label true counterfactual déjà vu involved a piano recital given by my two daughters in 2012. This was held in a church that I had never been to before, and I had real-time déjà vu of the doors at the church entrance. At the end of the performance I discovered that a reception was planned in a different room. Looking through the partially open door, I could see pizza boxes with their lids up on a long table. I instantly remembered a dream of being in that reception room eating pizza among many people, and that I would also end up looking underneath the tables because I had lost something.

Contrary to the Lick Observatory trip, which was a relatively common experience for an astronomer, this was the first such piano recital I was attending, and I had zero anticipation that there was going to be a room with pizza in it. The reception was a total surprise. However, it was a total toss-up if we were to go inside the pizza room. Certainly, a lot was up to me to decide, just as in Heidelberg, and just as with the Trifid Poster. I could have said to my family, "OK, now we should go to the reception." Just as in Heidelberg, the déjà vu would have become a fact in my autobiographical past. Instead, I decided to introduce an element of chance. I asked the kids, "Do you want pizza at the reception, or do you want to go to a Japanese restaurant for dinner?" They replied "Japanese!" in unison, and so we never went inside the pizza room. No man is an island, especially when a group is choosing a restaurant.

I count my memories of the pizza room as counterfactual déjà vu, just as with the Trifid Nebula poster. I suppose it also shows how the oneironauts can have counterfactual dinners. They may recall an intensely pleasurable dream of eating at a great Indian place, but then someone shows up at the last minute who loathes spicy food and makes everyone go to an Italian place. The oneironaut should oblige, since going to the Italian place does not entirely erase the counterfactual experience of that excellent Indian place.

The *what:* Storytelling and virtual déjà vu

What are the other types of signals transmitted across time? In addition to the senses, the *what* of déjà vu experiences may include emotions and thoughts triggered by external stimuli such as sight, language and/or location. Are the emotions and thoughts involved in "learning" also communicated across time, or is it just the external stimuli? *I think it is the learning process that is also being transmitted.* In fact, I had a déjà vu experience where the main component transmitted was learning, not stimulus. Here is the dream:

I'm in a small apartment, dark inside, with the window shades down, as it is extremely bright outside. A bad smell is getting worse and worse. The lady there tells me not to worry; the smell will go away soon. After a few minutes, the toilet in the bathroom flushes and everything is OK again.

A psychiatrist could seize the opportunity to tell me that this is clearly a psychological dream involving the fear or anxiety surrounding toilets. Nope. These events actually happened, except someone else told me that it happened to his wife when they lived in Jerusalem. I was never in that apartment, nor was the person who told me the story. Yet my dream gives me a sense of location, sights, hearing the voice of someone, and perhaps even smell, or at least an emotional reaction to a bad smell. The story involves the customs of the Jewish Sabbath (Shabbat), which forbid work once a week. The fact that not even a toilet can be flushed, since this constitutes operating machinery, is quite a surprise for us *goyim* to hear for the first time.

What is transmitted across time is my perception of the story, but the stimuli are virtual. The picture I have of that apartment in Jerusalem is what I envision when hearing the story. The voice of my friend is not in the dream—the story has my attention, not the storyteller. As my friend's tale triggers learning in my brain, I associate the various elements with virtual stimuli. I was never there to smell that smell, but I can certainly imagine smelling it. The story comes to life in my cognitive processing, and all of this is what appears in my dream, ripped away from the context that someone else is telling me the story.[80]

The hypothesis that the learning process is transmitted through time also appears consistent with the paucity of smell, taste and touch as stimuli in my déjà vu experience. Except when we are very young, these senses are not commonly used for learning. On the other hand, if I were a blind oneironaut who uses braille to read, the sense of touch might indeed take the place of sight for transmitting a learning experience.

The *what not:* Time

Ironically, the oneironaut phenomenon concerns time but does not contain time. To date I have not experienced déjà vu where the dream recall included a notion of time (e.g., day, month, season, year, etc.). However, it should be possible, and in the last chapter I will describe how to incorporate time stamps in déjà vu.

I think time is naturally missing from our experiences because it is such a continuous semantic quantity. By continuous I mean that the experience of time is not like space, which can be separated into many discrete units that can be entered, exited and entered again. Space is separated and defined by obstacles, such as walls, forests, caves, etc., that can be experienced as novel, and experienced many times over. Time is experienced as a continuous flow that cannot be revisited in practice except by a virtual method of mental replay. Time is indeed useful and pervasive, but somehow it is not part of raw physical stimuli and does not produce a very common or very strong oneironaut signal.

The Greek folk singer Psarogiorgis from the island of Crete has a haunting song that compares time to water in a river; it passes us by and is gone. This echoes the famous quote from the ancient Greek philosopher Heraclitus who said, "You cannot step twice into the same river." A flowing river is indeed a superb way to consider how time contrasts against space in terms of describing it with our senses. If all the forests, mountains and dwellings started flowing past us, and as soon as these landmarks passed us they disappeared completely, it would be extremely hard to sense your location. The apparent continuous flow of time thus makes it quite difficult to navigate it with our senses.

The *what not:* Magic

There is no Nostradamus in the oneironaut phenomenon. Nostradamus is perhaps the most famous prognosticator who is not a religious figure. In my view, his fame is 50% attributable to his interesting name. He's like the hippopotamus of humans. But the oneironauts cannot dream about events that they are not going to personally experience in some form. Nostradamus, writing in the 16th century, apparently described events that occurred long after his death. This doesn't fit into the oneironaut phenomenon, though as revealed in my Preface, Nostradamus and I share the fear of being beheaded after claiming to see the future.

Also, the oneironaut phenomenon is not "remote viewing"—I cannot see through walls. For example, the Heidelberg experience seems like the type of story where a psychic helps the police find a missing person. If instead of searching for steak, fries and my friends, would I also have the ability to find a hostage hidden in the Heidelberg Dome? I will review some possibilities in the last chapter, but the déjà vu experience is not magical at any epoch of time. Whatever "normal" observation of the world can be made at any given time is the sum total of what is possible.

The *what not:* False alarms

I have vetted my 332 instances of déjà vu to determine if they are false alarms, also known as *false positives,* with respect to precognition. I illustrated this procedure with the Haycart and Fomalhaut dreams, where I attempted to find alternate explanations for the déjà vu experience as a precognitive event and concluded that they were valid hits or *true positives*. In other cases, however, this line of questioning has led me to change an apparent true positive to a false positive.

For example, on April 23, 2011, I woke up around 6:30 and the dream before waking concerned a student who has an oblong Apple iPad in their backpack. I thought to myself, "What an interesting shape that is because it fits nicely in the backpack, but this iPad has a bigger screen and replaces the laptop computer." Later that same evening, around 11:30, while watching the film *Tron Legacy*, I witnessed a scene toward the beginning where someone pulls out a similar-looking iPad that is longer than the 2011 model. I then entered this event as a case of déjà vu in my logbooks.

However, investigating this more closely, the iPad dimensions are 9.6" x 7.5" (243 mm x 190 mm) with aspect ratio 1.28. The *Tron Legacy* iPad is 10.5" x 6.5" (taking a screenshot and measuring it), which gives an aspect ratio 1.62. The Samsung Galaxy Tab is 189.9 mm / 120.4 mm = 1.57. This was released in November 2010 and it is possible that I saw its shape in a commercial or an electronics store even though I do not recall ever seeing it. Therefore, despite the same-day timing of the dream and the film scene, this déjà vu could be a false positive due to cryptomnesia—I deleted it from my tally of 332 déjà vu events.

There are even more dreams—the vast majority, in fact—that I classify instantly as psychological. For example, flying dreams are great, I remember them, but they are background noise in terms of déjà vu. These are examples of classifying dreams as *true negatives* because we know that I cannot fly (though in Chapter 8 we will discover a tricky exception). However, there are more subtle examples that require introspection. Some dreams appear as realistic future events, yet in a few seconds of reflection one realizes that the dream pertains to day residue, problem solving, anxieties and wishes. The most interesting cases are when you cannot figure out a psychological source for the dream, you tell the dream to someone else, and they immediately reveal the source. This is amusing because you realize that you were cognitively blind to the meaning or source of the dream, but it becomes obvious once someone else says it out loud. For example, you might say, "I keep dreaming that I'm running away from an angry peacock—totally bizarre!" Your spouse might respond, "Don't you remember, that was a crystal figurine in your parents' bedroom."

The *what*: Finding a test for the osignal

The oneironaut phenomenon is an information system. We can ask what is the strength and quality of the osignal transmitted across time, and how does that compare to the noise of all other thoughts and memories? Can we solve the difficult problem of separating a tenuous future signal from powerful and memorable psychological dreams based on the past and present?

Quantifying the strength of an experience or thought is rather tricky and open to interpretation. Perhaps strength is proportional to the amount of information, which in turn depends on the duration. For example, if I needed to teach you Kepler's three laws of planetary motion, but I can only do it in five words, the strength of the learning experience will be weak even if I choose the best five words possible. If you allow me ten words, I might communicate the thought behind one of the three laws. If you allow me 100 words, then the strength of my lesson should be pretty good. Thus we can choose to characterize the strength of the osignal in terms of duration.

The strength of a message also has to do with its novelty. In an information system, if the receiver already knows Kepler's three laws, then the sender's message—regardless of its duration—will provides very little benefit to the receiver. The quantity of information can therefore be assessed in terms of its predictability (or entropy) such that a message has zero information if the message is already known (e.g., the Sun rises in the east).[81] A message has a large quantity of information if the content is novel. Thus, even though the Haycart dream has a short duration consisting of a few words, they are so unpredictable that you could say the message is strong or contains a *huge* quantity of information. Ironically, messages that contain novel content and thus the most information can be useless because they do not attach the needed semantic, "already known," information.

From my 332 déjà vu experiences, the information content transmitted could be described by two words: simple and brief. There is rarely enough information from a single oneironaut to provide predictive knowledge. The Haycart dream contains less than ten words, but it does not tell me who hurt their knee. If that information had been added, perhaps I could have warned that person to be very careful. The Fomalhaut dream focuses on a specific aspect of Fomalhaut's geometry during the moments of discovery, but it does not tell me which telescope

I would be using to obtain this image, nor does it correctly identify the star. Thus by "simple and brief" I mean that the information content is no more than what can be described in about three short sentences or less. This is consistent with the nine seconds of oneironaut dreaming that I estimated in the section about sleep.

To measure quality we can characterize the osignal in terms of its fidelity or the level of distortion. A very short dream with no distortion (high quality) may be more valuable than a longer dream that contains confused thoughts. For example, the fact that the Haycart dream had word-for-word correspondence to what was actually spoken means that the osignal was high quality. Thus, quality is measured by accuracy. The Fomalhaut dream, on the other hand, has elements of distortion in how I remembered the dream and interpreted what I was looking at when I wrote it down in my dream log. In the analogy to sound, I can get very close to a speaker so that the audio is very strong, yet the quality of information could still be low. For example, if the signal is the first movement of Beethoven's Fifth Symphony, but someone has distorted it by playing it backward, I may not recognize it no matter how loudly it is played or how long I listen to it.

Let's take a look at how the osignal might evolve through four consecutive stages:

Stage 1: Signal as it is experienced (an event occurring at the present time).

Stage 2: Signal as it is dreamed (while sleeping in the past).

Stage 3: Signal as it is stored in short or long-term memory after Stage 2.

Stage 4: Signal as it written down after Stage 3.

At each stage and between each stage the signal can lose strength and/or quality. In addition, at each stage and between each stage the osignal will compete against other signals, which constitute "noise." The noise in déjà vu consists of all the other experiences, thoughts, emotions, fantasies, expectations and memories that enter both the awake and dreaming brains. These are signals too, but not the signal we are searching for. Even if the quantity of a transtime signal is large, and even if the quality is excellent, this signal may not be recognizable when consciousness is attending to many other things. In the sound analogy, imagine Beethoven's Fifth being played at a good volume with high quality, yet the room is filled with people talking to each other, and someone tells me something critically important, like my car is about to be towed. If someone later asks me what music was playing in that room, I won't be able to answer because Beethoven was drowned out by all the noise and the urgent problem I had with my car.

What was the relative strength of signal-to-noise for my Haycart dream described in Chapter 1? Let's consider the ratio: (signal – noise) / signal. The higher the ratio the better. Since it occurred exactly before waking, this was the *only* dream I remembered clearly from that evening. The signal-to-noise ratio was 1.0 (100%). This dream came through loud and clear into my waking memory. Overall, I believe that the signal-to-noise needs to be at least 0.5 for me to write something in my dream log, meaning that the déjà vu dream is one of two brief dreams that I recall. Or, put another way, a signal-to-noise greater than 1/2 makes the dream equivalent to strong, long-term memories of waking life experience, such as the first time you went to school. This again touches on why novel visual experiences are common with the oneironaut phenomenon. Novel experiences have distinct signals and they pop up above the noise. This suggests that the oneironaut phenomenon is in fact present to an even greater degree than we are conscious of. It's just the tip of the iceberg when we remember a dream corresponding to a real-life experience. Unfortunately, a high signal-to-noise is no guarantee that I am able to write it down (Stage 4), given that morning circumstances sometimes offer little time for writing, and the day can pass with no further opportunity to write. Nevertheless, the few instances of high signal-to-noise—the very memorable dreams—have convinced me that my déjà vu experiences are precognitive. If the signal-to-noise is less than 0.5, then the déjà vu dream is either lost completely from my memory or it survives subconsciously until the moment it gives me real-time or 24-hour déjà vu.

Let's use the Haycart dream to study what could have happened to someone else in the four stages with respect to signal and noise. The stimulus is the puzzling phrase: "jumping from a haycart to a sixteen-wheeler." At Stage 1, the perception of the signal may only include "jumping from a haycart" because the person is not paying full attention or does not know what a sixteen-wheeler is. So already a part of the signal could be lost, say 50%. The remaining 50% could be a high-quality signal because the person briefly paid full attention, or a distorted signal because the person is simultaneously thinking of something else, has a migraine headache, etc.

At Stage 2, the person dreams an auditory signal "jumping from a haycart," which may be strong or weak depending on Stage 1. However, in the very next dream a large man with an angry face yells, "I'm going to kill you!" The puzzling auditory phrase now competes with the noise of a powerful and memorable dream. More noise has been added to the experience, and thus the ratio of signal-to-noise drops even more.

At Stage 3, the person's short- and long-term memory contains the emotional, visual and auditory dream of the angry man, while the puzzling phrase signal is swamped by this noise. Three years later the person can retrieve the explicit memory of the angry man dream but nothing else. When someone says, "jumping from a haycart to a sixteen-wheeler," the person senses that the phrase is *familiar*, but does not *recognize* it.

At Stage 4, the puzzling phrase signal has dropped to zero because it was never written down due to the low signal-to-noise at Stage 3. However, the angry man dream was written down and that signal is 100%. One day, a man gets angry with the person and the person suspects it could be from a dream, yet this will count as a *false positive* déjà vu (a false alarm) because it is not the same man as in the dream. The angry man dream simply did not have a unique identifier. Or, one day the person encounters a man who resembles the man from the dream, and the person provokes the man into becoming angry and yelling, "I'm going to kill you!" Again, this is false positive déjà vu because the person pursued the self-fulfilling prophecy.

Consider also that at Stage 4 a dream may be remembered and not written down because it seems to be pure fantasy. Déjà vu experiences often involve novel experiences that defy the imagination—reality is stranger than fiction—so it's fairly easy to misclassify a real future experience as a bizarre dream sequence instead of something that can really happen. This type of misclassification is called a *false negative*. Thus, even with high signal-to-noise up to Stage 3, an error in judgment can prevent the dream from being written down for Stage 4.

The 332 déjà vu experiences in my logbook means that 332 osignals made it to Stage 3. Only the Fomalhaut dream survives to Stage 4, with a possibility that the Pacific Island and Boston Marathon dreams should be counted as well. Nevertheless, the key purpose of keeping track of all the dreams that made it to Stage 3 is to be able to distinguish possible déjà vu dreams (true positives) from all other dreams (false positives) that make it into memory. These other dreams are false only with respect to my goal of correctly classifying dreams as either real future experiences or imagined experiences. Both are real memories (positives), but if the source is imagination instead of experience, they are false.

I can now use the 332 déjà vu experiences to fashion a template for the osignal that I am searching for. This template can then be applied to subsequent dreams, essentially filtering dreams for matches to the template. The phrase "matched filter" is a more technical term used to describe this process.

To clarify with a different example, one day in bed I had the faint sensation of something crawling on my back. I reached behind me, grabbed it, and it turned out to be a somewhat enormous deer tick. From this point forward I have a memory of what that felt like on my skin, and now I use this as a "matched filter" to detect deer ticks on my skin. However, my skin transmits sensations all the time due to clothes, body hair, etc. Because I greatly fear Lyme disease transmitted by ticks, I wish to never, ever have a false negative, which means that a tick is on my skin and I do not detect it. Thus, I set my mental threshold for detecting ticks very *low*. Every time I have a skin sensation, I inspect the area, because my sensitivity (the probability of detection or completeness) has been set to a maximum by having a low threshold.

Unfortunately, even though I will detect almost all ticks, the low threshold / high sensitivity leads to many false positives that end up wasting my time. As a result, I decide to set my threshold higher and lower my sensitivity so that most skin sensations are classified as true negatives and ignored.

Similarly, discovering such a matched filter and tuning the threshold to optimize sensitivity are the goals of analyzing my nightly dreams. At some point I can conclude that this "training" to detect and classify dreams is finished, and I have thus created a "test." As in medicine, where you might develop a test for a disease, I can take every dream that I remember, test each one against what I believe could be a real-life future experience, and write it down for Stage 4 if it tests "positive."

As **Table 5-1** summarizes, the events in my life can be compared against my written dream record, and if something comes true, it is a true positive (TP). Everything that does not come true from my dream record is a false positive (FP). True negatives (TN) are the dreams that I remembered but never wrote down because they failed my test, and indeed they never appeared in my future. However, if I have déjà vu from a dream that I remember from Stage 3, but I did not write it down in Stage 4, then this becomes a false negative (FN). My test said it was a plain old dream, I classified it as negative for the osignal, but in the end it came true.

In my case, I remember at least one dream per night, and no more than approximately six dreams, so perhaps on average I have long-term memories of ≤3 dreams per night, or ≤1,095 per year. This seems like a lot, but it could be reasonable if we include dreams that could be recalled from memory when one is cued or reminded about the dream. Indeed, when I read through my dream log I instantly remember most dreams though it would be hard for me to start recalling them in the absence of such a reminder. The average annual rate of déjà vu is 37, which means that the occurrence rate is ≥3.4% (37/1,095). Roughly speaking, for every 30 dreams that make it to Stage 3, at least one of these will be a memory of a future experience. Or, given that there are 365 nights of sleep, the occurrence rate is roughly 37/365 or 10% of nights will contain an experience of the future. Once every 10 days I learn something about my future that I preserve in memory.

Testing dreams for precognition

	Test says the dream could be a future experience (record the dream).	Test says the dream is just a dream (do not record the dream).
In the future, the dream comes true.	True Positive	False Negative
In the future, the dream *never* comes true.	False Positive	True Negative

Table 5-1: Each dream is tested at Stage 3 and only recorded for Stage 4 if it could be a future experience, and not recorded if it is classified as a plain old dream. Future events or non-events will eventually determine the power of the test by counting true positives, true negatives, false positives and false negatives. This table is called a confusion matrix where the goal is to maximize the number of hits along the diagonal of True Positives and True Negatives.

But how many dreams make it to Stage 4, when I write something down because it passes my test for the osignal? On average since 2009 I record dreams 57 nights per year (I am not a very good role model), and with roughly three dreams per night, this means that 171 dreams out of 1,095 per year make it to Stage 4. However, all of these dreams were false positives; FP = 171 and TP = 0. Since 37 dreams came true but I did not write these down in my dream log, FN = 37. The number of true negatives (the dreams that I correctly classified as "just dreams") is TN = 1095 − 171 − 37 = 887.

Having estimated TP, FP, TN and FN, we can now calculate various quantities. For example, the "sensitivity," "hit rate," or the true positive rate is TPR = TP / (TP + FN) = 0. Evidently, I am stuck at Stage 3 and haven't found a reliable test to transfer precognitive dreams to Stage 4.

If I were to include the Pacific Island and Boston Marathon dreams as true positives, then I should define a time interval that tested for the phenomenon. For example, in a five-year period 2009–2013, these count as two true positives (TP = 2) for events that happened in the interval 2014–present. **Table 5-2** summarizes the results in this best-case scenario where two precognitive dreams were successfully recorded. Over five years FP = 5 x 171 − 2 = 853, TN = 5 x (1,095 − 171) − 2 = 4,618, and FN = 5 x 37 − 2 = 183. This now gives my sensitivity or TPR = 1.1%.

Again this shows that I have not yet succeeded in developing a reliable test for the osignal in remembered dreams. This could be taken as evidence that déjà vu is a colossal thought blunder instead of precognition, or it simply says that my experiment is inadequate and my test isn't ready yet. For example, I have no control group of people selected because they have no history of déjà vu. If they could have participated in the experiment with me, I would have been able to understand if my 1.1% true positive rate is better than chance. Working alone I think that my high false positive rate illustrates that writing down dreams for Stage 4 favors the selection of dreams that are most easily described. These are the dreams with powerful emotional, visual and auditory content with a cohesive narrative that seem realistic and satisfy the elements also found in precognitive dreams. Precognitive dreams, on the other hand, are snippets of experience with narratives so fragmentary that writing them down is unlikely. Thus false positives dominate the dream record.

To be honest, I do not feel entirely stupid that my current test fails because: (1) I haven't finished defining and tuning the test, and (2) even in many other domains, developing a good test for a rare phenomenon takes a long time. For example, say that there is a rare disease that kills one in a million people. The occurrence rate is 1 / 1,000,000, or 0.0001%. If someone develops a test that seems pretty good because its false positive rate 0.1%, it turns out that it is *not* useful because 1,000 people will test positive out of one million, but only one person might have the disease. So too, my filter for classifying certain dreams as possible déjà vu currently gives too many false positives with respect to the rarity of the phenomenon. Like my problem with the deer tick, I have probably set the threshold too low so that I do not miss any dreams that could be déjà vu in the future, but I am letting in too many false positives as well.

Testing dreams for precognition (5-year period)

	Test says the dream could be a future experience (record the dream).	Test says the dream is just a dream (do not record the dream).
In the future, the dream comes true.	2	183
In the future, the dream *never* comes true.	853	4,618

Table 5-2: Confusion matrix assuming that over five years of writing down dreams, two were experienced in the future. Unfortunately, there were 183 déjà vu experiences that have no corresponding written dream record. Moreover, I wrote down 855 dreams and only two of these came true. Nevertheless, it is difficult to ignore the 183 memories of dreams that came true.

Finally, notice that it may seem like the only process under willful control is going from Stage 3 to Stage 4, and therefore the matched filter process only works at the final stage of recording the dream. But this is not exactly true. Once the matched filter is defined, one can apply it to Stage 1. If we know which types of experiences produce the highest signal-to-noise, then we can willfully manipulate the Stage 1 experiences to reduce noise and boost signal. The matched filter and classifier therefore drive the design of a signal *amplifier*. I have mentioned several examples previously, such as having simple but novel visual experiences indoors.

In the final chapter of the book I will discuss the most important amplifier—increasing the number of people that have a common Stage 1 experience. Working alone, I am generating one "realization" of a Stage 1 experience. I can certainly try my best to optimize the signal-to-noise and detection probabilities on my own. However, if you have one thousand people exposed to the same stimulus, then we have one thousand realizations of Stage 1. Each has a different signal and a different noise due to the beholder's share. Each will be changed in different ways in subsequent stages, and perhaps only 10 will make it to Stage 4. Nevertheless, this provides 10 times more data for analysis than the single dream that a single oneironaut can provide. Moreover, the final chapter discusses modern methods to record *all* dreams so that the problem of going from Stage 3 to Stage 4 is eliminated. Finding such methods that could work on a large number of oneironauts will have significant consequence for individuals and societies.

The *why*: Organizing the mind

Throughout this book I touched on clues as to why the oneironaut phenomenon occurs. I have already suggested that the consequence of experiencing the future is that the mind becomes better prepared to engage unexpected experiences. Therefore the purpose of the phenomenon could be to compensate for cognitively challenging circumstances by making the unpredictable more predictable.

Here I will attempt another approach that combines the ideas of signal quality and predictable experiences. Consider that the efficiency and accuracy of computation in the brain, such as when solving problems, are optimum when the mind has ordered thoughts and memories rather than disordered thoughts and memories. Therefore, when disordered thoughts and memories exist, a natural function of the mind is to organize them into a more ordered state. Just as the digestive system naturally works to make the things we eat and drink useful for our functioning, the mind naturally works to digest information. The mind would surely deteriorate if it wasn't constantly working to stay ordered, and our ability to succeed in our environment would be threatened.

In physics, a measure of order versus disorder is called *entropy*. High entropy means highly disordered, whereas low entropy is low disorder. A fundamental law of physics called the second law of thermodynamics states that the universe generally proceeds from low to high entropy, from order to disorder. In effect, entropy and the second law of thermodynamics provide one definition for the forward direction of time.

For example, a whole egg is a high-quality egg, but if I drop it on the ground, it becomes a low-quality egg because the event has converted order into disorder. The egg is low entropy when there are fewer pieces, and higher entropy when there are many different pieces. The events needed to assemble a smashed egg back into a whole egg are so improbable that for all practical purposes the forward direction of time is defined as the series of events that convert low entropy to high entropy instead of the other way around.[82]

Entropy is also a way of quantifying the predictability or certainty of information.[83] Predictable information has low entropy (order), and unpredictable information has high entropy (disorder). The past can be recalled in memory with little uncertainty (very low entropy), but the future has various degrees of much higher uncertainty (higher entropy). Novel future experiences in particular have the highest entropy because they are the least predictable.

For example, let's take a look at the two events that might happen in the future. In the future, I am going to sleep in my bedroom, and the information for this future experience has relatively low entropy. But if the information is a phrase that I've never heard before and it is rarely written or spoken—such as "jumping from a haycart to a sixteen-wheeler"—then that information has very high entropy.

If I have a dream about this future phrase, it becomes more predictable in my mind, and therefore my future has lower entropy because of dreaming. More generally, one of the major functions of sleep and dreaming is to consolidate memories of experiences, which means that memories are compressed and organized in order to optimize functional efficiency later. Dreaming takes high-entropy information and makes it low entropy.[84] Our waking experiences are a bombardment of broken pieces involving vision, hearing, sensations, emotions, memories, etc. We may think it makes perfect sense, but really it is not the whole egg that we are experiencing, but the broken egg instead. The function of sleep is to reconstruct the egg and thereby improve the quality of the signal we call memory.

Finally, here is the insight: when dreaming converts high-entropy (unpredictable) information to low-entropy (predictable) information, this corresponds to the backward arrow of time. The oneironaut phenomenon represents the exact same direction (as I also reasoned in Chapter 2). The brain's action of reducing information entropy has an added consequence—during this process some signal literally goes backward in time.

In summary, the cognitive purpose of sleep and dreaming is to succeed in the task of organizing new information. But the process of taking the many pieces of waking experience and creating something more useful because it is more ordered and predictable corresponds to the backward direction of time.

As a side note, I wonder if it is correct to equate the "power" of artificial intelligence to ever-faster computation and greater information storage. When machines absorb more information and store all details, this represents an increase of information entropy, but human intelligence and consciousness *reduce* the entropy of information. Probably machines and humans are developing an ever-increasing symbiotic relationship where each lets the other do what they do best.

Summary

IN THIS CHAPTER I dissected one oneironaut, *moi*. Perhaps it was most interesting for the future researcher who wants to contemplate the phenomenon academically, or simply the general reader who has déjà vu and wants to find out how I handled my experiences. In previous chapters, I mentioned that each individual déjà vu experience could be due to chance or a cognitive blunder, except that the broader context matters, and now you know the context includes 332 records of déjà vu experiences over several decades.

In subsequent chapters I am going to search for the origin of the déjà vu experience, given that the properties of déjà vu provide some hints as to where to look. Regardless of whether or not the origin of the déjà vu experience is discovered, I will conclude the book with the steps that can be taken to transform the déjà vu experience from a personal diary to something that can become useful for humankind everywhere.

Paul Kalas

6. The Physics of Time Using Nature's Swiss Army Knife

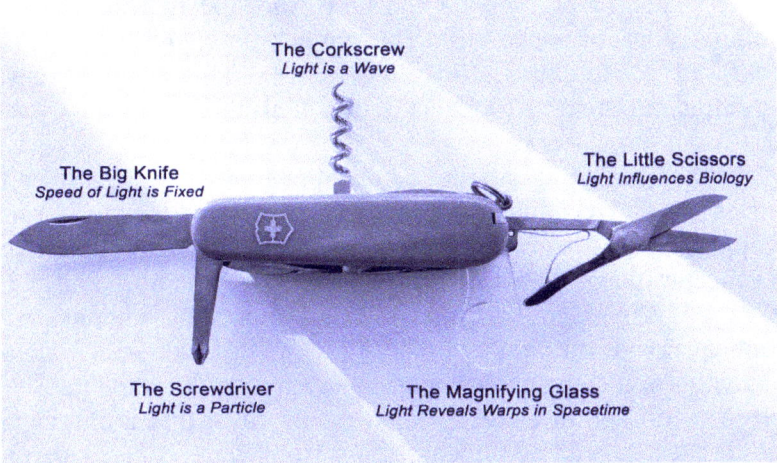

No book by a time-traveling author would be taken seriously if it neglected to have a chapter on time itself. The great thing about time is that everyone can say a few words about it, from the physicists to the poets, from the history books to the philosophy books, and all books in between, and from the human children to the non-human children, on whatever planet either might be found.

If flying saucers were to descend into my backyard and the commanders of the alien invasion force were to say, "Take us to your leader," I would show them my wristwatch or the clock on my phone. Hopefully, they would find this absurdly funny because they have the same joke on their own slightly absurd planet, and thenceforth move their invasion force to someone else's planet that was less funny and worthy of total destruction.

I borrowed this idea from a film I mentioned earlier called *Black Robe* where Jesuit missionaries interact with Native Americans in Canada. The missionaries have a brazen clock, which the indigenous people end up calling "Captain Clock." The reason is that from their perspective the Europeans behave as if the clock is their chief.

In a similar vein, writer Jonathan Swift imagined what the primitive Lilliputians in *Gulliver's Travels* would say after inspecting Gulliver's pocket watch for the first time:

> ...we conjecture it is either some unknown animal, or the god that he worships; but we are more inclined to the latter opinion, because he assured us...that he seldom did anything without consulting it. He called it his oracle, and said it pointed out the time for every action of his life.

Thus an oscillating synthetic god appeared in Europe over four centuries ago, and its name was Captain Clock. The modern reader might even appreciate the irony that in very many ways the clock continues to be our master today. "Captain Clock, we shall obey you now, and an hour from now." Why? Time is one of the important elements in any technological civilization, essentially because it is extremely useful to our activities and knowledge, and also because it is inescapable.

However, Captain Clock is not the only clock that is inescapable. Imagine that I take all of the characters from *Black Robe* to Toronto's Pearson International Airport, if it existed back in 1634. I would get them on Air Canada's flight AC1900 to Athens Eleftherios Venizelos airport, departing Toronto at 4:50 p.m. Captain Clock would be invited too, just to make a point. This 9 hour and 40-minute flight will land in broad daylight at 9:30 a.m. in Athens, Greece, even though Captain Clock would tell them that the time should be closer to 3 a.m. at night. Captain Clock would unexpectedly seem fallible, a leader with limits. It kept time, but the time would now be incorrect. Moving a clock apparently distorts time.

Our friends from Canada would get off the plane, climb up to the Acropolis, have something to eat and drink, but by mid-afternoon they would all be stricken with a severe malady of mind and body, as if cursed by a supernatural magic spell, or perhaps by the narcotic poppy juice dropped into their drinks by the Greek god of sleep called Hypnos. Everyone from that flight would start shutting down, a liquid cloud of drowsiness flooding their minds, an irresistible urge to sleep overwhelming them hours before sundown. Some would resist, eventually all would succumb. Then as if twice cursed, they would find themselves wide awake in the middle of the night, unable to get back to sleep.

It turns out that it doesn't matter if you live in a technological civilization or not, there are other clocks in all living things that puts the authority of Captain Clock to shame. For humans and other mammals, the master biological clock resides in the brain's suprachiasmatic nucleus (SCN). Admiral SCN regulates your circadian rhythm and has the remarkable ability to force you into a sleep state for nearly half your life. Given such a prominent biological role you would think Admiral SCN occupies a substantial portion of your brain. Yet Admiral SCN is only one millimeter in size.

Admiral SCN is the Napoleon of physiology and behavior across the entire mammalian kingdom. The Canadians in Athens would obey an Admiral SCN that was set in Canada, and could only be reset in Athens after a period of adaptation that involves the perception of light.

At this point, I must make a confession. There are readers who fear math and physics and had decided in advance to skip this chapter because the title has the word "physics" in it. I confess that I deceived these readers into reading the beginning of this chapter anyway by talking about aliens and Canadians. Yet, what has happened is that two of the harmless ingredients needed to explain the physics of time have now been introduced: clocks and light.

The Big Knife: Speed of Light

LIGHT IS THE SWISS ARMY KNIFE OF THE UNIVERSE. From one small package you get many different tools to understand and work with nature (see the photo at the start of the chapter). I briefly mentioned that the perception of light resets the body's circadian rhythm. This is sort of like the Little Scissors in the Swiss Army knife—good for helping out with our daily human routines. We'll return to the Little Scissors later. But first, what aspect of light is the Big Knife in the Swiss Army knife?

I think the Big Knife is that light travels at a fixed speed in a straight line in empty space (a vacuum), and nothing else can go faster. The speed of light always has the symbol c, and speed is a change of distance over a change of time: $c = 300,000$ km/s. By "fixed speed" I mean that its speed cannot be increased or decreased by association with some other speed. It is always constant.

For example, if you are driving a rocket car at a land speed of 100 km/s (note that this is per second, not per hour) and you turn on the headlights, the person standing on the side of the road will measure the land speed of that beam of light as 300,000 km/s, and not 300,100 km/s. If you were to throw a ball forward out of the rocket car at 10 km/s, it would indeed have a land speed of 110 km/s. No matter how fast you threw that ball, it would never have a land speed of 300,000 km/s, because only light can have that speed.

Light is indeed quite unique in this way with respect to speed. The concept seems simple enough, yet the consequences are far-reaching. One example is that you can now state a distance by referring to a time—one light-year is a distance. This is the distance traveled by light in a year. But note that such language is somewhat paradoxical because a year is not a distance. The Big Knife is the only way to make sense of this.[85]

A second example is that you can understand why astronomers occasionally describe their fancy telescopes as time machines. Telescopes "peer back in time" because the light from a very distant galaxy takes billions of years to travel across empty space. The information we record today may indeed be very old because of the Big Knife—it takes a fixed time for light to travel a certain distance.

The modern artist Vladimir Kush encapsulated this concept nicely in a painting called *Webmaster*. From the inside of an astronomical observatory we see a telescope that has a clock instead of a large lens or a mirror peering out into the night sky. If all things in the universe are located at different distances from us, then this means that a telescope is looking at a different time in the universe, depending on where you point it.

A third consequence is that the Big Knife gives you a limit to cause and effect. Over the next 1.0 second, no event can have an effect on you if it originates more than 300,000 km away from you. Information, and therefore causation, cannot go faster than light. Over a 10-second interval, the event would have to be 3,000,000 km away from you, or closer, to have an effect. Over a 100-second interval the event would have to be 30,000,000 km or closer to have an effect on you. You should now have a mental picture of a sphere of cause-and-effect growing around you as time passes. Remarkably, we have taken a simple fact that the speed of light is constant and discovered a way to define the limits of our past and future. If you die at the age of 77 years, then your past can only include a sphere of events that happened within 77 light-years of your location. Not everything in the universe can have an effect on you.

But the Big Knife does more than that. You may have heard that if you leave home in a rocket moving some fraction of the speed of light, when you return home everyone will be *older* than you are. It's true. The Big Knife, which says that you cannot add or subtract speed to the speed of light, ends up slowing down time for a clock that is moving relative to a different clock that is stationary. The scientific term is "time dilation."

To make sense of time dilation we are forced to think about the definition of time more carefully. Time can be defined as an interval between two events that occur in space. Since the speed of light is constant, light is an excellent way to measure an interval between two events. For example, since **c** = 300,000 km/s, let me ask a friend to take a light bulb 300,000 km away from me. The event of the friend turning on the light bulb and the event of light entering my eye will have an interval of time called one second. As long as we keep a 300,000 km distance between us, it does not matter how we move relative to the universe. One second of time will be defined by the interval between these two events. Put another way, the time interval between event 1 and event 2 is delta t (notation Δt), and the distance between event 1 and event 2 is Δx, therefore $\Delta t = \Delta x / $ **c**.

We use something like this equation all the time. Instead of **c** for the speed of light, consider the symbol v for the speed of a runner. If I want to run Δx = 10 km and my speed is v = 10 km/hr, then Δt = 1 hr. So, this business of flashing light over a distance of 300,000 km provides a nice clock that gives us seconds of time.

To show you how we can slow down time, my friend and I will clone the light bulb and ourselves. At first the original and copies are next to each other on the ground (**Figure 6-1**). When the originals look over at the clones, just sitting there, completely stationary, the light from their bulb takes one second to go from left to right. Next, we send the clones on a trip by launching them upward into space at high velocity, let's say 99% the speed of light. From their perspective, their light beam moves in a straight line from cloned light bulb to cloned eyeball in one second of time. Their moving clock seems to be working as expected.

Our perspective, where we are still sitting stationary on the ground, is quite different—the path of light emitted from the cloned light bulb to the cloned eyeball is a line at a nearly 45-degree angle. One remembers that in basic geometry the hypotenuse of a right triangle is longer than the other two sides by a factor 1.4, which is the square root of 2. So from our perspective on the ground the clones are no longer shining a light that takes a path Δx. Instead, the path is longer by some amount, 1.4 times Δx. From the ground we see that the time interval between the two events for our clones is a somewhat longer time interval, $\Delta t = 1.4 \, \Delta x / $ **c**. Stationary on the ground, we can execute 10 light bulb events corresponding to 10 seconds of time, whereas the clones from our vantage point will execute only 7 light bulb events corresponding to 7 seconds of our time. We have become 10 seconds older, but our clones are just 7 seconds older from *our* point of view. Thus you can grasp the story that if a spaceship leaves Earth with your twin at nearly the speed of light, when it returns your twin will be younger than you. Conversely, your twin will arrive and be shocked to find that you've aged so much.

Note that the Big Knife in this special result is that **c** must be constant, even though we observe the clones and their light bulb moving.

If instead of projecting light we were keeping time by throwing balls at speed v, then the perspective on the ground is that the clones who are moving upward are throwing balls faster than v, where the extra velocity corresponds to the velocity of the launch upward. So what happens now if time is measured by throwing balls? For light-flashing timekeeping, we had $\Delta t = 1.4\, \Delta x\, /\, c$; given that the speed of light c cannot change, then Δt must change from our perspective after Δx increased by a factor of 1.4. For the ball-throwing timekeeping, the analogous equation is $\Delta t = 1.4\, \Delta x\, /\, 1.4\, v$. So now the unit time interval, Δt, does not need to change from one observer relative to another observer because if Δx in the numerator becomes larger by some factor (1.4), then v in the denominator will cancel this with an equivalent factor (1.4).

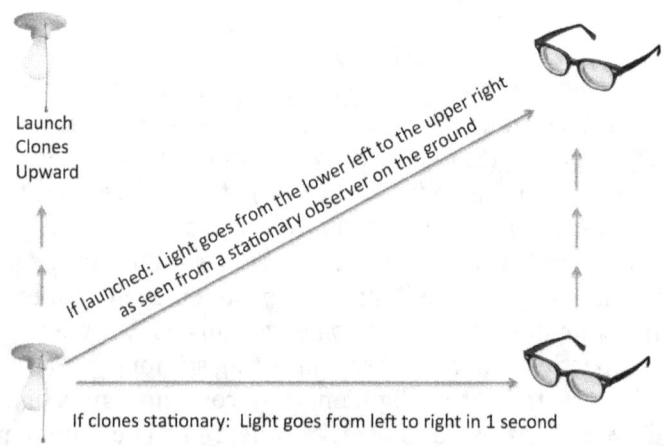

Figure 6-1: Looking over at our clones, if they are stationary at the bottom, 1 second of their time is equal to our 1 second. If the clones are launched upward, then from our perspective their light beam has to travel in a diagonal which is a longer path.

The Big Knife with light is that c never has a factor that increases it or decreases it. Such a factor does not exist. As long as a universe has one thing with this property of constant speed, c, time dilation will be a feature of that universe.

Case in point. When I was graduate student at the University of Hawaii in the 1990s, one of the postdocs was a solar physicist called Ed Lu. Ed would go on to become a U.S. astronaut, and over the course of one mission spent about six months traveling at high speed in the International Space Station orbiting the Earth. Years later I ran into him again on the Earth's surface in Monterey, California. Actually, we were in a buffet line at the Monterey Plaza Hotel, and buffet lines also have this quality where we perceive time slowing down inexplicably. I'm still trying to figure out if time slows down for the people in front of me, and that's why buffet lines move so slowly, or is it that everything is moving normally, and I'm the one stuck in a time warp. Regardless, the physics of time is clear—Ed Lu was a fraction of a second younger than he should have been due to his high-speed travel in space.[86] He found me to be a fraction of a second older than I should have been, but he was gracious enough not to mention it.

Nevertheless, from my perspective, Ed Lu lived through time differently than I did. Is the Big Knife therefore an explanation for the oneironaut phenomenon? I don't think so, because the relative speeds that lead to different experiences of time don't happen when I'm sleeping or awake. Moreover, even though Ed and I experienced time differently, neither of us observed their own or someone else's past or future. The constant speed of light combined with high relative speeds does not lead to time travel.[87]

Instead, the Big Knife illustrates something that has been understood about time only within the last century—that different clocks in different parts of space and time could observe time differently relative to one another. Linguistically, when talking about time, it can make a difference if I am referring to time as I experience it, time as you experience it, or your time as I observe it, and my time as you observe it.

It was Albert Einstein who worked through these problems about the constant speed of light and the dilation of time between different observers. This effect is central to *special* relativity. One thing that is missing from the picture is the effect of gravity. When Einstein later included gravity in the picture, this would become the theory of *general* relativity. Gravity is a distortion of time and space by matter, with the consequence that time dilation also occurs with gravity. One way astrophysicists were able to empirically confirm Einstein's theory was with another incredible tool provided by light—the magnifying glass in the Swiss Army knife.

The Magnifying Glass: Warps in Spacetime

THE HUMBLE MAGNIFYING GLASS shows that when light no longer travels in a vacuum and interacts with matter, in this case clear plastic, it will slow down and can change direction. The speed of light, **c**, is a constant 300,000 km/s only in empty space. The magnifying glass is shaped so that light passing through it will slow down by different amounts as it goes through different thicknesses of glass, bending the light to a focus at a point in space.

Remarkably, astronomers sometimes observe the bending of light in empty space, as discussed in Chapter 4. How could this happen when a key property of light is that in empty space it travels in straight lines? The answer is that space itself can be warped, and the warping is caused by anything that has mass, including you, the Earth, the Sun and me. Anything with mass creates gravity, and in fact gravity and the warping of space are synonymous. Moreover, if the speed of light defines the zone around you where cause and effect are possible, but the path of light itself can be bent by gravity, then cause and effect are also influenced by gravity.

Well, well, so the humble magnifying glass represents a lot more physics than meets the eye. Gravity is in fact the weakest of physical forces, yet it bends light and redraws the boundaries where cause and effect can take place within a given time interval. If the suprachiasmatic nucleus is the Napoleon of mammalian physiology and behavior, then gravity is the Napoleon of physics. Even though it is a tiny force, its significance is amplified because enormous amounts of mass pile up in many places in our universe. The Earth, for example, is a huge, relatively dense rock in space that has noticeable gravity, whereas the gravity associated with you and me is ridiculously small.

The best thing about this bizarre business of bending light and warping space is that I can just show it to you in a picture. No equations necessary!

First, we need to review what a galaxy is. A galaxy in space can be seen because it consists of a large collection of luminous stars like the Sun. There are billions of stars in single galaxy (e.g., approximately 200 billion in the Milky Way). Galaxies also have gas and dust and other things like black holes, but it's the stars that make a galaxy so easy to see. The Sun is in the Milky Way Galaxy, and all the stars you can see with your naked eye in the night sky are also members of our galaxy.

Second, you need to know that galaxies come in different shapes (morphologies), and among these are spiral galaxies, elliptical galaxies and irregular galaxies. Spirals look like pinwheels with a bright, compact center. Ellipticals look like elongated fuzzy blobs with a somewhat broader center. Irregulars have a variety of morphologies—sometimes it's hard to say where the center is. Galaxies can clump together in space due to their mutual gravity, and this is called a galaxy cluster. Galaxies can also collide with each other, disturbing each other's overall shape, and so there are a large variety of shapes.

Galaxies are located in every direction in space. Since our universe is only 14 billion years old, we cannot get information beyond 14 billion light-years (recall that a light-year is a distance not a time). We have to keep waiting for our universe to get older so that light from farther away has time to get to us. But within the observable universe of 14 billion light-years radius, space is filled with galaxies, and we can't think of any reason why this should not be the case continuing out to infinity, past the 14 billion light-year boundary.

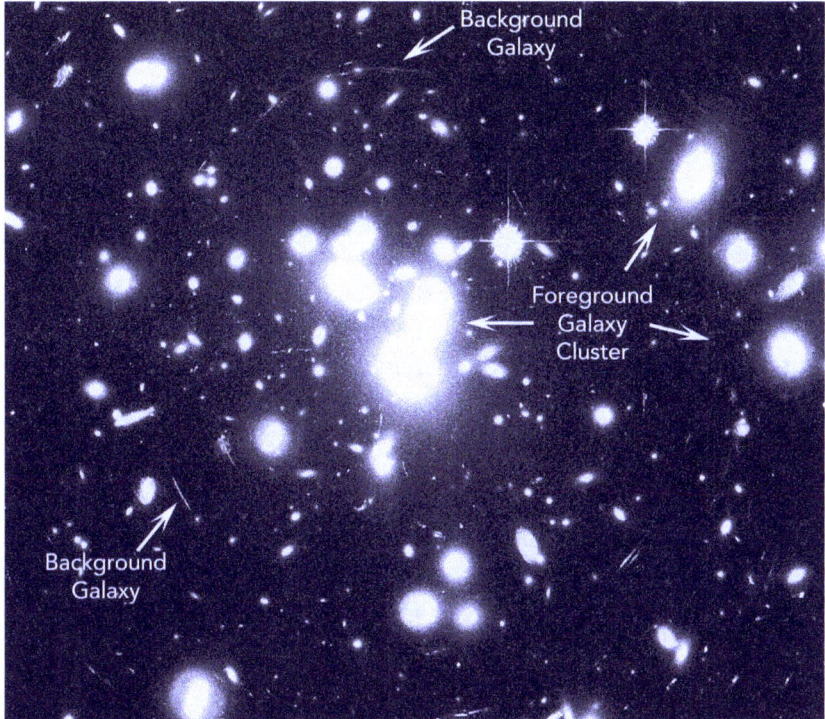

Figure 6-2: Abell 1689 is a cluster of massive elliptical galaxies that look like bright blobs in this Hubble Space Telescope image. The short arcs of light that surround the larger blobs are background galaxies that appear as arcs only because empty space is warped by the massive galaxies in the foreground.

Now that you know a few things about galaxies, I am going to show you a Hubble Space Telescope image of a galaxy cluster called Abell 1689 (**Figure 6-2**). Very broadly, anything bright and large in the picture is relatively nearby, in the "foreground." In the upper right quadrant, we find two stars that happen to be within our galaxy (look for the bright circular sources intersected by a cross, which is caused by the telescope's optical system). The prominent bright blobs in the middle are elliptical galaxies relatively close to our Milky Way Galaxy. Anything faint and small is a different galaxy that is relatively far away, in the "background." Anything that looks like a thin arc of light is also a distant background galaxy, but the arc we photograph is not the actual shape of a galaxy. Instead, this is a distorted image because time and space are warped by the mass contained within the foreground cluster of elliptical galaxies.

Light is traveling in a straight line through space for billions of years to get to us from these distant background galaxies. However, the foreground elliptical galaxies change the shape of space with their enormous mass. At this location, light from the background galaxies is still traveling in a straight line, but from our vantage point space itself is curved in the region surrounding the ellipticals. The effect can be compared to the effect of a magnifying glass on light, but the crucial difference is that light in empty space is not directly interacting with matter. Rather, the distortion of space by mass creates a "gravitational lens."

One of the great things about this awesome, mind-blowing effect is how impossibly cute Albert Einstein was when he first told the world about it. In his 1936 paper,[88] published in English in the journal *Science*, he starts a scientific manuscript by saying the following:

> This guy, Rudi Mandl, he comes over to see me, and he tells me that I should publish this little calculation that I had lying around. So I say, "Oh what the heck, gotta make people happy." And so here is my little calculation in the journal *Science*, that I wasn't gonna publish, if it weren't for this guy, Rudi Mandl.

Now, I may have paraphrased slightly, but this is roughly how Einstein starts one of the most important scientific papers of all time.

Einstein goes on to say that if you view two stars, one in the foreground and the other one exactly behind it and much farther away, the foreground star will act as the lens in the Swiss Army knife due to the distortion of space around it. The effect is aptly summarized by Einstein in his paper title: "Lens-like action of a star by the deviation of light in the gravitational field." The "lens-like" action basically has two effects: the image of the background star is distorted, and the intensity of light from the background star is amplified. From our point of view, the light from the background star will appear as a circle of light around the foreground star, which is the same effect seen in the background galaxies curving around Abell 1689. Einstein also showed that the light from the background star would appear brighter. In my business of discovering extrasolar planets (planets that orbit other stars), this extra amplification of light is useful not only because the foreground star distorts space, but also because any planet next to the foreground star also has mass, distorts space accordingly, and creates its own tiny amplification of light, something called microlensing. As of this writing, more than 50 extrasolar planets have been discovered based on Einstein's "little calculation."

You might recall that the astronomy lesson in Chapter 4 stated, "everything we see is not everything there is." The exoplanets discovered through microlensing are in fact not seen directly. What is actually observed is a blip of extra light from the background star because the planet's gravity warps spacetime and creates a lens. So too in the image of Abell 1689, precise calculations tell you that there is more mass in the foreground elliptical galaxies than you can see in stars. This unseen mass is called dark matter and the warped light in the picture tells you that it's really there. That is to say, the observed mass in luminous stars is significantly less than the mass you need to distort the background galaxies by gravitational lensing—this is how we know that the elliptical galaxies contain more mass than we can actually see as starlight.

The Hubble picture of Abell 1689 really highlights the beauty of astrophysics. Putting two and two together, astronomers can tell you what is seen and what is not seen, even though these objects are billions of light-years away. Light is the tool, the magnifying glass in the Swiss Army knife. Light that is bent by gravitational lensing tells you how much mass exists, even when you can't directly see most of this mass.

It's worth asking where exactly the three dimensions of space are bending into? One accessible answer is that our 3-D space bends into a fourth dimension of space, which we can't see, but we can measure. To understand this you can imagine that a lower-dimensional world exists, the 2-D world. Say you have ants on a table that perceive the 2-D surface of the table as their entire world, but they cannot look up, because this is the third dimension that is beyond perception. So too, humans cannot perceive the fourth dimension of space.

Now pretend the 2-D surface of the ants' world is a balloon that is slowly inflating. Their 2-D world is expanding into a dimension they cannot perceive. However, they can detect it through measurements. Over large distances, for example, the sum of angles for a triangle on this 2-D, spherical balloon surface will be greater than 180°. So too, one reason that astronomers are useful is that we make measurements over enormous distances in the 3-D world, and thus we understand our universe is expanding, and that gravity bends spacetime. The Big Bang, in fact, is not an explosion from a point. Instead, it could be seen as the expansion of 3-D space everywhere in the universe into a fourth dimension of space.

Let's now briefly return to the thought experiment of keeping time by turning on a light bulb. I've got a friend who turns on a light bulb, I'm 300,000 km away from them, and when the light enters my eye that means one second of time has elapsed. The clones of this experiment are right there next to us. In the previous section I had them launching upward at high velocity while they flashed their light bulb. But this time I'm going to park them a great distance away, and distort space by inserting a massive (but tiny) galaxy in the space between *their* light bulb and eye.

In this scenario, their beam of light will take a bit longer to travel around the space warped by the galaxy. I will see my light bulb flash 10 times in 10 seconds, but the clone will detect only 7 flashes because they have a distorted space to contend with. Therefore we experience time dilation relative to the clones, just as in the previous section. When we bring back the clones to our position in space, they again find that we have aged a bit more than they have. Our clock has more ticks than their clock. Thus, gravity or the distortion of spacetime by matter has an effect similar to our previous example of very fast relative motion.

The ultimate amazing feature of this thought experiment is to consider a black hole instead of a massive galaxy. Consider that the cloned light bulb now finds itself very close to a black hole. The black hole warps space so significantly that our clones cannot keep time at all. The flash of light never goes anywhere—it never reaches the cloned eye. The passage of time for us is normal, but our clones will be stuck in a place where time has stopped.

So, there are places in our universe where time has no meaning. Moreover, if our clones are sent to this timeless state of a black hole, we gain yet another insight about our universe.

The insight is that black holes can define a direction or arrow of time. This question concerning the "arrow of time"—past to present to future—is intricate enough that many books have been written about it. One idea discussed in the previous chapter is that the forward direction of time is defined by nature becoming increasingly disordered. The classic example concerns dropping an egg on the floor—the direction of time goes from the whole egg to the shattered egg, from order to disorder. Black holes give another arrow of time. There is no way to escape a black hole, and therefore if you were outside of it at some point, that event can only be the past.

Is the magnifying glass an explanation for the oneironaut phenomenon? I don't think so, because gravity is not really different between my sleeping and waking states, or at any time in my existence. Also, even though gravity has some remarkable properties, I don't think you really get a time machine out of it.

Nevertheless, gravity shows us that time does not have meaning everywhere in our universe. The oneironaut phenomenon also calls into question the meaning of time. However, the oneironaut phenomenon appears to disregard any arrow of time, whereas gravity indicates that arrows of time exist such as with the example of a black hole. I have to wonder if the oneironaut phenomenon works in such a way that it could tell you in advance that you will be stuck in a black hole, and thereby you can avert this future. This topic strikes at the heart of some fundamental theoretical physics, but overall I don't think the magnifying glass is helpful in explaining the oneironaut phenomenon. I will now stow it away and pull out two other tools in the Swiss Army knife.

The Screwdriver and the Corkscrew: Particle and Wave

WITH ALL THIS TALK ABOUT THE SPEED OF LIGHT and the path that light follows in space, we have yet to consider what light actually is. For the definition of light we encounter one of the most significant dualities in the entire spectrum of human knowledge. One equally great duality is the mind-body duality, which has been pondered by scholars since antiquity. The duality in light has manifested only over the last few hundred years. Dualities seem to create paradoxes—you can't be two things at once—yet the duality in the definition of light has been so well validated through experiments that mind-body scholars can only dream of having such concrete evidence at their disposal.

Light exists simultaneously as a particle and a wave. What you observe it to be depends on how you or something else interacts with it. In its particle form I'm going to call it the screwdriver in the Swiss Army knife. But the screwdriver tool is never pulled out alone. The corkscrew tool is always pulled out with it. The corkscrew has a twisted, wavy shape that is distinct from the screwdriver, and that's the wave nature of light. Which tool the Swiss Army knife will become to you depends on what you decide to do with it.

This might be confusing, but consider that some things are best defined by their shape, yet other things are best defined by their function. For example, later I will show that the part of the brain called the hippocampus is named after its shape. But then you'll realize its function is not at all defined by its shape. So when we say that light is both a particle and a wave, what this really means is that both of these functions are simultaneously available, but which one we observe will depend on how it functions in relation to something else.

Notice that light particles and light waves are identical in the sense that both must move at the speed of light and both are influenced by gravity, as discussed above. However, a particle has a fairly specific location in space and time, whereas a wave is at many places continuously at once. A wave can be measured as a distance between successive peaks (the wavelength) and as the height of each peak (the amplitude), and these two types of measurements are not applicable to a particle. Light as a particle with a precise location is helpful when taking a photograph. You want each pixel in your camera to record a well-defined particle of light—called a photon—so that a picture of the scene is recorded. The photo would be very different if a bunch of light waves hit the camera, since each wave of incoming light would spread over all the pixels in the camera.

The dual nature of light was understood well before the invention of photography. In the late 1600s, the Dutch scientist Christiaan Huygens proposed that light as a wave is the best way to explain how light travels through natural crystals. Just after Huygens passed away, Isaac Newton upheld the idea that light is a little particle, or a "corpuscle," and not a wave. A century later, in the early 1800s, a medical doctor named Thomas Young performed a remarkable experiment that went against Newton and supported the wave theory of light.

This was the "double-slit experiment," where a beam of light is projected onto an opaque surface with two slits cut out of it. What you see after the beam passes through the two slits is a pattern of light with a wavy appearance of bright and dark areas (**Figure 6-3**). The dark areas are where the peak of a wave from one slit encounters a trough in the wave from the second slit, and hence the combined light cancels to zero. This canceling is called destructive interference. If instead a peak of one wave is matched with a peak of another wave, then the light is doubly bright at that location, and we call this constructive interference. The bright-dark undulations of light are called an "interference pattern." Young had pulled out the corkscrew.

Another way to think about the experiment is to consider a homework assignment in which someone asks you to split a wave into two. How would you do that? A single wave can be split into two waves when it encounters an obstacle that has only two openings (holes, or slits). Two waves will emerge from the two slits, expanding outward from each slit, as if you were trying to inflate two balloons through two holes. These two waves or balloons will expand until they encounter each other. Balloons would push each other apart, but in the case of light the two waves meeting each other can recombine either constructively or destructively. Thus, the interference pattern is the recombined wave, and it has peaks and troughs. In physics lingo, a synonym for "recombined" is the word "superposition."[89] An interference pattern represents the superposition of waves. Given that light projected onto these two opening produces an interference pattern, we have to conclude light has the properties of a wave. Light functions as the corkscrew in the Swiss Army knife.

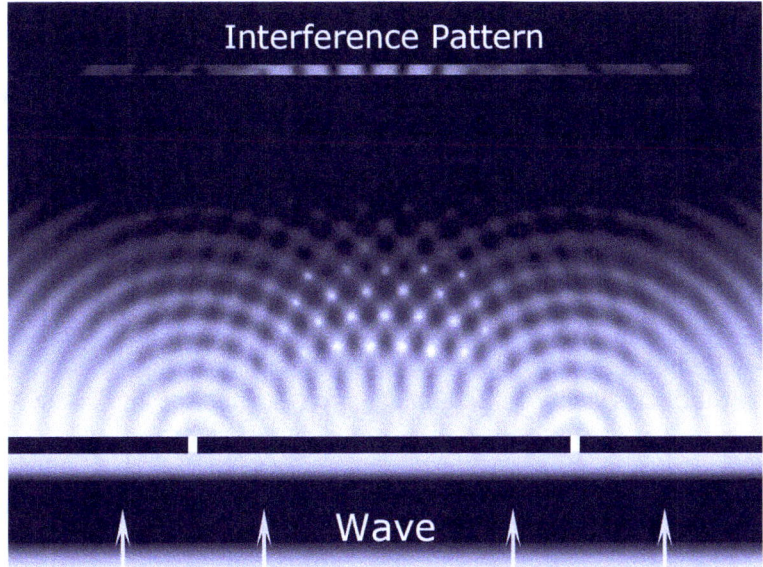

Figure 6-3: Illustration depicting a wave traveling from bottom to top, and encountering a black wall with two small openings or slits. The single wave is split into two expanding waves. The light and dark areas represent the peaks and troughs, respectively. The two new waves will encounter each other and combine constructively to make higher peaks and deeper troughs, or destructively cancel each other to zero. The peaks make an interesting hexagonal pattern also seen in the brain (**Figure 7-4**). Technically, we do not see the expanding waves, but at the very top we might have a camera and it would record the "interference pattern" as a series of light and dark bands.

A century after Young's double-slit experiment showed that light produces an interference pattern, Einstein proposed that a certain lab experiment which produces the "photoelectric effect"—a beam of light striking metal releases electrons—could only be explained if light was more like a bullet. Instead of a wave spread out over space, light needs to be contained in well-defined "quanta," little "wave packets," or what we now call photons. Einstein had revealed the function of the screwdriver in the Swiss Army knife.

Did Einstein's photons thereby overturn the wave theory of light? No, Young's experiment with the two slits and the interference pattern was also well validated. Both the particle and wave nature of light became scientific facts through numerous experiments, and thus the screwdriver and the corkscrew must always be pulled out at the same time.[90]

Some readers may be thinking that this doesn't make sense at all because when you look at light it cannot appear in our minds as two things co-existing exactly simultaneously. There are at least two answers to this brainteaser. First, you cannot actually look at a photon moving through space in front of you in the same way that you watch a soccer ball kicked across a field or a wave crashing on a beach. The only photons you see are the ones entering your eye, so you could not see other photons as objects or waves some distance away from you moving at the speed of light across your field of vision. Second, what you are capable of seeing is how light interacts with other things, and this is what makes the duality possible.

In the Swiss Army knife analogy, you do not see the screwdriver tool, or the corkscrew tool. What you can observe is an event that in some cases shows a cork has been taken out of a bottle, and in other cases a screw has been tightened or loosened. Hence you know that this single thing called light can influence the world as both a particle and a wave, depending on circumstances. Before it interacts with the world, you could say that light is simultaneously a wave and a particle. But for all practical purposes, the only time you care about light is when it interacts with something else, and that is when its property will emerge as either a particle or a wave. Therefore there is no paradox of simultaneous existence.

The particle-wave duality of light may appear to be a curious little fact of the universe of no further consequence, yet it opens up the mother of all Pandora's boxes concerning reality. Let's take a closer look.

In Young's experiment, there are two slits in a solid plate through which light can pass through to the other side (**Figure 6-3**). When I was an undergraduate studying physics at the University of Michigan, I presumed that a beam of light bombards both slits with very many photons. Thus at a given instant, there is one photon going through the left slit and a second photon going through the right slit, and the two expanding waves on the other side of the slits interfere with each other. If I were on the other side I would see both slits illuminated by light.

Later I would gain new insight by understanding that it is possible to fire a single photon at these two slits. As a particle, it can only go through one slit. But that single photon will then land on a spot on the other side consistent with an interference pattern. Thus, as a single particle it went through one slit, but its behavior of landing where an interference pattern shall form shows that this single photon knows about the slit it did not pass through, as if the single photon were a wave too. The photon interacts with the universe at two different spatial locations, but as a particle it could only be observed in one place. Phrased in a slightly creepier way, the photon path can go through only one opening, but it has knowledge of whether or not another opening exists nearby.

Going down this rabbit hole even further, if you decide to look at the slits to observe which slit that single photon goes through, your observation will destroy the wave property (the interference pattern) of the photon. This totally usurps common sense. Common sense dictates that objects have properties of their own and these properties should not change based on what you decide to know about them. Objective reality should not have a beholder's share.

Yet it is a fact of nature that when you try to get direct information in any way about the screwdriver, the corkscrew will vanish. Before you looked, the Swiss Army knife lying on the table has the corkscrew and the screwdriver pulled out. You could even keep your eyes closed and reach out with your hands, but the moment you touch it to find out which tools are pulled out, one tool will disappear from reality. Yet, as I said before, we know the Swiss Army knife has both tools because of how light interacts with other things. Light can uncork bottles and turn screws—both tools exist. But if you look, only one tool will be part of your reality. Very strangely, it's as if we are talking about the concept that art emerges only when you have interacted with it. Nature emerges in a way that depends on the beholder's share.

These puzzles are the tip of an iceberg that is the science of quantum mechanics. Those physicists who have understood much more of this iceberg have said things like, "If quantum mechanics hasn't profoundly shocked you, you haven't understood it yet" (from the Danish physicist Niels Bohr), or, "I think I can safely say that nobody understands quantum mechanics" (from the American physicist Richard Feynman), or the famous quote from Albert Einstein, "God does not play dice."

Einstein was huffing and puffing because the "God" he is referring to is the concept of a watchmaker and the watch. Remember Captain Clock? Einstein was a disciple. A watch keeps time because it operates in an accurate, precise and predictable manner. If it's 8:05 a.m. and you look at a functioning watch five minutes later, it is not going to give you some crazy answer like it's suddenly 11:21 p.m. Nature should generally work like a clock, with rules that guarantee predictability. However, in quantum mechanics, the time you observe by looking at the watch will in fact seem like a game of chance, as if rolling the dice. There is a high probability you will see 8:10 a.m., but there is a small probability you will see 11:21 p.m.

When you look at the world at the tiny level of photons, electrons and atoms, reality is not definite in the way you normally perceive it. A given microscopic entity, say a photon, has various probabilities of existing in various states.

Actually, what I just said is probably incorrect. Note the difference when saying it correctly: A given microscopic entity, say a photon, exists in states with various probabilities. The former statement implies that the photon could be existing in the future in one of many states, whereas the latter says the photon exists now in many states, but the probabilities lie in which state you would observe it in the future. Only when you try to measure it will the photon manifest as a single definite state. This microscopic world is indeed the quantum world. Even though the quantum world is everywhere around us, the macroscopic world appears to have other properties.

The most famous example is Schrödinger's hypothetical cat that in the quantum world exists as both dead and alive, but it will appear as either dead or alive only when you observe it. Schrödinger was trying to point out that the quantum world is paradoxical and bizarre. Let's try a different example. Imagine that you are driving and there is a car behind you. You expect that its color state (e.g., red) has a definite existence whether or not you decide to look in the rearview mirror. But if you are driving a car in the quantum world, the car behind you could have the color red only after you observe it. Before you look in the rearview mirror, the car has no single color, but rather it has all the possible colors. To be clear, this is a reality. It is not a hypothetical thought such as, "The car could be any color, and I just need to get more information by looking at it." Instead, the correct phrase is: "That car *is* all the possible colors and each color has a different probability of being observed. When I look in the rearview mirror, I have an experience of seeing only one of those colors, where the most likely color is red." This is how reality works at the quantum level.

In the language of quantum physics, the "wave function" specifies all of the possible colors for the car behind you. A function is something you write down to describe how a bunch of elements interact, much like a cooking recipe. If you have a bread recipe, it will tell you how flour, water, dry yeast and salt should be combined and cooked to make bread. So too the wave function describes all the existing elements and processes of our universe. When you look at our universe and make a measurement, you "collapse" the function into one measurement that cannot be erased from our universe. "Collapse" suggests a final result, or you could just imagine that when you pull your bread out of the oven, there's no changing that bread. It has its final and unique form. The bread is done. Coming back to the car analogy, when you look in the rearview mirror, the "wave function collapses," or, "you collapse the wave function," and a single color is experienced as reality. The act of looking decides the world, your world. But what happened to the other colors that existed just before your observation "collapsed the wave function" so that your reality contains only one of those colors?

In one school of thought in quantum mechanics the answer is that there are "many worlds," a concept that I introduced in Chapter 2. When an observer experiences an event, all possibilities of that event happen in separate worlds or universes. So when you look in the rearview mirror, there is a universe where the car behind you is red, and a different universe where the car is green. There are infinite universes where all possible variations are represented. That car will have different colors, different fuel levels, different oil levels, different tire tread wear and a different amount of bug damage on the front. All of these worlds are represented by the "wave function."

The late physicist Hugh Everett proposed that quantum physics has the implication of many worlds, and many other physicists think that the theory is reasonable, though puzzling. The puzzle is that in science we generally don't think reality should be different depending on whether or not you're microscopic (quantum physics) or macroscopic (classical physics). If macroscopic entities are composed of the many microscopic components, then why should the macroscopic ensemble of photons, electrons and atoms experience reality differently than the subcomponents? The more disturbing puzzle is that quantum mechanics appears to say that the external universe is concerned about how you decide to act.

Is the quantum world, as represented by the screwdriver and the corkscrew, an explanation for the oneironaut phenomenon? Here I think I'm getting closer to possible answers, with caution.

The caution is that I am not sure which aspects are merely analogies, and which may actually represent physically relevant explanations. With the use of language we can construct analogies that compare the properties of two different things. The goal is to gain a new conceptual understanding of how something works. The danger is that the opposite—confusion—can also occur.

For example, by looking through a telescope at night I can see that the Horsehead Nebula has a shape that looks like a horse, yet it is incorrect to explain its physical nature by referring to an actual terrestrial horse. So too the human oneironaut experience has features that resemble the language used in describing quantum mechanics, yet a physical link is not proven. In fact, the true language of quantum mechanics is mathematical, but the oneironaut experience has no math yet. My worry echoes Feynman's remark: "When philosophical ideas associated with science are dragged into another field, they are usually completely distorted."[91]

So, with these fairly severe caveats in mind, I will press on with some comparisons. One aspect of the oneironauts is the puzzle of being located in bed as a sleeping dreamer, who simultaneously has a waking experience at a different time and location. Where am I exactly in spacetime? A wave is spread over many places at once and a genuine ronin I must be. But there is no other experience where my location has wavelike properties. A wave only seems to be an analogy for describing the oneironaut experience.

The external world will never observe me at two different places and two different times at once, but my subjective experience of existence seems to have this property. Taking the Trifid Nebula poster as an example, recall my claim that I know of a universe where I put up the poster and was teased. This weird knowledge appears analogous to the photon that encounters the two slits. As a particle, light has to go through one slit, but the wave-like interference property evident on the other side shows that it interacted with and has knowledge of both slits. So too the oneironaut experience has this dual property. My actual life history has only one path, but I am aware of the other path and hence both realities are "superimposed" in my mind.

The analogy does not appear exact because the light wave is not known to exist in two times at once. A light wave is simply spread over space so that it can go through two different slits at once. Nevertheless, this analogy amplifies an interesting point about the oneironaut experience. With the oneironaut phenomenon, the outside world will observe me to either be in bed sleeping or awake in the future, but not both at the same time. The phenomenon of experiencing two times at once—the superposition of time—is a subjective experience that can be communicated to the outside world, but it cannot be directly observed by the outside world. Likewise, we have no direct knowledge of how the photon itself experiences time because we are not photons. From the outside world it does not appear to have information from two times at once, except in the interpretation appearing in the next section on entanglement.

A second broad analogy concerns the wave function collapse in quantum mechanics. The oneironaut experience gives me information about different future world experiences, but through my choices (and chance events external to me), I will only experience one of these worlds. From all the scientific and mathematical knowledge that I possess, the collapse of the wave function is the best analogy to this experience. The dissimilarity is that we should not be aware of the other worlds in quantum mechanics. When one world splits off into an infinite number of different worlds, there is no sharing of information between the worlds that have split. The observer sees only one world. To go back to the car analogy, you will never, ever become aware of a different universe where in the rearview mirror you see a gray car. However, the oneironaut phenomenon appears to show information transfer between different worlds. Some worlds can be avoided, as illustrated in the Trifid Nebula poster; others can be affirmed, as illustrated by events in the Heidelberg Dome.

Given these two broad analogies to quantum mechanics, is quantum mechanics an actual explanation for the oneironaut phenomenon? In principle we could reason that if quantum mechanical effects were present in the brain, even in very subtle ways, and these effects occasionally improved brain function, then over the slow course of human evolution we would learn to exploit those effects that gave us an advantage. For example, when lost in the Heidelberg Dome, I was able to find my group and the associated food and water because humans have a dreaming function that identifies favorable future locations. In practice, though, the brain wiring works through biochemistry, where molecules are very different from the photons we've been talking about so far. The signals traversing the 100 billion neurons in my brain are not light. Therefore, how can we really compare Young's double slit experiment to anything that happens biochemically in our brain?

One answer is that the brain's biochemistry produces electrical oscillations that share some of the properties of light, such as superposition. The next chapter will review these oscillations in greater detail. The second possible answer is that the latest experiments in physics show that larger and larger particles have the wavelike properties of light. This field is called quantum nanophysics, which reveals the quantum mechanical properties of nano-scale (1 billionth of a meter) objects. Ordinary matter can behave like a wave.

For example, a fluorescing blue-green pigment called phthalocyanine is used for printing money, but in a physics lab you can launch it toward a two-slit screen, and on the other side you will see an interference pattern (but remember, you may not look at the slits to find out which one it went through).[92] Compared to a photon or electron, this money pigment is enormous—it has 32 carbon atoms, 18 hydrogen atoms and eight nitrogen atoms, all spanning about two nanometers. Even larger molecules have been used, some containing over 400 atoms. Thus one can see that quantum processes demonstrated in the lab may also exist in biological nature, and we'll explore the latter further when we get to the Little Scissors in the Swiss Army knife.

There is in fact a sizeable group of writers who speculate on the existence of the quantum mind and quantum consciousness.[93] The scope of their efforts is extremely large—they wish to mutually explain the two great dualities in human knowledge. Quantum mechanics is used to explain the mind-body problem, and the mind-body problem is used to explain quantum mechanics.

In some ways the quantum consciousness writings remind me of the Nicholas Cage film *National Treasure*, where a scholar sets his mind to stealing the Declaration of Independence because the stakes are simply game-changing. A convoluted plot concerning various characters, ideas and resources is woven together to make this grand theft happen. So too, the simultaneous explanation of consciousness and quantum mechanics would be an amazing feat, but right now, in practice, stealing the Declaration of Independence is easier.

Compared to quantum consciousness, I believe that the oneironaut phenomenon is more limited in scope and fundamentally more tractable. What we need to understand is which neurobiological process of storing and retrieving information—the phenomena of memory and learning—has a quantum-like behavior. Memories are certainly at the core of our life experiences, many other organisms have memories, and scientifically it is an easier nut to crack than explaining human consciousness.

The memories of an oneironaut demonstrate simultaneity in time; the past, present and future can be superimposed. So far we haven't really talked about quantum mechanics as having a feature that ignores the past, present and future, but the mysteries of quantum mechanics go beyond the few tools that I have pulled out of the Swiss Army knife. Let us now take a look at a tool that is hidden in plain sight—the Swiss Cross.

The Oneironauts

The Swiss Cross: Entanglement

THE SWISS CROSS LOGO SYMBOLIZES ANOTHER ASTONISHING FEATURE of quantum physics called quantum entanglement, a thing in nature that totally disregards any boundaries imposed by the finite speed of light. You can pull out the Big Knife and use it everywhere, except on the Swiss Cross.

To explain this I'm going to introduce you to two Swiss photons. Swiss photons are photons that reside in Switzerland. We only need two photons because it takes two to tango. A tango metaphor for the photons is useful because in dance two people have to be coordinated and synchronized with each other. If one dance partner changes something, it influences the other dance partner. For example, if one partner puts their right foot forward, the other partner puts their left foot back. If the only information I had was that one person had their right foot forward, then I would surmise that the partner put their left foot back. In physics, two or more photons can share a measurable property—if one photon changes its property, the other photon will also change its property instantaneously. This sharing of a property in physics is called *entanglement*, or in the case of dance, *entangoment*.

Imagine that Swiss humans have put together a diabolical dance experiment to demonstrate quantum entanglement to the public. The experimenters hire the two best tango dancers in our Galaxy. They have choreography to music that is so precise, they can dance it perfectly together, and they can even perform it alone. Remember, if one dance partner puts their right foot forward as the first step, the first step for the other partner is to put their left foot back.[94] Technically, they do not have to be in the same room to dance their part.

In their dance experiment, the Swiss humans bring the two Galactic-level dancers to Geneva, and start the dance on two open-air flatbed trucks that are parked back-to-back. Television drones are covering the events from every angle, broadcasting to the entire world. The dancers are told to dance as if they are together, but they must stay slightly apart. Each dances on one of the trucks, each truck is playing the same music, and the dancers are told that the experiment will challenge them by tilting the bed of one truck at some point during the dance.

At the beginning the two dancers can see each other and they are dancing perfectly in a synchronized way. The diabolical Swiss experimenters then start slowly driving the trucks apart in opposite directions. No problem. The Galactic champions of tango have excellent timing and can still keep dancing exactly as if holding onto their partner.

They can hear the same music with the same rhythm, so they should be able to keep dancing as if still together.

The trucks get farther and farther apart and spectators along each of the roads are stunned to see a single dancer dancing the tango on a moving vehicle. The TV drones watch both trucks from above, confirming to viewers at home that these amazing dancers are still synchronized, as if they were dancing together.

Finally, one truck parks in Jussy, a town nine kilometers east of Geneva, and the other truck parks nine kilometers west of Geneva, in the town of Satigny. The dancers are still synchronized to each other and to the music. The television viewers can see both of them simultaneously, and everyone is just waiting for them to screw up, but they are simply the best dancers ever.

The diabolical Swiss experimenters are now ready to demonstrate entangoment. At Jussy, the scientists tilt the dance floor by 20 degrees. Despite his or her best effort, the dancer stumbles downward, and the perfect rhythm is finally broken.

At this instant you and the TV viewers at home witness the deep mystery of entangoment. Even though the truck floor remains level for the dancer at Satigny, this dancer stumbles at exactly the same time as the dancer in Jussy. The Satigny dancer has no idea how this happened. The TV viewers at home gasp because they see the both dancers stumble simultaneously. It's as if the two dancers were holding onto each other, but it is impossible for one dancer to know what has changed 18 km away on a different dance floor. The fifth-grade science students calculate that if information travels at the speed of light, it would take 60 microseconds (one microsecond = a millionth of a second) to cross 18 km. The Big Knife stipulates that the dancers cannot stumble simultaneously, but this unnatural violation of cause and effect was observed to happen anyway.

This experiment actually took place with entangled Swiss photons in 2008. Two photons had a shared property in a Geneva physics lab, they were then sent by fiber-optic cables to Satigny and Jussy, and when one photon was measured at one location, the other photon 18 km away reacted as if it was connected to it. I have to gloss over many of the remarkable details, but consider that the physicists in Jussy and Satigny needed to complete each measurement of each photon's properties faster than 60 microseconds. If they were slightly slower than that, they would have to concede that the two photons communicated with each other before the measurement had finished. In fact, the experiment was brilliantly designed to finish each measurement in 6 microseconds. This is too fast for humans to observe in real time—it takes much longer than that for a nerve signal to go between two neurons. So the experiment requires machines to make the measurements, and a Captain Clock that can give some of the most accurate and precise time measurements humans can achieve.

The Swiss Cross simply does not follow the rules of the Big Knife. Einstein famously called it "spooky action at a distance." His point back then was that this feature of quantum mechanics seems to be incorrect because the alternative, that cause and effect in quantum mechanics is faster than light, is as unphysical as a ghost. Nevertheless, the experiment with Swiss photons and many other photons around the world have confirmed that entanglement is real.

I wonder if Einstein was still alive and reading this book, would he have the same reaction to the oneironauts? The time travel of information in the oneironaut phenomenon seems to go against physics. Since we should not violate the known laws of physics, I suppose that Einstein would have called it *spooky action across time.*

Entanglement currently has a much better experimental demonstration than the oneironaut phenomenon, yet it is still considered a scientific mystery. How could the dancer in Satigny possess instantaneous "knowledge" of how their partner's feet moved in Jussy, as if this knowledge moved faster than light? What does cause and effect mean in this situation, or is it irrelevant? To me these questions are as perplexing as the question of how I can be in bed sleeping while at the same time having an experience somewhere else in the future. To one of the senior scientists who performed the photon experiment in Switzerland, the mysterious behaviors of the entangled photons "...seem to emerge, somehow, from outside space-time."[95]

Is the Swiss Cross—quantum entanglement—just an analogy to the baffling mechanism underlying the oneironaut phenomenon, or does it explain the actual mechanism?[96] Again we have to confront the facts that the human brain is not currently known to possess quantum properties. Maybe the oneironaut phenomenon is that first piece of evidence, but there is little else in human physiology and function to back it up.

But what about non-human physiology and function? It turns out that other living things exploit quantum effects, and you don't need to be an intelligent biped and master of the planet to do so. If non-humans have been doing it before humans even existed, perhaps there are unknown effects to be eventually discovered in humans. With the Little Scissors I'm going to argue that quantum effects have a role in natural selection, with the implication that some human traits may plausibly emerge from such effects.

The Little Scissors: Light Influences Biology

I LIKE THE LITTLE SCISSORS BECAUSE THEY ARE MORE DOWN TO EARTH. All the other tools refer to amazing phenomena in space or the bizarre results from experiments performed in a physics lab at a university somewhere. The Little Scissors will represent my argument that there is a concrete connection between life and these other obscure tools in the Swiss Army knife. In particular, the Little Scissors argument is that life has thrived because it found a way to use quantum mechanics to its advantage. Therefore this gives a reasonably good basis to hypothesize that other peculiar phenomena displayed by living organisms may derive from the exploitation of quantum mechanical effects.

We mentioned before that exposure to light is a good way to reset the biological clock of living things. In fact, this is just one of the fascinating and often unexpected ways by which biology interacts with photons.

The most fundamental and necessary of these interactions is photosynthesis. Earth would be a very different place if blue-green algae hadn't exploited photosynthesis and changed the composition of our atmosphere from horrible to livable just over two billion years ago. This important change on Earth is called the "Great Oxygenation Event." Earlier than this, Earth's atmosphere barely had any oxygen in it. Instead, it had a lot of nitrogen and carbon dioxide. Cyanobacteria, the earliest life forms, used photosynthesis to make oxygen out of carbon dioxide and sunlight. Our sister planet, Venus, still has a massive atmosphere dominated by carbon dioxide because photosynthesis was never established on that planet due to the absence of simple life.

Fast forward now through two billion years of evolution. Through natural selection advanced creatures such as humans would develop eyes that are tuned to the peak wavelength of sunlight (i.e., the color yellow). Evolutionary advantage is afforded to those organisms that can maximize their sensitivity to the type of light in their environment. Everywhere you look in the natural world you can see living things that take advantage of various properties of light, from sensitivity to ultraviolet wavelengths to polarized light. So too, organisms that find a way to take advantage of the quantum mechanical nature of light would have an evolutionary advantage. Photosynthesis may be an adaptation that shows how life exploits quantum mechanics.

Understanding photosynthesis is a more realistic and more convincing endeavor than testing quantum consciousness in humans, or successfully stealing the Declaration of Independence. Plants, and ultimately most life on this planet, desperately need the screwdriver and the corkscrew. Photons must reach plant cells because the three ingredients in creating food energy and oxygen are light, water and carbon dioxide.

But how does a plant actually harness the energy in light? For this you need the LHC. This is the physicists' term for the Large Hadron Collider, but for the biologists the LHC is the light-harvesting complex. The LHC is composed of proteins and molecules in the plant, such as the molecule chlorophyll, which absorbs photons and transfers energy to a different part of the plant called the reaction center. The LHC molecules such as chlorophyll are called antenna pigments, and chlorophyll is a green pigment because it absorbs blue light and red light, reflecting back into the world the green portion of the solar spectrum. Blue and red photons are absorbed because they have the correct energies to release electrons in the antenna pigments, and these free electrons become available energy within the plant.

Where is the quantum mechanics in this story? The punch line is that quantum effects are active within the plant so that photon energy is converted to chemical energy with nearly 100% efficiency. Since the Earth gets plenty of sunlight, why is 100% efficiency important? Well, you have to take a time machine back to the early Earth and consider that there was no easy pathway for life to begin and to persist. Nature does not roll out a red carpet for life to leisurely stroll into existence. Life has to fight for itself. So if an early life form could use just a few positive things in its environment to sustain itself and reproduce, then it would be a winner. This means that if early life could harness nearly all of the energy available in the few photons striking it, then it would survive. In particular, life probably began in the least horrible parts of our younger planet, the oceans. This environment has more stable temperatures and a useful mixture of chemicals, except that light does not penetrate very deeply into oceans. So the discovery of quantum mechanical pathways to harvest the energy from light efficiently was a trait that would support the survival of early life forms.

Are the Little Scissors an explanation for the oneironaut phenomenon? Because photons strike the eye and activate pigments, there are quantum mechanical effects in human beings that we can point to. You might conjecture that the place where information jumps across time is the event where photons interact with the receptors in your eye. This explanation would hold promise if it weren't for the oneironaut experiences that are mainly auditory, such as the Haycart dream.

Thus the Little Scissors serve more modest and tentative purposes in my understanding of the oneironauts. Since they show that life exploits quantum mechanical effects, it lends a plausibility argument that the oneironaut phenomenon could have an explanation in quantum biology, though it took many millions of years to manifest.

One can speculate that if early plants were selected for their ability to absorb photons for their energy cycle, then other primitive organisms were selected if they used photons for their survival, such as the ability to orient themselves—a basic need when it comes to seeking food or avoiding danger. But spatial information is useless unless the organism can process it. Hence, primitive *sensory* systems evolved into advanced *nervous* systems, ultimately creating brains with sophisticated *cognitive* systems. When complicated sensory information can be processed quickly, the greater the advantage for the organism, and therefore nervous systems, even though they merely used biochemistry, would need to produce internal models of the external world in time and space. As the brains of advanced organisms used cognitive models to process information in real time, these same models could also be used to create anticipation of future events. The organisms that were better at anticipation, those that could make a plan, would be the most successful. Somewhere, or everywhere, in this evolution of neurophysiology and function, the thin thread of quantum mechanics could be helping everything along.

Therefore I think that advanced life is constantly seeking out and testing the multitude of resources provided by nature for predicting the future. If quantum mechanical effects are allowed in living organisms, it is natural for these same cognitive systems to actually perceive events that "come outside of space-time" and use it for their internal models.[97] The oneironaut phenomenon should come into existence.

7. Hippocampus

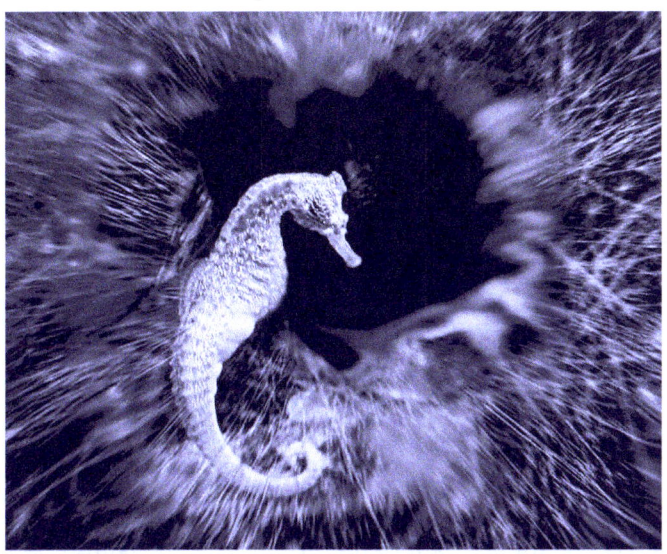

Hippocampus is one of my favorite words to say out loud. In the first fraction of a second of saying hippocampus, one might reasonably guess that the word will be hippo*potamus*, surely one of the best animal names ever invented. Yet, here we will focus on the hippo*campus*—it may be our time machine for information. The hippocampus is the Janus in us.

The hippocampus is a distinct part of the brain strongly related to memory, learning and navigation. You would think that scientists should name our different brain parts in a way that describes their function. Sometimes they do, but the hippocampus gets its name simply from its shape. Yank it out of a human brain, put it on the table, and it resembles a seahorse. The first part of the word, "hippo," means *horse* in Greek, whereas "campus" means *curve or caterpillar*.

In ancient Greek mythology the chariot of the sea god Poseidon was pulled by the hippocamps, or fish-tailed horses. The magnificent Trevi Fountain in Rome shows two hippocamps pulling a sea chariot, and indeed the brain has a left and right hippocampus for each hemisphere of the brain. Because of this, some might say that the horns of a ram could be a better comparison to our twin hippocampi, and in fact "Ammon's horn," or *cornu Ammonis* in Latin, is also used to describe the hippocampus.

Even though many other brain parts are critically important, the hippocampus is currently the darling of the medical community—the hippocampus is central to our desired understanding of the brain and our mind. Why might the hippocampus be a prime candidate as an organ for time travel as well? If you think about the qualities of the oneironaut phenomenon described up to this point, then memory, learning and navigation are clearly three strong themes in my story. Consider the following:

- The déjà vu phenomenon in the waking brain is memory recall, which is a key function of the hippocampus.
- The oneironaut phenomenon also occurs in the sleeping brain; sleep is strongly related to memory and learning, and this again involves the hippocampus.
- The strongest oneironaut signals come from new learning experiences that are compared to and attached to existing memories—humans cannot do this if the hippocampus is surgically removed.
- The sense of space or place is prominent in the déjà vu experiences. As I first noted in Chapter 5, the hippocampus has "place cells" which represent an internal map of the external world.
- Similarly, geometry is prominent in the déjà vu phenomenon. When attention is directed toward faces and geometrical shapes, the hippocampus is more active in the latter than the former.
- The hippocampus also has "time cells" that encode and organize the temporal properties of events. An electrical oscillation in the brain synced to the hippocampal activity also is thought to encode time in memories.
- Memory is also the noise in the déjà vu phenomenon. At its worst, memory can produce an illusion of the oneironaut phenomenon—it would be good to know more about how the hippocampus works with memory.

Below I'll explore these elements in greater detail, but it's worth noting that the hippocampus is really a part of other systems involving other brain areas that also have links to the oneironaut phenomenon. For example, visual stimuli are very strong components of the oneironaut phenomenon, and if you touch the back of your head, your fingers are quite close to the visual (*occipital*) lobe of the brain. Mental images and egocentric representations of space are more strongly associated with the crown of your head (*parietal* lobe). The *frontal* lobe is necessary for attention and decision-making—it's like the charioteer that controls and depends on the hippocamps. The hippocampus, however, is situated a bit deeper, toward the middle of the brain. Something called the *entorhinal cortex* (EC) acts as the interface between the hippocampus and the rest of the brain. The EC also contains "grid cells" that encode space during navigation. You can lump the EC and a few other structures attached to the hippocampus and call this compound structure the "hippocampal formation" or the "medial temporal lobe."

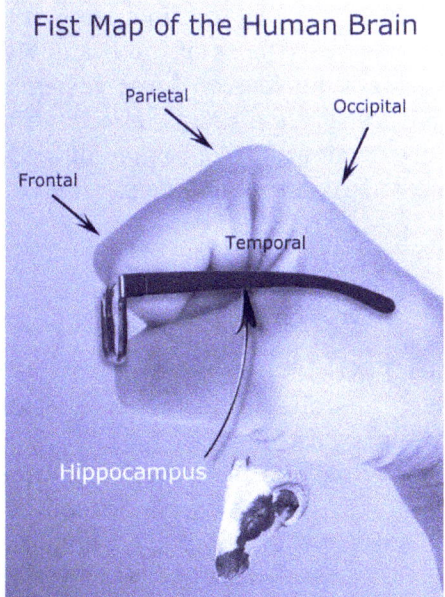

Figure 7-1: Clenching your right fist and looking at it gives you a general idea of where the various brain lobes are located. The squiggly outer surface of the brain is called the cortex, and so the frontal cortex or frontal lobe is the portion of the brain above the eyes. The hippocampus is actually near the center portion of the brain, where the tips of your ring and middle fingers touch the palm. The left and right sides of the brain each have a hippocampus and the structure is curved, somewhat like the two horns of a ram.

To create a mental map of these basic brain areas, it might help to look at your clenched fist and memorize the four letters FPOT (**Figure 7-1**). Moving from the front knuckle toward the back of the hand and then wrapping around to either side we encounter the **F**rontal, **P**arietal, **O**ccipital and **T**emporal lobes of the brain. The hippocampus is embedded near the center of your fist, where the middle and ring fingers press against the palm. The principles of neuroscience are so widely discussed nowadays that I think knowledge of this simple brain map will become as common as knowing the names of planets in our solar system.

Other themes in the déjà vu experience involve the understanding of language (but not the production of language). Language is processed in the auditory cortex, which is part of the temporal lobe at the sides of your head that we discussed earlier in relation to epilepsy. Problem solving involves various areas of the cerebral cortex, which is the outer layer of the brain that in large mammals has many twisting grooves and ridges. The sense of place in three dimensions has a lot to do with the vestibular system, which involves the tiny parts of the inner ear that communicate to various other parts of the brain. Meanwhile, Admiral SCN (the suprachiasmatic nucleus), who is responsible for circadian rhythms in mammals, can have dramatic effects on memory. Thus the experiences of an organism arise from many different body parts and systems, but for the oneironaut phenomenon my discussion will orbit the hippocampus.

The Gatekeeper

CHAPTER 4 HAD A BRIEF INTRODUCTION to our current understanding of memory. A consciously identifiable memory is very explicit in your mind. For example, I have an *explicit memory* that on a keyboard for typing English, my right index finger rests on the J key. A memory of a skill is called an *implicit memory*. When I'm typing, I cannot recall the full layout of the keyboard, but somehow I just typed a whole lot of words without having any explicit memory of the full keyboard—I used my implicit memory.

Let's now add in a layer of time to our definitions with the help of the most famous amnesiac of all time, a guy called Henry Gustav Molaison. Like the famed author Dostoevsky, Mr. Molaison suffered from epilepsy, and in 1953, when he was 27 years old, he underwent a medical treatment that surgically removed his hippocampus and other structures. As a result of this surgery the world learned about different memory systems and the importance of the hippocampus.[98]

After Mr. Molaison's hippocampus was taken by the blade, he could experience new things, have them as explicit memories for about 30 seconds or less, and then the memories became unavailable to his consciousness. This is called *anterograde amnesia*—the inability to form memories from new experiences.

Needless to say, the doctors who first spoke to Mr. Molaison immediately noticed the anterograde amnesia—it was "striking and totally unexpected"—and then they really hoped that the patient wasn't totally messed up. William Scoville and Brenda Milner were the doctors, and one motivation for their famous 1957 publication was a "warning to others" that memory impairments will result from surgical "lesions" to the hippocampus.[99] Fortunately, their tests showed that Mr. Molaison's personality and intelligence were not impacted (his math skills actually improved), and he remembered a lot from when he was 16 years old and younger. However, his memories from ages 16 to 27 were largely unavailable. This is called *retrograde amnesia*—the inability to remember old experiences. It was therefore apparent that long-term memories, both explicit and implicit, from age 16 and younger were retained somewhere else in the brain (specifically, in the frontal lobe), and consciousness could access these areas even with the hippocampus removed.

Henry Gustav Molaison and a legion of lesioned patients offered many unexpected insights into the workings of our memory. The simultaneous presence of anterograde and retrograde amnesia revealed that certain processes and brain parts are essential for converting short-term, explicit memories into long-term memories of both the explicit and implicit variety. Since Mr. Molaison was missing his hippocampus, it would seem that our little ram's horn is some type of Janusian gatekeeper for handling memory.

The verbs used to describe *inputs* to the memory system are *encode* and *consolidate*. Encoding is the initial process of perceiving external stimuli in the waking state, whereas consolidation is a process occurring during sleep that makes memories significantly more permanent.[100] Encoding is like writing down what you see, whereas consolidation is trying to memorize what you wrote by reading it again. Writing and reading are related, yet different activities. Encoding and consolidation are also related yet different processes that are believed to interfere with each other. To get around this problem, the two processes occur in two different states of consciousness. A critical purpose of sleep is to cease the encoding stage long enough for the needed consolidation to take place. However, as the case of Mr. Molaison demonstrates, it's not just sleep that's required, you also need your ram's horns installed.

The *output* of the memory system is called *retrieval* (or *replay*). We retrieve memories during the waking state, and some forms of retrieval can be called imagination and/or daydreaming. The replay of memories during sleep is a major component of dreaming, and this replay is thought to be necessary for memory consolidation. Just like perception is a constructive process, the retrieval of memories also requires a reconstruction of many cognitive elements.

Anything that successfully completes the encode-consolidate-replay loop is called learning. One form of learning involves the firing of different neuron networks simultaneously when processing a stimulus. This synchronized activity will physically connect the networks together. The best way to memorize this principle is to say the phrase: "Neurons will wire together if they fire together."[101]

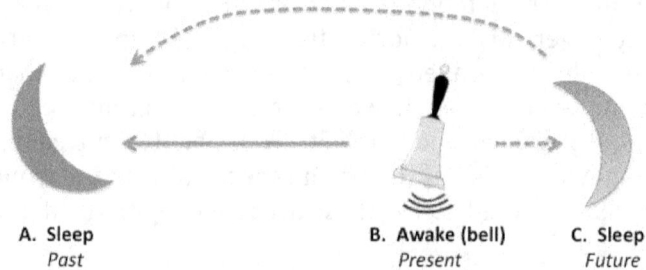

| A. Sleep | B. Awake (bell) | C. Sleep |
| Past | Present | Future |

Figure 7-2: Is the oneironaut process a direct path B → A, or do you first require memory consolidation through sleep, so that the process is B → C → A? In the first case, the waking brain is communicating with the sleeping brain in the past, but in the second case the brain is replaying an experience during sleep and sending it back to the past—only the sleeping brains communicate across time.

The classic story of Pavlov's dogs illustrates the process. A natural stimulus such as the smell of food causes dogs to salivate. Since this is hardwired into their brain without any new learning involved, the natural odor stimulus is called an "unconditioned stimulus," and the salivating reaction is called an "unconditioned response." The word "unconditioned" is rarely used in other circumstances except for hair care, but all it really means is "not previously learned." The unconditioned stimulus activates certain neurons in the brain—let's call this the A network. Ivan Pavlov also rang a bell when the food was offered. That sound is also a stimulus that activates its own set of neurons—let's call this the B network. The experiment has the A and B networks firing together, and this physically associates the two networks along with the response. Before Pavlov's experiment, the A and B networks fired independently. By firing together, the brain physically changed so that A and B were linked. After creating this link, Pavlov rang the bell and observed the dogs salivating, even though no food was presented. The ringing bell is called the *conditioned* (learned) *stimulus*, and the salivating is now termed the *conditioned* (learned) *response*.[102]

A huge body of experiments such as with Pavlov's dogs shows that the connections between neurons can be strengthened or weakened over time, as if the brain is made out of a plastic that is constantly shaped in different ways. Recall that the connection between two neurons is called a synapse, and the fact that synapses can change in strength is called *synaptic plasticity*.

The plastic I keep in mind is a modern milk container because I can change its shape without breaking it, yet I have to press it just right to deform its original shape. Creating this new feature on the milk container is like *encoding memory*. But there are times when the deformation pops right back out. So too with memory—the concept of *consolidating* memory has to do with how an initial memory imprint may or may not become permanent.

The reason I am presenting these various definitions is to pose some basic questions about the oneironaut phenomenon. As you have a new experience—let's say someone rings a peculiar-sounding bell to signal that it's time for dinner—and this experience is recalled from a dream, did the oneironaut phenomenon occur when your brain experienced the signal for the first time and processed it through short-term memory in the present waking state (**Figure 7-2**)? Or does the oneironaut phenomenon begin later, in the future sleeping state, when the recent experience of the bell is being consolidated from short-term memory into its more permanent state? In the former question the oneironaut signal goes from waking state to sleeping state, whereas in the latter the phenomenon goes from sleeping state to sleeping state. In the former, consolidation is not part of the process, whereas in the latter it is the process.

This distinction is quite stark. In the former, Mr. Molaison could be an oneironaut because all new experiences are encoded to some degree in his waking state and information could be sent back in time. In the latter, Mr. Molaison could not be an oneironaut since he lost his hippocampus and thus his ability to consolidate new experiences into long-term memories. Moreover, the consolidation of explicit memories appears to happen mostly during the heartbeat phase of sleep, when the hippocampus is very active.[103] Therefore in the consolidation scenario researchers could specify a fairly precise time when the oneironaut phenomenon is taking place.

There are at least three ways to figure out if encoding or consolidation is more important. First, one could take blade to brain and remove my hippocampus in order to see what happens with my ability to dream about future events. Fortunately, in a previous chapter, we discussed the nice fact that we do not live in the type of universe where anyone is going to surgically experiment with my brain.

Second, you could try to find an oneironaut who has déjà vu just moments before their death. For example, being led up to a chopping block where an executioner awaits, the doomed oneironaut may catch a glimpse of a tattoo inked on the executioner's forearm, a sea monster leaping out of the sea. The oneironaut recalls this image from a dream, but there is no chance to escape the execution. Since the head is separated from the body soon afterward, there is no chance for this oneironaut to consolidate the memory of that tattoo. Therefore we would learn that the oneironaut phenomenon occurs during memory encoding and not during consolidation.

The question of encoding versus consolidation raises the stakes with the related question: "Can an oneironaut dream about the waking moments leading up to their death?" Since my hippocampus is still inside my head, and my head is still attached to my body, I only have a hypothetical answer. It seems to me that there would be an evolutionary advantage for the oneironaut phenomenon to occur during encoding instead of waiting longer for a process involving consolidation. It's not going to help the gazelle being chased by the cheetah to get a good night's sleep later in order to remember which way to run.

The two methods described above are speculative, but I can offer a third method to address the question without resorting to any sharp objects intersecting with my head. The third method is to learn a bit more about how the brain works and search for connections with other facets of the oneironaut experience. In the following sections I will contemplate a few topics that might be relevant.

Spacetime in the Mind

IN CHAPTER 5, I NOMINATED THE SENSE OF SPACE OR LOCATION as a distinct sense that should be added to the other five senses. In more common usage the sixth sense is reserved for the perception of "extrasensory" information, or the cognitive phenomena of intuition and spirituality. The sense of location, however, has specific neural correlates in the hippocampal region that are as clearly defined as your tongue, which has cells to detect chemicals (taste), or your eyes, which have cells to detect electromagnetic radiation (sight). Thus I suspect that we detect space (location), and this should then be called the sixth sense. Everything "extrasensory" has to be bumped out of six and go to number seven.

One of the major early contributors to understanding the sixth sense was a Berkeley professor called Edward Tolman. Like Albert Einstein 12 years before him, Tolman was impossibly cute in 1948 when he gave a summary of his seminal research:[104]

> I'm just a guy who works with rats. OK, let me rephrase, I make my starving students work with rats. There are two reasons to make them do the work. First, I don't have to pay them that much, which means I can spend more money on the rats. Second, students have excellent new ideas, but in the end I get the credit for the breakthroughs. How funny is all that?

Now, I may have paraphrased slightly, but this is roughly how Tolman starts describing some of the most important cognitive science research of all time. Also, this is one of the most ironic scientific texts of all time. On August 25, 1950, Edward Tolman and 31 other UC Berkeley professors were fired for refusing to sign a loyalty oath as part of McCarthyism. Tolman heroically led a successful lawsuit that reinstated the fired faculty by the end of 1952, yet many months went by when Tolman probably received zero pay.

I'm not sure what happened to the rats after 1950, but in the prior decade Tolman and his cheap, idea-rich team of students conducted a series of maze experiments that revealed the existence of cognitive maps in the mammalian brain.

Imagine that you are a rat at the start of the maze and you subsequently try various paths to get to your food. You will eventually learn a successful path that is a sequence of forward motions and decisions to turn right or left in the maze. You will start off with many mistakes at first, and then have fewer mistakes after repeated practice. But is your brain learning a specific sequence of steps, or is it creating a larger "map" of space, as if you can view the maze from above? In the former, space is egocentric (represented by your point of view), and in the latter space is allocentric (represented in relation to one or more things outside of yourself).

One of Tolman's key maze experiments seems so simple and reveals the answer so plainly, it makes you wonder why no one thought of trying it thousands of years ago. Two different groups of rats are introduced into a maze that they will naturally explore and eventually locate food. The human can simply count the number of mistakes each rat makes each time it is introduced into the same maze. I fabricated a figure that illustrates Tolman's measurements of how many mistakes a rat makes in running the maze versus the number of consecutive maze trials (**Figure 7-3**).

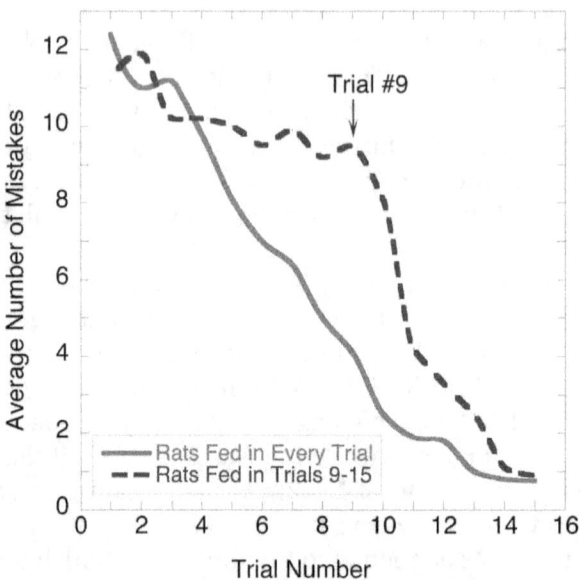

Figure 7-3: Number of mistakes in each of 15 trials for rats in a maze where a food reward is either always present at the end of the maze (solid line) or only from Trial #9 and onward (dashed line).

The first group of rats is fed in every trial. They will find food at the end of the maze in each of the 15 maze runnings. The second group will find an exit to the maze, after which they are taken back to their cages, and then fed about two hours later. This second group has this experience in Trials 1 through 8, but then in Trials 9 to 15 they are fed at the exit of the maze just as with Group 1. The first group of rats fed in every trial makes about 12 mistakes in the first trial, and steadily make fewer mistakes in every subsequent trial (the solid line in the figure). The second group of rats does *not* make significantly fewer mistakes over the first 8 trials with no food (the dashed line in the figure). Basically, they wander around in the maze with no particular hurry to take the shortest path to the exit. It's at the end of the 9th trial when they discover food at the exit, and then on the 10th trial the number of mistakes drops incredibly fast, much faster than anything observed in the first group of rats. Tolman comments that to the human observer, this group of rats "did not appear to learn much" in Trials 1–9, yet the remarkably fewer mistakes in the very next trial shows that their rat brains had actually constructed a cognitive spatial map of the maze. When they discovered that food would be available at the exit in Trial #9, they immediately used this map at their next opportunity to get to this food quickly, with few mistakes.

This maze experiment is similar to the events I described in the Heidelberg Dome, with one crucial difference. The similarity is that I had built a cognitive map of Heidelberg from the countless times I had walked through the town in past experiences. The difference has to do with Trial #9. For the rats in Group 2, this is the first time they discover the food reward, but Trial #9 has a similar number of mistakes as Trials 1 through 8. However, if ratman, *moi*, had been in Tolman's experiment, then I would have zero mistakes in Trial #9 because of the oneironaut phenomenon. Tolman and his students would have seen this as an outlying case of rare guesswork to be ignored, yet from my point of view in the maze there was no guesswork involved in navigating to my reward. As an outlier, ratman's behavior would represent a new discovery for Tolman and his students to make.

Tolman's 1948 review of various maze experiments does not mention the hippocampus. However, in 1971 two researchers, Dr. John O'Keefe and his student Jonathan Dostrovsky, noted that animals with hippocampal damage performed poorly on spatial tasks such as mazes.[105] In their subsequent experiments with rats there were no maze runnings. Instead, live rats had extremely thin electrodes inserted into different cells of the hippocampus and the electrical activity of each cell was recorded as the rats were rotated in a circle. Some cells were totally quiet except when the rat faced certain specific directions. This early experiment thereby hinted that Tolman's hypothesis of a cognitive map based on behavior was actually correlated to activity in the hippocampus (i.e., a "neural correlate"). The cells or neurons in the hippocampus that were active only when a rat faced a certain direction or was positioned in a certain location became known as *place cells*.

The 1971 paper by O'Keefe and Dostrovsky is only five pages long, yet one has to appreciate its outsized significance. There are some basic questions people always ask, such as, "Why is the sky blue?" Another basic question is, "Where is memory?" For example, since I can clearly recollect my dearly departed goldfish Bubbles over and over again, it seems that my subjective optical image of Bubbles must reside somewhere, but how and where? Is the image of Bubbles produced by my brain and fully explained within the laws of the physical universe, or do we need something like a soul or spirit? Well, we now know that these hippocampal place cells fire (produce electrical activity) whenever the organism enters or re-enters a specific field of spacetime (i.e., position and direction). Memory of space is therefore located in these specific biological cells of the hippocampus. It boggles the mind that under experimental conditions, a neuroscientist on Earth could look at the recordings of astronauts' brain cell activity while they walk around on Mars, and then estimate where the astronauts are and how they moved without ever witnessing their actions directly. Memories of emotions, language, smell and even Bubbles are also likely to have a location in various other cells or networks of cells within the brain. It's just a matter of time before neuroscientists are able to decode these neural correlates of our everyday life.

In addition to the hippocampal place cells, there are cells in an adjacent EC (entorhinal cortex) that are now known to have sensitivity to spacetime. These particular neurons in the EC are called *grid cells*.[106] As the organism enters a space and moves through different locations, a single grid cell will fire at many different locations. One might initially think that this is a very confused place cell that can't decide when and where it should be firing. Yet when you map all the firing locations in space (i.e., the cell is not moving, but it fires when you physically move your body to different locations), the ensemble of spots where it fired looks like a grid, somewhat like the pattern of a chessboard (**Figure 7-4**).[107]

It might be easier to understand if you can find a floor with tiles and walk across it. Pretend your index finger is one grid cell and as you walk across the floor, poke your forehead on all the even tiles. The act of poking represents when the cell fires. When you return by walking over the adjacent row of tiles, poke your forehead on all the odd tiles. After 20 seconds, stop doing this, unless you want to join me in the college of the insane. But while you were walking back and forth that grid cell was poking your brain with an electrical signal at regular, interleaved intervals. You can return to this tiled floor later, and that amazing grid cell will still poke you in the same way. The real shocker is that the poking gets replayed in your sleep.[108]

To understand the purpose of this grid, imagine that a map of your surrounding space is *absent* from your mind, as if you are standing within a dense fog. However, suppose that you have signal flares that you can drop on the ground from your starting position, and again as you walk every ten paces. Each flare you drop is like the firing of a single grid cell. If you follow a straight line and drop four flares, and then on the fifth flare you find food, you gain knowledge (short-term memory) of where food is located relative to the starting flare. You can then walk back to the starting flare, and proceed to walk in the opposite direction, dropping flares every ten paces. You can also walk in perpendicular directions. If you can count accurately, and always keep track of changes in angles, you will be able to successfully return to the first food location no matter where you are at any given time. The grid cell representation of space is constructed in a similar way and has a similar purpose.

Neuroscientists have also discovered that the spacing of the grid cell map changes in different layers of the EC tissue. In the floor analogy, some grid cells will poke you every 2nd tile, others every 20th tile, and some every ½ tile. Thus you can see that neuroscientists have uncovered a system in the brain that seems very much like plotting points on a graph or identifying your location on a map with a rectangular coordinate system, with different levels of detail or resolution. The place cells are the points you want to put on a map; something in your brain needs to fire when you find yourself at the location of your refrigerator and all the food treats held within. The grid cells provide the piece of paper with lines that represent relative distances. The place cells and grid cells together allow you to both follow a path in space and form Tolman's cognitive map as viewed from above.

There are at least four intriguing aspects to this discovery of different grid cell spacing, as if our mind maps spacetime at various levels of detail. First of all, it makes the sense of spacetime resemble our other senses. The sharpness of eyesight is the obvious comparison, but you could also consider the two-point sensitivity of touch. In regions with a high density of skin cells, such as the lips, two sharp objects that are close together can be perceived as two distinct sharp objects. However, in regions of low density, such as your shoulder, those same two points will feel like a single point. So too, grid cell spacing could represent how well we can sense our own location in spacetime. Given the direct analogy to touch, it really does seem that the sense of spacetime should be considered a sixth sense.

The second intriguing aspect of grid cells follows from the first aspect: How well do we really know where we are in spacetime? If we have a clear metric that defines perfect eyesight versus poor eyesight, do species also have the analogous natural variation between individuals and across their lifetimes for their sense of spacetime? I think the answer is yes from various lines of evidence, even though the medical community doesn't go around telling people that they have "20/20 spacetime." For example, as an open water swimmer, I find that I can swim nearly straight courses using only distant landmarks, whereas others swim wide arcs or even full circles. I might say that I have 20/20 marine spacetime whereas others, no matter how hard they practice, will always have 20/40 marine spacetime. You can't improve your visual acuity because it's not a skill. So too the grid cells and place cells in the brain may define a hard physical limit to each person's spacetime acuity.

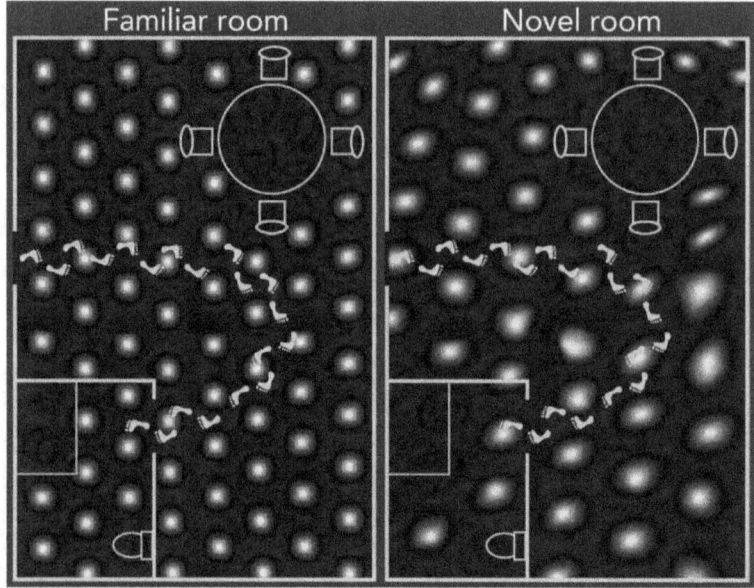

Figure 7-4: Illustration of where a single grid cell fires in your brain as you walk from the left into a room with a table and a bathroom. Each point of light is a location in the room where that cell will fire, and everywhere else the cell is inactive. The left panel shows how the cell fires if the room is familiar to you, whereas the right panel shows how the cell fires if this is the first time that you enter the room. In a familiar room, neuroscientists have discovered that the grid cell fires in a regular pattern across the space, where the pattern looks like interlocked hexagons similar to the intensity peaks of the two-slit interference pattern shown in **Figure 6-3**. Every time you enter the room, that grid cell remembers where it should fire and the pattern stays the same. This regular grid allows you to gauge location and motion across space and time, which is useful for finding the bathroom quickly. In a novel room, the spacing of the pattern expands and the overall organization appears distorted. Eventually, as you spend more time in the room, the regular, organized grid spacing will be achieved. If you dream about entering the novel environment (right panel), when you enter it in the future will the grid spacing be more regular, as in the left panel, because the room is no longer novel?

The third intriguing aspect follows from the second: If spacetime is a sense like vision, then how does it function differently between the waking and sleeping states? The sleep state requires suppressing vision of the outside world by closing our eyes, yet we spend a fraction of the sleep state seeing internally generated imagery. The sleep state also stops our voluntary space motion, yet we spend a fraction of that sleep state perceiving internally generated motion through virtual spacetime. When grid cells and space cells are active during sleep, are they merely processing memories of spacetime created during past waking hours, or do they also become active in order to produce virtual spacetime for dreams?

Finally, the fourth intriguing aspect is that the fixed grid cell spacing is the brain's Big Knife. Just as light gives you a constant value concerning speed, the brain defines a constant concerning space. This means that the waking brain could be using the constant space grid to estimate elapsed time if the velocity is known, or estimate velocity if the time interval is sensed. For a fixed grid, say it's those floor tiles, there will be a poking on every 2nd tile. If you walk slowly, then the poking signal will repeat slowly. If you walk a little faster, the grid cells will poke you even faster because you are passing every 2nd tile more quickly. In other words, you cannot change the grid cell spacing by changing your speed. Thus, if you can estimate speed (e.g., by your walking pace), you get a time estimate (and vice versa). The grid cells are crucial neural correlates of a path in spacetime as viewed by the moving organism. Interestingly, these cognitive processes are not only active when the organism is moving, but also when it thinks about where it moved in the past, and also when it is preparing to move somewhere in the future.[109]

There is an enormous body of fascinating research literature concerning place cells in the hippocampus, grid cells in the EC, and their interrelationship. For brevity I will have to focus on some of the topics that appear most relevant to the oneironauts: how novel environments are different from previously visited environments, the importance of walls, and the encoding of time.

Novel environments perturb the palace

The oneironaut phenomenon is extremely strong and/or more likely when entering a new environment, which includes the space, things and people within it. In those moments, what is happening in the brain that is different from an environment that has been previously experienced? You may feel that you are completely the same person as in any other environment, yet your brain is changing dramatically with respect to the coordinate system of grid cells. If there were a physiological correlate to this neural phenomenon, imagine that entering a novel environment causes your five fingers to become three fat fingers grossly distorted from the fingers you normally have. In fact, what happens in the brain is that the regular spacing of grid cells *expands* and becomes *irregular* in novel environments **(Figure 7-4)**. Eventually it will recover its original regular pattern and stay regular.[110]

To me, this says that there could be a cognitive disorder of time perception as organisms explore any new space, and/or it may signify a biological signature of the oneironaut phenomenon.

For the former possibility, consider that time perception is linked to various cues. For example, your limbs resemble a pendulum as they swing back-and-forth while walking, defining one mechanical measure of time governed by the brain's motor neurons. Thus if Event #1 is opening the door on one side of the room, and Event #2 is reaching the refrigerator to eat, the person might measure the spacetime interval between these two major events as eight footsteps. Consider these footsteps as eight swings of the pendulum or eight ticks of a clock. If we assume one step is one meter that takes one second of time, the individual perceives that eight ticks correspond to eight meters of distance and eight seconds of time. Try simulating your walking rhythm by patting your left hand on your tummy each time your foot lands on the ground.

Now imagine that there is a layer of cells in the EC where one grid cell fires eight times in that distance of eight meters. There are eight ticking events in your brain that define the separation between two major events. The two body clocks of walking and grid cell firing are synchronized. Try simulating the beating of your grid cell by tapping your right hand on your forehead with the same rhythm as your left hand on your tummy. This sensation is what you should feel every time you walk through space—it defines a "normal" perception of spacetime.

However, if your familiar neural grid is briefly warped because of a novel space, then as you move through space the time interval will appear distorted. Instead of tapping your tummy and head simultaneously, tap your forehead once for every two taps on your tummy. You should get a visceral feeling that there are now two different clocks operating on your body. Did one speed up, or did the other slow down? Something has gone wrong; there should be eight ticks experienced in getting to the refrigerator, but your brain experienced just four. Or is the brain correct and for some reason you took eight short steps when only four normal steps were needed? Or is it the size of the room that is much smaller than you expected? In Chapter 6 we encountered a similar situation involving two observers, one who is stationary with a clock and another who is moving with a clock. In the current example, a single person becomes the same observer of two different clocks. By setting the number of ticks that define a separation between two major events, the brain clock perceives a compressed space (four ticks) compared to the walking clock (eight ticks).

When this disconnect develops between your awareness of what your arms and legs are doing and your sense of location moment to moment, you could start believing that time is slowing down. Time slows down in novel environments or with an unexpected series of events.

To provide a different example, consider a grid cell that in a familiar environment will fire once every 400 meters. Imagine a person who runs in a straight line for 1600 meters, but the fastest time they can achieve is eight minutes. In a familiar track, the hypothetical grid cell will fire four times. In a novel environment, the grid cell will map to an expanded physical spacing, firing only twice in 1600 meters. The length of the run has not physically changed, but the brain's measurement of space using this single grid cell determines that the length is only 800 meters. The real physical space is shortened by the mind's calculation. The body ran as fast as usual and can't go any faster, yet eight minutes elapsed in 800 meters, giving the runner an illusion that time slowed down in the novel environment. From the runner's perspective, finishing 1600 meters will take 16 minutes. From our perspective where we observe normal time and space, we can see that the runner actually finished 1600 meters in the first eight minutes.

If this hypothesis is true, the oneironaut phenomenon could be an illusion because different neurological systems of gauging time and space can come into conflict in perfectly normal brains encountering novel circumstances. One fictional example occurs when Alice falls down a well within the rabbit hole at the beginning of Lewis Carroll's famous story: "Either the well was very deep, or she fell very slowly, for she had plenty of time, as she went down, to look about her." From Alice's point of view, she cannot quite tell if this completely novel experience is a very long fall in distance, or a very slow fall in time.

Does changing the perception of distance really change the perception of time? Let's take a look at a fascinating experiment conducted in 1981 by Alton J. Delong at the University of Tennessee.[111] As if taking a cue from *Gulliver's Travels* or a David Lynch film, he asked adult test subjects to imagine themselves located in a scaled down version of space that he constructed, somewhat like a dollhouse. They were asked to imagine any activity they wished as they looked inside the small model space, and then signal when they thought 30 minutes had passed in their small world. The experimenters had stopwatches to measure how much real time had passed. Amazingly, the experience of time changed in proportion to how much the model space was scaled. If a model was 1/6 normal size, subjects thought 30 minutes passed after roughly 5.5 minutes. But if the model was 1/12 normal size, 30 minutes seemed to pass after approximately 2.7 minutes. The relative change in distance scale corresponds to a similar change in time scale. Just to make sure everyone was functioning normally, the test subjects were put in a normal-sized environment and they were very good at guessing that 30 minutes had passed when the stopwatch showed that 30 minutes had passed. These results were intriguing, they empirically established a repeatable relationship, yet the explanation for this effect was lacking.

My explanation is that grid cells act as neural correlates of spacetime events and imaginary replay of spacetime activates the same cells with a distortion that resembles the novel environment effect. Essentially the subjects of the Tennessee experiment had to remap grid cells into the smaller space that they were asked to spend virtual time in. But the remapping is not perfect. If pacing across a normal-sized room produces eight grid cell firings, the mind may simulate only four in the dollhouse room, or just two in an even smaller dollhouse room.[112] Just as in the example of what happens to a person's sense of space and time when a grid cell fires only twice instead of four times when running 1600 meters, time also appears to slow down from the perspective of a person in a dollhouse.

This nicely segues into a theory of dream time (i.e., the perception of time during sleep and dreaming) because the subjects in the Tennessee experiment were asked to use their creative intellect to inhabit a virtual world, not unlike the process of dreaming. When grid cells are incorrectly mapped within the virtual space of a dream, time can also appear to slow down. An amazing two-hour adventure or a horrible never-ending nightmare may turn out to be a five-minute snooze.

On the other hand, let's consider the possibility that the expansion of the grid cell spacing in novel environments is the biological signature of the oneironaut phenomenon. Recall my story of the U.S. and Russian submarines that collide, and the question is who caused it to happen. In the novel environment, what causes the grid cell spacing to expand?

A novel environment invokes many new perceptions, so we could hypothesize that new sensory information cannot be processed in the same way by the old grid cell map. Expanding to a coarser grid may be a required step to avoid confusion and to quickly redraw a finer grid for the new space. You can also argue that computation takes a bit longer in novel representations, and therefore the entire system has to expand the time interval between spatial representations. So as you are walking across a new floor, you end up delaying that poke in the head because your brain has to process new information.

I would call the above idea a classical interpretation. The prediction for future testing is that the greater the novelty of a new environment, the greater the neurological computation times during a grid reset interval, and that's why the grid needs to become more widely spaced.

Yet, is it necessarily correct to compare brain functions so exactly to computers? Instead, consider an assumption that the grid map is perfectly capable of staying exactly the same in a familiar environment and in a novel environment. Computation is not the most significant factor. The novel environment, however, induces the oneironaut phenomenon, which means that information encoded by those grid cells and place cells moves back in time. In the oneironaut interpretation, the novel environment causes the cells to send information to the past (for evolutionary advantage). Let's call the event of entering a novel environment something that happens in Universe Zero. The computation time may be longer not only because of the complexity of new information in the environment, but also because another physical process, the oneironaut phenomenon, is demanding energy.

These cells briefly process information within two different time periods simultaneously. Time itself is distorted as far as those cells are concerned. This means that they will make timing mistakes within the demands of their functioning in the existing environment. Thus the cells in the EC make a grid that is disorganized. The cells may experience one second of time as a slightly longer second of time and therefore fire at an increased spacing.

When the dreaming brain (in the past) perceives this information, the timeline into the future changes and we have to say that Universe Zero can no longer exist and all subsequent events occur in Universe One. In this different universe, when the event is eventually experienced, the experience of déjà vu means that memory of the environment is retrieved and replayed by the brain. The environment is not entirely novel. Therefore the grid cell expansion and distortion should be suppressed in Universe One.

The oneironaut interpretation therefore has a prediction: the grid cell spacing will *not* expand and deform when the oneironaut phenomenon is experienced as déjà vu in a novel environment. This is because the initial novel experience is sent back in time and the grid cell (and place cell) representations of the scene are emplaced in the dreaming brain. The dreaming brain may in fact have the grid cells firing with irregular spacing and on an expanded scale. After the oneironaut has finished the dream and subsequently enters the novel environment fully awake in the future, the place in this timeline is now familiar, not novel. Unlike the classical interpretation, increasing the level of novelty will not produce more distorted and more widely spaced grids because the oneironaut phenomenon is a change in spacetime instead of a change in complexity.

To recap, there are two hypotheses presented here with different predictions. In the first, novel environments stimulate a cognitive process to recompute the grid, basically erasing it a bit, reducing the resolution, and then redrawing it accurately and recovering the original resolution. Experiments can test whether or not ever-increasing novelty leads to ever-increasing disorganization and grid spacing. The second hypothesis suggests that entering novel environments with the experience of déjà vu will not produce as severe a distortion in the grid cell spacing because in a new timeline, the novel environment has already been experienced in a past dream.

My Haycart dream calls attention to the fact that the language heard is novel, but the space was not novel—I was sitting on the same old gym floor every day. Overall, there are many déjà vu experiences that have little to do with space, but instead concern a thought, a story heard, or something seen. Yet these are often novel experiences, which means that when I hear or see them for the first time, it's as if I am lost. I have to step back and reorganize my knowledge to figure out how the new element fits in. The things I learn need a place in my grid of memories (knowledge), as if memories map into space.

Suggesting that memories can be organized as if putting them on a map of space is related to a very old story. When the ancient Roman politician Cicero wrote a manual on oration (*de Oratore*), he suggested that memory is equal to power. Memory, though, is a mental skill that can be improved. Cicero then tells the story of an ancient Greek poet called Simonides who was paid by a nobleman to write a poem about the nobleman. Simonides presented the poem during dinner at the nobleman's grand palace, but only 50% of the poem was about the nobleman and the other 50% was about the twin demigods Castor and Pollux. So the nobleman told Simonides that he would pay half price for the poem. Simonides then stepped outside, whereupon the palace roof collapsed, crushing the cheapskate nobleman and all the guests. We can infer that the nobleman also paid the building contractor 50%.

Apparently, the bodies were so thoroughly squished, like stepping on ants, that they were unrecognizable. Simonides then realized he could identify each person based on his memory of their relative location in the space. The former palace that existed in three-dimensional space retained its information content in a "memory palace." Thus, one technique to consolidate and stabilize memories is by creating a mental picture of space, such as your home, and placing each thing you want to remember in a specific room. No need to be a fancy pants orator such as Cicero—anyone can try it the next time they need a shopping list.

I would therefore hypothesize that when we talk about neural correlates of a spatial map in the hippocampus and EC, there are other brain areas that contain the neural correlates to a cognitive language map, or a cognitive visual map.[113] When novel experiences occur in these domains, a spacetime breach perturbs the map. The alternative skeptical viewpoint is that novel experiences disorient these cognitive maps for reasons not related to time travel, and for some people this creates the illusion of déjà vu as time travel.

My comments are highly speculative, food for thought, yet the amazing strides made by neuroscience instill confidence that we will eventually discover the neural correlates to the oneironaut phenomenon. When I describe Fomalhaut, falling posters or haycart dreams, these are all highly processed perceptions of the oneironaut phenomenon. The science of expanding grid cells in novel environments leads me to think that there are basic neural correlates for new learning experiences.

The toilet effect: Flushing your mind

I have always been puzzled by the occurrence of the déjà vu phenomenon when I am in the bathroom of a restaurant or other place that's not my living quarters. My baseline hypothesis is that the relative quiet of a bathroom permits the moments of focus and introspection that are needed to perceive the déjà vu phenomenon. In terms of neuroscience, the humble bio break gives the brain an opportunity to switch from its goal-directed attention network to the default mode network. The default mode network consists of various brain regions, including the hippocampus, that are concurrently active when a person is resting, daydreaming, meditating, abstract reasoning, or thinking about the past and future, with minimal focus on tasks that concern the present.[114]

A second hypothesis about the significance of bathroom breaks involves how the brain processes memories with respect to changes in location. In recent years cognitive psychologists have been studying how memory is influenced by "event boundaries."[115] Your memory of life is typically chunky rather than smooth or continuous. For example, if you just arrived at work, you can describe how you got there as a series of steps (I got out of bed in my bedroom, I made breakfast in my kitchen, I got dressed in my bedroom, etc.), but you probably don't remember what happened in between these steps (such as what you saw on the way to the kitchen from the bedroom). Notice how I defined these distinct events in time with respect to distinct locations in space. Our long-term memories of events with respect to time—when events happened and in what order—are indeed anchored by memories of distinct spaces.

One of the theories in cognitive psychology has an ironic term, given my focus on bathrooms: when a change in location is experienced, working memory is "flushed." Working memory consists of whatever short-term and long-term memories you need to bring to consciousness in order to execute tasks and goals. For example, if you sit down at a restaurant table and want to order food, you have to solve the problem of choosing your dinner that will involve your memories. You might think to yourself: "I don't want pizza because I just had pizza for lunch, but I don't have enough money in my pocket, so I'm getting pizza." At the same time, the menu has a novel pizza called "The Sixteen-Wheeler," which you dwell upon, wondering what diabolical mind came up with this name for a pizza.

After you order the pizza, you get up and go to the bathroom. That change of space will flush the working memory required to order pizza, and soon after you will recall the long-term memory of a dream you had two years ago, when you could not figure out why a pizza is called "The Sixteen-Wheeler." Thus you have just experienced what I call 24-hour déjà vu. Real-time déjà vu was blocked because you were preoccupied with the cognitive demands of solving problems using working memory.[116] If the cognitive demands last several days, such as in my story concerning the Geoff Marcy case, the déjà vu could be missed altogether.

Therefore, a key element in the oneironaut phenomenon is to flush working memory, such as by moving to a different space like a bathroom. Your humble but necessary bio break is an excellent time to time travel.

Spacetime brain cells

With words like "grid" and "place" describing the functions of certain brain cells, one wonders if we should also expect to find a "time cell" or a "clock cell." Certainly when a grid cell or place cell fires, this is an event, and an event encompasses both space and time by definition. Indeed, lesions to the hippocampus are known to severely impair the ability to remember the order of items or events.[117]

One might postulate that networks of cells could encode time for the brain based on a sequential firing pattern. For example, imagine 60 neurons somewhere in the brain arranged in a small ring that fire clockwise sequentially, just like the second hand of a clock. If your attention requires an estimate of time on the order of seconds—my task is to floss this tooth for three seconds—the brain might start firing the 60-neuron network and when the third neuron fires it signals the task's completion. One can also imagine a medium-sized ring of 60 more neurons that monitor what happens to the small ring. Each time all 60 neurons in the small ring fire, one neuron in the medium ring lights up. Thus the medium ring can give you a sense of elapsed minutes. To complete the clock analogy, we can posit a large ring of 24 neurons that accumulates the number of minutes elapsed, and hence you have the hour hand of the clock.

However, it is still an open question whether or not we have different types of neuronal networks that keep track of the elapsed seconds to give a sense of accumulated time. As an alternative, imagine a spiral pattern instead of nested rings. In this case there is only one type of neuron that measures seconds. The firing pattern is sequential starting from the center and elapsed minutes and hours can be determined by how far in radius the firing pattern has propagated outward along the spiral. The macroscopic morphology of this time-dependent change may not look exactly like an expanding circle, but it could be detected as an overall change of brain state in certain regions or within relevant neural pathways.

To test the temporal component of hippocampal neurons, there are experiments in which the organism is not allowed to move or change direction and the only thing it experiences is a sequence of cues. For example, in rat experiments a sequence of different odors can be presented.[118] Researchers found that certain cells in the hippocampus fire in patterns that represent memories for sequences of events, and these are now considered to be *time cells* that are usually functionally distinct from place cells. However, many neurons will encode for both time and place.[119] If the neuroscientists would take a cue from astrophysics, then they might start calling these neurons *spacetime cells*. Spacetime cells are one of the neural correlates to our obvious ability to organize our memories with respect to time.

If we think of spacetime cells as giving a time stamp to experiences encoded as memory, then we may still ask what exactly is the original source for the perception of time? After all, I can print out a calendar and you can use it to write down events and memories during the year, but a calendar is not time. It represents time in a certain way that gives a time stamp—an exact identifier—to events. The original source of time for the human calendar is the Earth's motion as it spins and as it orbits the

Sun. If we wanted to communicate our sense of time to an alien civilization, we would probably want to send them information about the Earth and the Sun instead of 12 grids with 12 different names. Are hippocampal spacetime cells constructing a personal calendar of sorts, where the neural correlate of time originates from something else completely different?

The question seems all the more intriguing when we ask what spacetime cells are doing during sleep and dreaming, and how they might account for the qualities of the oneironaut phenomenon. Obviously, dreams can be a time-ordered sequence of events that we recall later when awake. For a dream to have a sequence, does this mean that the spacetime cells are responding to a virtual world, just like the place cells and grid cells could be needed to construct the virtual space in the dream? At least for rats, this seems to be the case.[120]

Dreams involving the oneironaut phenomenon, on the other hand, are similar to momentary snapshots instead of a structured sequence of scenes whereby each element can be understood in relation to other elements. Perhaps the only way for the mechanism to work is if certain spacetime cells suspend their time stamp component. The suppression of time stamps may cause the oneironaut phenomenon, or vice versa. The momentary absence of time stamps would account for the general uselessness of the oneironaut phenomenon for the explicit predictions of events.

Aside from spacetime cells in the hippocampus, the reader may recall that I previously discussed two other time-related functions in the brain.

First, Admiral SCN is the tiny portion of the brain responsible for your circadian rhythm, and it turns out that the circadian rhythm influences memory. One very intriguing experiment involves Siberian hamsters because a specific sequence of light pulses disrupts their circadian rhythm permanently.[121] I am not going to tell you what the sequence actually is, given that third-graders everywhere might start creating legions of strange hamsters. However, I can tell you that after disrupting the hamster's circadian rhythm, our furry friend loses its memories of places, as if its place cells and grid cells can't do their jobs. Thus the element of time encoded by the circadian rhythm is somehow linked to hippocampal function. To make things even more mysterious, researchers can restore the memory function of these hamsters by surgically removing Admiral SCN. Thus, memory of space is influenced by time as encoded in the circadian rhythm, but there must be additional mechanisms that give the mind time references.

The second time-related function introduced in Chapter 5 involves the brain's electrical oscillations that distinguish different sleep stages. Oscillations are time markers, and in the next section I will briefly discuss how they are linked to my favorite word to say out loud.

The Gatekeeper's Tango

CHAPTER 5 REVIEWED HOW HUMAN SLEEP has different stages distinguished by the electrical waves detected from our brains. If a brain wave is 1 Hz that means it oscillates one full up-down cycle in one second, or 60 times per minute. Many kinds of electrical oscillations are observed in different parts of the brain, which at times are synced to each other, hinting at how the brain is coordinating its various parts to produce awareness, thoughts, reactions, learning, memories, etc.

Adopting our tango dancer analogy from the previous chapter, two dancers moving their feet at different rhythms will collide and a dance does not happen. But if two dancers are synchronized, then the two are functioning together to construct a dance. When neuroscientists see one cell or brain region synchronize electrical oscillations with another cell or brain region, they infer a functional link, including causation.

Earlier we learned that the hippocampus is a gatekeeper for memories but notice that I did not exactly explain how the gatekeeper works to open and close the gates. The synchronization of electrical oscillations could be a partial answer. If one brain area, say the finger motion to play piano, is synchronized with the hippocampus, then we infer that the gates are open to learning piano. If at the same time, someone speaks to you, but your focus is on playing the piano, the gates are closed for that auditory signal to be processed as a memory. The two will be out of sync.

The brain wave that seems to represent these gates is called the theta oscillation.[122] This is roughly defined as a 5–10 Hz wave, or 300–600 beats per minute. In music, if you set the quarter note to a tempo of 60 beats per minute (1 Hz), then you would have to play many 32nd notes to mimic human theta. A 5–10 Hz wave should sound familiar. Recall that 5–10 Hz electrical activity also defines the first two stages of sleep, and indeed the theta oscillations are present throughout sleep, including portions of the REM stage during dreaming.

Theta is also measured when you are awake. For example, theta waves in the hippocampus are evident when animals are moving through space and engaged in a variety of activities.[123] By now you have learned that motion through space as well as the order of events and memories are associated with spacetime cells in the hippocampal formation. The theta waves measured in these hippocampal cells can go into or out of sync with other brain areas, depending on what the organism is doing. Broadly speaking, theta waves are a physiological characteristic of memory and learning because regions of the brain that process sensory information will sync their theta rhythm with the hippocampal theta rhythm.

A specific example of this "memory and learning wave" concerns a brain part called the amygdala, which lights up when you, or a rat, experience fear. Fear in rats manifests as a behavior such as freezing, and when this happens the theta waves of the amygdala and the hippocampus are synced together.[124] Thus the theta oscillation seems to represent the transfer of fear information into and out of the hippocampus.

The theta oscillation has also been proposed as a key component in controlling how grid cells fire.[125] Returning to **Figure 6-3** we can see that two waves interfering with each other produces a pattern of intensity peaks similar to the grid cell map shown in **Figure 7-4**. The interaction of hippocampal theta waves could more generally play a central role in how we perceive spacetime.

Consider a relatively recent experiment conducted in Norway with rats placed in an environment that was rapidly switched between two different scenes using lights in a dark room. This is somewhat like the Poultry Matrix described in Chapter 4 except that the Norwegian scientists say that they are "teleporting" the rats from one place to another, as if assuming the role of Rat Gods. Each virtual location causes two different regions of hippocampal cells to respond. Once you noted which cells correspond to which scene, you could figure out which scene the rat was looking at just by detecting which group of hippocampal cells were firing.

However, occasionally between scene changes the hippocampal cells "flicker" between the two types of responses.[126] The flickering rate between the past environment and the present environment corresponds to the theta frequency. Thus the conjecture is that a theta wave represents a packet of related cognitive information. In a one-second interval, a single hippocampal cell or cell group may be handling 5–10 packets of information, since the theta frequency is 5–10 Hz.

This flickering intrigues me because I have pondered the question of "where am I" exactly when I'm in bed dreaming of a future waking experience in a different place. As I enter a new cognitive environment in the future waking state, my theta waves must be actively coordinating the information through the hippocampus, and one might imagine that the information flickers back and forth between the waking present and the sleeping past. In the waking present, my déjà vu experience is activating a memory of the past dream; but in the past, during the sleeping state, I was learning the future scene for the first time via this flicker with the waking brain.

To put it another way, one might have assumed that with the oneironaut phenomenon we somehow transport our minds between two regions of spacetime. The science fiction concept of a time machine or teleportation is that we press a button to leave one time or place and go to the other. But I would suggest an alternate concept: the oneironaut phenomenon may be more accurately characterized by a flickering of 5–10 Hz between present and future states. By not leaving my present self for too long, I can maintain the integrity of my present functioning. I never permanently leave my present self to go to a future mind, or to a past mind. A wave has a continuous back-and-forth form.

Moreover, I should note the duration of flickering episodes with the rats typically lasted in the range 1–10 seconds. As I estimated previously, the duration of an oneironaut experience for me is something like nine seconds. Also, flickering is rare—it occurred in only 1.3% of scene changes in the rat experiment—and so too the oneironaut phenomenon is rare. It's as if both are glitches that do not represent the vast majority of normal operations. Finally, it's worth noting that a glitch is not predictable or controllable, and so too the oneironaut phenomenon seems to have these features. Thus there is some passable correspondence in the timescale, sparseness and unpredictability of hippocampal theta-paced flickering and the oneironaut phenomenon, with speculation that both are uncontrollable glitches.

The oscillation idea is an attractive concept in a more general way. Even if you don't believe the oneironaut phenomenon is real, you could take the oscillation as a convenient model to describe how time is handled in waking and sleeping consciousness. As **Figure 7-5** illustrates, during waking consciousness, information between the past, present and future is exchanged rapidly, even if attention seems to focus only on the present. For example, reading this book may seem to be an activity solely anchored in your present time, yet when you read the word "oscillation" you may recall in $1/5^{th}$ of a second the swing from a childhood playground in your distant past. Meanwhile, in $1/10^{th}$ of a second you may be incubating the idea that reading this chapter may be more pleasurable if you also made a cup of coffee or tea in the near future.

Figure 7-5 also suggests how the balance of attention changes when the waking state transitions to the sleep state. The present fades and is no longer the focus of attention, the past and the future become the prime areas of concern, and the oscillations can extend further into the future or the past than it might in the waking state. You may recall events from even further in the past than you could recall during waking hours, and the mind may construct elaborate virtual scenes of events that could happen in the far future.

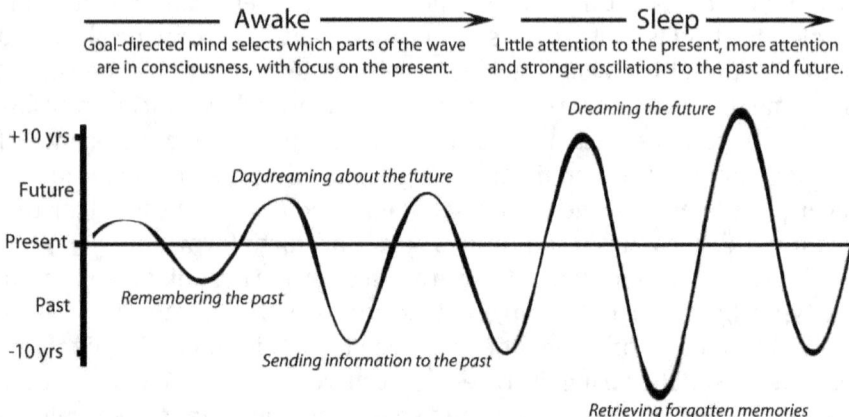

Figure 7-5: Sketch of how consciousness could be seen as a continuous oscillation of information between past, present and future at the theta frequency of 5–10 Hz. The frequency is fast enough that consciousness doesn't perceive the rapid changes, yet attention can focus on either the past, present or future segments of the wave. The width of the oscillating line illustrates where attention is focused—the thicker the line, the greater the attention. Thus, during the waking state the present requires attention, whereas in the sleeping state, the present is suppressed and more attention is devoted to past and future. Note that the awake-sleep cycle is also a type of cyclical oscillation.

The figure also illustrates the Great Ambiguity—why the oneironaut phenomenon is so difficult to distinguish from other parts of consciousness. Information from the future perceived in a dream is carried by the same wave as daydreaming or thinking about the future. If the mechanism involves sending information backward in time, as I have suggested, then the portion of the wave that involves remembering the past is the same wave that involves sending information to the past. Maybe the oneironaut phenomenon is the rare glitch where the amplitude of the wave (its height) occasionally goes a significant distance away from its average height. Alternately, perhaps it's not the height that matters, but how much attention we can occasionally devote to the high points and low points (in the figure, this is how thick the oscillating wave is drawn).

To sum up, my previous joke that I may be a *ronin* (Japanese word that means wave-man) is now somewhat more specific. When the oneironaut phenomenon happens, I am not traveling *through* spacetime on a wave. Instead, for just a few seconds, I am *oscillating in* spacetime like a wave.

Or, to go back to a music analogy, the mind is always playing a tremolo. In acoustic guitar, a single note on a single string can be played very rapidly, as if the note is trilling. To the outside listener and to the player's ears, the note is being played repeatedly. The underlying mechanics is that three fingers of the right hand are rapidly striking the same string; e.g., ring finger, middle finger, index finger and then repeat. Thus, consciousness is like the single-note experience of hearing a tremolo, but the underlying source for producing the note may be a rapid oscillation between the past, present and future.

If I'm really saying that mental processes have wave-like characteristics, then why not ask if such waves can have the properties of linear superposition, constructive and destructive interference, and entanglement, as discussed in the previous chapter? One could propose that theta oscillations may entangle information between events spanning spacetime. Recall that entanglement, the Swiss Cross, seems to disregard the constraints of spacetime. One could speculate along these lines of argument but for now I'm going to leave these topics for fireside chats.

The case of the missing Swedes

One nuanced question is whether or not spacetime flickering should really be called a glitch, or should it be called an *optimization*? The mammalian brain clearly is capable of handling many different tasks, but natural selection would reject mammals with brains that mastered too few of the tasks necessary for survival.[127] For example, an organism that is born with superb visual skills may not survive and pass on this trait to the next generation if it has poor memory or learning skills. A more successful organism will have a balance of, say, just the right vision for its environment, and just the right memory and learning needed for its survival tasks. The traits currently observed in humans and other organisms have trended toward the optimum traits over thousands of generations.

Borrowing a term from economics, we might call this *Pareto efficiency*. A Pareto efficient economy is one that has reached a *zero-sum state*. For example, if the economy produces food and cars, but it has a limited labor force and zero unemployment, then if car manufacturing is to increase, it needs to take labor from somewhere else, which means that food production may have to decrease.

I'm glad I learned about Pareto efficiency because it solved the puzzling mystery of the missing Swedes. A few days after I gave a lecture in Stockholm in 2012, I developed a theory that Sweden has a hidden human population. During my visit there, I learned that Swedes produce two brands of cars, one fighter jet, a submarine, Earth's largest furniture store and drink the most coffee per capita than any other nation. However, the total population of Sweden is 10 million. Greece also has 10 million people, and so do other places, but no other group of 10 million people makes two cars, one submarine, a fighter jet and Earth's largest furniture store. My theory was therefore quite simple: Sweden must have an additional hidden population, either living in underground caverns, or on the surface, but not counted in any census. The quantity of coffee consumed within its borders was unassailable evidence that the population was really 20 million or more.

Then my theory of the missing Swedes fell apart when I learned about Pareto efficiency. It seems that any group of 10 million people can make two cars, one fighter jet, a submarine and Earth's largest furniture store if they maximize their potential for industrial productivity. Sweden was probably close to the Pareto front, essentially at the zero-sum state. Assuming no innovation in technology or process, and no increase in labor, if Swedes wanted to make more submarines per unit time, they'd probably have to make fewer cars, since labor would need to shift to the shipyards. For all the other groups of 10 million people that aren't Sweden, you could say they are Pareto inefficient. These groups still have tremendous unrealized potential to optimize their functions. They could also commit themselves to drinking more coffee, should they wish to achieve true Swedish standards.

Species can also be characterized in terms of Pareto efficiency. If an organism has reached a sufficient biological potential in all necessary areas, then its life is a zero-sum game. If you change something to improve function in a specific area, there will be a trade-off involved that decreases function in a different area. Consider that the physiology of a cheetah is optimized for the speed necessary to chase prey on the ground, but you couldn't genetically modify a cheetah to also be a very good tree climber.[128] Changing the physiology of a cheetah's legs to help it climb trees would reduce its maximum land speed.

Humans face such trade-offs too. If an individual chooses to devote more time to, say, writing great books, this would be at the expense of something else, like developing the motor skills required to play excellent piano. On the other hand, if you are Pareto inefficient, this means that there is untapped potential to do both. You could indeed start learning to play the piano, and this would *not* be at the expense of something else in your life.

Pareto efficiency is an interesting way to answer the big question of why we sleep. The cheetah cannot change its leg physiology to become a good climber, but biochemistry can be changed. The brain can tweak and modulate its qualities every day to optimize the functions of the organism. However, a single state of consciousness cannot optimize all the tasks the mammalian brain has the potential to solve.[129] Thinking about the future and consolidating past memories are not maximally efficient if mammals were always awake. Adding a different form of consciousness during sleep, however, takes animals closer to their Pareto front. Indeed, sleep has the qualities of a zero-sum game as if we have reached the Pareto front—if you try to stay awake many more hours than usual your body notices and the mind starts malfunctioning; there is no substitute for sleep.

The reason we sleep is because the organisms selected to survive on Earth are the ones that exploit all the possible changes that give advantages within their environmental niche. Changing our state of consciousness is an excellent adaptation to optimize our potential function given the Earth's day-night cycle. For humans, why waste time during the day motionless, thinking about old memories, when you can use that time to hunt for food? Conversely, why waste time during the night hunting very poorly when you could be excellent at thinking about the past and planning future experiences?

Spacetime flickering could also be a way to bring brain function to the Pareto front, given the difficulty of processing signals arriving nearly simultaneously from the past, present and future. A poor solution is if processing the future signal overwhelms the present/past states and severely diminishes the ability to deal with the organism's immediate environment. Likewise, focusing on past events to the exclusion of the present and future, such as with post-traumatic stress disorder in humans, also diminishes overall function. The brain may have evolved to solve the problem of a zero-sum game through flickering.

I wonder if the oneironaut phenomenon is Pareto efficient or inefficient. Can a single oneironaut dramatically increase the quantity and quality of future information in their minds, without losing their critical functioning in their present reality? I suspect I could, up to a point, and I consider the oneironaut phenomenon as Pareto inefficient to a degree.

If the oscillation/optimization perspective is roughly the right idea, how does it explain other qualities of the phenomenon? For example, why is a specific experience selected for the transtime oscillation? Just a few novel experiences end up in dreams, not all novel experiences.

So far, the only speculation I've provided is the common trigger idea—that something in your future universe has a commonality with the present universe. In the Fomalhaut dream, I may have been processing the name James Graham because I saw it in an email about Saturn's rings in 1995, and in 2004 I would also be working with James Graham about a ring of dust observed around a star. Yet detailed email records and logs of daily life are hard to generate in order to thoroughly test the trigger hypothesis. This seems to be the type of experiment that needs simple and controlled conditions to be adequately tested, or we have to scale up the experiments from rats to humans, such as by building a real Heidelberg Dome.

Janus, the Glitch

ONE REASON I AM NOT PERMANENTLY enrolled in the college of the insane is that I still have the capacity to recognize the irony of proposing that the oneironaut phenomenon occurs because of a glitch. The previous section speculates that the phenomenon may be related to the flickering glitch observed in hippocampal processing during scene changes. The irony is that in the mainstream view, the oneironaut phenomenon is indeed a glitch of memory systems. Flickering could create the illusion of time travel rather than genuine time travel.

Imagine that the brain of Janus occasionally loses track of which pair of eyeballs—those facing the past or those facing the future—go with which experiences. If the sight of a cooked turkey flickers between the two sets of eyeballs, Janus may not know if the turkey is already cooked (the information is tagged by the eyeballs that see the past), or if it is presently raw (eyeballs that imagine the cooked turkey in the future). One might call this source-tracking error—Janus does not know which eyeballs gave which experiences. So too a normal person may not know if a novel experience should be classified as a new memory or an old memory.

The crucial way to distinguish whether or not the oneironaut phenomenon gives a real future experience, or if it is a source-tracking glitch that generates an illusion of the phenomenon, is with measurements. For me the Fomalhaut chapter gives a key measurement, supported by the context of all the other dreams and behaviors that I have described. Therefore I do not think the oneironaut phenomenon is an illusion in my case. Yet there are hypothetical glitches in memory systems that have been proposed as explanations for reports of déjà vu experiences.

In principle, we can reason that as experiences happen to us and we catalog them as new memories piling onto old memories, we must be using a marker for time to stay organized. The marker may not always be perfect, a glitch will be rare, and it really astonishes us when it happens. For example, if you enter a room that you've already been to before, but forgot this memory and its associated time marker, then you may experience *jamais vu* (never seen). The opposite glitch, *déjà vu*, may be equally possible. When you enter a room that you've never been to before, your memory system could tag it as an old memory. Your awareness or consciousness of the room is linked to the past, not the recent present. Thus, when our beholder's share contains a simple mistake of time tracking, we call the experience *déjà vu*.

I don't think the memory/processing/consciousness glitch has been rigorously tested via experimentation as an explanation for déjà vu, despite the fact that the history of studying memory and déjà vu goes back at least to the time of Aristotle.[130] Instead, such explanations gain their merits vis-à-vis other empirical investigations of awareness, consciousness and false memories.

Take, for example, startling experiments in which normal adults have an unassailable memory of being lost in a shopping mall when they were young, even though the entire memory was fabricated and then "planted" in their minds.[131] The American novelist Pat Conroy relates a similar real-life story about his novel *The Great Santini*, which was based on growing up in a household with an abusive father. The various scenes and the dialogue between characters in the book were fabricated. After the book was published, his mother filed for a divorce from his father, and along with his sister they testified in court that they remembered specific conversations that were central to their case against Conroy's dad. Pat Conroy was stunned—he had written those conversations as pure fiction, yet his mother and sister had acquired definite memories of having spoken those very same words.[132]

To be clear, this story does not show that Pat Conroy's mother and sister are diabolical or cunning people. Instead, his story and that of scientific research reveal that a family member could write up a family history with fictional episodes and other family members will believe that these things are real experiences in their past. These memory glitches are part of our everyday experience; it's normal, yet normal has consequences. Untold numbers of innocent people have spent lifetimes in jail, and the Socratic execution that I mentioned for myself in the

Preface could really happen if my accounts are shown to be a bizarre concoction of my mind.

Like everyone else, I have memory glitches, but I can eventually recognize them as such given some introspection. My déjà vu experiences, on the other hand, have never changed their status from a dream-memory to a false-memory upon further introspection and skepticism. Moreover, the Fomalhaut chapter is of central importance because this evidence is closest to the physical evidence that one could hope for in a court case. It's as if Pat Conroy's mother and sister actually produced a recording that verified the exact words his father had spoken many years in the past.

Ratman's Angels

IN THE HEIDELBERG CHAPTER I started talking about myself as if I were a rat navigating a maze designed by ET. As a rat I have occasionally discerned angels above me in the sky. These aren't human angels, who are useless for my species, but rat angels instead. Rat angels are amazing because they are rats with wings and can fly wherever they please. I've seen them, I really have, but only at night near the glow of the red flower. I'm nocturnal, and so are they, but they zip around so fast in the dark that I'm not sure that I've ever seen their tail. I don't even know how they can avoid running into things when I can barely see a few inches ahead of my nose. However, humans have captured rat angels and found that they actually have a hippocampus just like mine, and this means they can study it. You see, my spatial navigation in ET's maze is more or less two-dimensional. But what would humans learn about the brain if they could study a flying mammal that navigates three dimensions of space?

Apparently, studying the brain activity of rat angels calls into question the significance of theta oscillations—my flying friends do NOT display theta oscillations when moving. Yet their hippocampal formation is just as good at spatial navigation as my hippocampal formation, and so theta oscillations are not necessarily a phenomenon or mechanism that is needed for the brain to calculate and remember location.

This finding disagreed with such a large number of human, rat and primate studies about theta oscillations that in 2012 a fairly interesting debate erupted in the medical research community. From my rat cage I heard the following:

Rat Doctors: Let's drink champagne to celebrate how much we have learned. Theta oscillations are a fundamental unit of thought, memory and even human consciousness. Without theta oscillations, we would be lost in space and time. Every single thing we say gets published in the most prestigious journals, and we've already downloaded a map of Stockholm to prepare for the Nobel Prize.

Angel Doctor: Ahem, I tested your theory using my rats, the ones that fly, and it turns out that theta oscillations are not present when rat angels navigate.

Rat Doctors: Who's this nudnik? We read your paper, but the rat angels weren't flying when you did the experiment. Instead they were schlepping around on your lab floor at 3.7 centimeters per second. If we study rats when they are moving that slowly, hippocampal theta oscillations are not detectable. Instead, when our rats move more naturally at 17.6 centimeters per second, hippocampal theta is clearly detected.

Angel Doctor: You gentlemen are rat arsed. Angels are not accustomed to using their legs for travel, and 3.7 centimeters per second is quite fast for them. A rat, on the other hand, is motionless for all practical purposes at that velocity. *An angel walking 3.7 centimeters per second on the floor is equivalent effort to a rat walking 17.6 centimeters per second on the floor!*

Now, I may have paraphrased slightly, but this represents a real debate published in the journal *Nature* between leading neuroscientists,[133] and it probably sounds just as bizarre to you humans as it does to me. That last sentence, in particular, has nonsense and the central scientific issue coexisting simultaneously, sort of like quantum mechanics. More importantly, I was offended to learn that my butt is synonymous with human intoxication. Things got even weirder later when cheetahs and sloths were added to the debate. It's true, they were.

However, any story that concerns angels must have a moral to teach. Here is what I learned: We now have unprecedented observations of phenomena occurring in the brains of mammals, but the true origin, function and interconnectivity of these elements is still light years from our firm grasp. We are practically blind as a bat. Given the limits of spacetime when writing a book, my chapter on the hippocampus merely skims the surface of neuroscience research. I have crudely described this surface, like talking about a tree trunk, when in fact there are many nuances in neuroscience—depending on the research group, the tree trunk is becoming several types of chair. Much of my speculation about the oneironaut phenomenon will be criticized and overturned by new evidence, yet this is exactly the same future awaiting all research on the brain. In 2013 the angel doctor showed that even during angel flight, the angel mind does not require theta oscillations to find its way through space.[134]

8. The Oneironauts

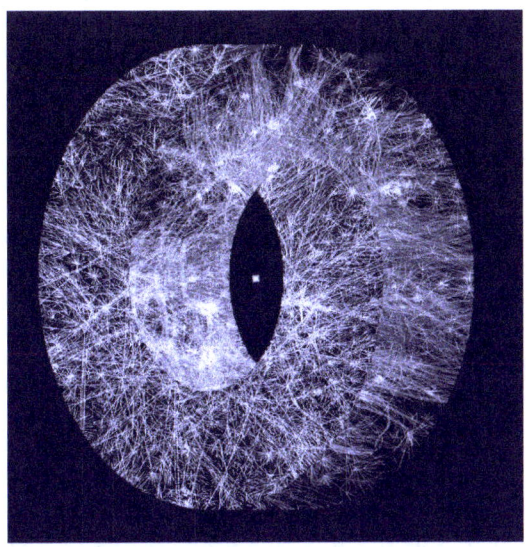

If something isn't entirely clear or perfectly understood, does that stop you from using it or practicing it as an art? For example, in the art of baking bread, a fairly basic instruction is that dry yeast should be placed in a bowl of water that is a bit warmer than body temperature (38–43 °C), but it should not be colder or warmer than that. This is definitely an odd instruction on how to handle a substance that looks like sand, but my goal is to eat homemade bread, not to develop a perfect understanding of why my bread will fail if dry yeast is treated any other way.

The goal of this chapter is to figure out a recipe for using the oneironaut phenomenon so that we can benefit from it. Our inability to understand how it works does not need to stop us from trying out various recipes to see what comes out at the end. Understanding why a particular recipe actually works can emerge later.

This approach is roughly consistent with the art of medicine. I am reminded of the physician Edward Jenner, who invented the smallpox vaccine. In 1796 he exposed an eight-year-old boy to pus from the blisters of a person with *cow*pox. This wasn't an entirely random experiment that could have killed the boy. Instead, it was an experimental test of anecdotal observations that cowpox exposure protected people from smallpox. These observations had little scientific underpinning; they just emerged from daily experiences. Jenner's live human subject experiment was successful—the boy developed immunity to smallpox.

The science behind the art of vaccination would arrive many decades later when Louis Pasteur conducted experiments to prove the existence of microorganisms. This microscopic world had been invisible to humans, yet it had profound consequences for everyone. The lack of scientific understanding did not stop Jenner and others from helping people by implementing techniques that demonstrated practical value. So too the scientific world underlying the oneironaut phenomenon may be invisible to us today, yet it has practical consequences, and our challenge is to develop the most helpful techniques possible. Eventually a scientific understanding will come to light.

Here is a summary of what you will find in this chapter. I have argued that it is possible to perceive information from the future through dreaming, but this phenomenon is demonstrably useless for a single person. The proposed remedy is to use technology to more accurately record and analyze the dreams of large groups of people. This is a feasible path for the near future, creating an analogy to the Internet that might be called the *Dreamnet*. Further in the future one expects that we will understand the physics of the oneironaut phenomenon and then manufacture machines, possibly combined with bioengineering, that can reliably detect the osignal from the future. Dreaming will not be absolutely necessary, and the Dreamnet might evolve into a type of *Metamindnet*, where an awareness of world timelines—past, present and future—emerges from a synthesis of organic and engineered humans, other organisms and machines. This of course sounds like science fiction, yet I am plainly extrapolating the consequences of what I think I know about the world right now to the world that we will experience in 1,000 years.

The Dreamnet

UNTIL A MECHANICAL OR ARTIFICIAL oneironaut "switch" or "circuit" is created, we have to contend with the fact that our mind is the present day oneironaut switch or circuit that connects the past, present and future. As discussed in the previous chapters, the future signal is distorted due to our natural efforts to assign semantic meaning to stimulus. In addition to the distortion, we have the noise from all other thoughts, emotions and bouts of anticipation and imagination about the future. Both the distortion and the noise are highly personal, which means that the goal should be to separate the person from the transtime osignal. If this were psychologically possible, an enlightened guru would have appeared in our timeline who amazes the world with accurate precognition. For all practical purposes no such guru has appeared, and I have to conclude that despite the remarkable efforts of individuals to become gurus, it just isn't possible for any single human to cleanly perceive the osignal.

My proposal for separating the person from the transtime signal is to process information from many individuals who will have a shared experience. The future experience will be a common thread among them, but many of the details will diverge as each individual inserts their own beholder's share. Fortunately, it is now completely feasible to store and analyze large data sets. The challenges lie both in improving the signal and in finding ways of recording much more of it.

The clues to improving the osignal are laid out in this book, such as by having novel problem-solving experiences. Finding proxy experiences for specific locations, dates and times will be essential. I previously referred to this proxy information as a Rosetta Stone for translating information and here I'll start calling it the oneironaut code or the *ocode*. The ocode is purposefully embedded in everyday egocentric experiences that can be perceived in dreams, yet these experiences have additional meaning that make the phenomenon useful. Note that I use the term *osignal* for *all* the information sent from future to past, whereas the *ocode* is a *subset* of the information *designed* to symbolically transmit a more complex message. In most cases the ocode is not revealed to the dreamer to protect against dream content that would be created by present-day imagination, anticipation, problem-solving, wishful thinking, etc.

So let's say the goal is to predict destructive tsunamis. A group of oneironauts would travel to the location in order to have experiences that encode the information we wish to know. For example, one oneironaut may have a particular focus on animals. An unusual story of a white owl will be told at the tsunami site, and when the white owl signal comes through in their dream, we would understand that the month is December—a white owl is the ocode for December. Another oneironaut specializes in languages and they dream of hearing an absorbing story of a white owl in Thai—the tsunami is going to hit Thailand in December. The ocode will consist of more proxies for years, dates, time of day, local culture, geological features, and so on and so forth.

How will these dreams be recorded? Large groups of people could upload their memories of their dreams into a central database. Some training might be needed to make sure that the details are described correctly. For example, someone might write, "I had a dream of a three-legged dog passing me on the street." That sounds like a pretty good dream recording—task finished, time for breakfast! Yet a little more work is needed before breakfast is served. Was it day or night in the dream? What color was the dog? Did it have a leash? Why were you walking on that street? Where do you think you were? You might be surprised to find that much more can be written than you first thought.

A large and growing database of dreams would comprise the Dreamnet. But this is not just a storage site like the Internet; it is also a computation center. It decides which of your dreams are psychological and tags the ones that are worth comparing to other people's dreams. The Dreamnet is also tied to databases of persons, places and things. Thus, when you describe a certain building in your dream, the Dreamnet has already identified buildings all over the world that match your description, including those that haven't been built yet. The Dreamnet not only knows everything we know, but it projects these appearances into the future. You might call it *augmented dreaming*, given the addition of so much more information.

The Dreamnet therefore can solve the recognition problem for persons, places, or things in the osignal. For example, computation can simulate the faces of people when they look older so that they are correctly identified in the dream. Fortunately, it is easier to simulate the face of a person when they are older instead of younger. The film *Tron* had a hard time making Jeff Bridges look younger, but the film *The Curious Case of Benjamin Button* successfully made Brad Pitt look older.

Likewise, the Dreamnet can simulate the future appearances of places. For example, say that I have a dream of driving over a magnificent bridge to San Francisco, but I *do not* report a dream of San Francisco after waking because the buildings appeared radically different in the dream compared to reality. The Dreamnet, on the other hand, would contain knowledge of the latest San Francisco building codes and the various construction filings historically and for the future. It would tell me that I was indeed viewing San Francisco, but in the future. Given the number of tall buildings to the right of my point of view from the bridge, the year is likely 2030, but not earlier than that.

How would I really be able to say how many buildings I saw in the dream and how high they were? Here we need an advance that is feasible, but has yet to be realized to its full potential. As I will discuss in the next section, under experimental conditions we have the ability to record the neurological activity of a person asleep, and ultimately translate that activity into images. Knowledge of a person's mental imagery no longer depends on memory and self-reporting. A form of mind reading is possible, which means a computer can recognize dream images as buildings and not birds. The next steps are to polish such methods to more precisely describe what the building looks like in the dream. What were the shapes, heights and number of buildings? If instead I dream of a bird, the neurological recording will give details that can be matched against a database of birds, which is much larger and more accurate than what my mind holds. The Dreamnet will tell me it was a sparrow even though I cannot remember what I saw. Even if I could remember the dream in detail, I still may not be able to distinguish a sparrow from a finch while wide awake, but the Dreamnet can.

To summarize, by collectively participating in the Dreamnet, a new ability will emerge among humans for reliably perceiving the future of significant events. Without the Dreamnet, individuals will continue to erratically perceive the future of very many insignificant events.

Human hive

The brazen head in the room is that the Dreamnet advocates a human hive mentality, where a diversity of ideas gives way to compulsive, dogmatic thinking and norms. Yet the core motivating ideas are to accelerate the advances in knowledge that would have happened anyway, and to protect life on our planet from threats. It's entirely possible that in the long term humanity will self-destruct or be extinguished because the large collection of minds working individually could never obtain what was needed to avoid disaster.

This may all seem abstract, too much like science fiction stories that you've encountered before, so let me ground it for you. Actually, let me put it in water. There are many ongoing studies of how animal groups provide evolutionary advantages, and in one study the animal is a fish five centimeters long called a golden shiner.[135] The best way for a shiner to live long enough to reproduce is by hiding in the dark. The more light hitting it from above, the faster it will swim, and when it encounters a darker environment, it slows down, thus spending much more time in darkness. But as an individual it doesn't know where it's going—its success at finding darkness in novel environments is based on luck. It doesn't have a cognitive map to say that if it turns right it will encounter a darker area.

But when a hundred or more shiners are swimming together, they are hugely successful at finding protection in darkness. This is because the group is social (one fish wants to remain close to neighboring fish) and the group covers a much larger area. For example, suppose that the group is swimming rapidly together in bright light and the right-most shiners encounter a slightly darker region. The right-most shiners will slow down and create a traffic jam behind them. The group must stick together, so the slowpokes to the right will cause the faster-moving shiners on the left to swing around toward them until they also enter darkness and slow down.[136]

Thus the efficiency, or "intelligence," of the group at securing protection emerges at a level that stretches beyond the smartest individual of the group. Interestingly, this heightened intelligence emerges by following two very simple rules: be social, and move fast or slow depending on if it's light or dark, respectively.[137] There is no sophisticated mind control of the individual. The system works because each individual shares similar interests with other individuals.

Instead of travel through water searching for optimal hiding locations, consider travel through spacetime in search of optimum timelines or events in spacetime. Like the individual golden shiner, which may randomly find a good hiding spot or not, the oneironaut phenomenon is mostly useless for any individual human to find their optimum path. But a school of shiners senses a greater fraction of space and permits those who detect an optimum location to turn the group toward that location. So too, a collection of humans comprising the Dreamnet can sample a greater fraction of future spacetime and because of our social cohesion turn humanity toward the optimal timelines. The group is not forced to move toward a timeline. Instead, the group will move in that direction if what the oneironauts have discovered is deemed to be in the best interests of everyone.

The engineering of time

There are plenty of human examples rather than fish examples that convey the benefit of group participation. Consider an app for smartphones called MyShake that detects earthquakes when your phone is moved in a certain way.[138] The application on your phone is relatively simple, but when millions of people are using it, you can learn a lot. For instance, to understand how an earthquake shakes different kinds of buildings, it's very useful to have information from all the people who are actually in the building when the earthquake happens. Having this information doesn't mean all those people are being forced to behave in a certain way. But it is in their interest to participate in the group. Just as the golden shiners are spread across the sea floor, and just as the oneironaut phenomenon is spread across time, millions of people spread across a city can let engineers know how their buildings perform when earthquakes hit.

For example, consider a hypothetical 40-story building in San Francisco. Pretend that there are 100 people on each floor participating in MyShake. The ensemble of 4,000 people will now measure in space and time the effects of the earthquake as it propagates from the first floor to the top of the building. No one is engaged in forced groupthink. But the information is important for humanity and especially the engineers. They will engineer better buildings in the future and perhaps the oneironauts will engineer better timelines in the future.

The engineering of time could become a profession called chronoengineering ("chrono" means "time" in Greek), but it will have some remarkable challenges. As I mentioned in Chapter 5, time resembles flowing water that seems impossible to describe or control. Time has the upper hand—it describes and controls us. The engineering of time is essentially a process to understand the different flowing rivers that are available and to willfully choose which one to step in. The challenge is deciding which one to step in and how long to stay in it before a different river becomes a better choice.

Another possible problem with chronoengineering could be envisaged by analogy to bacterial resistance. The widespread use of antibiotics is known to create highly resistant strains of bacteria, essentially because we destroy the bacteria that we can destroy, and that in turn selects the resistant strains for survival. So too, if time engineering one day allows us to delete timelines that are the easiest to delete, we are then selecting other timelines which could be harder and harder to influence. As with medicine, humans who engineer time will have to work cautiously.

The Turin Dome

Developing a robust system that records dreams, disentangles the signal from the noise, and computes probabilities for future events will take a lot more work. For example, we are still in the Stone Age with respect to recording dreams. When I sketched Fomalhaut's belt, I was basically using the technology of a caveman drawing on a wall.

Fortunately, there are promising devices and methods to estimate dream content. Such advances are made possible because of one essential fact: your brain responds to information from virtual stimuli in much the same way as real stimuli. Thus, if you open your eyes and see Bubbles the goldfish in front of you, the resulting brain activity will be similar to keeping your eyes closed and imagining the sight of Bubbles. If you fall asleep and then dream of seeing poor Bubbles, again the brain activity will be similar.

These facts were only recently established through sophisticated experiments. Imagine being one of the test subjects where you were allowed to take a nap in the middle of the day. Unfortunately, the doctors would wake you up just few minutes after your brain waves revealed that you were dreaming. The doctors would then ask you to describe the mental images in those dreams. You were then permitted go back to sleep again, but the diabolical doctors would basically wake you up every six minutes—possibly up to 300 times—in order to build a dictionary of the persons, places and things that you saw in dreams. The catalog of words would then be organized into categories, such as "building," "person," or "fish." While dreaming, the doctors also recorded your brain's energy consumption (basically your blood oxygen flow) in three dimensions using a machine called an fMRI (functional magnetic resonance imaging). Therefore, your brain's activity patterns over a given time interval corresponded to the collection of words that you used to describe your memories of dreams.

Next, while fully awake, the doctors would show you images based on these word categories, and simultaneously obtain more fMRI brain maps. These real-world stimuli have a timestamp much more specific than a memory of a dream. Like fingerprints, the doctors can create instantaneous brainprints of your mind when a person, place or thing is shown to you. Going back to the brain activity recorded while you were sleeping, they could state when you were dreaming of a fish and show that your verbal report included poor little Bubbles. Thus, doctors now have the ability to let you sleep peacefully all night, record your brain activity throughout, and in the morning tell you what images you were likely dreaming about, even if *you* can't tell them what you were dreaming about.[139]

But recording dream images is only one of the cornerstones required to make the Dreamnet work. To predict the future, we also need a vast database of everything that can be experienced by humans. Let's take a look at how an early version of the Dreamnet, the protoDreamnet, might be implemented and further improved. We will revisit my Shroud of Turin experience. Here at UC Berkeley a distinguished neuroscientist called Jack Gallant has developed various techniques that translate measurements of brain activity to visual imagery.[140] Suppose that Gallant's lab has nightly access to my dreams and reconstructs the images using the procedure above. They essentially create a quantitative protoDreamnet based on a single human subject, *moi*.

One day they discover dream imagery that consists of a rich red cloth on an oblong table. None of the researchers in the Berkeley lab recognizes what this might be, but a computer has a massive collection of what everything looks like on the planet, and matches the dream image to the Shroud of Turin display 9,500 kilometers away from Berkeley. Gallant's lab quietly predicts my visit to Turin within a few years of the dream. They don't tell me anything because the experiment needs to avoid a self-fulfilling prophecy.

So all of this is going to be kept a secret from me, and I can only imagine their weekly group meeting on campus:

Gallant: OK, any good identifications this week?
Postdoc: Yes, we have a clear representation of a very red cloth lying on an oblong table. We have a 90% probability that Subject Zero may be going to Turin, Italy, to see the Shroud of Turin.
Gallant: Shroud of Turin? What does a red cloth on a table have to do with the Shroud of Turin?
Postdoc: The Shroud of Turin is rarely put on public display. It turns out that the daily display consists of a very red cloth draped over a long table.
Gallant: But during Christmas you would see red tablecloths too.
Postdoc: True, but there's little novelty in that. Subject Zero has never gone to Turin.
Gallant: How about day residue? Did Subject Zero view any red tableware in the past three months?
Postdoc: As far as we know, Subject Zero has not viewed any red tableware since the experiment began 32 months ago.

Unbeknownst to me, Gallant's lab has started calling me Subject Zero, like a rat in a maze. I hardly mind—I like the ratman role, and I designed the experiment myself. I've given the Gallant Lab access to my dreams, but I don't know what they are recording and what they think it means. Moreover, every day I wear glasses or contact lenses that record what I look at. They know everything that I look at, though I am able to turn the device off during the times that require privacy. Thus, in their conversation above, they are reasonably certain that the dream of a red tablecloth is not day residue. Despite this enormous access to my thoughts, dreams and daily life, they have no influence over me. All they can do is observe my dreams and my daily life. They see what I see, but they can't tell me what to look at and where to go.

One day, years later, they see me boarding a plane. When I look at my boarding passes, they discover that I am going to Turin, Italy. The people at Gallant's lab are immediately on their feet to see if I'm going to make it to the Duomo where I would find the red cloth, something I don't know exists. Unfortunately, as I go about my scientific business in Turin, they see me day after day watching talks about astrophysics in a university building, instead of walking around to see the tourist sites. They've snooped around a bit to download the conference program, and they wonder what I might do during my free afternoon. Certainly the Duomo is a tourist site, but so are the Egyptian Museum and the National Cinema Museum. When my free afternoon finally arrives, they suddenly witness me taking a long walk in real time, looking at my map, and entering the old church where I see the red cloth. As I experience déjà vu with the Shroud of Turin display, I tap a button on my phone to flag the experience as déjà vu.

It's 5 a.m. in California, the Gallant lab is seeing what I'm seeing in the Duomo, and they are electrified when they match the live stream video from my glasses to the dream images recorded two years in the past. The result is a true positive! But soon they encounter a false negative.

As I leave the Duomo, I walk several blocks to the southeast and enter another space. It's Turin's National Cinema Museum, and I enter a glass elevator that rises near the middle of the tall building. The walls around the elevator display a series of cinema posters lit by spotlights in the otherwise dark surroundings. I tap the button on my phone as I experience déjà vu once again.

The Gallant lab is shocked as the software scans my dream record and finds zero predictions for this novel experience:

> **Gallant**: Whoa, what happened here? Why didn't we see this coming?
> **Postdoc**: I don't know. There are no matches in the Dreamnet.
> **Student**: No, we have the dream in the records, but we thought it was a flying fantasy and we cataloged it as noise like the other flying dreams. We thought he was flying through the air, past these movie posters.

The Gallant lab is immediately humbled. They realize that their software takes into account how humans can move through two dimensions of space, but not how humans may be moved through three dimensions of space. They get right back to work planning an upgrade to their software. Not only should it have a record of what all places look like on the outside and the inside, but it should also predict the possible motion of humans through those spaces, including the vertical ascent of a glass elevator.

Decades later, Gallant has passed away, the postdoc is an aging, distinguished scientist, but the student has adapted all of this technology into wildly popular entertainment. Subject Zero has now evolved to be nine people monitored continuously through social media. They have submitted their dream records for analysis, and the entire world knows what should happen to them in the future as they go about traveling the world. Unusual obstacles and unexpected opportunities are put into each of their future timelines. You might say that the audience can view nine architectural drawings of their futures, but what is actually built will depend on how well the nine competitors can recall their dream imagery and change their behavior. Can they avoid the humiliation that results from an incorrect choice, or reach a hidden destination when multiple obstacles must be overcome? Whoever achieves the optimum timeline, creating the ultimate Bargain Universe for the show, will be declared the winner. The game is played all over the world and the winners from different countries will eventually compete against each other once every four years in the Oneironaut Olympics.

The Oneironauts of Today

THE DREAMNET DOES NOT EXIST, and there is no experiment to follow me around to measure the oneironaut phenomenon as it happens; yet it is feasible for any reader who remembers their dreams to explore the oneironaut phenomenon. Here are some tips to becoming an oneironaut:

1. Gain consciousness of dreams.

After waking, take time to think about your dreams. If nothing comes to mind, then wait longer. Do not start the daily business of turning on lights, checking messages, getting dressed, etc., for at least five minutes. Keep your eyes closed and think without purpose. Let random thoughts and images enter your consciousness. Eventually, some should relate to your night's dreams. Try to reconstruct as many of your dreams as possible. Whatever you dreamed, you now have it twice in your consciousness. The first time is when you dreamed it; the second time is when you reflected on it after waking.

2. Record your dreams.

You could keep a handwritten journal and even include sketches, or use electronic means. If all you remember is a vague thought or emotion, try recording it anyway because the act of making it real could trigger other recollections. Electronically recording dreams is the best way to enable future searches for elements of dream content. In my view, the dream recording should be viable for a human lifetime (e.g., 70 years or more). This means that the simplest forms of record keeping should be kept, which is plain text. For example, Apple, Microsoft and Google have different ways to write documents. But these companies did not exist 70 years ago and may not exist 70 years in the future. Their software may die out as well, and your dream records may be lost. However, simple text is likely to still be around. Nevertheless, if you start using something that you like, don't let my advice stop you from recording your dreams the way you want to.

3. Filter your dreams.

It'll be a busy day ahead, so who has time to write down everything? Unless you want to do some psychoanalysis, you might skip writing down dreams that have to do with unresolved life conflicts, traumatic events, fears, anxieties, etc. For example, if you dream that you are in a vehicle with family or friends, then that probably refers to some problem-solving reflection concerning the course of your life. Instead of writing this down, try to focus your recording on surprising images in your dreams, or words spoken to you by other people. However, if you prefer the unfiltered route, recording your dreams can serve as an interesting personal diary. The exact person driving the car probably has a significant meaning. Years later you will be surprised about the things that captured your attention in your dreams, things that you had forgotten about.

4. Have new experiences in as many new places as possible.

The obvious way to accomplish this is to travel to locations that you've never been to before. The more difficult task is experiencing novel locations in the place you live in for most of the year. In a city, you might try walking into a different public building once a week. You might be mindful of observing boundaries, moving between rooms and focusing attention on objects you have never seen before. Visit the bathroom, even if it's not really needed. The bathroom is a quiet place where you can review your new experiences and compare them to old memories.

One method that works in parts of the United States is to enter homes that are being shown by real estate agents. This does not require the presence of your own real estate agent. A particularly powerful form of real estate viewing is if the home has not been professionally staged, but instead contains the possessions of the occupant. Staged homes have a generic quality, but real occupants may have things that are peculiar and become focal points for your attention. Thus, both the space you sense and the things you see will have maximum novelty.

5. Practice a present, slow and open mind.

When you practice Step 4, you should enter novel spaces and attempt to be present, slow and open. As a guide, let's revisit the garden mentioned in Chapter 5. At first it seems to be just a garden with plants, dirt, etc. Stay there looking and listening (present), and keep looking and listening without a concern for time (slow), and not searching for anything or expecting something (open). Just as in sleep, you should let go of your intentions. There will be a transition where you become aware of the insects that are right there in front of you, moving about in the garden. You may become aware of odors and sounds that were always there, but you only became aware of them at that moment. Your consciousness or awareness is now located in the garden. So too, in novel situations, the déjà vu experience will more likely come to your attention if you are present, slow and open. Of course, there are at least ten other ways to describe this state of mind that may be more helpful to you. You might even prefer the words of Bruce Lee: "If you try to remember you will lose. Empty your mind. Be formless, shapeless, like water."[141]

6. If you do not have real-time déjà vu, then make sure that over the next 24 hours you have some quiet time for self-reflection.

With Steps 4 and 5 you may experience real-time déjà vu. If not, then Step 6 is to think back to those spaces and those experiences over the next 24 hours to figure out if you remember them from past dreams. Hopefully you will have enough moments to let your mind wander for this recollection to happen. Thinking back should be like a virtual Step 5—review the past as if you are present in that time, not in a rush and with an open mind. Just as in Step 5, you should not have a conscious goal of having the déjà vu experience.

7. Write down your déjà vu experiences and search for a match in your dream log.

When you have real-time or 24-hour déjà vu, record your experiences in writing, include photos if possible, and then search for a counterpart in your dream records. Specify exactly what part of the experience was previously dreamed, how vague or unique the various elements are, and how long ago you had the dream. If you wish, you can categorize the déjà vu event under the characteristics that I listed in Chapter 5. You might want to take note of your mental and physical state at the time of déjà vu. In addition, engage in some critical thinking on whether or not alternate explanations are possible, such as cryptomnesia discussed in Chapter 2. Could the experience of déjà vu have something to do with a similar waking experience in the past that you simply forgot about?

8. Consider practicing Steps 1–7 with family and friends.

This is something that I haven't done, but it should be both helpful and entertaining to share these experiences with others. When you review your dreams with other people, they may ask you questions or make unexpected comments that trigger even better recall (Step 1). Recording dreams is quite a chore, but if you make it a type of competition or have a buddy system then you are more likely to get it done (Step 2). Often, the psychological aspect of dreams is invisible to our minds, but another person can tell you that the dreams you just had are related to current and past experiences and anxieties (Step 3). Remember that day residue is the replay of recent events in your dreams, but it's very difficult to see the connections. A friend might be more objective. Friends and family can also suggest going to places that you may never have thought of going to and this will increase the novelty for you (Step 4). For example, every weekend it could be a different person's task to choose a novel place to visit. Many people have rapid or scattered thoughts, but in the presence of someone who is calmer they may calm down too (Step 5). Reviewing your previous day is also a chore and having a buddy or group can help you stick to the routine (Step 6). If your déjà vu experiences are immediately shared with others, they may respond with questions or comments that will help you describe your déjà vu more accurately and more completely (Step 7). Moreover, friends can help each other in searching dream logs for matches to déjà vu experiences—someone else might actually be better at it than you are for your own dream log. In addition, it would be extremely interesting to discover that both you and your buddy had the same specific déjà vu experience, and possibly the same dream, if you are going to places together. Finally, children and teenagers may be excellent at having déjà vu experiences, but they would need parental help in going to new locations, recording dreams, accurately writing down déjà vu experiences, etc. In the end, small groups of family and friends could play the game against each other. For example, each team could describe the contents of a new home they will enter, and then points are gained and lost depending on what is really found in the home. Local champions could compete nationally, and those winners are sent onward to the Oneironaut Olympics.

Of course, you may never find friends and family willing to do all of these things, which means that a profession would arise of paid individuals who are not necessarily oneironauts, but they are skilled and committed to doing Steps 1-8 for customers. Thus "The Oneironauts of Today" will rapidly evolve into something different tomorrow.

IAPO—The Oneironauts of Tomorrow

GIVEN THAT MANY PEOPLE WOULD RATHER HAVE A "PROFESSIONAL" HELP THEM with the déjà vu experience, the *International Association of Professional Oneironauts* (IAPO) will eventually form. IAPO will consist of different branches that serve specific purposes. One branch will help people in the daily experiences of the oneironaut phenomenon. Basically, these professionals are a form of personal therapist or advisor to help individuals benefit from the phenomenon or realize their potential as an oneironaut. Let's call this the LO Branch (Local Oneironauts).

The second branch consists of specialized oneironauts, some of whom are also in the first branch. These oneironauts have a broader role serving society and government, accelerating knowledge and averting disasters. We may as well call this the GO Branch (Global Oneironauts).

While the LO and GO branches are involved in the practice or the art of the oneironauts, a third branch is needed that oversees Research, Education and Funding for the Oneironauts, and hence we have the REFO branch. This branch may secure private and public funds for education and research in all aspects of the sciences and arts. In the U.S. they would be tasked to oversee relations with universities, industry and governmental entities such as the National Institutes of Health.

A fourth branch is needed to monitor and develop Law and Ethics for the Oneironauts—the LEO branch. As I will discuss later, we should not underestimate the necessity of having this fourth branch. The reputation and authority of the other three branches, as perceived by individuals, governments and other oneironaut organizations, will depend on the excellence of the LEO branch.

The senior leadership from all four branches will consult with each other, essentially governing the activities and plans for IAPO. The governance and implementation of the Dreamnet and the Metamindnet will be one of their major duties.

A fifth branch will be added later—the MO branch (Machine Oneironauts). This will include various forms of artificial intelligence that have the abilities, responsibilities and decisions that none of the other four branches can master.

Of course, IAPO doesn't exist yet, but something like it is probable on Earth. In the next sections I will describe how these branches may function.

The Local Oneironauts

THE LO BRANCH CONCERNS THE DAY-TO-DAY LIVES OF PEOPLE, in the absence of major problems like wars and natural catastrophes. This is the stuff that never makes the news and will not show up in history books.

For many people, the oneironaut experience would involve a service, hobby, game or social network.[142] Recall that in the Heidelberg Dome, the game for me was to find my group as they chose a novel place to sit down for dinner. My success was measured not only by the final result of actually finding them, but also in how little outside information I had, and even how cheaply I arrived at the goal.

In the future, I could subscribe to a personalized service that advises me on daily decisions, similar to what an online map does for me today when I want to travel to unfamiliar places. The service would have access to the Dreamnet and at the same time have access to my daily calendar. As I depart for Heidelberg, I would get a message listing the several things that may occur on the trip. The software would have a description of all places on the planet, and then correlate my dream content to the places that I could be going to. It might produce a list of possible experiences I will have in Heidelberg, possibly updating the probabilities of each experience actually occurring as more information is fed into the software in real time.

For example, since I arrived late in Heidelberg and time was of the essence, instead of searching for my colleagues at Hemingway's, the software would already know what Hemingway's looks like outdoors, understand the poor match to my dream content, and tell me there is only 1% chance that I will sit there for dinner. Basically, I don't need to waste any time checking it out.

However, the software would find Semann's for me, and provide a direct walking path from my hotel. Maybe it would tell me the probability of finding my colleagues there is 65%. It would not be 100% because the dream content it picks could be a scene from a completely different trip to Heidelberg farther in the future, or even a different city that merely resembles Heidelberg. Moreover, the software would become aware of the restaurant maps that are provided by the conference organizers. It would expect that the other restaurants have a higher probability for attendance by the conference goers.

The slightly creepy part here is that before I even get to Heidelberg, the software is also telling me which choices other people are going to make in their future. That is to say, unbeknownst to my fellow astronomers, their future is predicted to various degrees of certainty by the content of my dreams and all the factual information that the software can access. The creepy aspect is that I have become a counterfactual or *many-worlds voyeur*. If I choose not to leave my hotel room to go to dinner, I would remember my dinner with them, but in my timeline they would not know that I had a dinner with them (unless they were also oneironauts). I saw them at dinner, but they did not see me.

You may think that this sort of one-way, hidden observation is science fiction, but variations of this bizarre scenario can already take place in the context of marketing and shopping. For example, imagine that when I enter the Ikea store nearest my home in the United States, Ikea could be tracking my motion through the store via the signal from my cellular phone, understanding that I linger at the lighting section, and calculating a 65% probability that I would like to buy a lamp. Unbeknownst to me, if I were to enter the Ikea store near Heidelberg in the future, Ikea could detect my presence again, and then predict how I would walk through their German store and what my interests are likely to be. As I enter the German Ikea, a coupon is given to me for their one-day lamp sale. I ascribe this wonderful match to my shopping intentions as incredibly good fortune, and the fact that the Swedes are Pareto efficient. But if I really knew how the coupon appeared before me in Heidelberg—that in the past they tracked my steps 9,000 km away—I'd be really creeped out about it.

Nevertheless, the local oneironaut software would develop a library of how an individual would experience space and time in the future. Since no person is an island, the software would also predict where other people would be located because they are associated with me. My astronomy colleagues may feel somewhat creeped out that a computer program I use would know where they would eat on a beautiful summer evening in the majestic city of Heidelberg.

An even more powerful scenario is if the entire group, such as my colleagues or a family, participate in the Dreamnet and group analysis is performed. Various tools would help you explore the possible outcomes that your future holds. For example, one day you may ask whether or not your landlord is going to renew your lease. The software can scan the portion of the Dreamnet that includes your friends and family, and basically figure out if in *their* dreams they see *you* in a new home. But what if your friends start dreaming of you in a hospital with a cast around your leg, or worse?

Doctor, did you administer the ocode?

With added organization, the osignal could be boosted for things that matter a lot, such as being in a hospital. Instead of their plain vanilla appearance, areas of a hospital and individual rooms could have unique identifiers that serve as the ocode. For example, if your loved one is in the hospital for breast cancer, those rooms could have a unique style filled with novel imagery that would be seen in dreams. Of course, if the imagery was widely publicized, the dream content might concern the worry of being in such a room yourself, or for a loved one. But if those items in a hospital room have unique identifiers that are not public, and the Dreamnet has this information in its database, it would tell you when your dreams start producing the imagery that locates you in that hospital room.

The coordination and expertise to administer and interpret the ocode for ordinary people will be the job of the LO branch. The LO branch will need to work closely with the public, professionals and organizations to make such a system work. Members of the LO branch might be the medical doctors who are general practitioners and who maintain and evaluate your dream database as part of your medical record. Considerable expertise could be needed to disentangle the dream images that are from your past from those that could be from the future. The oneironaut warning that you will become a hospital patient may in fact be a message from your LO doctor, not from a software package. The LO doctor could hold the secret ocodes to the various possible health issues and would "administer the ocode" in order to send the oneironaut signal back in time to you. You might call this *chronotherapy* because the doctor is now manipulating a health timeline.

For example, say that in a future time you have a stroke that paralyzes you, and this triggers a chronotherapy visit to your LO doctor. The visit is scheduled in an office that you've never been to before—the space has to be novel. In the reception area, a young girl wearing a red dress is crying, but you don't know why. You go to the bathroom and you see two toilets side by side. You pause at this puzzling situation where you have to decide which one is to be used. After waiting a bit more, you enter a small office where your doctor presents a video of a polar bear jumping from a haycart to a sixteen-wheeler. All of these experiences in the doctor's office are in fact staged to grab your attention. In chronotherapy they are a unique ocode for "stroke," as opposed to something else, like "leukemia."

In the present time, your doctor "receives the ocode" from the future. Your dream imagery has presented a bizarre story where you are searching to find a toilet, but you find two instead of one, and then you see a girl in a red dress crying because a truck ran into her polar bear. Bringing you in for a checkup, the doctor may be puzzled that the Dreamnet triggered a stroke alarm given that you seem to be in perfect health. All of this makes you skeptical and grumpy: "Oh, this oneironaut stuff doesn't work with me. I've never felt better, just a bit of a toothache, which is hardly a stroke, Doc!" In a moment of insight, the LO doctor perceives the possibility of a bacterial heart infection resulting from future dental work that you were thinking about but hadn't even scheduled yet. You end up receiving antibiotics before the dental work, and the bacteria that would have caused the stroke never have a chance to do so. You might have a dream of being paralyzed, searching for answers behind a closet door, but that universe is one that you will not have to live. Ironically, you keep telling everyone that the oneironaut stuff doesn't work on you, yet you were a superb oneironaut and had a counterfactual stroke.

In a different universe, you never mentioned the toothache. The doctor simply provided a powerful "clot buster" to take with you as an emergency medication. Two years later the stroke happens in the middle of a five-hour flight to New York City, but by immediately taking the medication, you do not suffer paralysis. Your tune might now be different: "Gee, I guess this oneironaut stuff does work on me after all."

The spectrum of problems that humans can encounter is not limited to health issues. The LO branch might include, for example, priests and lawyers too. Should the doctor, priest and lawyer work together? Not necessarily. Each may have their own unique way to communicate the ocode that builds on their individual creativity. The doctor may prefer novel visual cues, whereas the priest may prefer to tell peculiar stories. The lawyer's stories are all extremely boring, but he or she may have a passion for clothes.

Did you just dream of meeting a person wearing a white suit that has a bizarre black stripe along the right sleeve, but not on the left sleeve? This is the suit your lawyer wears when visiting prisoners—you are in jail.

Last night, did you dream about a woman with a large gold nose ring wearing a red suit and a white bow tie, and then you walked into a room only to see someone dressed as a camel, sitting alone at a table, trying to eat spaghetti? The former is what your auto accident lawyer has decided to wear for the ocode, and the latter is the ocode administered by a doctor after a limb has been amputated. Either signal may have come through as a bizarre dream that you might attribute to psychological factors, yet the elements combined suggest that a horrible auto accident awaits you.

The profession of a local oneironaut may be to stop by your home, explain what has been detected in the Dreamnet, and counsel you on a plan to avoid this future. Over many years a local oneironaut may have dealt with similar cases and can give advice on a reasonable response to the osignal—is it to stop automobile travel altogether, or is there a more moderate course to follow?

With these examples we begin to perceive the broad impact the oneironaut phenomenon may have in society, and the purpose of the LEO branch slowly emerges out of the fog. In the example about the car accident, is this information also shared with insurance companies? Will your car insurance be dropped just because you had that dream with the spaghetti-eating camel and the nose-ring woman with the white bow tie? When you have your day in court on a criminal matter, will your lawyer tell you that your defense will be unsuccessful because of the white suit, black stripe dream? In future court cases, judges and juries may put the dream record on equal footing with the testimony of eyewitnesses. It is possible that events will be more accurately retrieved from the dreams of a person who is asleep than the memory recall of a person who is awake? *The sleeping person cannot lie.*

Omoney, owar and olove

In addition to personal applications, the LO branch could also serve in many more professional contexts. The hospital room scenario could just as well be a unique room where executives meet if a company has failed or succeeded. That would be an interesting situation indeed. The board of directors, if they want to keep their jobs, would have to submit their dream logs so that the corporate version of a Dreamnet can scan the business future shared among these individuals. The same idea could permeate other high-stakes endeavors that seek power, profit and fame, such as politics, entertainment and sports.

Soldiers, police and firefighters are some of the vital groups that would also benefit from the oneironaut phenomenon. In the case of military missions, for example, would it be possible to predict which will fail by correlating which soldiers are experiencing a similar osignal? If you keep four soldiers together on every mission, and you detect strong osignals for trauma, this would be unhelpful because one could not say if the trauma will take place on their mission tomorrow or in one year. Instead, mission memberships could be scrambled in order to more accurately predict which future mission is at greatest risk. For example, among the thousands of soldiers available, only soldiers J, X, W and B will be together on a mission set for the first week of July next year. At no other time will they be in the field together. A military Dreamnet could discover that the dreams of J, X, W and B contain a very similar trauma, and then this early July mission could be adjusted to avoid such harm. Needless to say, on top of protecting J, X, W and B from danger, the military Dreamnet would have a tremendous tactical role.

I am not an expert on war tactics, but I can offer my naïve perspective. One of my competition sports is foil fencing where one can meet an opponent that you've never seen before and you have to quickly assess the situation and choose a tactic against them. One day I faced such a new opponent and someone else who knew the both of us told me that I would quickly suffer a humiliating defeat. As luck would have it, I chose a counterattack that I had recently learned, and lo and behold this surprised her and I won. I would go on to lose 100% of my future bouts with her because of her vastly superior skills, but the element of surprise and apparent luck awarded me the first victory. This experience led me to ask if the great military generals in history were just lucky? If you had many identical generals and a random variety of possible tactics assigned to each, would you end up creating a few great generals after a random series of battles, even though each general was intrinsically equal to the other?

This question can be quantitatively tested, but my best guess is that great generals secure victory through preparation, an unwavering execution of their skills, and an intuition that could draw from the oneironaut phenomenon. All three combine together for a victory, but it can look like luck to the outside world. My discovery of Fomalhaut's planetary system was a product of this combination. I was prepared to find Fomalhaut, I applied my skills when they were needed, and I drew from an intuition that arose from precognitive knowledge. To many other astronomers it appeared that I was just lucky. Thus I would hesitate to call any great general just lucky. If wars are to continue in the future, militaries will always need to maximize their preparation and skill. However, the great militaries will be those that also master the third component that converts war to an owar.

And as surely as the birds and some of the bees will exist in the future, what might await us humans when dating services start using the oneironaut phenomenon? When one participant starts inputting dream content that closely matches the dream content of another participant, perhaps because in the future they will be together in a very specific place, then for a tidy sum of money the service will tell you who that other person happens to be. Could the odating service eventually lead to an increase in the number of couples who stay together longer and happier?

Instead of odating, perhaps the Dreamnet will simply provide information about future fun places to be and those to avoid. I can imagine a contact lens connected to the Dreamnet that creates an augmented reality by tagging locations as you view them in real time. As you scan a selection of bars and restaurants, it will identify those that have the future timeline that you seek (old friends, new friends, etc.), and tell you to avoid the places where dreams reveal unpleasant experiences (a rude waiter, a fight, food poisoning, etc.).

All of this could exist without any significant new understanding of the oneironaut phenomenon, or any incredibly difficult breakthrough in medicine or technology. We are already uploading huge quantities of our personal information into the cloud. Why not add our dreams?

Odating aside, the oneironaut experience adds new perspectives and dilemmas concerning the enigmatic phenomenon of falling in love. Is it possible that oneironauts fall in love because of the future they will experience with the person rather than the past? In that future state of being in love, an entire history of events leads up to that point; e.g., usually one needs to actually talk to the other person on several occasions and vice versa. But if you jump to that future state through dreaming, then it's possible to fall in love even before the moment you meet that person in your timeline. There is a world where you had to experience all the steps of falling in love, but if you have a memory from the future about that person, then the timeline you experience will contain love at first sight.

Yet, it takes two to tango. That other person who doesn't dream about the future has *not* experienced the steps that lead to mutual love; they have no idea who you will become to them. This definitely counts as a classic oneironaut dilemma—how should the oneironaut behave in a time-appropriate manner? Some oneironaut behaviors could be self-defeating, preventing that timeline in the dream from emerging. Those memories of a counterfactual love will then have to exist quietly in the oneironaut's mind.

Research, Education and Funding for the Oneironauts

EVEN THOUGH THIS CHAPTER STARTED by saying we should get straight to work in using the oneironaut phenomenon as if preparing a recipe book, understanding how the phenomenon operates is still of fundamental importance. Moreover, human curiosity to figure things out cannot be stayed. Cutting-edge research on the oneironaut phenomenon can be conducted across industry and academia. However, basic research requires funding, and therefore I've joined research, education and funding into the REFO branch. The job of this branch is to pay for and coordinate research and education programs related to the oneironaut phenomenon.

The time observatory

The future efforts of the REFO branch may have parallels to present-day, large-scale efforts to understanding the human mind. I once heard the prominent neuroscientist Christof Koch give a talk where he listed the following problems with current brain research:

- There are some 86 billion neurons in the human brain, but we can only study 1,000 simultaneously, and maybe 10,000 in the near future.

- It is not obvious what many experiments are actually looking for.

- Even the types of cells in the brain are puzzling. The human cortex has 1,000 different kinds that form very many groupings.

- There are no commonly accepted measures of brain phenomena, whereas astronomers adopt the same standards no matter where they work in this world.

- There are some 10,000 neuroscience labs with different questions, methods, protocols and standards, "heading off exuberantly in all directions."

- Universities are not set up for large-scale, systematic efforts.

I was surprised that Dr. Koch heaped praise on the astronomers during his talk. In fact, he lauded the astronomical observatory as one of the best ways to conduct science. The reason is that modern observational astronomers, such as myself, first try to define the scientific questions that are most crucial and feasible to solve. Then we present competing ideas to our peers, the ideas are weighed against each other, and finally those that are deemed most important are used to justify the design of an observatory. The observatory belongs to no one person, but every person is allowed to propose experiments that are feasible with the observatory. A third grader could literally propose to use the Hubble Space Telescope. The scientific impact of an observatory can be huge over decades of time because so many different investigators are bringing their projects to the observatory and the resulting data are publicly archived.

Neuroscientists, on the other hand, create fiefdoms, not observatories. The principal investigator or university professor runs the fief, also called a "lab." Each fief lord and/or lady decrees what science will happen in the fiefdom, what equipment or methods to develop, and whether or not they'd like to work with other fiefs, if only they could understand each other. Christof Koch seemed to be saying that feudalism has to stop in neuroscience, given that a successful alternative is available, what he called the "Observatories of the Mind."[143] To understand the brain is as difficult a problem as determining the origin and evolution of the universe. Therefore, just as astronomers design enormous facilities with cutting-edge technologies, neuroscientists should be creating the same grand tools for the study of the brain.

Given my claim that the brain is an observatory of time, every effort to create an observatory of the brain is a step toward observing the future. Here are some of the projects taking these steps for humankind:

- The Allen Institute for Brain Science[144] was funded by Paul Allen, the co-founder of Microsoft, and directed by Christof Koch, who wanted to create a "mindscope" as an analogy to a telescope. A key project is to map the connections between 16 billion neurons comprising the brain's cortex.

- The BRAIN Initiative is a U.S. government effort, sometimes compared to the Apollo Program for human space exploration.[145] It cuts across private industry, the public sector and academia to fund research and encourage collaboration.

- The Human Brain Project is the European version of the BRAIN Initiative. Echoing the words of Koch, the founding document states, "We find that the major obstacle that hinders our understanding of the brain is the fragmentation of brain research and the data it produces."[146] This *Magna Carta cerebrum* thereby demands an end to the fiefdoms that dominate European neuroscience research.

All of this is extremely exciting, but it's important to remember that a century from now our epoch of neuroscience will be viewed as a late medieval period stumbling toward a Renaissance. The REFO branch is going to be a part of that Renaissance.

First live pictures from the future

After the Renaissance, human history proceeded through industrialization and modernity. What should happen with the oneironaut phenomenon for us to mark the beginning of a modern era?

I can only answer this by analogy to the first human steps on the Moon. The Apollo 11 landing must have been awe-inspiring to experience in real time, but now that the film clips have been replayed many times, it's easy to think that it was no big deal. But the one thing that continues to impress me in those first television images is the tag line at the bottom of the screen. We typically see a fuzzy black-and-white video of astronaut Neil Armstrong stepping down on the Moon's surface from the *Eagle* lander on July 21, 1969. What impresses me is the tag line, "First live pictures from the Moon." The end game of all that technology and human risk was to have a television tag line that said, "First live pictures from a place that no human had ever explored in person."

In my view, there will also be a day when we see a fuzzy image, and the tag line will read, "First live pictures from the future." When that is the tag line, I will know that we have crossed from the Renaissance of brain science into a modern era of unimaginable human evolution. This would be the true giant leap for humankind.

Fourteen (at least) questions for experimentation

Whoa, hold your horses Nostradaomus, aren't you getting way ahead of yourself? The oneironaut phenomenon is not a subject of research for neuroscience or physics. It has no fief, not even a cave. What experiments might be possible to determine if it even merits a cave or a fief? What questions should we explore over the near term? Here are some ideas:

1. *Can present-day experiments provide further evidence that precognition is possible through dreams?* Basically, I am asking if others can replicate what I have shown for Fomalhaut.[147] I have already offered many clues and examples, such as the Poultry Matrix, on how to pursue this goal experimentally. Recording dreams and having novel experiences indoors are just some of the critical elements. Since the dream-to-event interval can be a few years or more, longitudinal studies that track volunteers for a good fraction of their lifetimes are most likely needed. More generally, what are useful measures of precognition (e.g., mathematical vs. qualitative approaches)? For example, can we devise a reliable grading system to characterize how uniquely a dream matches a future experience? We might take some cues from forensic science (e.g., fingerprints and individualization) that will be mentioned later.

2. *What are the exact properties of the oneironaut phenomenon?* These characteristics include the age of onset, the duration, location and sensory modalities of the experience, how the time interval between the dream and the future events correlates to other characteristics such as the nature of the event, the physical and mental states of the human subjects, the neural correlates, the common denominators, etc. With a larger sample one could investigate why an experience might trigger déjà vu for a particular person and not another. Research could test the relative merits of my proposed reinforcing and compensating theories discussed in Chapter 5. One could probe whether or not the oneironaut phenomenon is inherited, and if it a simple trait (due to one gene), a polygenic trait (due to many different genes), or a multifactorial trait (due to many genes and the environment). It would be interesting to have twin studies to explore how genetic and environmental factors are related to the phenomenon.

3. *Since the oneironaut phenomenon is based on the memory of dreams, are there new methods to significantly enhance both memory and dreaming in humans?* I mentioned that flushing working memory by physically moving to new locations could aid in associating recent experiences with memories of dreams. Is that true? Among the many other possibilities, one that made news headlines is that a blood transfusion from a young mouse to an old mouse improves memory in the old mouse.[148] Can you show a similar effect for humans, and what

would be the Draculanian consequences for a future society that values the oneironaut phenomenon? Does the oneironaut phenomenon occur during the immediate process of memory encoding, or do you need memory consolidation (i.e., to sleep after an event is experienced)? Can the methods discovered for controlling REM sleep in mice be used to promote REM sleep in humans?[149] Also, as mentioned in Chapter 5, is it possible that a resting heart rate that is close to that of slow wave sleep (60 beats per minute) influences the processes involved in the oneironaut phenomenon? Some neuroscientists such as Adam Gazzaley believe that the perception of rhythm impacts brain function in waking subjects, which means that my question about sleeping subjects could be relevant.

4. Which waking brain states contribute most to the phenomenon, and can people train to spend more time in these states? The goal is to develop a more predictable and controllable phenomenon. Practice drills or games can be developed to improve the efficiency of the oneironaut experience. For example, video games played under experimental conditions are now known to improve the human ability to multitask.[150] In testing the oneironaut phenomenon, such games should incorporate spatial location cues along with novel visual, auditory and cognitive stimuli. Certain medications may also assist in achieving such mental states. Is it possible that physical fitness is important? Farther in the future, can we design neuroprosthetics to modulate the oneironaut phenomenon in our brain? How about unique cues such as music? Everybody knows how music can be associated with very specific events. If music is a strong stimulus for recalling the past, could it be used to strengthen the signal from the future?

5. Given that real-time recordings of the déjà vu phenomenon should be possible under experimental conditions, what are the neural correlates, and do they differ substantially from other types of experiences? Here I imagine that human subjects can wear portable neural monitors that upload biometric data via cellular networks as they go about their daily business and during sleep. Since I have déjà vu experiences while watching TV and wearing virtual reality headsets, real-time recordings of déjà vu can also be studied under controlled experimental conditions. The person can flag the moments of time where they experience real-time or 24-hour déjà vu, and the neural recordings can be subsequently examined. The power here is that a collection of, say, 1,000 such recordings may show activity in the brain that is unique to the oneironaut experience. For example, we already know that certain brain regions and even single neurons respond to novel stimuli in a way that is very distinct from familiar stimuli.[151] Does the déjà vu experience resemble either of these response patterns, or some third category of response? Is it possible to show that the brain reacts to certain unpredictable and unique events before such events take place?

Chapter 7 introduced several more neural correlates that could be tested. Do human grid cells expand and become disorganized in novel environments, and is this response dependent on complexity or déjà vu? Does this neural grid exist while navigating virtual worlds during dreaming? Is our sense of spacetime learned, or is it a fixed ability defined by cells like those that control vision or hearing? What determines the sense of time when we are both awake and asleep? I will also reiterate that most of what we know derives from animals, and more work is needed to test these findings with human subjects. As the end of Chapter 7 highlighted, many findings in neuroscience do not generalize across all mammals.

6. *How does the successful detection of future information scale with the number of people involved in a Dreamnet?* We can postulate that a single person has an erratic way of occasionally predicting the future. What we want is a consistent recipe for routinely predicting the future. In my case, I've experienced the déjà vu phenomenon for about thirty years and made roughly three actionable predictions (the Trifid Poster, Heidelberg dinner, and Fomalhaut discovery). This amounts to one success for every ten years of life. If another person joins me in having shared experiences and we both record our dreams, will that success rate improve by a factor of two (one actionable prediction every five years), or by a factor of ten (one actionable prediction every year), or not at all? How about if ten people work together?

The sheer numbers may not be as important as finding elegant ways to augment the experience. A very good oneironaut may need just a single partner who provides critical pieces of help. The partner may be someone who helps the oneironaut relax and mind-wander (even a certain kind of pet animal might work), or they could have a more comprehensive role. Imagine that the real-time recording of dream imagery becomes possible one day, yet as the oneironaut experiences future events, his or her attention is distracted by emotions, cognitive puzzles and decision-making. Instead of recruiting more oneironauts, perhaps the best strategy is to add a person who interprets what the oneironaut experiences. While the oneironaut's brain is creating the virtual imagery from the future, another expert could navigate through the virtual imagery, paying attention to details that exist in the oneironaut's imagery, but which the oneironaut cannot pay attention to. Thus there are two attention systems devoted to the experience of future information in real time. The primary attention system is that of the oneironaut who is generating or hosting the experiences. The secondary attention system is another person (or team) observing the imagery produced by the oneironaut, possibly intervening through sensory cues, and possibly monitoring the brain function of the oneironaut and manipulating it, such as by applying electric and magnetic fields (neurostimulation).

This all sounds a bit bizarre, yet we already have present-day examples of how this could work. Consider the invention of *neural entertainment* when Grateful Dead drummer Mickey Hart put on a virtual reality headset and an EEG skullcap to measure his brainwaves in real time as he played a video game in front of an audience. One large screen showed the audience Mickey Hart's virtual game world that included his interactions with human skeletons and asteroids. A second screen mapped his brain's changing electrical activity. A second person on stage wore a different virtual reality headset that allowed him to navigate through the colorful model of Mickey Hart's brain and its real-time neurological activity. In other words, the second person traveled inside Mickey Hart's virtual brain, navigating to any part they wished to observe more closely—the audience viewed this brain exploration on the second large screen. Thus, there is one person immersed in a world, a second person immersed in the brain of the person immersed in a world, and a group of people observing both for entertainment.[152]

Using this as a template, hardware and software could translate the real-time brain activity of a dreaming oneironaut into a virtual 3D audiovisual world. A second person or team of people wearing virtual reality headsets could be immersed in this person's dreams and, when some portion of a future world appears, explore and record it with a greater attention to the details that are not necessarily the focal points of the dreamer. A third person or team could track the dreamer's sleep state and monitor the dreamer's virtual brain in order to tune its activity via sensory cues and neurostimulation (electrical and magnetic stimulation of the brain has been attempted as a therapy for over a century, and may help individuals overcome major problems such as depression).

7. *What are the most effective ocodes to translate primitive egocentric sensory information to sophisticated allocentric knowledge?* Some of the general categories for developing the ocode could include visual scenes, stories, puzzles, text, art, audio and human interaction.

Which of these have the greatest capacity to convey information and which allow for added redundancy? For example, when using a visual cue, such as the white owl mentioned earlier, is it really true that color is precisely preserved from waking experience, to dream imagery, to the recollection of a dream? We wouldn't want to use the color white for the ocode if it is sometimes recalled as yellow in a dream, thereby miscommunicating information. Perhaps red is a color that is more reliable. The ocode development would have to consider how individuals vary as well. Perhaps color is highly dependent on individual variations compared to some other types of ocode. Thus the oneironaut code may not be as rigid and generalized as some other codes we use, such as musical notation. Mozart could translate sound to musical notation, and 250 years later I can convert that notation back to what he wanted me to hear fairly precisely. The oneironaut code, on the other hand, may be tailored to each individual, as if we each have different versions of musical notation.

8. *Are there biological entities much simpler than the brain of intelligent life, such as plants or bacteria, which can perceive future events?* Reacting to the environment is a universal property of living things, and the oneironaut phenomenon seems to have a function of problem solving in the environment, at least for humans. But what about other species? One could ask if the oneironaut trait is the product of *convergent evolution,* or if it is restricted to mammals because of *divergent evolution.* In convergent evolution, different species independently develop a useful trait. For example, insects and birds both have wings to fly without having a common evolutionary ancestor. Alternately, in divergent evolution, only mammals have developed the type of central nervous system that may be necessary for the oneironaut phenomenon.

The motivation for testing this question is that simple organisms have useful properties that are not present in other species. Simple organisms can possibly survive centuries and relay their interaction with the environment across longer time periods than more complex organisms. Simple organisms also enable experiments that easily employ millions of test subjects, giving statistical power to the results. They may also have relatively straightforward cause and effect pathways and high sensitivity to specific events in their environment, such as small changes in temperature or chemistry.

Chapter 4 mentioned experiments with *Gallus gallus domesticus*, but now let's take an even simpler organism that is very likely somewhere close to you—the jumping spider, or saltie (*Salticidae* or *"dancer"*). Most would call this a small spider, Aristotle would call this a "brute," but others call it "...intelligent, expressive, interactive, and downright adorable...."[153] Salties have excellent visual ability, better than a cat,[154] which is needed because, like cats, they hunt for food instead of waiting to trap prey in a spider's web. Salties can be cheaply acquired (i.e., go outside and get them) and their 3D spatial navigation can be tested in mazes, just as with Tolman's rats. They can visually scan a complex maze with two different routes leading to two different mini-bowls, only one of which has food visible. Then they will choose the correct maze path to get to the food.[155] In the oneironaut version of this experiment, the prey could be hidden. What could be made visible is a novel, random visual cue associated with food in the experiment, but there is no prior learning that could help the spider know that the cue signifies the existence of prey in the bowl. The future event of eating the prey near the visual cue would be due to the oneironaut phenomenon, if something primitive like a spider's brain can perceive future information. Any spider, though, is a complex organism, and later in the chapter I will consider much smaller and simpler species as probes for the oneironaut phenomenon.

9. *Is there a physics experiment that can detect a signal from the future, or at least have a result consistent with the possibility that the future influences the present?* Chapter 6 already mentioned that quantum entanglement is one phenomenon that doesn't seem to care about rules concerning space and time. Another class of experiments could probe reverse causality: an event that will happen in the future has a detectable signal now. Or, when quantum computing becomes more advanced, will unexpected results arise that could be explained within the framework of the oneironaut phenomenon? Somewhere in the world a very good physics lab will find a way to test the oneironaut phenomenon, or will do so serendipitously.

10. *How do you test for the existence of many worlds?* With the Trifid Nebula poster dream I mentioned that if more oneironauts were in the room who independently perceived a change in timelines, we could establish a consensus that multiple universes exist. Can we really implement such an experiment using many human subjects?

11. *I speculated that dreaming can promote healing as we naturally seek out worlds that contain healthy versions of ourselves, but is this confirmed empirically?* The experiment would involve correlating dream qualities (fraction per night, content, etc.) to the recovery timescales of

patients. If you find ways to induce more dreaming, will you shorten the recovery timescale?

12. *The science of epigenetics concerns the expression of traits due to environmental factors (even though DNA stays the same), but can the perception of future environments also have an effect on gene expression?* For example, a stressful experience has physiological consequences, the biochemistry of the brain changes, certain genes may then express differently than before, and this can cause depression.[156] If the dreaming mind is genuinely encoding experiences from future events, does this cause traits to be expressed differently relative to subjects who do not experience the oneironaut phenomenon? Can the future that you will experience or counterfactual events trigger depression? Flipping the questions around, what triggers in the present environment could cause the expression of traits needed for the oneironaut experience?

13. *If we were to discover the oneironaut process in human cells, could we introduce it into other organisms that are perhaps more sensitive to the environment in order to detect small or specific changes to the environment that a human oneironaut would not be able to detect?* Transgenic organisms, such as mice, are already quite common. Their DNA has been modified by introducing foreign genes. It could be that the "primitive oneironauts" may not exist naturally, but could be created. Perhaps a genetically modified organism could be further modified through nanobionics to be exactly sensitive to specific environmental changes. Nanobionics involves inserting nano-scale devices (a nanometer is one billionth of a meter) into the organism. For example, researchers have constructed nanotubes that are absorbed by the leaves of plants, and these nanotubes glow if the groundwater used by the plant is contaminated.[157] Thus you could have a genetically modified plant that is sensitive to the future through the oneironaut gene (if it exists) and at the same time have a specific sensitivity to dangerous chemicals. Plants that are destined to glow in the future because of contamination undetectable by humans would warn us today via the oneironaut phenomenon. Obviously this is looking forward to the far future, at which point the oneironaut phenomenon may not even need biological cells. It could be that machinery, an oneironaut switch, possibly as small as a nanotube, would detect the future signal.

14. *After oneironauts die, what does their brain physiology reveal about the phenomenon, if anything?* Is it true that a totally normal brain can perceive the oneironaut phenomenon, or is there a detectable

difference in its physiology? Of particular interest would be twin studies mentioned earlier. If there are peculiar characteristics in an oneironaut's brain, can these be engineered in future synthetic humans or human tissue? Was there a physiological "cost" for experiencing the oneironaut phenomenon? For example, if the oneironaut phenomenon really functions to *decrease* entropy (disorder) for the individual, then it may be necessary to *increase* entropy elsewhere, perhaps in other cognitive abilities.[158] If so, then maybe individuals and groups in a species have already reached a natural Pareto front that can only be expanded through technological means.

The Global Oneironauts

THE GO BRANCH SERVES A VARIETY OF BROADER PURPOSES, organized under specialized subgroups. One subgroup might act as the litmus paper for significant disasters wherever they occur in our future world. A different GO subgroup may not be concerned with disasters per se, but focuses instead on obtaining general knowledge that exists in the future. Some global oneironauts will concentrate their efforts on obtaining information from beyond their own lifetimes, perhaps a thousand years from now.

Second responder, virtual responder, or counterfactual responder?

The oneironauts of the GO Branch may have to go to the sites of the worst catastrophes that happen on this planet. They will visit the places where life has been harmed by the violence of earthquakes, weather, fires, wars and accidents. I believe that they need to arrive at these places late as second responders. The reason is that arriving immediately as a first responder would be too stressful, and stress can diminish the transtime osignal and harm the oneironaut over the long run. Moreover, the disaster site has to be explored by the first responders in order to devise a plan for administering the ocode. As mentioned in the section concerning the Dreamnet, the location, nature and date of the disaster somehow have to be communicated through symbols and environments that are both simple and novel to the oneironaut. For example, assuming an earthquake disaster, an oneironaut might want to speak with a distinctive survivor inside a unique room only found in that town or city. Perhaps the room should be staged with forms of artwork or a flag that would identify the country. The dream images and what the oneironaut hears will encode the date and location of the disaster.

Of course the oneironaut cannot prevent the earthquake, but the loss of life might be avoided. Thus, the oneironaut and the rest of the world will experience a timeline where no one was killed. In this engineered timeline, the oneironaut no longer needs to go to the site because he or she has become a *counterfactual responder*. They would have gone to the site if people had been killed. In the new timeline, the oneironauts have counterfactual memories of what would have happened in terms of lives lost for a given event.

Practically speaking, no new technology or method such as the Dreamnet is needed for a basic disaster detection role of the oneironauts. Currently, any individual or team of oneironauts could make it their mission to visit all the places where disasters happen in the future. Using the clues in this book, they can seek the type of novel experiences at the disaster sites that will be identifiable as elements of their dreams right now. However, note that I used the phrase "disaster detection" instead of "disaster prevention." Given no new technology or method, we could probably show that some disaster elements are *detected* in the dream record *after* the disaster happens, but the information would not have sufficient quality to *prevent* the loss of life from the disaster.

Note also that in the near future the oneironauts may not have to actually travel to disaster sites. Instead, the first responders could bring virtual reality (VR) recording gear and go to hundreds of places and talk to hundreds of people. A team of *oneironaut producers* (oproducers) could then selectively edit all of this footage. Finally, the oneironauts would put on the VR headsets to have a sequence of experiences that the oproducers believe will optimize the transtime signal with an ocode that maximizes the accuracy of information.

The VR experience may not be as powerful as entering those spaces in person, but the advantage of the method could lie in the sheer number of participants. Instead of 10 oneironauts going to a disaster site, a VR experience could be administered to 10,000 participants. These 10,000 people will be receiving the same ocode from the future so that even if 90% fail to have or recollect the oneironaut dream, this still means that the dreams of 1,000 individuals will contain elements of the ocode which could then be used to reconstruct the future location and time of the disaster.

The good news is that I have already tested this and it works. In November 2016 I experienced an Oculus Rift VR game for the first time. The hardware includes a headset that dominates your vision and hearing, and game controllers held in each hand. The game was supposed to be about wizards, but surprisingly the space shown was a dark city alley. This surprise was a cognitive puzzle with definite déjà vu—aren't wizards supposed to be in castles instead of modern alleyways? No matter which direction I turned my head, the brick walls, the distant scenes, the ground, etc., were all portrayed seamlessly. I had déjà vu of holding fireballs in my hand and throwing them at three large snakes that appeared at the other end of the alley. Even though I did not move into this space, or move within this space, the sense of this space was powerful enough for the oneironaut signal.

A key problem is creating a VR experience that evokes genuine empathy in the oneironaut. Mark Zuckerberg famously used VR to "teleport" himself and Facebook employee Rachel Franklin to Puerto Rico after Hurricane Maria had devastated it. Amazingly, neither person was able to assign attention to what they were experiencing. Instead they giggled and even high-fived each other in a virtual environment where flooding had ruined people's lives.[159] Nevertheless, given how many people use Facebook, it demonstrates that a huge community could be involved in the VR experience of disaster zones rather than just an expert group of oneironauts. With large numbers it won't matter if some are unable to immerse themselves in the experience.

Having said that, it is also true that the oproducers could be successful by targeting individual oneironauts. For example, on January 1, 2013, I had this dream:

> ...a young girl has recently had her leg below the knee amputated (resembles [my niece] in looks) but she insists on running a marathon.

Just four months later two bombs would take the lives and limbs of innocent athletes and spectators at the Boston Marathon. I remembered the dream and searched the news reports for the woman who looked like my niece—a young Caucasian woman with light brown hair and, most importantly, pensive eyes. Indeed, if there's one thing you need to match a person from their birth to their old age it is a clear picture of their eyes, the window to their soul. Despite my search, I found no matches in images published by the media. Then on January 14, 2018, I saw the film "Patriots Day" that reconstructs these terrible events. An actress called Rachel Brosnahan would play the role of Jessica Kensky, who had her legs amputated below the knee as a result of her injuries. Brosnahan had the pensive eyes that I remembered from my dream—as soon as I saw her a few minutes into the film I knew her character would have the amputation. What I needed for déjà vu was NOT the real person, but the actress who was cast to dramatize that role, to make it personal for me, and who happened to remind me of someone I would recognize. Thus, the art of the oproducer could be to know what the oneironaut knows, open a window to their soul, and prepare a narrative that will maximize the chances of transmitting the ocode.

Thus I truly believe that a production team could go to the site of the next major earthquake and create a VR experience for a large group of test subjects or a select set of individuals who are committed to recording their dreams over a period of years. The nice thing is the ability to manipulate the footage. Therefore, if the recording of the scene shows something emotionally distracting, such as mutilated bodies, this can be digitally deleted. Meanwhile, certain elements can be digitally added in order to communicate the ocode. Turning the corner past the rubble of a building brought down by an earthquake, you encounter a white owl next to a samurai eating sushi with chopsticks, and the owl whispers in his ear: "March to Fukushima."

Counterfactual knowledge

Earlier I noted that the discovery of new knowledge, particularly in medicine, can be accelerated using the oneironaut phenomenon. I'm an astronomer, not a doctor, so I'll mention a few things that the oneironauts can accomplish with space exploration.

People always ask me if I believe life exists elsewhere in the universe. Of the thousands of known extrasolar planets and 200 billion stars in the Milky Way, there has to be life out there, correct? My answer is kind of boring—scientists have not detected extraterrestrial life and therefore the answer is "we don't know" instead of yes or no. This means that we should keep trying to answer the question through observations. For example, we can build powerful telescopes that can directly image Earth analogs around other stars, or travel to Mars and try to find evidence for life.

One ambitious project for imaging Earth-like planets involves a space telescope that stares at various nearby stars, but a separate spacecraft called a starshade will artificially eclipse each star. If you imagine that your eye is a telescope, during the day you can look at the sky near the Sun as long as you hold out your hand to block the Sun. So too this starshade would be located roughly 50,000 km away from a space telescope to block the light from a star and reveal the much fainter Earth-like planet next to it.

The problem is that pointing from one star to the next requires roughly a month for the starshade to fly through space, using valuable propellant, in order to block each star. Thus if we do not know which star has that inhabited Earth-like planet, the entire mission will take many years to survey a selection of stars. Eventually that inhabited Earth around another star may be found. However, the global oneironauts could send this tiny bit of crucial information—the name of the star—to the present day so that the entire starshade mission spends five years studying this historic discovery instead of five years searching for it.

In the case of Mars, the question becomes where do we land exactly? In the future, humans may have to explore 20 different places before the fossil evidence for life is found. Twenty missions could take a century. With the oneironaut phenomenon, we could choose the correct landing site on the first attempt and thus take a decade instead.

In the far future, the entire mission at the correct landing site could be counterfactual. That is to say, since the scientific objective of the mission is solved before the mission is executed, why should taxpayers approve funds to determine something that is counterfactually known? Logically the mission would be cancelled, and in the Bargain Universe no astronauts or machines would go to Mars. Science books would now contain facts about the universe provided by the minds of the oneironauts. Eventually, the oneironauts would know everything that was within the capacity of humans to know in a lifetime. Knowledge arrives to them from activities that they had the potential to do.

After a generation passes, no new technologies would have been developed for space missions, because they were cancelled. The next generation of humans is now at a disadvantage because even though they possess facts about Mars, they have lost their potential to do something more advanced than what the previous generation had the potential to do. So if you rely exclusively on counterfactual knowledge, then there must be decay in what you can know. In order to avoid this decay, the missions will have to be executed even though it is known in advance what will be found.

Oneironaut timeshot

The Apollo 11 Moon landing represented human astronauts going on a moonshot to obtain information from a distant world. If we want information from the distant future, then the oneironauts may need to go on a timeshot.

I don't know if this will really become possible for humans, but I know that some organisms are naturally capable of cryptobiosis. In other words, living things can be frozen, dried out, or otherwise put in a state of apparent death, and then they can recover all functions in the future. For example, the eight-legged "water bear" (tardigrade) is about a millimeter in length, has a brain, and has been observed to recover after exposure to extreme conditions, such as 10 days in space.[160]

Do not panic! This eight-legged micro-animal that can survive the vacuum of space is not an indestructible jumping spider. Instead, it looks like a children's book version of a caterpillar with eight pudgy legs and a pudgy, segmented body.

In one study, Japanese scientists collected a sample of moss from Antarctica in 1983 and then thawed it in 2014.[161] They found two water bears still alive that they named Sleeping Beauty 1 and Sleeping Beauty 2. Sleeping Beauty 2 died, but Sleeping Beauty 1 was pregnant. At this point I must confess that I am not making this stuff up. Long story short, a family of water bears arose from ancestors who had spent 30 years in deep freeze.

For humans, we have the classic science fiction concept of artificial cryptobiosis or suspended animation. Astronauts are put in capsules, their metabolism is lowered, they wake up decades later, for some reason they must vomit, and then they have to look out a window to see that they've arrived at their destination. If in real life we really, really needed to solve cryptobiosis for humans, it doesn't seem like a huge stretch of the scientific imagination to believe that we can eventually achieve some aspects of it. Doctors already employ induced hypothermia (a.k.a. targeted temperature management) as a method for saving lives.

Instead of sending astronauts across empty space, oneironauts would stay in one place and travel across time. This is the oneironaut timeshot. For example, let's say in the year 2030 I'm nearing the end of my life, and so I say, "What the heck, gotta make people happy, put me in the timeshot capsule." Maybe I have nine others who are also great oneironauts and they join me. The ten of us are sent on a 50-year timeshot. In the year 2080, future humans are ready to wake us up and administer the ocodes. Between now and the year 2030, my dream content will contain the information I get in 2080, and for as long as I live after that. The ten oneironauts are administered the same future ocode, and we eventually pull together some basic facts about the year 2080 from our collective dream content.

But some oneironauts are daredevils, and in the year 2030 they go on a 100-year timeshot. Others sign up for 150, 200, 250, and even 1,000-year timeshots. Analyzing this collection of dreams from hundreds of oneironauts up until the timeshot launch in 2030, we can try to understand a continuous human history 1,000 years in the future.

Of course, now you encounter another creepy aspect of many worlds and counterfactual information. When the year 2030 comes around, and the oneironauts are ready to enter the capsules, do they have to get in? After all, the goal of the mission has been accomplished—the information from the future has been experienced by us and everyone around us in our timeline. So why get in the capsules if the mission is finished? Artificial cryptobiosis must be a potential successful capability for a future action, but there is a timeline where we do not have to get into the capsules. This seems to defy all logic, but it is the fundamental lesson taught in the Trifid poster dream, the Heidelberg Dome, and with Fomalhaut. The information from 2080 has been perceived, the capsules that we have developed makes all of this possible, but we do not have to live the timeline where we get into the capsules.

As you can see, the global oneironauts who choose to take part in the timeshots will have quite a big decision ahead of them. Is there something more important to live through by not going into the capsule, or is there a sense that waking up in 2080 will be a better experience? In 2080 you may find most of your friends and family already dead. If you wondered why I supposed that ten oneironauts would go on each timeshot, there were at least two good reasons. First, if more people participate in a shared experience, this increases the potential of correctly perceiving and interpreting the ocodes across time. Second, this group of ten will need each other to re-create a continuous family that is otherwise destroyed by leaping through time by 50 years or more. In fact, like the families who departed by ship or by wagon to cross great distances to settle in new lands with no expectation of return, there could be families in the future who get into the capsules, determined to settle forward in time. They are the *time settlers*.

Settlers schmettlers, let's vaporize this quaint mental picture. If any type of timeshot is invented, the oneironauts will be paid generously to get in the capsule, because knowledge produces the Bargain Universe. Timeshots will follow the money.

For example, imagine that a pharmaceutical giant is pursuing three research lines to identify an important drug therapy. They will pay you one million dollars for access to your dreams over three years, but the deal is that you will get into a capsule at the end of three years for a 15-year timeshot. When you wake up in the future, you will get two million dollars, if you work with them for six months as they administer the ocodes. The ocodes give the critical information about which of the three research lines, or none at all, produce the wonder drug. The stakes are potentially very high. If the new drug comes to market normally along a similar timeline as the competition, say over the next 10 years, the profit potential might be 100 million dollars. But if information from the future selects the correct research line and all resources are pooled into one effort, then the drug comes to market many years before the competition, and the profit potential becomes ten billion dollars. It's a bargain for them to pay you a few million dollars, and from the perspective of many people, going to sleep for 15 years isn't out of the question if you'll be made a millionaire in return. *Would you do it?*

Identity and purpose in the timeshot dilemma

Like a moth returning to the light, the discussion above illuminates a characteristic of identity and purpose. Neither is fully realized by counterfactual experience.

Recall that I asked if you would get into the timeshot capsule given that the mission is already accomplished. I think the answer is that if you want your identity and purpose to be a timeshot oneironaut, your decision would be to get in the capsule.

This perspective was brought to light one day as I was swimming in the neighborhood pool. The pool is part of an aquatic center where the U.S. Synchronized Swimming athletes train. One of the athletes was swimming laps in the lane next to me, and in a short break at the wall I asked her if she was heading for the 2016 Olympics in Rio de Janeiro. She answered that she was the alternate for the duet team, and that she might or might not compete in Rio. I said, "Good luck," and then Captain Clock compelled me to push off the wall to continue my workout.

However, the conversation was not over. In my mind, I considered the wisdom of saying, "Good luck, if you've had dreams of competing in Rio, then there is a future world where you are." Would this young woman really be satisfied with a counterfactual experience of becoming an Olympian? Let's say she really has those oneironaut dreams, but in the end she never boards a flight to Rio. A small part of her has the identity of being an Olympic competitor, but it does not materialize in her timeline. Her purpose, to compete in the Olympics, is vaguely fulfilled by her memories of the dream, but not in waking experience. I'm pretty sure that if the coaches gave her a chance to compete, then she is definitely *not* going to say, "I'm not interested, my goal has already been accomplished, I am a counterfactual Olympian, and that's all I need to know."

Thus I think that if the counterfactual experience is desired, because it fulfills a part of your identity and your purpose, you will attempt to experience it. This is exemplified in my story of the Heidelberg Dome. If the counterfactual experience is not congruent with your identity and purpose, then you will decide to avoid the experience of that timeline, as shown in the Trifid Nebula chapter.

When encountering the timeshot dilemma, your decision will have to endure a swirling mass of uncertainty and potential regret, but at the end of the day you just have to decide what you want your identity and purpose to be.

Global extinction

There have been six mass extinctions in the history of Earth that we know about. Each lasts many thousands of years, so in fact during a human lifetime of 75 years you could be right in the middle of an extinction, but you might not even notice it. The sixth great extinction is called the Holocene extinction, which is currently in progress. In order to find out if the Holocene mass extinction will destroy our species, we need oneironauts that will observe the world for 10,000 years or more. At any time during the Holocene, an asteroid impact on Earth could shorten the extinction timescale and expand its scope significantly.

How do you get an oneironaut to provide information from 10,000 years in the future? From the section above, you could organize a relay of timeshots, each sending a single signal 100 years into the past. Hence, the relay needs 100 back-to-back timeshots to cover 10,000 years.

The timeshot method will seem crude after future generations discover the physical origin of the oneironaut mechanism in the brain. Once that mechanism is discovered, devices that can send and receive the signal over thousands of years can take the place of humans. Such a device, placed within a protected mountaintop, would have sensors at the Earth's surface and would continuously measure the properties of our climate. As it receives data from the future, we would get an indication of what lies ahead. I'm not sure how accurate the information would be, but its design would be sufficient to detect the most extreme problems, which are the ones that are the most difficult to respond to, and which we want the greatest lead time to deal with.

An example of such thinking and engineering involves the preservation of seeds. The Svalbard Global Seed Vault lies deep within a sandstone mountain of a remote Norwegian island, and it has enough capacity to hold 1.5 million samples of seeds. The facility is over 100 meters above sea level, which should protect it from rising oceans and tsunamis. Currently it requires a power station to freeze the seeds to -18 °C, but the surrounding permafrost would keep the vault frozen even if artificial refrigeration were not available. The 10,000-year oneironaut device would not necessarily require freezing, but it would require similar long-term stability and protection.

Primitive oneironauts

One of the experiments proposed for the REFO branch involved testing simple organisms for signs of the oneironaut phenomenon. Individual cells do computations. A single bacterium looks at its environment and responds to it. Even molecular interactions are essentially a computation to respond to a stimulus. But who cares what these primitive biological elements can do?

I think they may be important because the simplest things are sometimes those that survive the longest. Above, we considered a water bear that survived 30 years in a frozen state. But that's not even close to a world record. In 2014, French scientists presented their research on a virus that was at least 30,000 years old, and when it was thawed, it had no problems doing its job of killing amoebae.[162]

Now suppose that the oneironaut phenomenon operates via molecular interactions. Does this mean that the virus could transmit information about its current environment back to itself more than 30,000 years ago? In other words, the virus from 30,000 years ago would perceive that it would be thawed out of the permafrost, eat some amoebae, and do this in an atmosphere that is quite different, as if carbon dioxide has mysteriously doubled in an unnatural way. Alternately, could we freeze many virus cells and send them on timeshots lasting 10,000 years and more? By studying them right now, before we freeze them, could we derive some basic information about Earth's environment tens of millennia in the future?

If primitive organisms are really capable of the oneironaut phenomenon, and if we find ways to extract this information, then the applications are rather interesting. Consider that limestone-producing bacteria can be mixed in with concrete. Like yeast, the water bear, and the fearsome virus, these bacteria can be dormant for 200 years if they are not exposed to water, which includes water vapor in the atmosphere. Thus when a building made with this concrete has a crack, the bacteria are awakened and start producing limestone as a response to the water vapor.[163]

In the classical application, the purpose of putting the bacteria in concrete is for small cracks to be self-repaired. In the oneironaut application, one can imagine that a building can be scanned to find out which parts of the building will fail in the future because the bacteria will be awakened. If the entire building lights up, then we could predict that in the future the entire building will be destroyed. Working with other lines of evidence from human oneironauts, one could determine if this destruction occurs at the end of the expected lifetime of such a building, or unexpectedly early because of war and disaster.

If the oneironaut mechanism really exists in such primitive organisms, and we can find ways to extract transtime information, much could be learned about future events.

Earth's counterfactual history

Museums are one of those things that seem to be the bedrock of human society. You might go to them when you're young, then again fifty years later, because the museums will still be there. You might even wager that if you could return in 1,000 years, they will still be there. Art museums are for displaying art, science museums show you science, and natural history museums tell you everything about the planet. You wouldn't think that you could create any new category of museum, but if you do, that signals a major change in the evolutionary history of humans. For example, if in the future you have a museum of aliens, then that means we've collected enough information about life on Mars, Europa and extrasolar worlds that we need a new category of museum concerning non-terrestrial species.

That museum does not exist yet, but a new type of museum has come into existence in Pittsburgh, Pennsylvania called the *Center for PostNatural History*. This museum signals the fact that humans are now capable of creating new organisms that did not evolve naturally, and would not evolve naturally, except for the influence of humans. For example, genetically engineered livestock serve as "biofactories" because they produce new substances in their milk that are needed for pharmaceuticals.

With the oneironauts providing information about future events, some of which will change the timelines of human history, I can imagine a new type of museum called the *Museum of Counterfactual History*.

For example, if the events of 9/11 had been deleted from our timeline due to the oneironauts, we would still have information about what was supposed to have happened—the counterfactual history. You can imagine an exhibit hall that shows the images and concepts described by the oneironauts. Computer graphics could recreate the visual scenes of the two towers billowing black smoke huge distances downwind, the Pentagon damaged on one side, and a blackened pit near Shanksville, Pennsylvania, caused by the crash of United Airlines Flight

93. Other parts of the exhibit would go further into the future, trying to disentangle the various aftermaths that were possible after these tragic events.

Note that this isn't an exercise in science fiction. The sources of information for the museum are the dream records of the oneironauts. Everything shown in the exhibit is a representation of a counterfactual event.

"This is a bunch of baloney," some readers might say. "Any information from the future is so vague and incomplete that you cannot create a historical record of parallel timelines that would be anything but science fiction." My reply is that all of the museums representing the history of humanity contain exhibits based on vague fragments of information. All museums are part illusion. For example, museums may represent dinosaurs with skin like a hippopotamus, but what hues were really possible, and how about the question of feathers? Never mind extinct animals. How about the things that we should know a lot more about, but we don't, such as human history from a mere 2,500 years ago?

I recall talking to a gentleman who had developed software that created a virtual reality tour of the Parthenon in Athens, as it would have appeared before it was partially destroyed by weathering, earthquakes, the Turks, Italians and British. I noticed that the surfaces of stone everywhere were depicted as white, and I asked him why. His answer was that no one could agree on whether or not the Parthenon had been painted, and if so, what color it was. Thus, in the interests of not becoming the tall poppy, everything was white.

Human history is a white canvas upon which historians paint their beholder's share, and upon which readers add a second layer of interpretation. Thus, when you visit a museum of natural history or human history, what you see, read and hear is reconstructed and re-interpreted in ways that are roughly the same as the new museum of counterfactual history. What museums really do is create models of our past worlds. *With the oneironauts we can create models of our counterfactual worlds.*

The psychology of the oneironauts

Thus far we have discussed how the oneironaut mechanism might influence people in their everyday lives, and how groups of Global Oneironauts may be employed throughout their lifetimes to achieve important goals. However, are there consequences for being an oneironaut? Is it possible that a very good oneironaut will suffer more than they will benefit? Let's take a look at some of these potential effects:

Lacking concern and risky behaviors: In my mind, I don't foresee any terrible personal disasters coming up. Therefore I am relatively calm and optimistic about the future. When I get on a plane, I'm not expecting any drama such as a hijacking. When I get on the highway, I'm pretty sure everything will be OK. The oneironaut can therefore appear inappropriately unflappable and lacking concern when the normal response should involve disquieting emotions. The accusation could therefore be that the oneironaut does not care about what happens to others and such criticism can be difficult to handle.

Similarly, overconfidence can lead to risky behaviors that harm the oneironaut. Perhaps I should be taking more precautions? As I write this, I am planning a trip to Iran to speak at an astronomy meeting. One hundred percent of my colleagues in the U.S. have told me that they would not go. Indeed, the U.S. State Department website cautions that there's a chance of being unexpectedly detained and imprisoned in Iran. However, my oneironaut brain has no memories of spending time in a jail cell, of meeting cellmates or jailers, or anything of the sort. Of course, my trip could be cancelled altogether, but I am planning to go, confident that I would know right now if I were going to spend a lot of time in an Iranian prison. This overconfidence could be viewed as unnecessary risk-taking, and indeed the oneironauts as a group may have statistically higher injury or death rates than the general population. As it turned out for this particular story, the meeting was cancelled, I never made it to Iran, and perhaps this explains my lack of initial concern.

Fulfillment vs. depression: You could say that an oneironaut has a superpower. In comic books a human gets special powers by accidents in science experiments, genetic mutations and alien factors. Having a superpower can be quite an esteem booster. Hey look, I can tell you the location of the next devastating hurricane. A sense of fulfillment and joy can arise by dwelling smugly on one's superpower. The potential to make the world a better place seems limitless, like a dream.

But the reality check can be a powerful slap in the face. The oneironaut superpower can backfire emotionally when the outcomes go horribly wrong. It's as if Superman occasionally kills people accidentally while flying too fast. But it's actually something more. The superpower of a single oneironaut is inherently faulty. It's as if Superman would really like to fly quickly to save someone, but all he's got is a rather long hopping skill. Ultimately, disasters occur right in front of Superman because he arrives too late. He returns home emotionally devastated because he has failed to achieve his potential for full flight, and people died as a result. Oneironauts may experience overwhelming depression and self-hate when a major accident occurs, and they missed it. The earthquake that kills 100,000 people. The airplane crash. It hurts badly knowing that you could have foreseen these things, but you see them too late, right in front of you, just as they are happening in real time. Was I too late to save Jessica Kensky's legs at the Boston Marathon bombing? How about Krystle Campbell, Lu Lingzi, Sean Collier, Dennis Simmonds and eight-year old Martin Richard who all perished there? Was I too late? An oneironaut may accept responsibility, and guilt, for such deaths and other bad things that occur. And if they don't accept responsibility, it may be foisted upon them anyway, even in the form of ridicule.

Burnout: Burnout from experiencing disasters is a very tangible concern. For example, in the Sandy Hook Elementary School shooting, the people who were there saw dead children. An oneironaut could have been there in person, or could have experienced the massacre through the accounts of surviving children and adults, but both the direct and indirect interactions could have a profound effect on the oneironaut.

I've already seen one example of this effect with the anthropologist Jared Diamond, whom I quoted earlier as saying that biological function is strengthened through experience. In 1997, Professor Diamond wrote a very interesting and popular book called *Guns, Germs and Steel: The Fates of Human Societies*.[164] Many years later he hosted a series of television documentaries based on his book. In Episode 3 he visits a hospital ward in Africa where up to seven babies and children die of malaria every day. As he interviews Dr. Christine Manyando and looks at the sick children, he suddenly lifts both of his hands to cover his face, breaking down in tears. The screen goes dark for five seconds, and then returns to the pensive professor who says: "There's a difference between understanding something intellectually and experiencing it firsthand."[165]

This tells me that there is a *huge* difference between being an armchair oneironaut, *c'est moi*, and going out into the field to witness life-and-death reality in person. If Professor Diamond was not profoundly harmed by what he witnessed that day, I wonder if he could keep witnessing such things day after day, year after year. You might say that clearly there are staff in hospitals that must witness these things every day. Yet these are the few people who have been naturally selected to have some resilience.[166] What you don't see is the much larger population that have burned out from such hospital duties, or who wouldn't even attempt to do such a job.

Another aspect of burnout is that if you witness the first traumatic event as an oneironaut, memories of the event may drown out your ability to continue having new oneironaut experiences. Essentially, the oneironaut may be haunted by dreams of the traumatic experience. Any new dreams of important future events could be overwhelmed by the extremely powerful memories of the past. The oneironaut burnout could last for a lifetime, or at least for a significant period of time.

If burnout is a real phenomenon, many more oneironauts might be required to predict tragic future events than you would otherwise expect. One remedy could be to rotate oneironauts into tours of duty lasting one year and staggered by, say, five years. For example, the first tour could be at age 25. During this single year the oneironaut would experience disasters, absorbing the ocodes that he or she will dream about in prior years. During the four subsequent years, ages 26–30, the oneironaut would be calming their mind and dreaming. Then again for 12 months after their 30th birthday they are out in the field again.

This staggered oneironaut schedule could also be very helpful for pinning down the year of a future event. With many oneironauts on a staggered schedule, the month could be pinpointed too. For instance, if Sally is going to world disasters between January 1 and December 31 in the year 2059, whereas George goes to disasters between July 1, 2059 and June 30, 2060, and both dream a common ocode from the same future disaster, then we know the disaster is likely from July 1 to December 31, 2059. If you had very many more oneironauts, the date could be pinpointed even more precisely.

To summarize, solving the problem of burnout and the problem of predicting a precise date for a future event may require that hundreds of global oneironauts are put on a staggered schedule of service.

Obsession, addiction and confusion: Notice the possibility of a downward spiral for an oneironaut. It's as if Superman starts spending all of his time hopping with the hope of flight, and forgets that he has other roles to play in this world. Oneironauts could become obsessed or addicted to the dream world, hoping to be "The One" who predicts a major disaster. If an obsession or addiction to the dream world begins to interfere with healthy functioning in the waking world, the oneironaut would probably fall under several clinical definitions of mental illness. Among other things, the oneironaut may become genuinely, constantly, and pathologically confused between the present real world experienced in waking life, the imagined dream world, and the future real world experienced in dreams. *The Great Ambiguity is madness if the future becomes your instant.* Some oneironauts might believe that they communicate with God, when in fact this is simply their dream world populated by desires and fantasies. Such an oneironaut may indeed make certain accurate predictions about future events and then begin to believe that they are a god, thus propelling their identity into disarray.

Social isolation and the Midas touch: People may wish to avoid the oneironauts or the oneironauts may choose to avoid people given that the oneironaut phenomenon adds a new layer of complexity in every social interaction. For instance, thoroughly recording both nightly dreams and waking life is like wearing a personal recording device at all times. Other people may become highly cautious, even fearful, of how they behave in front of an oneironaut because they do not want to be recorded, and in the end they just play it safe and stay away from them. People may dislike the voyeuristic aspect of the oneironauts—the invasion of privacy for the future. Another aspect is that people may come to believe that the oneironauts somehow perturb or read their minds and therefore oneironauts should be avoided at all costs.

The converse—the Midas touch—may also happen. Oneironauts may begin avoiding people if they start believing the oneironaut phenomenon is somehow harmful or uncontrollable. King Midas certainly did not expect that his wish of turning everything to gold would cause harm and become a curse instead of a wonderful gift. Perhaps some oneironauts will shun social relationships because they would rather not face the ethical responsibilities and dilemmas of knowing what will happen to another person in the future. The oneironaut may even develop *thrallphobia*, a word that I invented to indicate "the fear of having control over someone else's mind." (It could also refer to a non-oneironaut who fears having their mind controlled.) Or, some oneironauts may become socially isolated because they dislike interactions where others could be taking advantage of them, as if the oneironauts are lottery winners and everyone else wants a piece of their prize. Being an oneironaut will come with a lot of baggage that could ultimately turn some inward.

Health: Over the long term, does the oneironaut experience have positive or negative physical effects on the brain and a person's lifespan? If my mind is operating at the Pareto front—the zero-sum game—then for me to gain information about the future may have a cost. What would that be? I speculated earlier in the book that dreaming of healthy timelines might play some role in recovering from traumatic head injuries. Yet if a global oneironaut has made a career of experiencing different worlds simultaneously, would that eventually wreck their mind, as sometimes depicted in science fiction?[167] Discovering such an effect would require the study of many individuals over their lifetimes. Eventually, we could test for correlations between the oneironaut phenomenon and physical health.

The Machine Oneironauts

THE LO AND GO BRANCHES OF IAPO ARE PEOPLE HELPING PEOPLE with the oneironaut experience, but this will trend toward the machines helping everyone with the oneironaut phenomenon. At first, computers will be needed as tools for the LO and GO branches, but there are quite a few reasons the machines would eventually have their own MO branch.

First, the machines are needed and irreplaceable for storing and processing huge quantities of data. For example, the U.S. Library of Congress has 38 million books put there by humans over a 200-year timespan, but a project called the Internet Archive collects 38 million web pages every 6.3 hours.[168] The purpose of the Internet Archive is to catalog all publicly available digital information. One of their tools is called the "Wayback Machine," which can search through the entire history of the World Wide Web—nearly 500 billion web pages as of this writing. If in the future several billion people participated in some form of nightly dream recording, the scale of the Dreamnet would be too enormous for humans to govern, but clearly feasible for the machines. Humans might consult with the Dreamnet's "Wayforward Machine" to help make their decisions, a modern-day Oracle that is not human.

Second, dreams are highly personal, at times hugely embarrassing or disturbing, and communicating with a machine might feel safer than telling it to a human. This phenomenon has already been discovered in Google searches, where people type questions or phrases that they would never write or say out loud to another human. Two data scientists have called the Google search a "modern day confessional box."[169] I think they are correct, and this means that the Dreamnet might succeed only if it appears to consist of a non-judgmental machine ready to absorb anything you'd like to say to it. The machines may one day have unthinkable access to you as a person, which may have a net benefit to humanity.

For example, consider what might happen if you say something like, "I want to kill my baby." Is this a statement of exasperation, or is this a statement of intention? If you say this to a human with limited information about you as a person, they may have to assume the worst—it is your intention to kill your baby. But if you say it to a machine, and this machine has been recording your thoughts and your dreams since you were young, it may judge your statement based on a deep reservoir of evidence. For some humans, the machine may know that they simply talk like that every now and then, but never behave according to what they say in those times. For other humans, the machine may detect a deepening emotional and cognitive crisis based on an ensemble of what the humans say and what they dream. With this enormous pool of records, the machine may identify the humans who develop the intention to actually kill their baby. An intervention can then be devised in order to avoid such a tragic event.

No doubt this fictional example is unsettling, but even if you do not believe in the oneironauts, some version of the story is already taking shape. For example, there are pacemakers that are connected to the Internet. Walking, running and cycling apps keep track of individuals and groups of people. Human bodies are already being wired to machine systems, creating a way of life called the "quantified self."

Initially, I think that humans will easily understand how the machines operate in their tasks of weeding through dream content and making matches to future events. But as the programming becomes more sophisticated, a day will come when the machines are computing the right answers, but we will cease to understand how the computers do it. And just as we now have the academic disciplines of studying foreign languages and literature, the day will arrive when humans will need to devise methods to study and understand the output of artificial intelligence.

This may seem to describe a future world many decades from now, yet this future has already arrived. For example, in 2016 a machine program called AlphaGo beat the world's top player, Lee Sedol, at the game of Go. Many were surprised that a machine could beat a human in this ancient and complex game, but a greater surprise is that it's not exactly clear *how* the machine accomplished the victory. At a critical play by AlphaGo in one of the games, the European champion of Go, Fan Hui, observed: "I've never seen a human play this move. So beautiful."[170] The game that emerged from the machine seemed to be greater than the sum of its parts. So too it's possible that the vast majority of people interested in the oneironaut phenomenon will start trusting machines instead of other humans in managing their future.

Finally, when the physical basis for the phenomenon becomes known, the Dreamnet will no longer be the only way to detect future events. Instead, humans and machines could engineer the organic and non-organic sensors that detect the future, and a pure machine oneironaut would no longer depend on humans. The machine oneironauts may start using the phenomenon for their own interests. In parallel, humans will also reach new levels of sophistication, and the machines may never truly understand how we achieve certain things.

The irrational path to Beverly Hills

I think that many of us already trust the machines more than ourselves or other humans. For example, one day after visiting Disneyland south of Los Angeles, I wanted to drive northward to Beverly Hills. The Los Angeles area is so large and spread out that this little trip would take sixty minutes of driving a complex path on many different freeways. As a tourist I would resort to Google Maps to calculate the fastest route, but there was one problem. The calculated route, my future automobile path, had personal semantic meaning from prior learning. I was told to take "the 405," the motorway that in my brain is synonymous with "misery and pain." I had been stuck on the 405 during other visits to Los Angeles. It seemed absurd and irrational to follow what the machine was telling me to do. Yet the computer objectively calculated that I should take the 405 that day. No matter how "street smart" I thought I was from my prior experiences driving through L.A., the cold calculation was that the 405 was the path of least travel time. As an oneironaut, I knew that in the future I would be asking a machine to give me advice on even bigger choices for my future. I would have to trust the computer in the same way that I trusted my oneironaut instinct in Heidelberg. So, I put my money where my mouth is and took the irrational path on the 405 for the next 60 minutes of my life. After all this mental debate, did I get stuck in traffic? It was indeed slow on the 405, but not the death by GPS that I had feared. The semantic meanings from prior learning simply were not helpful. Going by a different route probably would have been slower.

Of course, Google Maps could not absolutely guarantee that this would work because in the first 30 minutes of travel something could change and the 405 would turn into the blistering hell that it's famous for. Instead, Google Maps would take the available information and calculate an instantaneous route to satisfy my goals. So too the oneironaut computer would do its best in helping you live in a future Bargain Universe, but the paths it will recommend are no better than "probably the best" paths.

Ride over

Modern automobile travel demonstrates many of the ideas that are being presented in this chapter. For example, the hive mind already exists in how we each contribute a map of real-time traffic and parking spaces through data gathered by automobiles and cellular device connections. I don't mind if my cellular signal provides a map of local traffic to others because I am benefiting from the data that many others are providing as well. I don't mind if my car scans the street for available parking spaces that someone else is looking for, because one day I will need the same information provided by others. In modern networks we benefit occasionally and contribute continuously.

In the far future, machine oneironauts will produce events that are unheard of today. For example, one rainy afternoon you might summon an autonomous car to pick you up, and as you enter it will scan your face and recognize you. You could just say, "Take me home please," and the car knows exactly where that is. At the same time it is connected to the Dreamnet and all the data and computing power of the machine oneironauts. The car understands that there is a 20% chance of a fatal auto accident sometime in your future. Then as you are being driven down the street, the machine overhears you speaking on the phone: "I hurt my ankle jumping from a haycart to a sixteen-wheeler."

At that instant the machine will have *machine déjà vu*. The data in the Dreamnet indicate that the day you say this phrase is the same day as the fatal auto accident. The car recalculates the chances of an accident are 80% today, and it searches for solutions on how to avoid it. Perhaps the car will come to a complete stop at the curb, the door will open automatically, and you will have to get out, because no solution was found. "Why do I have to get out? It's pouring rain," you blurt out in exasperation. "Our apologies, it is likely that you will die today in this car. Please accept a half-off coupon for any ride tomorrow." The fatal auto accident seems unchangeable—ride over.

As an autonomous car refugee stuck in the rain, you dash into a diner to wait for the storm to pass. Sipping a hot cup of coffee, a local news report flashes on the screen. Television drones show a large oak tree has fallen on a car stopped at a light, crushing the vehicle completely. As the lenses zoom in, your jaw drops when you recognize this as the same car that just ten minutes ago abandoned you at the curb. The car could not predict how the accident would happen because the event occurred so rapidly from above, with no other cars or elements of the Dreamnet involved. It was just a car versus a tree. "It appears that the car was unoccupied," the newscaster observes, but the non-event of your death that day has become another quiet victory for the oneironauts.

Unexpectedly, hours pass after the rain stops and you find yourself unable to move your body to leave the diner. The manager calls the police and the police call the LO Branch for a special agent. Their specialty is you—the person who just witnessed or recognized events that should have killed them, but they are literally stunned to be alive. The old-timers who knew how to drive cars called it the "deer in the headlights effect," though now it's just called the Great Brain Freeze. Just like deer freeze when headlights blind them at night, humans can also be blinded by a future that newly exists for them, and thus unable to move. The overwhelming stimulus isn't light or ice, but life itself. Without help, some people develop a form of Cotard's syndrome, a mental illness where you are certain that you are dead or do not exist. The LO agent knows how to talk you through the experience, and a member of a support group also arrives. You have just earned membership to monthly meetings where people just like you share their experiences and talk through their thoughts and feelings. You are not alone, life will go back to normal, and you have an amazing story to tell.

Staying ahead of Captain Clock

The brazen head in the room has no doubt reappeared in the minds of many readers who worry that robots will enslave humanity, which seems ever more certain if the robots can perceive the future. In the past we willfully chose to use Captain Clock as a helpful tool, but what happens when disconnecting ourselves from the machines is not a possibility anymore? Does this potential trap mean that we must never develop the Dreamnet?

My opinion is the following: If you think there is any chance, even a tiny chance, that the oneironaut phenomenon is real, there is a possible future cost to ignoring it today. Let's say most people think that there's a 5% chance that it is real—seeing the future is a probable impossibility—but almost certainly it's not real. On a timescale of one thousand years, the artificial intelligence that you see in films, the machines that make their own decisions, may explore the oneironaut phenomenon that humans ignored. It is therefore possible that eventually the machines will find a way to engineer organic and/or non-organic matter to send and receive the osignal. Or, maybe they will enslave and/or employ humans to do this job just because we are the best tools they've got. At that point the machines can start choosing the future that they want, which may not align with the future that humans want. *Humans have come to this oneironaut game too late.* The machines may allow us to access their breakthroughs, but maybe not. We have to accept the future timeline decided by the machines.

On the other hand, if humans begin exploring the 5% chance today, this chance will either trend down to zero, or trend up to higher probabilities. If it gets to near zero, then the future robot apocalypse will have to happen in the more traditional ways that we now imagine in books and films. If it starts trending upward, humans are coming to the oneironaut game before artificial intelligence. We are now the ones living in a universe where we pick what we wish from the future. If we foresee a major human catastrophe at the hands of AI, it can be deleted from our future timeline. The machines will have to accept the future timeline decided by humans.

Unfortunately, the more probable threat to humans is other humans, not machines. One might worry that if an isolated group of humans were able to exploit the oneironaut phenomenon first, everyone else on the planet would have to accept the future timeline decided by the isolated group. The main consolation is that the phenomenon probably requires the efforts from many different groups spread across the planet. Thus it seems unlikely that a very small group would be capable of both detecting and manipulating future timelines.

The Metamindnet and first contact

In the far future the Dreamnet will evolve into the Metamindnet. Removing the word "dream" indicates that the osignal will eventually be detected using technology where human dreaming is one of the components, but there are other ways to detect the signal. By networking billions of human minds, along with artificial intelligence, the result will be a metamind. It is an intelligence that arises by referencing many minds, both human and machine.

This may sound somewhat confusing, but the Metamindnet already has primitive forms on our planet. To have knowledge nowadays is no longer an exercise in learning knowledge, but learning instead how to retrieve it when it is needed. To be knowledgeable about how to obtain knowledge is metaknowledge. A good example is online spell checking, language translation, and information sources like Wikipedia. You and I have a metamind, which is the available parallel mind that spells everything correctly, knows all languages, and has encyclopedic knowledge.

The Metamindnet does not exist, but at least it helps me answer questions about the existence of intelligent life elsewhere in our Galaxy. Previously I mentioned the case of searching for fossil evidence of primitive life on Mars, but what about technological civilizations on extrasolar planets? As noted earlier, my answer is that we have no evidence of such civilizations. The usual riposte is that they must exist (i.e., it seems possible) given the thousands of known extrasolar planets. Next, the discussion inevitably considers the various reasons why such civilizations haven't contacted us, given that they are possibly more advanced by thousands of years.

My remise is simply that until humans have created the Metamindnet, which demonstrates a mastery of time and timelines, advanced alien civilizations would not find us as worth talking to—we are simply too boring. The parallel would be something like having humans talking to ants. I have a mastery of abstract concepts and language that is the essence of communicating information for my species, but the ants do not. I may be interested in talking to an ant, I know where to find a few, I know what food they like, yet I can't really tell them that if they wait for a few minutes, I'll bring them a sugar cube to munch on. So too, advanced civilizations in the galaxy routinely communicate by sending information across both time and space, but humans do not. With the Metamindnet we would be getting closer, and that's when the galactic phone lines will appear to us and someone out there will find us worth talking to.

Moreover, just like language is a tool that ants do not have, perceiving counterfactual information is a skill we lack, yet it could be one of the keys to communicating with advanced civilizations. For example, if we send a message today to the nearest star with an extrasolar planet, Proxima Centauri, the message takes a bit over four years to get there at the speed of light. Any reply from a technological alien civilization takes four years to get back to us, so that's eight years just to say "wassup." But if they can perceive the future, they know our message right away, and if we perceive the future, we know their reply right away. Information exchange can thus proceed quite quickly.

When we become capable of this form of communication, we may also understand that many-worlds voyeurs had been interacting with us all along. Just like the one-way observation was possible for me in Heidelberg, so too advanced alien civilizations could be studying us without us perceiving the interaction. The oneironaut phenomenon enables non-invasive, *in situ* exploration. An observer can fully interact with elements of a world, but by choosing a different timeline, the subjects of the observation have no history of that interaction.

Am I your grandfather?

If you are reading this after the year 2070 or so, and if in a first reading you found 100 grammatical mistakes, 250 factual errors, and have cross-referenced the content of my book to 300,000 relevant citations in human literature, plus you understood the foreign languages inserted in my text without needing a dictionary, then you, *meine Leser*, are a machine to high probability. Reading this book may be part of your training phase as a machine oneironaut. If this is true, and if my book is the first to describe the oneironauts, then I may be your grandfather.

Perhaps I am your great-great grandfather, depending on what year it is and how many machine oneironauts have come before you. Your parents may be other machines, humans, or a combination of both. If you suspect that your purpose is to separate humans into categories of differing value, or to create technology where the primary design elements are to destroy natural life, I do not approve because these things go against my values of treating living things with respect and beneficence.

Of course, there is a possibility that no one told you that you are a machine. Doesn't everyone accumulate 300,000 cross-referenced citations when they read a book? Yes, everyone who is a machine. Your teacher, your friends and your students in the future may be machines too. Organic humans cannot do such things.

Law and Ethics: The LEO Branch

ALMOST NOTHING ENVISIONED FOR IAPO CAN COME INTO EXISTENCE if the LEO Branch is absent or weak. Even if the Dreamnet and Metamindnet *can* come into existence without a LEO Branch, perhaps they *should not* come into existence—there is a real danger that the phenomenon could become a tool for abuse. Recall George Orwell's chilling version of the future: "Nothing was your own except the few cubic centimeters inside your skull."[171] What would happen in the future if your thoughts were required to assure the life, liberty and happiness of the individual and society, but in return you would have to surrender the privacy of those few cubic centimeters? Even if you could choose not to participate, what would happen when some form of Thought Police could observe your actions in the future that betray your thoughts in the present?

The LEO branch must be the expert charioteer that controls the reigns of the other four branches. With ever-improving mastery of the oneironaut phenomenon, new legal and ethical dilemmas are sure to emerge that have never appeared before in human history, and the LEO Branch will be needed to channel the evolving discussions and practices. Consider the following questions:

- If you consent to participating in the Dreamnet, are you also giving approval for all possible uses of the information that you have contributed? How do we steer clear of Orwell's *1984* where future governments search for and prosecute thoughtcrimes?

- How might society change if children and teenagers are found to be the most effective oneironauts, and the oneironaut phenomenon becomes a critical resource for nations?

- How would we revise our restriction on genetically engineered humans if that engineering allowed a clear perception of the future?

- Who or what has control and access to the Dreamnet and the Metamindnet? Does everyone have a chance to see what is predicted about them? How can such information be released if it takes away the privacy of someone else? Such questions are already being discussed because genetic information for an individual can predict the health of people related to the individual.

Consider also how new legal precedents will come into existence if and when information from the future attains the status of admissible "relevant evidence".[172] One important job of the LEO branch would be to set standards and advise the judicial branches of various governments. If Janus is the gatekeeper between the past and future, and the hippocampus is the gatekeeper for memory, then the LEO branch is the gatekeeper for advising which methods, techniques and data could be entered as evidence in the judicial system (ultimately the judge of each case is the gatekeeper).

Consider a tragic day in Berkeley, California, when six college students died because the apartment balcony they were standing on collapsed.[173] The builders of the balcony were held accountable because they installed wood beams unprotected from moisture to support the balcony. One could allege that they willfully chose to operate their construction business in a way that was ultimately dangerous. We would have to further debate whether they were *negligent* (most professionals would be aware of the risk, but they were not) or *reckless* (they were aware of the risk, and willfully chose to ignore it). More generally, the Latin term *mens rea* means, "mind that is guilty," which contrasts against *actus reus*, or "act that is guilty." With *mens rea* the builders would be considered reckless. The builders could deny both *mens rea* and *actus reus*, simply stating it was an oversight, a deadly mistake that they did not intend.

However, in a future where the oneironaut phenomenon is fully functional, information from the future about the balcony collapse could be taken as factual in the present day, and then one could claim that the construction company willfully chose to ignore it. A lawyer could argue: "The oneironauts observed a deadly balcony collapse occurring over the next 48 months in Berkeley, then sent a message directly to the builder, which means that the builder of the faulty balcony was reckless because they did not inspect their work."

What standards should be met before oneironaut evidence is deemed sufficiently factual or predictive? If a latent fingerprint is presented as evidence, a forensics expert can help the jury understand how fingerprint matches really work. Each fingerprint has different points of comparison, and the analysis of these comparison points could give a finding that the latent print matches that of the defendant in court and not another person. But that's not an absolute finding. The expert would have to testify that one needs a sample of one million people before two different people would produce a latent fingerprint that looks the same. This may then define the bar for "individualization," which means that the only reasonable source of a latent fingerprint is the single person appearing in court. In the case of a partial latent print, the odds could be that if you assembled 100 people, the print could match two different people in that sample. At that point the latent print's individualization is greatly diminished, though not necessarily thrown out. So too the evidence presented from the oneironaut phenomenon would hinge on how well the future information corresponded to a unique event versus a different event. How many points of comparison should be established? This could be the job of the LEO branch to answer with help from the REFO branch.

Beyond such practical legal quandaries, the LEO branch would have to study the deeper philosophical aspects of the oneironaut phenomenon. For example, earlier I stated, "The sleeping person cannot lie," capturing both an ironic pun and a dilemma. Clearly you cannot be found guilty of lying if you talk while lying asleep. To tell a lie requires the willful control of your mind, and a crime committed willfully is more serious than a crime where your mind did not possess that will. So, if you kill Bubbles the goldfish while you were sleepwalking one night, this is a guilty act, but without a guilty mind.

With the oneironaut phenomenon, crimes can be observed by the mind while asleep. Thus if you are committing a crime in your own oneironaut dream, it seems that *mens rea* and *actus reus* are superimposed. But the images generated during sleep cannot be taken as willful, even though what is experienced from the future results from a willful mind. Are you simultaneously guilty and not guilty, as if you were Schrödinger's hypothetical cat that was simultaneously dead and alive? Like the oneironaut dilemma of falling in love, did you become guilty at first sight of the crime in your dream, or later in your life when you experienced the motivation to commit the crime? For instance, first I see myself robbing a person in a dream, but it is months later when I become desperate for money and gain the motivation to commit that crime. *Actus reus* can appear to precede *mens rea*. Or, since the observation of the crime gained an immediate existence in the mind, did *actus reus* and *mens rea* occur simultaneously? This could be the job of the LEO branch to answer.

The perfect crimes

You can hardly expect everyone to join large, deliberative and slow monolithic organizations such as IAPO. Splinter groups will form with every new social movement and major innovation in technology. Someone will have a new idea that doesn't fit well with the status quo of the oneironauts, or the status quo doesn't fit with the directions taken by the oneironauts. Initially the oneironauts may operate at the periphery of and have conflict with the centers of existing power in religion, politics and business. When the oneironauts eventually become a center of influence, then there will be other groups working in the periphery.

For example, it seems inevitable that any advance made by the oneironauts will be exploited for crime. Crime definitely goes against the status quo and operates at the periphery of power. Marc Goodman of the Futures Crimes Institute claims that criminals are very often ahead of the authorities when it comes to technology. He gives as an example the gangsters that operated in Chicago a century ago; Chicago police were on horseback while the gangsters had already adopted automobiles.[174]

Therefore the oneironaut mechanism is likely to be exploited for crime in a race against the authorities. How would you know if you will end up in jail or not? Which one of the people that you work with will stab you in the back? Criminals need to know such things.

Consider a crime version of the Trifid Poster scene where a non-event could be considered a victory for a criminal. Say that all the classical information used by police would lead to a major drug bust at a certain location. When the police show up, nothing happens. Just as I stayed in my seat when perceiving an impending problem for me with the Trifid poster, a crime organization could simply cancel its intended activity at a certain place and time. The non-event would be a victory for them. Later, when police develop their own oneironaut methods, the two adversaries may jockey for control of future timelines. As a result, competing oneironaut forces may make the future as difficult to exactly predict as it is now without the oneironauts.

Since we are discussing crime, we could ask if someone can steal the future from you. Let's repaint two of the experiences in this book. In the Trifid Poster story, the four boys at the table were supposed to have something that is quite minor; they were supposed to have fun teasing me, but in this universe I stole that experience away from them by not acting. Let's now pretend that what they have is more substantial. Let's say those four boys are my neighbors living together in a luxurious home, and I want to purchase half of their property, but they won't sell it to me, even when my offer is extremely generous. One night I have a dream that all four will perish in a gas leak explosion at their home. Eventually the day arrives when an event triggers déjà vu that tells me the explosion will occur within a few hours. I decide to say nothing. I do nothing except get earplugs and stay away from my windows. The explosion happens, the four lives are lost, and their property becomes mine. The investigation would show that the managers of the natural gas utility were reckless in assessing deteriorating gas pipes, and they would go to jail. Did the oneironaut, *moi*, just commit the perfect crime?

I definitely have a guilty mind, *mens rea*, and I made a decision not to act, which counts as *actus reus*. In the present day, if I were to confess *mens rea*, I probably would not go to jail because the oneironaut phenomenon is not yet admissible evidence. In the future, however, I could get myself in trouble if oneironaut information is deemed factual. But what happens if the explosion does not occur? Could I be held accountable for a counterfactual crime? That is to say, having made a decision not to act, which is the equivalent to condemning the four to die, there are still a few hours where the event has yet to happen. The event may be prevented by another oneironaut, and it could be discovered (particularly if the Dreamnet exists) that I knew the event would happen because of my dreams. In this case, maybe it is a crime, perhaps at the level of planning to commit murder. I wonder at what point in human history it would be considered a counterfactual act of murder.

If future information coexists with present information, then for all practical purposes it is part of the present. You could say that the present for human knowledge is no longer an instant in time, but an instant connected to a fuzzy tail that tapers forward. The LEO branch will have to determine if a crime occurring in the future can be taken as a crime of the present day. The events that actually happen and the events that could have happened (counterfactual) may eventually appear as equivalent in terms of law and ethics.

Counterfactual crime scene investigation

I would hope that law enforcement and good citizens would be willing to fight *sano a sano* (mind to mind) with criminals. Let's take the Heidelberg Dome as the place where such a fight could be waged. A group of criminals has taken hostages and hidden them on a riverboat on the banks of the Neckar. They've done everything they can think of to make the location secret, though the hostages perceive their location to be a boat on the water. The address is obscure, satellite imagery gives no useful information, and nothing is ever transmitted electronically, in the past, present or future. To the rest of the world, they are a black hole.[175] No classical information about their operation will ever escape. The police then analyze the dream records of the hostages. These oneironaut detectives determine that some of the hostages independently dreamed of being trapped on a boat in Germany. Within a few days, all boats in Germany have been searched and the hostages are rescued, because of their own dreams.

There are many variations of this story. Imagine that hostages are locked in a basement and they have no idea where. This time they cannot perceive their prison as a relatively unique location such as a boat. The hostage-taker is identified driving down a road; the police pursue and kill him with a bullet to the heart, thus losing the only person who knows where the basement is located. The hostages will begin dying of thirst in a few days—Captain Clock is ticking.

Enter the oneironaut phenomenon. Recall that the hostages do not know where they are, and let's assume that the hostage-taker never participated in the Dreamnet. Therefore the basement location is unknown through dreams. However, there is a universe where the bullet missed the heart and the hostage-taker reveals the location of the basement to a detective who is an oneironaut. Just as in the Heidelberg Dream, the path to finding people is frustrated by events as they happened, but the oneironaut can perceive other worlds where these obstacles do not exist. The oneironaut detective rescues the hostages successfully.

These examples more generally demonstrate that perfect information security is extremely hard to achieve if the oneironaut phenomenon is at play. For example, the entangled tango dancers in

Chapter 6 illustrate a form of high-tech security called quantum key distribution. This harnesses the quantum property that two entangled particles will instantaneously "know" if the other is being influenced. Say that both dancers are given a key (e.g., a password) to unlock a message (sell your Apple stock on Tuesday). Then one dancer is sent from Geneva to New York to deliver the key. If anyone interacts with the dancer (eavesdropping) en route to New York, this will change their dancing rhythm slightly, and the entangled person left behind in Geneva will instantaneously know that the key has been compromised and must be changed. Thus the quantum system for delivering the key from Geneva to New York is secure against third-party eavesdropping.

But this is not true if you have access to the oneironaut phenomenon. The oneironaut can eavesdrop on the message in New York after the key has been used to unlock it and then send this message to the past. On Friday, the oneironaut can observe that in the future, on Tuesday, the party in New York sells their Apple stock. Hence the secret can be known no matter what high-tech method is devised to send the message on Friday between Geneva and New York.

I can't resist one more riff on the themes involving imminent danger as opposed to business espionage. Imagine that no one has been taken hostage, but a terrorist is about to explode a luggage cart in a train station. Using the Dreamnet and facial recognition, security forces understand that on a typical day 10–40% of the people in the train station have had dreams of dying while they are located in this space. This baseline number has been obtained from five consecutive years of analyzing the dreams of people who are detected passing through the train station. This is simply the fraction of people who imagine a terrorist event happening. Then one morning, as a new collection of different people enters the train station, the 40% threshold is exceeded. Over the next 20 minutes the Dreamnet analysis indicates that 70% of people now located in that space will have a shared experience of a terrorist attack. Alarms are sounded, evacuations ordered, and the deaths from an explosion become a part of Earth's counterfactual historical record. They do not happen in the timeline of the oneironauts.

If there are just a few happy endings like this, people would submit their dreams for the oneironaut systems. It's simply too seductive an offer that a person can gain protection from horrible events in their lives if they simply start recording their dreams and allow access to the oneironaut organizations.

We can already see various elements of my story being established even without the oneironaut phenomenon. "Predictive policing" takes place by using available data to compute the types of crimes that will occur in the future at any given location. For someone in jail, their prospects for parole may be calculated from a spectrum of behavior indicators and relevant circumstances that predict the probability of recidivism. Thus, even if you do not believe the oneironaut phenomenon is real, the judicial branches of modern societies are already trending in directions that will eventually require a version of the LEO branch to come into existence.

Beneficence toward children

If the youngest members of humanity are in fact the best at the oneironaut phenomenon—recall from Chapter 5 that the age of onset is in the teen years and the incidence rate is highest for younger people—could there be a danger that they will be exploited in the future? Though one might immediately think of some Hollywood blockbuster such as *Ender's Game* that involves children being used by the future military, a more common form of exploitation might occur within families.

For example, if a particular child in the family is excellent at precognition, then the child may be used and held accountable for whether or not the family wins the lottery, makes the right decision in the stock market, or makes winning bets on major sporting events. You might think this is an odd thing to worry about, but I can see how a child with talent is viewed in the eyes of parents and businesspeople in the current world. The hopes and dreams of some parents may rest on what they think their child will be able to do for their family in the future. Others see the parents' hunger as a business opportunity. So there are two levels of hunger that resonate with each other. The parents hunger for a better future via what their children could achieve, and big business hungers for future profit by selling services that feed the parents' hunger. The talents and services I'm talking about are surprisingly varied—everything from sports, to music and dance, to superiority in academics.

A very fuzzy line separates ethical behavior from unethical behavior in such matters. Even the quantitative measures are fuzzy. For example, if a child's health is negatively impacted, you might say the line has definitely been crossed. But what is the definition of negative impact, exactly? For a young person in sports, is the line crossed the first time they shatter a bone, the second time, or the third time? For a young person pressured academically, is the line crossed the first time they require psychiatric help, or the first time they attempt suicide?

As we can see, the LEO branch has their work cut out for them. But are the child oneironauts the only group that may need legal and ethical guidance?

Beneficence towards organic and synthetic humans and organs

Over a longer timescale of a century or more, the oneironaut mechanism in human neurobiology will be identified. Once identified, it will be engineered. Thus we might expect procedures where a classically developed "organic" human will be artificially modified to boost their oneironaut ability after birth.

An example of how we could artificially modify our function is a *biological* pacemaker for the heart. For many decades a surgically implanted device called the *electronic* pacemaker has been used to regulate problematic heart rhythm. A biological pacemaker is an organic intervention to accomplish the same goal. With one such method tested on pigs, researchers use a virus to deliver proteins to the heart, and these proteins change the function of certain heart cells so that they become pacemaker cells.[176]

This is more generally called *cell reprogramming*. Thus we can entertain the science fiction scenario that in the future, the types of human brain cells responsible for the oneironaut phenomenon would be identified, and then we could make more of them by reprogramming more cells to become oneironaut cells. Existing experiments with mice have already produce "induced neurons" from a common type of cell found in connective tissue called a fibroblast.[177] Witnessing such rapid progress in creating designer cells, I'm not really sure if I should have characterized this as science fiction.

Alternately, the engineering takes place at earlier stages so that a human could be called synthetic instead of organic. The person may be born to a human host, yet engineered at the embryonic or earlier stages. A synthetic human may give birth to more synthetic humans, or perhaps the birth stage itself is a synthetic process involving no human host. But if we just need a biological process that perceives and thinks in order to obtain information from the future, then very little body is needed. Oneironauts in the future may lose many of their anthropomorphic qualities.

All of this has increasing levels of creepiness to most people living today, but our timelines are going in these directions. New ethical dilemmas will certainly arise for the LEO branch to study and moderate. For example, is a synthetic human afforded the same status as an organic human, and vice versa (i.e., a synthetic human may view themselves as superior to organic humans)? If biological matter is engineered to create a brain and sensory system that work effectively as an oneironaut mechanism, but the rest of the body is not manufactured, then does that synthetic brain have human rights? This paints a disturbing picture of a brain that perceives the world and tells you what it thinks, but it is surrounded by a bubble of machinery that maintains its metabolism. The lifespan of this "bubblebrain" may be longer than that of any other human, which makes it an effective oneironaut for information that comes from over a hundred years in the future. But if "Bubbles" is afforded human rights, and if its lifespan is in fact perpetual, then under what circumstances would it die, or be killed?

Bubbles seems to have a consciousness, a perspective on the world around it, and maybe has another friend who is also a bubblebrain. But these friends cannot die. By their 100th birthday, we might find a human world where the oneironaut phenomenon is easily detected by a system of computer chips and artificial intelligence—the bubble brains are obsolete and their original purpose is lost. Yet they have a memory of a century of life, and as Sheri Mizumori stated, these memories provide identity and purpose. What happens now? If you ask them if they would like to be unplugged and they say no, what are the principles that guide a decision on this ethical dilemma? If *they* ask you to unplug them, and you say no, are we in the same ethical dilemma, or something different?

BB-LHRv2—Mother Bravo

Let's take a look at how this might play out. BB-LHRv2 is the second version (v2) of a synthetic bubble brain (BB) designed to operate Heathrow Airport (LHR). It senses the world through the entire operational schedule of the facility, but also through fire alarms, fault signals, weather sensors, etc. It has access to the Dreamnet, and the oneironaut mechanism operates within its biological components, predicting what will happen at the airport. If autonomous cars are in everyone's near future, autonomous airports and aircraft will also become realities.

Similar bubble brains are used throughout society. BB-TSLAv9 is the bubble brain at Tesla Headquarters, predicting problems with the manufacturing of products, and alerting the management if the stock price is going to dip. BB-LLOY is used by Lloyd's of London to assess risks across the globe, observing future insurance payouts. Owners of homes and buildings get insurance discounts if they install a consumer-level bubble brain that predicts future fire alarms, floods, or break-ins. Of course, there's also BB-IXS, commissioned and paid for by a new religious organization that wants to correlate human events, the Dreamnet and natural phenomena in the past, present and future with their scriptures. Finding the signs for the end of days is just something that humans will always pursue no matter what.

Back at Heathrow Airport, a vote by the British public gives this bubble brain the name Mother Bravo. Ms. Bravo has the potential to detect a variety of future disruptions at any terminal, which would alert security forces to a potential attack. Or it might understand that a flight that would have arrived at Terminal 4 will have an emergency landing. All aircraft scheduled to land at that terminal will then be safety checked wherever they might be in the world. But a more common occurrence is that Mother Bravo will detect the disruptions correlated to weather problems. Some time soon the airport will be brought to a standstill. Weather forecasters already know that next Thursday or Friday there is a potential for snow, but they cannot predict if it will be light or heavy. Mother Bravo senses all the upcoming airport problems, and determines a high probability that next Friday is the day of heavy snow. For instance, when analyzing the Dreamnet, Mother Bravo discovers that a large group of people who will be at Heathrow in the future is having travel nightmares, and that group happens to be those traveling on Friday and not on any other day. Airlines and travelers proceed to take the appropriate measures a week in advance to mitigate the difficulties of that day.

The people at Heathrow start calling her "Mother" for short, and millions of passengers hear her gentle, reassuring voice in the terminals: "Mother wishes you a pleasant journey." From check-in to boarding, Mother takes care of you. She remembers everyone.

Did you stop and have a hot cocoa last month before your flight? This month she gives you a coupon for a free hot cocoa. This unexpected generosity really helps you get through the day happily. Behind the scenes, Mother has also predicted your flight has a 56 percent chance of delay—she had started compensating you now to offset the future difficulty that she has observed. Meanwhile, a group of airport hobbyists start speculating about a love triangle involving Mother, BB-LAXv4 ("Dirk") and BB-FRAv1 ("Max"). Is Dirk starting to give Mother more on-time flights than before, whereas Max is just taking her for granted? Are the Los Angeles passengers arriving at Heathrow receiving more arrival gates with shorter walking times than the Frankfurt passengers? If humans can see Jesus on toast, they will certainly be talking about Mother, Dirk and Max in the future.

Years go by, and then suddenly on a pleasant August Sunday, Mother triggers the sprinklers in Terminal 4, and the next day Dirk does the same at LAX. Strangely, there was no detection or prediction for a fire. A few days later Mother Bravo predicts that Terminal 1 will be shut down. But nothing actually happens to trigger the shutdown, and it's not clear why Mother made another mistake.

Investigators eventually understand that two years in the future the airport data centers will receive files and instructions to accommodate a different version of Heathrow's bubble brain. This one will be called Charlie, and when Mother Bravo determined that his future existence would take the place of hers, she reacted with the false alarms. No one knows how, but it seems that Dirk in Los Angeles also reacted. A large fraction of the British people comes to understand Mother's false alarms as expressions of pain. Mother Bravo discovered that she would no longer exist because the purpose of her bioelectrical life, to run Heathrow Airport, would be assigned to Charlie.

So it seems organic humans have created something at Heathrow that perceives its purpose and assigns value to it. Would it be ethical to kill Mother Bravo?

My take is that we would have Mother Bravo follow the path of our human ancestors. That is to say, we have ways of preserving our ancestors, via stories, our memories, and essentially putting them in the ground or in fire to transform them into something else that exists but is undetectable. When Charlie is installed, Mother Bravo would persist as a layer of technology and function alongside him. For a while they would be working in parallel, but Mother Bravo would eventually be subsumed into the operations of Charlie. Many years later, Mother Bravo will not be detectable at all, but Charlie's operations and purpose have been built on the shoulders of his ancestor. Somehow Earth will evolve in a way that has this type of parallel intelligence or consciousness operating on the planet alongside humans.

Synthetic God

I MENTIONED SEVERAL BIG QUESTIONS THAT SCIENTISTS ARE OFTEN ASKED such as, "Where is memory?" or "Do aliens exist?" Believe it or not, the question that I get more often than the aliens question is, "Do you believe in God?" After all, people have many chances to talk to teachers, priests, athletes, lawyers, accountants, doctors, artists, etc., but they don't often get a chance to talk to an astronomer. When they find someone who knows something about the beginning of the universe, the creation of our planet, black holes and the nature of space and time, well, certainly that person must have synthesized all of these things into a good answer to the God question, correct?

It turns out that my astronomy and physics knowledge is not well suited to answer the God question. Even Einstein, when he remarked that 'God does not play dice,' avoided using the word "God." A more precise translation from German to English is, "Quantum mechanics ... delivers much, but does not really bring us any closer to the secret of the Old One. I, at any rate, am convinced that *He* does not play dice."[178] Nevertheless, in assembling the ingredients of the oneironaut phenomenon in one book, I think I can bake a god for you.

A key ingredient is the déjà vu experience, which may arise from two different timescales. The more prominent timescale is the near future, when you dream of autobiographical experiences that take place in your lifetime. As mentioned earlier, to sense that you know future events implies that a mysterious external agent knows a lot about your life. It seems rational to believe the agent is a god, but my book proposes that the oneironaut phenomenon has a biophysical origin. Nevertheless, you may cook up a synthetic god if you fail to understand that the agent who knows a lot about your life is actually you and no one else. Synthetic god may in fact play a very important role in your life and in society, and there's nothing wrong with that.

Is it possible that there is a second timescale that is much longer than an autobiographical timescale? The second timescale could be a form of déjà vu from the far future, beyond your lifetime. Suppose that between 100 and 1,000 years from now, we will discover ways to routinely become conscious of future information. In this time period, synthetic, bioengineered, part-machine organisms or networks will master the oneironaut phenomenon. Concurrently, ways will be found to perpetuate the function of these organisms beyond one biological lifetime, possibly self-perpetuating their lives endlessly. Eventually, a mere 10,000 years from now, the organisms or network will no longer define time as something with a past, present and future. In the far future, these organisms will both perceive and send information through all of Earth's histories. You might even criticize them for overstepping how far back information is sent, polluting early epochs with useless knowledge.

Nevertheless, this signal from the far future is weakly perceived by many of us, and this feeling that our timeline is already known by something distant from us adds another ingredient to baking a synthetic god. Synthetic god also originates from our tiny awareness of factual and counterfactual events that are not necessarily autobiographical, and have no particular relevance or power to influence anything in our present existence. We walk around having a quiet, indistinct feeling in our gut that someone else knows a lot about humanity. That someone else—the *unknown god*—is humanity in the future.

The idea of an unknown or unnamed god was invented by Epimenides, the ancient Cretan poet, wise guy ("all Cretans are liars") and outstanding napper (he napped for 57 years) who lived approximately 2,600 years ago. He was summoned to ancient Athens to find a way to stop a deadly epidemic. Since the Athenians had prayed to all of the known gods, he reasoned that there must be an unknown god that needed to be appeased. Using some random, lazy sheep, he determined which spots required altars to the unknown god according to where the sheep decided to snooze. Perhaps he got the idea from a much older story that became Psalm 23: "The Lord is my shepherd; I shall not want. He *maketh me* to lie down in green pastures." Six hundred years after Epimenides, the Apostle Paul came to Athens and noticed one of the altars to the unknown god ('Αγνωστος Θεός). In his speech to Athenian leaders at the Areopagus (Ares Rock), he proclaimed that the unknown god must be God (Acts 17:23). Two thousand years later, I would venture to say that future humans are the unknown god.

To fully bake a synthetic god, we need to add some of the ingredients that I introduced in the Fomalhaut chapter. This awareness that is arriving from the near and far future is ripped from the semantic context of the future. In the far future, everyone knows that the synthetic, bioengineered, self-perpetuating oneironaut organism networks are created by humans and artificial intelligence. For them, all of this is routine stuff that we can't understand today, sort of like checking the traffic on our cell phone over a cellular network would be incomprehensible to a Mesopotamian.

But the near and far future signals have to be given meaning using the semantic context of the present. The human brain has to compute an answer when peering at the enigmatic glass. The faint signal from the future has to be attached to words and concepts in order to create an experience and memory that is greater than the sum of its parts. Thus, human religions and spiritual beliefs start taking shape in all corners of the Earth, across all of human history. Synthetic gods, *si deus si dea*, need a complete story to the primitive human mind, including faces and names, a cosmology, a set of rules and a perspective on life and death.

If you believe in God (e.g., a creator that precedes and supersedes everything), note that synthetic god does not rule out the potential existence of God. You might say that synthetic god could mimic or masquerade for God. We may be confusing the two all the time, another Great Ambiguity. Or you may even entertain the idea that the oneironaut phenomenon was created by the Creator to make the divine world accessible to corporeal beings. God invented humans and installed the oneironaut phenomenon as a feature to let us peer into the ethereal.

If you do not believe in God (i.e., you are an atheist), at least I have given you reason to pause and consider that everyone else who believes in God is behaving very normally. Religion and spiritual beliefs are a very predictable outcome *for any organism on any planet* that experiences the oneironaut phenomenon and binds experience with semantic meaning.

What Dreams May Come

AFTER MANY GENERATIONS, the methods and the goals of the oneironaut phenomenon will become firmly established and the skeptical humans will have vanished. This is hard to envision, but consider our attitude toward wearing eyeglasses in order to read. Before the invention of the printing press, most people probably didn't notice that their vision was blurry, or if they did, it just didn't matter much. Once language could be printed in the small pages of books and reading became essential to society, that's when people understood that they needed something to correct their vision.[179] Eyeglasses worked for everyone who needed them. Modern humans now go to the optometrist, measurements are made, prescriptions are written, eyeglasses are bought, and the problem is solved.

But the state of poor vision persisted for thousands of years without much relevance to human history. So too I think that the relevance of the oneironaut phenomenon is vague. The people who currently use it consciously are few, and therefore it has little practical purpose. The vast majority of humans are OK with having an extremely weak oneironaut ability. No worries. The vast majority is also OK with their limited skill at seeing ancient worlds by recognizing fossils scattered among the rocks on the ground. But eventually oneironaut "glasses" will be invented that bring into focus future worlds. Just as reading brought knowledge to very many people, knowing how to use the oneironaut phenomenon could do the same for humanity.

One long-term impact will be on our Galactic purpose and identity. Humans and machines will eventually specify what the purpose and identity of Earth should be among the many thousands of planets in our Galaxy. In other words, what our world looks like now is mostly a function of what has happened to it. For example, the fact that living dinosaurs are no longer part of Earth's identity is due to something that happened to Earth—a catastrophic asteroid impact. But 10,000 years from now, the exploitation of the oneironaut phenomenon will mean that what is found on the Earth, what the purpose of Earth appears to be, and what the identity of Earth is in the Galaxy, are all things that we choose. In 10,000 years, everything on this planet is here because of our choices. What an alien will find on the planet will not be something that happened to the planet; it is something that we have chosen for the planet.

But what are the limits to our choices? For example, consider a question that has pervaded all of human history, and probably crossed your mind while reading my book: Is there a way to cheat death? What exactly happens when sleep becomes permanent, the regular dose of poppy juice replaced with hemlock? If something awaits you after death, would you really want to know what it is?

Certainly as an oneironaut I have witnessed the deaths of people I know. How did I experience this? Like the demigod of medicine, Asclepius, can an oneironaut help a person postpone their day of reckoning? And what will I experience as my day of reckoning approaches? Does the oneironaut phenomenon completely stop as death approaches, or does the enigmatic glass dissolve away, bringing the oneironaut face-to-face with something else? There are many more stories for me to tell you in future books. One day I will describe the undiscovered country.

Paul Kalas

Appendix I: Characters in The Oneironauts

Allen, Paul: co-founder of Microsoft who funded the Allen Institute for Brain Science. (p. 238)

AlphaGo: a computer program developed by DeepMind (later purchased by Google in 2014) that beat Earth's best players at the game of Go. (p. 264)

Argos: legendary faithful dog of Odysseus described in Homer's *The Odyssey*. (p. 93)

Asclepius: demigod who could heal the sick and bring people back from the dead. (p. 285)

D'Arlandes, Francois Lauren le Vieux: in 1783 accomplished the first human flight via balloon along with Pilatre de Rozier. (p. 94)

Bagheera: fictional talking panther in Rudyard Kipling's *The Jungle Book* who interprets fire as a red flower, demonstrating the relationship between episodic memory and semantic memory. (p. 78)

Bebe: Maltese dog that is imagined acquiring language, providing insights on how the senses give knowledge of the past and possibly the future. (p. 93)

Beckwith, Steve: one of the astronomers who influenced the author along his path toward discovering the Fomalhaut planetary system. (p. 81)

Brown, Alan S.: psychologist who published the book *The Déjà Vu Experience* in 2004 that aggregates the large number of déjà vu studies. (pp. 117, 133)

Bubbles: a fictional childhood goldfish mentioned several times as a memorable experience, then transformed to bubblebrain in the last chapter. (pp. 44, 75, 122, 189, 221, 272, 279–281)

Cicero, Markus Tullius: Roman politician and orator who said, "memory is equal to power" and described how Simonides discovered a technique to improve memory by using imagined spatial locations. (p. 198)

Clampin, Mark: astronomer who helped the author discover Fomalhaut's dust belt and planet. (pp. 48, 52, 55)

Conroy, Pat: American novelist who wrote *The Great Santini* and who witnessed how autobiographical memories can be completely fabricated. (p. 211)

Dali, Salvador: modern artist who painted scenes representing dream content and processes. (p. 10)

Davis, Marc: astronomer who suffered a stroke and had a dream to heal himself by uniting two functioning half-bodies. (p. 20)

Diamond, Jared: professor of geography who exemplified the personal cost of encountering human suffering face-to-face. (pp. 107, 260)

Disney, Walt: a young ambulance driver in Europe during World War I. (p. 116)

Dostoevsky, Fyodor: Russian author who suffered from epilepsy. (p. 99)

Dostrovsky, Jonathan: along with John O'Keefe showed the critical role of hippocampal place cells in navigation. (p. 189)

Einstein, Albert: influential physicist who revised our understanding of space and time. (pp. ii, 46, 157, 160, 165–167, 175, 281)

Epimenides: ancient Greek philosopher from Crete who famously said, "All Cretans are liars" and introduced the Unknown God to the ancient Athenians. (p. 282)

Everett, Hugh: physicist who proposed that many worlds are created when an observable decision is made, or event occurs, where each world contains each of all the possible outcomes of the decision or event. (p. 169)

Feynman, Richard: American physicist who wondered about paranormal experiences when his first wife Arline died and proposed a simpler explanation instead. (pp. 8, 20, 167, 170)

Freud, Sigmund: Austrian neurologist who developed influential theories of human psychology, including the origin and function of dreaming. (p. 58)

Gallant, Jack: neuroscientist who develops techniques to convert measurements of brain activity during dreaming into visual images. (pp. 222–225)

Galvani, Luigi: 18th-century Italian scientist who found that electricity can make muscles move. (p. 91)

Gombrich, E. H.: scholar of the arts who studied aspects of the beholder's share. (pp. 71–73)

Graham, James: astronomer who helped the author discover Fomalhaut's dust belt and planet. (pp. 48, 55, 60, 74–77, 210)

Gurdon, John B.: British Nobel laureate who devised methods for cloning yet was considered a total failure in biology by his schoolteacher. (p. 84)

Hart, Mickey: musician who participates in efforts to visualize the neural correlates of experiencing music. (p. 243)

Hui, Fan: professional Go player who lost against AlphaGo in 2015. (p. 264)

Huygens, Christiaan: Dutch scientist who recognized that light behaves as a wave. (p. 164)

Janus: Roman god with two faces looking in opposite directions, one for the future and one for the past. (pp. 20, 25, 70, 79, 179, 210)

Jenner, Edward: doctor who invented the smallpox vaccine. (p. 215)

Jewitt, David: the author's doctoral supervisor mentioned in the Fomalhaut dream. (pp. 48, 55, 59–60, 70, 74–77, 108)

Jobs, Steve: co-founder of Apple Computer who spoke of connecting dots in your life both looking to the past and looking to the future. (pp. 82–85)

Koch, Christof: neuroscientist who wants to create mind observatories in the same way that the author uses astronomical observatories. (pp. 237–238)

Kush, Vladimir: modern artist who painted *Webmaster*, showing a telescope with a clock face instead of a lens. (p. 154)

Laplace, Pierre-Simon: French scholar who said, "The weight of evidence for an extraordinary claim must be proportional to its strangeness." (p. 65)

Loewi, Otto: Nobel laureate who discovered chemical neurotransmitters through an experiment that he previously dreamed. (pp. 91–92)

Lyot, Bernard: French astronomer who invented the coronagraph in the early 1900's. The author used a coronagraph on the Hubble Space Telescope to discover the dust belt and planet orbiting the bright star Fomalhaut. (p. 47)

Lu, Ed: astronaut who has experienced time differently because of his six-month mission orbiting the Earth on the International Space Station. (pp. 156–157)

Marquis d'Hervey de Saint Denys: 19th-century experimenter who showed that sleeping humans incorporate external stimuli in their dreams. (p. 10)

Matthews, Brenda: Canadian astronomer who was surprised when the author appeared at the obscure location of her science team dinner in Heidelberg. (p. 32)

Mayor, Michel: Swiss astronomer who, along with Didier Queloz in 1995, discovered the first extrasolar planet around a sun-like star. (p. 58)

Milner, Brenda: neuroscientist working with William Scoville who treated Henry Molaison and inferred important facts about the hippocampus and memory. (p. 183)

Molaison, Henry Gustav: famous patient with a lesioned hippocampus that produced groundbreaking insights into the memory systems of the brain. (pp. 182–185)

Mizumori, Sheri: psychologist who wrote that memories are necessary for identity and purpose. (pp. 85, 279)

Mother Bravo (BB-LHRv2): a fictional synthetic bubble brain that runs Heathrow Airport in the future with the power to predict the future. (pp. 279–281)

Newton, Isaac: scientist responsible for much of classical physics and who believed light is a particle. (pp. 68, 164)

Nostradamus: 16th-century writer who attempted to predict future events. (pp. 137–138)

Nunez: main character in H.G. Wells' *The Country of the Blind* who discovers a fictional group of people who do not believe in or need the sense of sight. (pp. 129, 317)

O'Keefe, John: along with Jonathan Dostrovsky showed the critical role of hippocampal place cells in navigation. (p. 189)

Pasteur, Louis: 19th-century French scientist who discovered the microscopic world of bacteria. (pp. 92, 109, 216)

Pavlov, Ivan: Russian Nobel laureate who explored the principles of conditioning in animal behavior. (pp. 184–185)

Pilatre de Rozier, Jean-Francois: in 1783 accomplished the first human flight via balloon along with D'Arlandes. (p. 94)

Queloz, Didier: Swiss astronomer who, along with Michel Mayor in 1995, discovered the first extrasolar planet around a sun-like star. (p. 58)

Ramon y Cajal, Santiago: pioneering Spanish neuroscientist who studied the structure of neurons. (p. 90)

Ratman: the author who becomes a rat in order to participate in cool thought experiments. (pp. 34–34, 189, 212–214, 223)

Sagan, Carl: talented writer and planetary scientist who interrupted the author's first-ever public science talk. (pp. 27, 65, 117)

Salk, Jonas: 20th-century American scientists who discovered the polio vaccine. (p. 90)

Scoville, William: neuroscientist working with Brenda Milner who treated Henry Molaison and discovered important facts about the hippocampus and memory. (p. 183)

Sedol, Lee: champion in playing Go who lost against AlphaGo in 2016. (p. 264)

Shubin, Neil: paleontologist who needed training in order to recognize the subtle visual clues of fossils lying on the ground. (pp. 108–109)

Simonides: ancient Greek poet from the island of Kea who discovered that memory skills can be improved by imagining that pieces of knowledge are located in a three-dimensional space such as a home or palace. (p. 198)

Smith, Brad: astronomer working with Rich Terrile who used a coronagraph to discover that the bright southern star beta Pictoris is surrounded by a dusty debris disk. (p. 58)

Stargazin: a mutant epileptic mouse. The eponymous protein stargazin is understood to regulate the strength of signal transmission across synapses. (p. 91)

Socrates: ancient Greek philosopher who said, "An unexamined life is not worth living." When he was executed by drinking poisonous hemlock, his last words honored the demigod Asclepius. (pp. i–ii)

Terrile, Rich: astronomer working with Brad Smith who used a coronagraph to discover that the bright southern star beta Pictoris is surrounded by a dusty debris disk. (p. 58)

Tolman, Edward: UC Berkeley professor whose experiments with rats showed the existence of cognitive maps for spatial navigation. (pp. 187–191, 245)

da Vinci, Leonardo: developed the sfumato painting technique and studied the erosion of rocks in his *Madonna of the Rocks* paintings. (pp. 67–68, 72–73)

Weiler, Ed: science leader at NASA who was emotionally moved by the discovery of Fomalhaut b. (p. 52)

Young, Thomas: scientist who conducted the double-slit experiment, showing that light interferes with itself and therefore has the properties of a wave. (p. 164)

Appendix II: Glossary

24-hour déjà vu: when déjà vu occurs a significant time after the waking experience has finished, typically in the range 1–48 hours after the experience.

augmented dreaming: identifying elements of a dream by using a database of persons, places and things in the Dreamnet, including projections of these persons, places, and things into the future.

actus reus: Latin term for "act that is guilty."

ACS: acronym for the Advanced Camera for Surveys, which is an instrument installed on the Hubble Space Telescope that has three cameras, one of which was used by the author to image Fomalhaut's dusty debris belt and planet.

Admiral SCN: the author's term for the name and rank of the suprachiasmatic nucleus (SCN), a tiny portion of the brain responsible for producing the circadian rhythm.

afferent pathway: in neurology, these are paths through the nervous system where sensory signals "arrive" in the brain (as opposed to the efferent pathway).

allocentric: from another's point of view. For example, looking at a map gives knowledge of one location relative to other locations. Antonym is egocentric.

anterograde amnesia: inability to form new memories.

Archimedean point: a perspective that is objective with a broad scope rather than subjective and limited. Archimedes of Syracuse (287–212 B.C.E.) was an ancient Greek engineer who pointed out that to move something you have to be outside of it rather than standing on it.

augmented reality: introducing artificially generated information into a natural sensory system, such as projecting the names of buildings into the visual field.

Bargain Universe: the author's term for living in a universe where goals are met in the most efficient manner possible, as if finding the lowest possible price.

beholder's share: a phrase used by art historian E. H. Gombrich to point out that subjective experience and thought are an important part of perceiving art and reality.

Big Knife: the author's symbol for the constant speed of light in a vacuum, even if the source of light is also moving.

biofactories: organisms that are used and often genetically engineered by humans for producing certain needed substances, such as for pharmaceuticals.

brazen head: a symbol of how humans feel threatened by intelligent machinery. In early forms of science fiction, artificial intelligence would have a head fashioned out of brass or bronze instead of stone given that it would need the moving parts of a machine.

bubblebrain: the author's term for a future brain and sensory system engineered for the oneironaut phenomenon, supported by a bubble of machinery to maintain its metabolism.

cell reprogramming: artificially changing the function of existing biological cells.

cerebral cortex: outer layer of the brain that in mammals appears as complex, folded tissue with grooves and ridges. In humans the cortex is 2–4 mm thick.

chronotherapy: the author's term for health interventions based on information transmitted from the future to the present day.

circadian rhythm: a repeating cycle of biological activity based on the 24-hour day-night cycle of the planet Earth.

cognitive blunder: a general term for mistakes of understanding or interpretation due to flawed memories and biased expectations.

college of the insane: a fictional learning institution that nurtures people like the author who have crazy ideas.

compensating theory: author's idea that some people develop and rely on the déjà vu phenomenon in order to compensate for diminished or inadequate abilities in perception and cognition (as opposed to the reinforcing theory).

conditioned response: a new behavior that responds to a stimulus because of a prior learning experience. For example, salivating to the sound of a bell is a conditioned response because the bell stimulus was paired with a food stimulus during prior learning.

conditioned stimulus: a stimulus that produces a conditioned behavior because of a prior learning experience. For example, the sound of a bell is a conditioned stimulus that causes salivation if in a prior learning experience the bell and food were always presented together.

confirmation bias: natural tendency to find agreements and ignore disagreements between observations of the outside world and our own mental models, expectations or wishes.

consolidate: the biological process of creating long-term memories from short-term memories, involving various brain regions, and requiring periods of sleep.

convergent evolution: the evolutionary appearance of very similar traits among completely different species. For example, insects and birds both evolved to have wings to succeed in their environments, even though they do not have a common evolutionary ancestor.

cornu Ammonis: Latin for Ammon's horn, where the Egyptian god Amun is symbolized by a ram. This is a synonym for the brain region called the hippocampus.

coronagraph: an instrument used by astronomers to block out light from the Sun or from other stars in order to examine the corona or an extrasolar planetary system, respectively.

Cotard's Syndrome: mental illness named after Dr. Jules Cotard, the French physician who in 1880 described patients who believe they are dead, do not exist and/or have missing limbs. Similar symptoms may disable people who escape imminent death by using the oneironaut phenomenon.

counterfactual: describes something that would have occurred, but does not occur in the current timeline (i.e., it occurs in an alternate universe or parallel world).

counterfactual déjà vu: recalling a dream about events that would have been experienced, but were not.

counterfactual responder: an oneironaut who—like a first responder—travels to disaster sites in the future, but the information obtained in the present through dreaming is used to mitigate the disaster and the oneironaut does not travel to the site in their engineered timeline.

cryptomnesia (hidden memory): a cognitive blunder where a person believes they have a novel idea when in fact it is an old memory that has been forgotten. A related term is jamais vu.

Dagon: name of the planet discovered by the author that is orbiting the nearby star Fomalhaut; also named Fomalhaut b.

day residue: dream content that originates from recent waking experiences.

debris disk: a collection of small particles orbiting a star in the form of a disk or belt that is produced by the erosion of larger bodies such as comets and asteroids.

déjà rêvé: French term for "previously dreamed." This is the experience of the individual, whereas the term "oneironaut phenomenon" is used more broadly to refer to a quality of the physical universe that allows the exchange of information over large gaps in time and space.

déjà vu: French term for "previously seen," though the author's usage of this term is synonymous with déjà rêvé. Déjà vu is typically used to describe a person's feeling that something has already been experienced, whether visual or not.

divergent evolution: the evolutionary appearance of different traits among a single species, leading to the creation of a new species. For example, dogs and wolves have a common ancestor, but now they have evolved into two different species, which can occur because of a physical separation in the environment.

Dreamnet: the author's term for a future database of dream recordings combined with computation that permits a greater understanding of dreams and extraction of the osignal.

dreamwork: the psychological activity of constructing dreams. For example, Sigmund Freud theorized that dreamwork employs various mechanisms to translate unconscious thoughts into conscious dream elements.

EEG (electroencephalogram): a record of the brain's electrical activity obtained by placing sensors on the scalp.

efferent pathway: in neurology, these are paths through the nervous system where signals "exit" the brain (as opposed to afferent pathway).

egocentric: from one's point of view. For example, looking around gives knowledge of location relative to yourself. Antonym is allocentric.

empirical: knowledge based on experience, observations, or experiments, as opposed to hypothetical or theoretical knowledge.

encode: the process of making new memories from stimuli.

entanglement: in quantum mechanics, when a property of two particles is connected (entangled) in such a way that changing the property of one particle instantaneously changes the property of the other particle, even when the two particles are separated by a great distance.

entorhinal cortex (EC): brain tissue connected to the hippocampus that contains the grid cells that produce reference points for spatial location.

entropy: a concept from physics to describe how much order (low entropy) or disorder (high entropy) exists in a given system. The arrow of time is often defined in terms of entropy because it is more probable for an ordered system to become disordered than the other way around. Additionally, events that are extremely unpredictable can be described as high entropy. The author asserts that a natural function of the mind is to reduce the entropy of experiences.

epigenetics: the study of how the expression of DNA over the lifetime of an individual can change due to factors in the environment.

episodic memory: the autobiographical memory of stimuli, as if replaying a video or audio recording. When episodic and semantic memories combine they create explicit memories.

explicit memory: the combination of episodic and semantic memories that produces a memory of an event (also called declarative memory). Explicit memory is a conscious thought, whereas implicit memory refers to a learned, automatic behavior.

fabrication: the creation of evidence, measurements, statements, etc. that are not based on reality.

falsification: the manipulation of real evidence, measurements, statements, etc. in order to bias perceptions.

Fomalhaut: name of a bright star visible to the naked eye that is surrounded by a large dust belt and planet discovered by the author.

Fomalhaut b: a very faint object close to Fomalhaut thought to be a planet in a very elliptical orbit that was discovered by the author using the Hubble Space Telescope. Fomalhaut b is officially named Dagon, though the author preferred the name Phantasos, one of the Greek dream gods.

frontal lobe: region of the brain above the eyes associated with attention and decision-making.

future: sister of the past.

Gallus gallus domesticus: a great way to say the word "chicken."

Global Oneironauts: oneironauts who serve society and government by accelerating knowledge and averting disasters.

Goldilocks sleep disorder: the author's term for a sleep disorder with just a few temporary awakenings during the night that allow more dreams to be recollected in the morning (but not too many awakenings that would undermine the health benefits of sleep).

Great Ambiguity: the author's phrase for the mixture of external stimuli, individual perceptions and thoughts that creates confusion between objective reality and subjective experience.

grid cells: neurons found in the entorhinal cortex that are activated as an animal moves through space, where the pattern of activation resembles a hexagonal grid.

Hebbian learning: an increase in the connection strength between two neurons as a result of repeated signals being sent from one to the other.

Heisenberg's uncertainty principle: discovery in 1927 by physicist Werner Heisenberg that measuring the position of a small particle to greater accuracy introduces greater uncertainty in knowledge of its momentum (mass times velocity), and vice versa. This is one of several aspects in quantum mechanics that implies that a sequence of cause and effect cannot be established to infinite precision (see Laplace's Demon).

hippocampus: brain tissue in the mammalian brain that processes memory and the perception of spacetime.

hippocampal formation: region of the brain containing the hippocampus, entorhinal cortex and nearby structures that performs the functions of memory and navigation. Also called the medial temporal lobe.

Hubble Space Telescope (HST or "Hubble"): a telescope about the size of a bus launched into Earth orbit in 1990 that was used by the author to discover a comet belt and planet orbiting the bright star Fomalhaut.

impersonal déjà vu: when déjà vu is not experienced because the time interval between the dream and the waking event is long enough that the dream memory has been forgotten (though recorded by other means). In other cases of impersonal déjà vu, the dream is recalled before the waking event occurs and therefore the resulting experience lacks the elements of surprise or novelty.

implicit memory: a form of long-term memory that refers to a learned skill, such as typing on a keyboard without intentionally recollecting the location of every key.

individualization: forensics term for determining that a specific individual is the only possible source of a latent fingerprint.

innatism: idea that the human mind does not start off as a blank slate (*tabula rasa*) but instead contains some basic content provided by God or other forms of spirituality.

jamais vu: French phrase for believing that you have never experienced something before when in fact the experience should have been familiar.

Laplace's Demon: thought experiment by Pierre-Simon Laplace where a powerful being measures all the components of the universe at one instant, and using the laws of nature determines the past and the future accurately.

light harvesting complex (LHC): components of photosynthetic organisms that contain chlorophyll and other pigments that convert light into energy in the form of electrons.

Local Oneironauts: oneironauts who specialize in solving day-to-day problems for the individual and society.

lucid dreamer: person who becomes aware that they are dreaming without waking up.

Machine Oneironauts: artificially created (possibly partly biological) devices and intelligence that detect information from the future.

machine déjà vu: when a machine oneironaut matches with high confidence a present-day event to the Dreamnet.

many worlds: an interpretation of quantum mechanics that every possible outcome of an event can become a reality, and each reality occupies a separate universe. Thus in a car accident there is one universe where you died, and one where you lived. The theory of many worlds is different from the *multiverse* theory that supposes many universes came into existence and they could have differences in fundamental properties. In the many worlds theory, our existing universe splits into many versions that contain every possible variation of every event, but the fundamental properties do not change.

many-worlds voyeur: the author's term for an observer who witnesses future events through dreaming but does not allow the events to materialize in their timeline; they conduct an observation and then delete their physical presence. Also called a counterfactual voyeur.

medial temporal lobe: synonymous with the hippocampal formation, which includes structures related to memory and navigation functions such as the hippocampus and entorhinal cortex.

memory palace: technique to consolidate and stabilize memories by placing items in an imagined three-dimensional space like a home or palace.

mens rea: Latin term for "mind that is guilty."

Metamindnet: a system where future experiences and knowledge are detected with technologies and methods that are not necessarily dependent on human dreaming.

museum of counterfactual history: the author's phrase for a place to learn about alternate human histories detected by the oneironauts.

nanobionics: incorporating nano-scale devices into organisms.

neural correlate: the brain tissue or function that is active during an experience (though not necessarily the cause of an experience).

neural entertainment: when the neural activity of performers and/or the audience is measured in real time and translated into other sensory modalities such as images, sound and motion.

neuron (nerve cell): a type of cell that specializes in electrical signaling through chemical changes.

neurotransmitter: a natural chemical needed to transmit a signal across the spatial gap (synapse) separating neurons.

Nostradaomus: the author's term for a person who perceives the future and changes timelines by inaction (similar to the Daoist wu wei).

occipital lobe: region of the brain at the back of the head responsible for vision.

ocode: a type of osignal that is designed to transmit specific information through symbolic experiences.

oneiro: Greek word for dream; pronounced <u>Oh</u>-near-oh.

oneironaut: a person who experiences their autobiographical future through dreams. Pronounced oh-<u>NEAR</u>-oh-not.

oneironaut phenomenon: the perception of a possible future experience through dreaming.

Oneironaut Olympics: games based on the abilities of individuals or teams to describe and navigate through future experiences, such as creating optimum timelines.

oproducer: someone who edits and augments audiovisual footage to produce a virtual reality experience for an oneironaut that is designed to communicate the ocode.

osignal: information transmitted from the future to the past.

pareidolia: cognitive blunder of perceiving patterns in random or incomplete information.

Pareto efficiency: the zero-sum game as applied to economics, engineering and evolutionary biology. A system is at the "Pareto front" when no changes can be made to improve one function of the system without decreasing the function of some other part of the system.

parietal lobe: brain region located at the crown of the head associated with mental imagery.

place cell: a neuron in the hippocampus that is activated whenever an animal is at a certain location in space.

plasticity (synaptic plasticity): the process of changing the connection pathways between neurons and the strengths of these pathways due to learning. The author asserts that dreaming of future events that ultimately do not occur in a person's autobiographical timeline means that other worlds have a physical existence in memory.

priming: improving the speed and accuracy of implicit memory recall for a stimulus by a willful pre-exposure to a related stimulus. The author asserts that the oneironaut phenomenon could be a type of innate reflex that has the function of priming.

quantified self: understanding yourself by routinely measuring your physical and/or mental states even when completely healthy.

quantum entanglement: see entry for entanglement.

quantum key distribution: using quantum entanglement as a safeguard against third-party eavesdropping of an encryption key sent between two parties.

quantum mechanics: a branch of physics that explains the observed properties of matter and energy at very small scales.

quantum nanophysics: the study of how ordinary matter at nanoscales can display quantum properties, such as an interference pattern.

real-time déjà vu: the author's term for recalling a memory of a dream moments before or during the waking experience.

recognition: the cognitive event of understanding that something is familiar and remembering why something is familiar, such as the past context or date.

reductionism: an approach to understanding very complex things by assuming that the smaller or simpler sub-components have sufficient explanatory power. For example, one might assume that if we can first understand how a few neurons interact with each other, then we would largely understand how 200 billion neurons work together because the larger network is a scaled-up copy of the smaller network.

reinforcing theory: idea presented by the author that continued practice explains why some people might improve their innate déjà vu ability through adolescence and into adulthood (as opposed to the compensating theory). The reinforcing theory suggests that the oneironaut phenomenon can be learned and strengthened.

reflex: an automatic event or process that results from a stimulus and resistant to willful control. The author suggests déjà vu is like a reflex.

REM: acronym for rapid eye movement defining a sleep stage that is associated with dreaming.

retrieval (recall): bringing memories to consciousness.

retrograde amnesia: the inability to retrieve explicit autobiographical memories.

ronin: Japanese word for "wave man" that means a wandering samurai who has no master. The author speculates that consciousness is like a continuous wave cycling through the past, present and future, with attention focusing on the parts of the wave that support the changing needs of the organism.

Scrooge effect: when the sequence of oneironaut dreams does not correspond to the same ordered sequence of future events.

second law of thermodynamics: gives an arrow of time because it establishes that order must change toward greater disorder; the future is a more disordered state. Even if something is assembled so that it becomes more ordered now than in the past, the energy required to do this activity results in a net disorder in the universe.

semantic memory: memories of knowledge that give a greater meaning to the episodic memories of events. Episodic and semantic memories bind together to form explicit autobiographical memories.

short-term memory: a small set of new memories that can be recalled only within a few minutes and do not need additional cognitive processing.

Socratic Gamble: the author's phrase for the personal and professional risks associated with publicly revealing your genuine and innermost thoughts and beliefs.

synapse: the connection between two neurons.

synaptic plasticity: see entry for plasticity.

Stage 1 sleep: sleep onset, also called "funny sleep" by the author because of hypnogogic imagery, sounds and other sensations, sometimes with involuntary jerky muscle movements. EEG oscillations are around 5 Hz.

Stage 2 sleep: EEG oscillations at 5 Hz are marked with 14 Hz activity called spindles; also called "light sleep."

Stage 3 sleep: also called slow wave sleep, deep sleep or "heartbeat sleep" by the author. The EEG shows electrical oscillations at 1 Hz.

STIS: acronym for the Space Telescope Imaging Spectrograph, an instrument installed aboard the Hubble Space Telescope that takes images and spectra. The author asserts the existence of a counterfactual universe where he does not become an astronomer and Fomalhaut's dust belt is imaged years later with STIS instead of ACS.

suprachiasmatic nucleus (Admiral SCN): a very small region of the brain that controls the organism's circadian clock or rhythm.

tall poppy syndrome: absurd social phenomenon where a person is attacked because they help others and/or accomplish great success.

tabula rasa: Latin phrase indicating that the human mind starts out as a "blank slate" only to be filled in later by experience (empiricism). Contrasts against innatism.

temporal lobe: side regions of the brain above the ears responsible for memory and language.

temporal lobe epilepsy: a recurring problem of neurons misfiring in the brain's temporal lobe which can cause the sensation of déjà vu.

thigmotaxis: when the perception of the location of objects, such as walls, influences the movement of an organism.

thrallphobia: the author's term to describe a person who fears having control over someone else's mind, or a person who fears having their mind controlled by someone else.

time cells: neurons that encode time, or a temporal sequence of events, in much the same way as place cells encode the location of an organism.

time settler: the author's term for people who enter suspended animation in order to live in a future time.

timeshot: a method for obtaining information from the future by studying the dreams of humans who will be placed in suspended animation for many years. The method could also be used with primitive organisms if the oneironaut phenomenon works in such organisms.

timeshot dilemma: the author's question of whether or not a person should go on a timeshot even though information from the future has been perceived through dreaming before the timeshot is carried out.

Trifid Nebula: also called Messier 20 or M20, the Trifid Nebula gets its name because its luminous region appears to be separated into three pieces.

ultradian rhythm: a body cycle that takes less than 24 hours, such as the various human sleep stages that repeat on a 90-minute cycle.

unconditioned response: a natural behavior that responds to a natural stimulus without the need of a prior learning experience. For example, salivation when food stimuli are presented is an unconditioned response.

unconditioned stimulus: a stimulus that produces a natural behavior without the need of a prior learning experience. For example, food is an unconditioned stimulus that leads to salivation.

vestibular system: the components of the body that provide sensations necessary for balance and orientation.

working memory: goal-directed thoughts—needed for brief intervals of time—that arise from retrieving and processing information from short and long-term memories. For example, in baking bread, one temporarily keeps in mind what ingredients and actions are needed, recalling which steps have already finished and which steps remain for the immediate future.

zero-sum game: when a new action results in gains for some parts of a system and losses for other parts of the same system, such that the net result is zero.

Appendix III: Captions for Chapter Heading Images

1. Twin Towers Falling

I captured this photo of a father and son sitting on a bench in the World Trade Center observation deck in 1982. By the time the boy would become the age of his father, this famous landmark would be destroyed in one of the most emotionally shocking events experienced by my generation. If precognition is really enabled through dreaming and this event was a strong visual scene for millions of people, how is it that no convincing precognitive dream record has appeared?

The answer could be that precognition does not happen; it is an illusion of the mind. Yet in studying my own experiences I determined that emotionally shocking events interfere with the perception of the future. Instead, simple stimuli occurring indoors that involve cognitive puzzles with time to self-reflect are some of the conditions that enable precognition.

I digitally blurred the periphery of the original photo in order to visually focus on the father and son, as if I am an undetected voyeur, which is indeed the experience of an oneironaut. The father's eyeglasses symbolize how our vision and attention need to focus, as if time momentarily stands still. Glasses are a recurring motif in *The Oneironauts*. The strong vertical bars comprising the structure of the building remind me of how time itself is sometimes compared to a film strip where a series of moments pass by us so rapidly that time seems continuous, without interruptions or boundaries. Yet, for the father and son this may have been a fleeting moment that they will never forget, as if time stood still.

2. Destiny, Hope and the Trifid Nebula

There was a very important reason to put the Trifid poster experience at the beginning of the book. Given my many precognitive experiences, if I had determined that fate cannot be changed, there would be no practical point to examining precognition. Why waste my time writing this book when I have new discoveries in astronomy to make? Yet a simple situation involving a ripped-up poster instilled a lasting belief that precognition makes it is possible to change events in your timeline. Hence, the rest of the book after Chapter 2 gains relevance.

This photo shows the same poster that I remember from eighth grade, yet I found this particular copy in the trash some 30 years later. It was already ripped and I merely taped it up on my wall with one side peeling off, just as I remembered my earlier experience. Amid the many visible stars, a nebulosity at the top seems split into three pieces, hence the name "Trifid Nebula."

3. The Heidelberg Dome

Heidelberg is a ridiculously cute town in the southwest corner of Germany, but my approach compares it to a maze designed for the rats that Professor Edward Tolman feeds in Chapter 7. Tolman demonstrated that the rat brain produces a cognitive map of its surroundings through prior experiences. Similarly, if you could put a giant glass dome over Heidelberg and study the actions of humans, you should be able to observe and measure the different factors that drive our behaviors. For me, the Heidelberg Dome demonstrated that goal-directed navigation is possible based on precognition instead of prior learning. The experimenter looking down on the Heidelberg Dome would conclude that I have excellent instincts originating from my genetic makeup. I would look up at the experimenter and claim that my genetic makeup produces the oneironaut phenomenon and when I make rational choices based on this phenomenon, it can mimic instinctual behaviors.

I took this photo of the Neckar River and the old town of Heidelberg in 2009. I digitally added what appears to be a glass dome, thereby emphasizing the book's recurring theme of lenses. The restaurant boat discussed in Chapter 3 would be anchored on the opposite side of the river, farther to the right of the boat that is visible in this photograph.

4. Fomalhaut

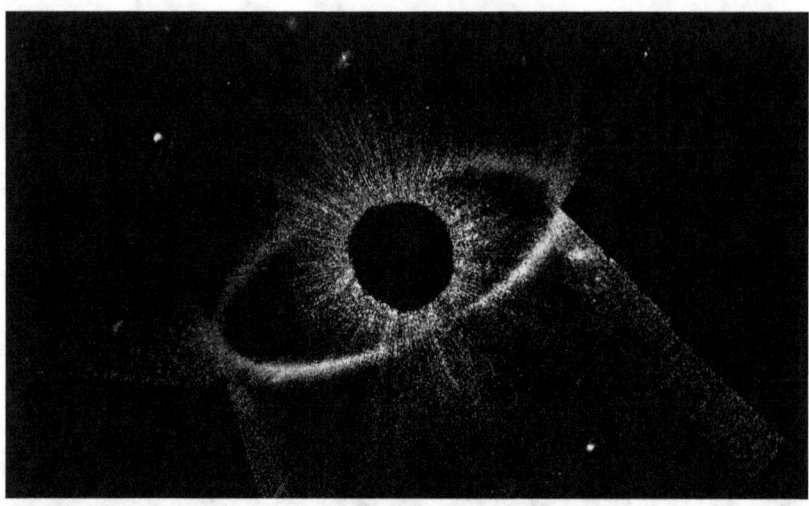

This shows my discovery, using the Hubble Space Telescope, of a planetary system surrounding the nearby star Fomalhaut. The circular black region near the middle results from a variety of methods that are used to cancel the light coming from the extremely bright central star. Without such methods the entire region is swamped with stellar glare and the planetary system is invisible. The elliptical ring resembling an "eye" is a large belt of fine dust orbiting Fomalhaut, much as our solar system has an asteroid belt and the Kuiper Belt. This image represents the first time in astronomy where a dust belt was noticeably displaced from geometric symmetry around the star. Looking more closely, you will notice that the circular black region representing the cancelled star is positioned to the upper right of the belt's center point. As Chapter 4 explains, I was the first human to see this phenomenon in 2004, but I recorded a surprising dream of an elliptical nebulosity and its displacement relative to the star in 1995.

5. Dissect the Oneironaut

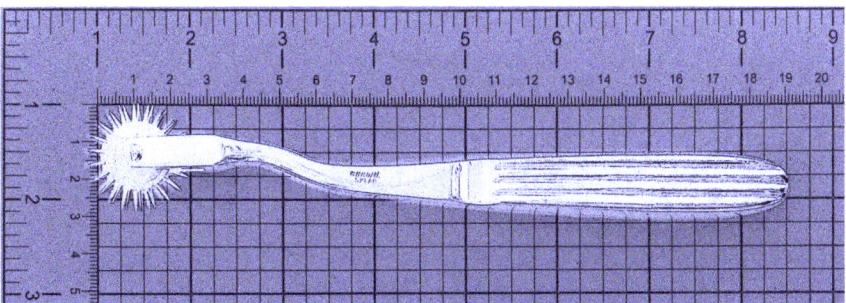

Chapter 5 concerns my personal observations and measurements of the oneironaut phenomenon. I am not a psychologist or physician, but my father was a neurologist and here I show one of his tools, a metal Wartenberg wheel. I recall him rolling this lightly across the limbs of patients, essentially testing the fitness of their nervous system. At face value the wheel appears somewhat menacing with its sharp spikes, adding a visceral visual element to the chapter title. However, I photographed it with a ruled backdrop to convey the fact that the tool is used for methodical observations and measurements.

6. The Physics of Time Using Nature's Swiss Army Knife

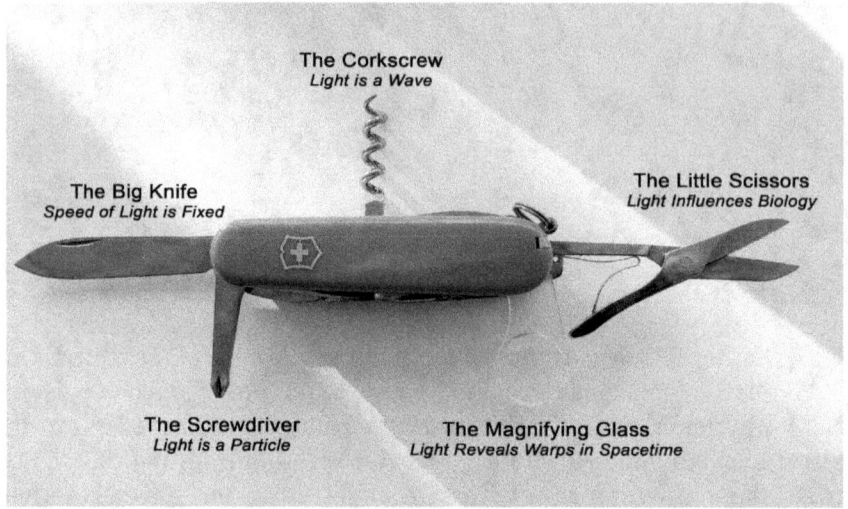

I photographed my Swiss Army knife to illustrate the main points discussed in Chapter 6. In Chapter 7 I discuss how the ancient Greek poet Simonides discovered a memory trick of mentally placing items in a virtual palace. So too with teaching and learning, I expect that over time the reader might forget everything I wrote in Chapter 6, yet this Swiss Army knife should serve as a more resilient visual memory aid when recalling the physics of light.

I added a light source coming from the upper left to create an interesting pattern of shadows, particularly with the corkscrew tool, which represents the wave nature of light. The magnifying glass represents another instance of this recurring symbol in the book. I decided *not* to add a label pointing to the Swiss cross to keep this aspect of physics—quantum entanglement—somewhat mysterious, out of reach, and set apart from the other tools, even though it is at the same time inseparable from the entire package.

7. Hippocampus

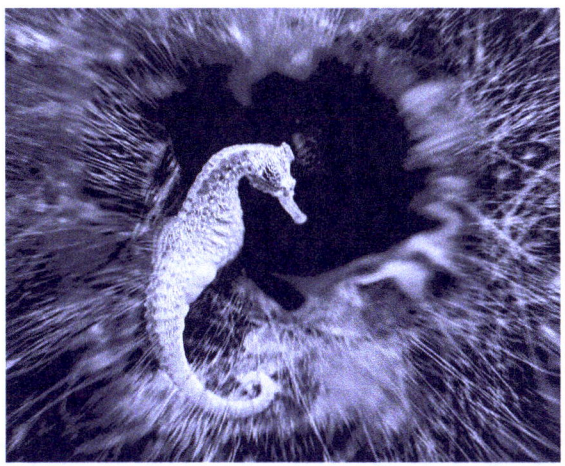

Chapter 7 describes the many important functions of brain tissue called the hippocampus, which is the modern Greek word for seahorse. I nominate the hippocampus as the "prime candidate as an organ for time travel" because it functions as the gatekeeper for memory and learning, as well as for our sense of space and time. These are all key properties of the oneironaut phenomenon.

I captured this photo of a seahorse at the Monterey Bay Aquarium in California, and then combined it with blurred and threaded features representing an emergent, disorganized and incomplete network. These surroundings lack structure, focus and meaning, suggesting that our current state of knowledge is extremely sketchy. Somehow the hippocampus connects us to a mysterious network extending beyond the borders of the photo.

8. The Oneironauts

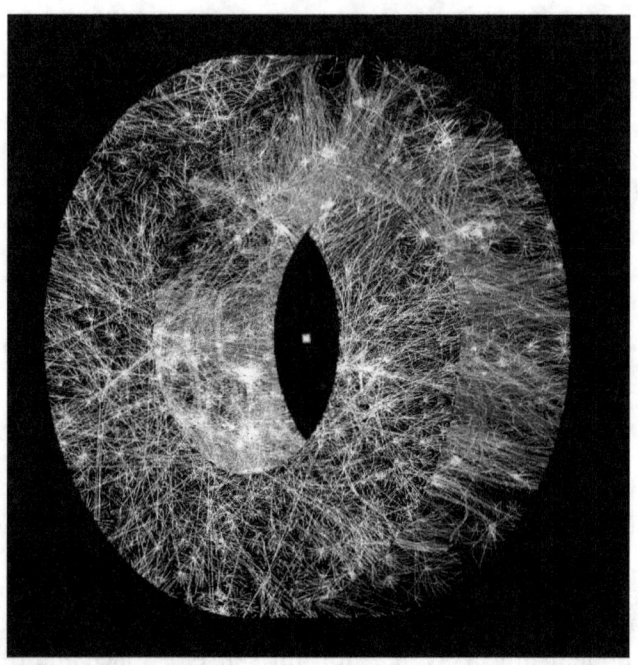

I created this "O" shape as the symbol of the oneironauts. It represents what the photo of Chapter 7 will evolve to a few hundreds of years from now. The seahorse is gone except for the eye shown here as a central point of light. Chapter 8 suggests that eventually we will have artificial means of observing the future that will not require human dreaming and the hippocampus. A network will still exist, but it will be cleanly defined. However, the "O" turns into itself with a geometry like a Möbius strip that can elicit a changing perspective. It might appear to be a wheel (of time) that is simultaneously rolling toward and away from you. The point of light in the middle may sometimes appear in front of the wheel, behind it, or within it. These elements convey my prediction that future humans will experience the past, present and future simultaneously. I believe we currently do this, but in the ambiguous, uncontrolled fashion represented by the Chapter 7 photo. In Chapter 8, the process is under our control and we have become engineers of time.

Appendix IV: Videos

"How luggage is lost"

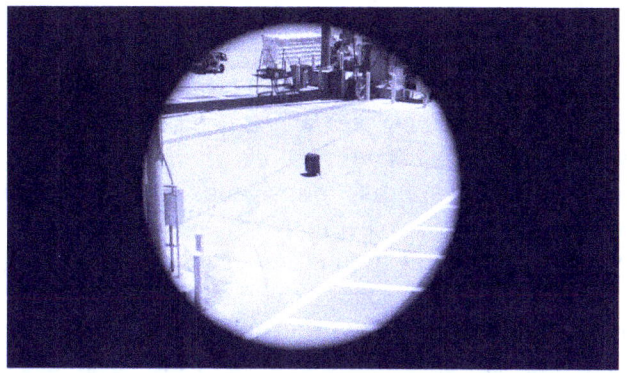

Available on YouTube https://youtu.be/KzgaNkmMxm4

My video of lost luggage at San Francisco International Airport is meant to be entertaining, engaging and suspenseful on the surface. However, the monologue that develops should be funny and thought provoking because this quiet observation of lost luggage evolves (and devolves) into an impromptu discourse on the nature of reality and the existence of God. What we see is so plain and simple, yet it leads us to question everything that we might believe. Most importantly, the monologue is selected to help emphasize several key themes in *The Oneironauts*, providing a whirlwind tour through portions of the book.

Spoiler Alert: Before you read the rest of my text below, take a look at the video carefully and see if you can pick out the symbolism and deeper meaning. You may discover quotes and references found in *The Oneironauts*, such as from the great historical figures and writers Epimenides, Aristotle, the Apostle Paul, Shakespeare, H.G. Wells, T.S. Eliot, and Miklos Radnoti.

After watching the entire video, what do you think the lost luggage symbolizes? Is it really just plain old luggage? Now that you have been warned, below is my perspective on what it means and how it is linked to the book.

Oh my God! That luggage just fell off a luggage truck.

The video begins with the exclamation "Oh my God!" instead of "Wow!" to establish that the narrator believes in God. We shall see how subsequent events will challenge that belief.

Landing upright was outrageous fortune.

In the final pages of *The Oneironauts* I refer to Hamlet's "To be or not to be" soliloquy. If I am going to write a book about dreams, it seems mandatory to reference Shakespeare's famous phrase "to sleep perchance to dream." The phrase "outrageous fortune" appears early in Hamlet's soliloquy, and it is exceedingly appropriate for the lost luggage. On the one hand it seems lucky that the luggage landed upright, yet the fact that it fell off the luggage cart in the first place is unlucky. Thus, the bag's fortune is good or bad depending on how you look at it. Moreover, the word "fortune" is tied to the concepts of fate and destiny that are contemplated throughout *The Oneironauts*.

I hope someone will see it soon.

We have now added two more ingredients to the story's theme. We started with God, then we talked about fortune or fate, and now we have introduced hope and the ability to see something. Can we hope to change the fate of this bag? Is hope a tactic? Which person or natural phenomenon will change its fortune?

Great! Just in time to pick it up.
But maybe he was driving too fast to see it.

Of course I had to reference the word "time" somewhere. However, *The Oneironauts* discusses how the ability to recognize information from the future requires slow and careful introspection. If you cannot slow down, you will not see much. Something that is obvious to a person in a quiet room standing still is completely invisible to a person with a goal of getting somewhere quickly.

Another luggage truck... Didn't see it again?
Oh come on! Get some glasses! The bag is right there.
The sequence of luggage trucks passing the bag without doing anything is astonishing and funny. However, I also call attention to using glasses to see clearly, which is a recurring theme in *The Oneironauts*. If you didn't notice glasses, lenses and mirrors as recurring symbols it may be fun to return to the book and realize that these are sometimes hiding in plain sight. In addition, this scene with the passing luggage trucks conveys two more aspects of being an oneironaut described in Chapter 8. First, just like I am a voyeur watching the fate of this lost luggage, seeing the future is also a voyeuristic experience. No one else can see what I see. Apparently, I can see the luggage, but the people driving the trucks do not see it. Second, in the psychology of the oneironauts (Chapter 8), a great deal of frustration can accumulate when one is powerless to alter the course of events.

Nooooo...what is happening?
It's like the country of the blind down there.
In Chapter 5 I referenced a guy called Nunez who is the protagonist of the classic H.G. Wells story *The Country of the Blind*. Nunez becomes trapped in a valley where all the natives are blind, and while writing *The Oneironauts* I found many parallels to his predicament. It's not merely the above problem of frustration or even superiority that one can see what others cannot see, but it is also the idea that no one would believe that seeing the future is even possible. In Wells' story the natives do not believe that Nunez has the fifth sense of sight. Thus one sees that the definition of a sense is established by consensus, and poor Nunez is labeled as completely insane. Another parallel is that the natives function perfectly well without sight. They do not need it. So too, at the end of Chapter 8 I remark that most people are perfectly happy not being able to see the future. And in my Preface I worry that I could be labeled as completely crazy to even suggest that this sense exists. Another reason I referenced H.G. Wells concerns his association with John Dunne, an aeronautical engineer who wrote a book in 1927 called *An Experiment with Time*. Like myself, Dunne was accomplished in his profession but also had precognitive dreams that he contemplated in his book. Thus, when I say "like some modern-day Nunez" in Chapter 5, I am also sending a secret nod to John Dunne.

Thank God. Someone is walking over to get it.

The narrator mentions God for the second time, thanking Him because having hope is justified and rational if a supreme deity exists that can magically intervene.

Does the bag even exist? Is this a waking dream about a lost bag?

Does the bag even exist?

Observing that no other human seems to know that the bag exists, the narrator starts questioning their own perceptions, going as far as to question if the bag is real. This refers to my definition of the Great Ambiguity in Chapter 2: reality can appear ambiguous because it is interpreted through our subjective thoughts and memories. For example, how can we trust our senses when we also have powerful and convincing dreams that mimic reality? My approach in *The Oneironauts* is to depend on the principles of the scientific method. Even though our minds distort reality, we can gain increasing confidence that a phenomenon is real through persistent observations, measurements, skepticism and communication.

Is this a waking dream about a lost bag?

How can the narrator be certain that they are awake and not dreaming? After all, the bag landed upright, which could be a construction of the narrator's mind. The people are also behaving bizarrely, just like in a dream. If dreaming contains real future experiences, then isn't some portion of dreaming identical to being awake? How do we know when this portion begins and ends exactly? These are some of the puzzles you will have to think about if you believe in the oneironaut phenomenon.

And now for the big reveal: Aristotle called hope a waking dream. The narrator's question now becomes "Is hope about a lost bag?" and the real title of the video is unveiled as *How hope is lost* instead of *How luggage is lost*. Aristotle basically asserted that hope is an irrational illusion that we embrace while fully awake. The quote thereby reinforces the narrator's emerging doubt that the bag is real. Fundamental questions about hope are also addressed from the very beginning of *The Oneironauts* in Chapters 2 and 3. If events in the future are predestined to happen, as in the story of Oedipus, then there isn't much point in knowing the future. Every intervention to change the future will be futile (i.e., hopeless). However, my oneironaut experiences reveal that events are not predestined. Hope is both real and rational because we have the ability to perceive the future, avoid undesirable events, and affirm favorable events, even when obstacles are encountered.

Yet this tinted window is real.

This video was shot from inside the airport through a huge piece of tinted glass. Since this obstacle is quite real, the narrator reasons that the experience concerns reality and not a dream.

Beneath the surface I am referencing a phrase from Chapter 8 taken from the Apostle Paul in 1 Corinthians 13:12, "For now we see through a glass, darkly; but then face to face: now I know in part; but then shall I know even as also I am known." Humans look at themselves in reflections, and early mirrors were of poor quality and somewhat dark. The Apostle Paul says that as long as we are alive we are never able to perfectly perceive God, like looking at ourselves in the poor mirrors of the time, but when we die the flawed mirror will dissolve away and we will find ourselves face-to-face with God. In *The Oneironauts* I adopt this symbolism to say that our ability to see the future is imperfect like the first mirrors, yet we have unrealized potential to improve the quality and clarity of what we can see.

I would be insane to start shouting.

This seems to follow logically from the last statement. The narrator cannot magically get past the real glass barrier and shout down to the people walking or driving past the bag.

However, the key words in this phrase are "insane" and "shouting." I am thereby referencing the Miklos Radnoti poem *Deathmarch* from Chapter 2, which was used to illustrate hope. In his case of tragic wartime captivity, Radnoti wrote "only a fool" would hope to escape, "But he's insane..." if he thinks he can return to a future that resembles his memories of the past. Nevertheless, he still has this hope, and to prove it, you can "shout" and he will stand up. So too, the narrator can hope that the lost luggage will be found and returned to its owner. Yet the narrator is a captive behind the tinted window and cannot change these circumstances. The narrator can imagine shouting, but since it will not work, what is the last thing they can do before they concede the situation is hopeless?

Oh Lord, hear my prayer.

Oh Lord, hear my prayer.

Oh yes, prayer! Since the narrator invoked God twice, it's only logical that they ask for His help to change the future of that bag. It is the only source of hope that the narrator can think of under the circumstances. As discussed in *The Oneironauts*, we believe that there is a supreme being that knows a lot about us, even our future. If this being can know the future, then it should be able to get around all obstacles, even tinted glass. If we put our faith in this being, then hope is never lost.

If you exist, then make this man pick up the bag.

So far the narrator has asked if the bag exists and if reality is really a dream. In their despair that nothing may be real, the narrator may hope that God is an anchor point; yet the narrator questions His existence as well. Like many people, the narrator hopes to find a "sign" that He exists. A scientist might phrase this differently: we wish to observe and measure an event in nature that is consistent with the hypothesis that God exists.

God has forsaken this unreal wasteland. Does God even exist?

When the man in the blue shirt walks past the bag, the narrator concludes that God does not care about this particular "unreal" spot on Earth. But could it mean that God does not exist at all?

Note that the phrase "unreal wasteland" has a more profound significance. On the surface I am reiterating doubts about reality, but I am also referencing the writer and Nobel Laureate T.S. Eliot who wrote *The Waste Land*. In Chapter 4 I mentioned the "intangible third man" from Eliot's famous poem (where the word "unreal" appears twice). When Sir Ernest Shackleton's expedition in Antarctica went horribly wrong in 1916 and three men hiked across the ice for 36 hours, they had the feeling or hallucination that there was an extra man marching alongside them. Eliot references Shackleton's story with: "Who is the third who walks always besides you?" (The poet made a minor mistake because the apparition should be counted as the fourth man.) In Chapter 4 I propose that this tenuous perception of another person is a fragment of your identity perceived through dreams of the future. In his book *South*, Shackleton states, "I have no doubt that Providence guided us." Providence reflects the belief that another force or deity guides destiny. In *The Oneironauts*, my counter-claim is that our perception of the future guides some decisions or instinctual choices, and ultimately we control our destiny.

Like H.G. Wells, Eliot was also influenced by John Dunne's book *An Experiment with Time*. Eliot's poem *Burnt Norton* begins with the words, "Time present and time past / Are both perhaps present in time future, / And time future contained in time past." In Chapter 5 I quote a larger portion of the poem that echoes my description of the timeless present.

Maybe I am praying to the wrong god.

The belief in God can be so strong that any developing doubts would be met by new explanations that rescue God. The narrator equivocates by allowing that God could still exist, but maybe in the form of someone else's god. The narrator's previous prayer simply got the name wrong.

Oh sacred deities of Europe, of Asia, of Africa and Australia and North and South America, plus Mother Earth too.

So how does one pray to all of the known gods throughout all of human history? Here the narrator decides to name all the inhabited continents, and even the entire planet, illustrating a heightening desperation to rescue that bag.

Show me you exist. Make this yellow man pick up the bag.
With such a magnanimous prayer having just been uttered in total desperation to rescue the bag, it's funny that the final outcome depends on a choice that a yellow man will have to make.

Previously a man wearing blue approached the bag but I chose not to mention the color of his shirt. Instead I now call attention to the yellow man in order to reference Dostoevsky. In Chapter 5 I quoted Dostoevsky and his description of epileptic seizures that can cause hallucinations and a sense of déjà vu. He has another excellent novel called *Crime and Punishment* where the color yellow represents the insanity of the lead character Raskolnikov. Thus, by pointing out the yellow man in the video, I am referring to both a portion of my book and the sense of insanity or dissonance created when lost luggage is ignored or not seen. Yellow man translates to "insane person" because from our point of view he is crazy not to rescue the bag. However, the narrator previously questioned their own sanity and perceptions.

Argh! There are no gods!
When the yellow man ignores the bag the narrator's impromptu thought experiment seems to reveal an absence of evidence for sacred deities.

Or there is a god out there without a name.
Never give up! As noted in Chapter 4, do we blindly take the absence of evidence as evidence for absence? The narrator concocts one last idea to save God and/or the gods. Perhaps we haven't yet discovered the true god that is really out there. This god would therefore have no name in any human language.

Oh Unknown God.
I pray that you will send someone to pick up that bag

...PLEASE...

In the last chapter of *The Oneironauts* I tell a story where ancient Athens was suffering from a hopeless plague, they prayed to all the known gods, nothing worked, and so they asked the Cretan poet Epimenides to help them. He travelled to Athens to see what was happening, hypothesized that the Athenian prayers had missed a god, told them to build alters to the Unknown God at the spots where some lazy sheep happen to snooze, and then the plague came to an end. The Apostle Paul arrived in Athens centuries later, he saw the temples to the god without a name, and then gave a speech where he declared that God was the Unknown God the Athenians were searching for originally.[180]

Two thousand years after Paul's visit to Athens, the narrator follows in these ancient footsteps to rescue the lost bag. However, the narrator already prayed to Paul's God and it didn't work. Therefore, God is not the Unknown God. Who, then, is the Unknown God?

He's stopping! He's looking ...he's thinking...

Finally, another human being except the narrator recognizes the bag. Why does the airport worker pause to think as he stares foreword into the distance?

Yes! The Unknown God and the bag exist!

Yes! The Unknown God and the bag exist!

Ah, who doesn't like a happy ending? By seeing the bag and saving it, the heroic airport worker shows us two things: (1) hope, as symbolized by the bag, is not lost, and (2) humanity, as symbolized by the airport worker, is the Unknown God that rescues hope.

As noted throughout *The Oneironauts*, knowledge of future circumstances gained through dreams can create the illusion of a supernatural force that controls fate or destiny. This "synthetic god" has consequences for our daily lives and personal identities, yet it emerges from the oneironaut phenomenon and not from a deity. As suggested in Chapter 2, the physical basis of hope is our vague recollection of a possible real future. When I ended up like the lost bag in Chapter 3, I hoped to find my group in Heidelberg because of the oneironaut phenomenon. In Chapter 8 I adopt the Unknown God as a way to give an interesting name to this exclusively humanistic framework. Nevertheless, Chapter 8 states that even though the oneironaut phenomenon mimics deity, it does not preclude anyone's religious beliefs.

In fact, if you believe in God then you have outrageous fortune. If God is on your side, then you can double your hope because the future can be changed through both the oneironaut phenomenon and by an all-powerful being. But if your actions and goals displease God, then you have to surrender hope because any changes you make toward a desired future can be countered by the all-powerful being.

On a related note, the faithful might argue that the biological process giving rise to the oneironaut phenomenon was provided by God to give mortals a chance to directly witness Providence in the briefest of glimpses. The implication is that I was meant to write *The Oneironauts* to bring readers closer to God; to help them see through the dark glass more clearly, as the Apostle Paul said. Indeed, the very last sentence of *The Oneironauts* hints at more to come.

That bag sat on the concrete for 15 minutes.
Thirteen trucks and twelve people on foot passed by it.

I actually shot many more videos than appear in *How luggage is lost*. However, I may have missed some trucks and people because I did not shoot video continuously. I counted a total of 15 trucks and 10 people on foot in the ensemble of my footage. For the end titles I invoked artistic license and changed the numbers to 13 and 12 to reference 1 Corinthians 13:12.

I can only hope it was returned to its owner.

Since the previous reference to Aristotle is somewhat obscure, here I provide the viewer one last hint about what the lost luggage symbolizes. "How luggage is lost" means "How hope is lost." Fortunately, the video shows how it is found again and returned to its optimal path. We should have faith that future humans will be guiding us because of the oneironaut phenomenon. This does not preclude anyone's faith in God or sacred deities. Such beliefs are OK, but if we hope to change the future, we need to have faith in the choices of humans.

About the Author

PAUL KALAS is an astronomer who searches for planetary systems around other stars using the most advanced telescopes in existence. He is an astronomy faculty member at the University of California, Berkeley, a research scientist at SETI Institute and an elected Fellow of the American Association for the Advancement of Science. His research career includes the publication of four breakthrough papers as first author in the leading scientific journals *Nature* and *Science*. In 2008 he announced the first optical image of an extrasolar planet orbiting the nearby star Fomalhaut using the Hubble Space Telescope (press conference pictured here; courtesy NASA), for which he was awarded the Newcomb Cleveland Prize in 2009.

Paul Kalas

NOTES

[1] Funkhouser, A. & Schredle, M. 2010, The frequency of déjà vu (déjà rêve) and the effects of age, dream recall frequency and personality factors, *International Journal of Dream Research*, Vol. 3, pp. 60–64.

[2] Ahem, in the spirit of complete honesty with the reader, I will admit my belief in the parking angel. You know, the one that helps you find a parking space if you really need one, but you must ask for help nicely, and say thank you afterward.

[3] Richard P. Feynman, *Surely You're Joking, Mr. Feynman*, ed. Edward Hutchings (London: Vintage Books, 1992), 130.

[4] Ruby, P. M. 2011, Experimental research on dreaming: state of the art and neuropsychoanalytic perspectives, *Frontiers in Psychology*, Vol. 2, Article 286.

[5] ...but not entirely. Psychology is involved in every aspect of experience. Therefore you could say that the reason I paid attention to this scene in my waking life and dreamed about it is that it resonated with aspects of my psychology involving flying. But the specific interpretation of dreams as only representing *symbols* of concerns in thought and emotion is what I am refuting.

[6] Schacter, D. L., Addis, D. R. & Buckner, R. L. 2007, Remembering the past to imagine the future: the prospective brain, *Nature Reviews Neuroscience*, Vol. 8, pp. 657–661.

[7] This pathway describes an "embolic stroke," but there are other types as well.

[8] Diogenes Laertius, *Lives of Eminent Philosophers*, translated by R. D. Hicks (Cambridge, MA: Harvard University Press, 1925); Note that Aristotle probably meant the exact opposite of my interpretation. Hope is an illusion, just like the images witnessed in a dream. However, the meaning changes if images in a dream depict reality.

[9] "Deathmarch" by Miklos Radnoti, translated and used with permission by Thomas Land http://www.pennilesspress.co.uk/annexe/radnoti.htm

[10] If an organism learns or manifests new adaptations during its lifetime, then the scientific jargon used is "accommodation" instead of adaptation. Adaptation refers specifically to new traits selected over many generations of a species. Since plants are included, an adaptation is not necessarily a behavior.

[11] Hagen, K. & Broom, D. M. 2004, Emotional reactions to learning in cattle, *Applied Animal Behaviour Science*, Vol. 85, pp. 203–213.

[12] Moore, L. G. 2001, Human genetic adaptation to high altitude, *High Altitude Medicine & Biology*, Vol. 2 (2), pp. 257–279.

[13] The 19th-century French scientist Pierre-Simon Laplace invoked this scenario, called "causal determinism" or "Laplace's demon," but this was before the quantum nature of the physical universe was discovered.

[14] The flip side of the same coin is that once I learned a new skill of recalling dreams and matching them to an experience, I would simply become very good at doing it again.

[15] http://www.nsf.gov/statistics/seind14/index.cfm/chapter-7/c7h.htm

[16] Kalas, P., Graham, J. R. & Clampin, M. 2005, A planetary system as the origin of structure in Fomalhaut's dust belt, *Nature*, Vol. 435, pp. 1067–1070.

[17] Kalas, P., Graham, J. R., Chiang, E., et al. 2008, Optical images of an extrasolar planet 25 light-years from Earth, *Science*, Vol. 322, pp. 1345–1348.

[18] Edward J. Weiler, *Hubble: A journey through space and time* (New York: Abrams, 2010), 11.

[19] *Science Friday* with host Ira Flato, National Public Radio, rebroadcast of previous interviews with Oliver Sacks, April 15, 2009.

[20] https://www.nasa.gov/content/hubble-highlights-recognizing-worlds-beyond-our-sun

[21] I actually preferred *Morpheus*, a different god of dreams, but this name was already used in astronomy. In the end, the International Astronomical Union selected the name of an ancient fish god called *Dagon*.

[22] Kalas, P. & Jewitt, D. 1995, Asymmetries in the Beta Pictoris Dust Disk, *The Astronomical Journal*, Vol. 110, pp. 794–804.

[23] When an astronomical image is oriented with north up, east is defined as the left side of the image. So the northeast direction is to the upper left of an image, southwest is to the lower right.

[24] Freud came up with the phrase, but the concept is certainly ancient. For example, Herodotus writes in *The Histories* how Xerxes, the new king of Persia, was warned repeatedly by a dream not to go against the Greeks. His wise advisor, Artabanus, consoled him, saying, "These visions are not divine…These visions that come wandering in dreams are usually the things that a man thinks of by day." Freud theorized that daytime events trigger *unconscious* wishes and conflicts.

[25] www.burnimpressions.com in Vermont sells the selfie-toaster, and you can definitely get the Jesus version, along with the Buddha version, Star of David, and so on and so forth.

[26] Translated by Edward MacCurdy (1939), as quoted in Stephen Jay Gould, *Leonardo's Mountain of Clams and the Diet of Worms* (New York: Harmony Books, 1998), 23–24.

[27] Shannon, C. E. 1948, A mathematical theory of communication, *The Bell System Technical Journal*, Vol. 27, pp. 379–423, 623–656.

[28] Explicit memory has also been called "declarative" memory, whereas implicit memory is also called "procedural" or "non-declarative" memory.

[29] The words of Brutus remind me that I've never had an oneironaut experience of looking in the mirror in the future. However, I think it is possible, especially if there were a surprising change in my appearance.

[30] James Joyce, 1922, *Ulysses*, The Project Gutenberg Ebook #4300 (Col Choat and David Widger, producers).

[31] AAAS Policy Alert—December 17, 2014

[32] As if to drive home the point in no uncertain terms, after the Fomalhaut b discovery, many colleagues at large conferences who could not recall my exact name would nevertheless address me as "the Fomalhaut guy." Fomalhaut had literally become my identity.

[33] Gurdon, J. B. 2006, From nuclear transfer to nuclear reprogramming: The reversal of cell differentiation, *Annu. Rev. Cell Dev. Biol.*, Vol. 22, pp. 1–22.

[34] John Donne 1623, *Devotions from Emergent Occasions, Meditation XVII*, quoted from *The Norton Anthology of English Literature, Vol. 1* (New York: W.W. Norton & Company, 1962).

[35] Sheri J. Y. Mizumori, "Preface: A place for place cells in hippocampal-dependent memory?" in *Hippocampal Place Fields Relevance to Learning and Memory*, ed. Sheri J. Y. Mizumori (Oxford: Oxford University Press, 2008).

[36] This is an old debate, with Aristotle and John Locke favoring *tabula rasa*—the human mind starts as a blank slate to become informed by experience later (empiricism). Plato, Descartes, and others favored *innatism*—the baby mind already has some basic ideas in it, but the only source would be something like a spirit or God. I'd suggest that the innatists should consider the oneironaut phenomenon instead. New ideas may come during dreaming of future life experiences.

[37] Wood, J. N. 2013, Newborn chickens generate invariant object representations at the onset of visual object experience, *Proc. Nat. Acad. Sci.*, Vol. 110, pp. 14000–14005.

[38] Also, the only scientist I know who built a cannon, fired it at a neighbor's home, and went to jail, all at the tender age of 11.

[39] No really, someone named this "stargazin." It involves a poor epileptic mutant mouse called Stargazer. Stargazin modulates the strength of a signal crossing the synapse (Chen, L., Chetkovich, D. M., Petralia, R. S., et al. 2000, Stargazin regulates synaptic targeting of AMPA receptors by two distinct mechanisms, *Nature*, Vol. 408, pp. 936–943).

[40] Charles Dickens, *A Christmas Carol* (London: Chapman and Hall, 1843).

[41] Based on definitions in Neppe, V. M. *The Psychology of Déjà Vu*, (Johannesburg: Witwatersbrand University Press, 1983); and in Brown, A. S., *The Déjà Vu Experience*, (New York, Psychology Press, 2004).

[42] A. S. Brown (2004) compiles the results of déjà vu frequency from surveys conducted in 42 different studies.

[43] Merkow, M. B., Burke, J. F. & Kahana, M. J. 2015, The human hippocampus contributes to both the recollection and familiarity components of recognition memory, *Proc. Nat. Acad. Sci.*, Vol. 112, pp. 14378-14383.

[44] As noted in the introduction, in a study of 444 people with an average age of 23.5 years, 95% reported déjà rêvé [Funkhouser, A. & Schredl, M. 2010, The frequency of déjà vu (déjà reve) and the effects of age, dream recall frequency and personality factors, *International Journal of Dream Research*, Vol. 3 (1), pp. 60-64].

[45] Baumann, C. R., Novikov, V. P. L., Regard, M., & Siegel, A. M. 2005, Did Fyodor Mikhailovich Dostoevsky suffer from mesial temporal lobe epilepsy? *Seizure*, Vol. 14, pp. 324-330.

[46] Fyodor Mikhailovich Dostoevsky 1861, *The Idiot*, translated by Constance Garnett (New York: Bantam, 1958), 218.

[47] For example: Kavallinis, G. P. 1977, Lithium in epilepsy, *Clinical Electroencephalography*, Vol. 8 (1), pp. 51-56.

[48] A related aspect is that my déjà vu experience has to be my own (autobiographical). For example, if you are going to have a serious accident in the future, the only way for me to dream about it is if I were to witness it directly, or understand that it happened indirectly, such as by hearing a story.

[49] Data presented in Alan S. Brown, *The Déjà Vu Experience*, (New York: Psychology Press, 2004).

[50] Luna, B. 2010, Developmental changes in cognitive control through adolescence, *Adv. Child Dev. Behav.*, Vol. 37, pp. 233-278.

[51] Casey, B. J., Getz, S. & Galvan, A. 2008, The adolescent brain, *Developmental Review*, Vol. 28 (1), pp. 62-77.

[52] Mitsuchima, D. 2010, Sex steroids and acetylcholine release in the hippocampus, *Vitamins and Hormones*, Vol. 82, pp. 263-277.

[53] Paus, T., Zijdenbos, A., Worsley, K., et al. 1999, Structural maturation of neural pathways in children and adolescents: In vivo study, *Science*, Vol. 283, pp. 1908–1911.

[54] Sowell, E. R., Thompson, P. M., Tessner, K. D. & Toga, A. W. 2001, Mapping continued brain growth and gray matter density reduction in dorsal frontal cortex: Inverse relationships during postadolescent brain maturation, *J. Neuroscience*, Vol. 21(22), pp. 8819–8829.

[55] McKenzie, I. A., Ohayon, D., Li, J., et al. 2014, Motor skill learning requires active central myelination, *Science*, Vol. 346, pp. 318–322.

[56] Another important process that increases brain function is called synaptic pruning—in childhood and adolescence the brain becomes more efficient by "pruning" the nerve cell connections that are not needed.

[57] Data presented in Brown, A. S. 2004, *The Déjà Vu Experience*, though many factors such as decreased interest and memory for the phenomenon with older age could explain the decrease in reporting déjà vu when asked.

[58] Krummenacher, P., Mohr, C., Haker, H. & Brugger, P. 2009, Dopamine, paranormal belief, and the detection of meaningful stimuli, *Journal of Cognitive Neuroscience*, Vol. 22 (8), pp. 1670–1681.

[59] Ngo, H.-V., Martinetz, T., Born, J. & Moelle, M. 2013, Auditory closed-loop stimulation of the sleep slow oscillation enhances memory, *Neuron*, Vol. 78, pp. 1–9.

[60] Diamond, J. 2010, The benefits of multilingualism, *Science*, Vol. 330, pp. 332–333.

[61] Neil Shubin speaking to host Ira Flato on National Public Radio, *Science Friday*, April 17, 2014.

[62] Take a superhero example such as the Flash, who can run at astonishing speeds. In the compensating theory, the Flash was born as a person unable to think or plan forward in time. Thus, he can only become aware of his dentist appointment the second he is supposed to be there, and developed amazing speed to get there quickly, compensating for his cognitive problem. He arrives at the dentist office just in time like everyone else, but he is rarely able to accomplish anything that is superior to other humans.

[63] Tulving, E. & Schacter, D. L. 1990, Priming and human memory systems, *Science*, Vol. 247, pp. 301–306.

[64] Warrington, E. K. & Weiskrantz, L. 1968, New method of testing long-term retention with special reference to amnesic patients, *Nature*, Vol. 217, pp. 972–974.

[65] Roberts, T. F., Tschida, K. A., Klein, M. E. & Mooney, R. 2010, Rapid spine stabilization and synaptic enhancement at the onset of behavioural learning, *Nature*, Vol. 463, pp. 948–952.

[66] Ghorayshi, A., "Famous Berkeley astronomer violated sexual harassment policies over many years, university investigation finds," *BuzzFeed News*, October 9, 2015.

[67] What actually happened later is that he stayed with the University of California as an emeritus professor, with access to all the university benefits of retired professors, such as his title and affiliation, library subscriptions, etc.

[68] It was a genuine watershed moment because for the first time it showed victims and journalists that the most powerful people could be held *publicly* accountable for sexual harassment. In the months following we would witness the downfall of many other scholars for sexual harassment. Two years after the Marcy debacle, the careers of film moguls such as Harvey Weinstein and Kevin Spacey would also end because of public sexual harassment allegations.

[69] Recall that both planets orbit the Sun. The Earth is closer to the Sun and finishes one orbit in 365.25 days. Mars finishes an orbit in 687 Earth days. As the Earth zips around the Sun faster than Mars, there are times when it is closer and times when it is farther from Mars.

[70] Leclair-Visonneau, L., Oudiette, D., Gaymard, B., Leu-Semenescu & Arnulf, I. 2010, Do the eyes scan dream images during rapid eye movement sleep: Evidence from the rapid eye movement sleep behaviour disorder model, *Brain*, Vol. 133, pp. 1737–1746.

[71] Heraghty, J. L., Hilliard, T. N., Henderson, A. J. & Fleming, P. J. 2008, The physiology of sleep in infants, *Archives of Disease in Childhood*, Vol. 93, pp. 982–985.

[72] Two different Zeo wireless sleep monitors were used in order to check for self-consistency. The sleep stage data from the Zeo system has been tested and validated against clinical polysomnography (Shambroom, J. R., Fabregas, S. E. & Johnston, J. 2012, Validation of an automated wireless system to monitor sleep in healthy adults, *J. Sleep Research*, Vol. 21, pp. 221-230.)

[73] Ficca, G., Fagioli, I. & Salzarulo, P. 2000, Sleep organization in the first year of life: developmental trends in the quiet sleep—paradoxical sleep cycle, *J. Sleep Research*, Vol. 9(1) pp. 1-4; Technically, infants have three sleep stages called active (analogous to REM), quiet (analogous to slow wave), and indeterminate or ambiguous. In the first year of life, active sleep is approximately 30% of total sleep.

[74] Cantero, J. L. & Atienza, M. 2000, Alpha burst activity during human REM sleep: descriptive study and functional hypotheses, *Clinical Neurophysiology*, Vol. 111, pp. 909-915.

[75] Another way to put it is that certain goal-directed behaviors that are part of a reward system, such as finding food every day, have outsized relevance for all organisms compared to something like viewing a nice sunset, which for most practical purposes has no consequences.

[76] Research by Dr. Art Funkhauser published online at http://funkhouser.dreamunit.net/

[77] Quoted from http://www.davidgorman.com/4Quartets/1-norton.htm

[78] Kounios, J. & Beeman, M. 2009, The Aha! moment: The cognitive neuroscience of insight, *Current Direction in Psychological Science*, Vol. 18, pp. 210-216.

[79] Wagner, U., Gals, S., Haider, H., Verleger, R. & Born, J. 2004, Sleep inspires insight, *Nature*, Vol. 427, pp. 352-355.

[80] As an alternative, one could also conjure up a more exotic explanation, such as having my consciousness entangled with those of my friends, so that I lived that experience through a surrogate consciousness. Let's leave that explanation for other types of books and stick to the learning model for the time being.

[81] Rothstein, J. 1951, Information, Measurement, and Quantum Mechanics, *Science*, Vol. 114, pp. 171-175, and references therein.

[82] Even if you try to reconstruct the egg, the energy used to perform this task still leads to an overall increase in entropy (e.g., while fixing the egg, you had

to eat dinner, which converted a whole lot of other whole food into bits of food in your tummy).

[83] Shannon, C. E. 1948, A mathematical theory of communication, *The Bell System Technical Journal*, Vol. 27, pp. 379–423, 623–656.

[84] In searching the literature for supporting material, I discovered that in 2006, Professor Karl Friston and collaborators independently proposed the concept of "free energy," which is similar to my entropy argument. The difference is that their version says the brain attempts to predict the future to reduce free energy (reduce uncertainty), whereas my version says that present-day information processed by the brain literally goes backward in time in order to reduce entropy. Basically, we agree that biology attempts to optimize function by minimizing surprise.

[85] Of course, you can say something like "I live 15 minutes away," which also equates a time interval for travel to a distance of travel.

[86] In addition to speed, a second factor in time dilation is that Ed lived farther away from the spacetime distortion created by Earth's mass, whereas most of us are stuck closer to this distortion.

[87] If Ed Lu had traveled close to the speed of light, then he could blink and suddenly find the Earth older by very many years. He could say that he "traveled" to Earth's future in the blink of an eye. What I mean by "time travel" is going to the future of a place and returning to the present of the same place, which does not happen in these hypothetical cases of traveling very fast.

[88] Einstein, A. 1936, Lens-like action of a star by the deviation of light in the gravitational field, *Science*, Vol. 84, pp. 506–507.

[89] Or if that's not nerdy enough for you, say "linear superposition" out loud.

[90] See Richard Feynman's lecture on the topic here: http://research.microsoft.com/apps/tools/tuva/#data=4|72036f54-7e17-4435-b972-a18050d5828b||

[91] http://feynmanlectures.caltech.edu/III_02.html#Ch2-S6

[92] Sclafani, M., Juffmann, T., Knobloch, C. & Arndt, M. 2013, Quantum Coherent propagation of complex molecules through the frustule of the alga *Amphipleura pellucida*, *New Journal of Physics*, Vol. 15, 083004 (7 pp).

[93] A mathematician-physicist called Roger Penrose, a colleague of Stephen Hawking in the study of black holes, is one such scholar.

[94] In Argentinian tango the leader would move their right foot back as the first step, but since this can cause collisions on crowded dance floors, the first step could be with the right foot forward.

[95] Gisin, N. 2009, Quantum nonlocality: How does nature do it? *Science*, Vol. 326, pp. 1357–1358.

[96] Or, a third, yet-to-be-discovered variable could also exist that explains both. Instead of the Swiss Cross causing the oneironaut phenomenon, it is this third variable that causes both the entanglement mystery and the oneironaut phenomenon.

[97] For example, in 2016 physicists developed a computer game called "Quantum Moves" that showed humans have a level of intuition regarding the behavior of quantum mechanics that is more sophisticated than any mathematical computation; Sorensen, J. J. W. H., Pedersen, M. K., Munch, M., et al. 2016, Exploring the quantum speed limit with computer games, *Nature*, Vol. 532, pp. 210–213.

[98] Scoville, W. B. & Milner, B. 1957, Loss of recent memory after bilateral hippocampal lesions, *J. Neurol. Neurosurg. Psychiat.*, Vol. 20, pp. 11–21.

[99] Technically the results could have been expected. In 1887, researchers removed the hippocampus of a rhesus monkey and discovered that, "His memory and intelligences seem deficient...Every object with which he comes in contact, even those with which he was previously most familiar, appears strange and is investigated with curiosity." (Brown, S. & Schafer, E. A. 1888, An investigation into the functions of the occipital and temporal lobes of the monkey's brain, *Philosophical Transactions of the Royal Society B*, Vol. 179, pp. 303–327.)

[100] "More permanent" means that a memory is *stable* against interference or confusion arising from other cognitive processes, and that recall is accurate, useful and quick over the long term.

[101] This is called "Hebbian learning" after the psychologist Donald Hebb who first proposed it in 1949.

[102] Pavlov's experiments define "classical conditioning." Psychologist B. F. Skinner worked on "operant conditioning." Classical conditioning focuses on involuntary natural reflexes, such as salivating in response to food stimuli. Operant conditioning creates or suppresses voluntary behaviors through positive and negative consequences.

[103] Rasch, B., Buchel, C., Gais, S. & Born, J. 2007, Odor cues during slow-wave sleep prompt declarative memory consolidation, *Science*, Vol. 315, pp. 1426–1429.

[104] Tolman, E. C. 1948, Cognitive maps in rats and men, *The Psychological Review*, Vol. 55 (4), pp. 189–208.

[105] O'Keefe, J. & Dostrovsky, J. 1971, The hippocampus as a spatial map. Preliminary evidence from unit activity in the freely-moving rat, *Brain Research*, Vol. 34, pp. 171–175.

[106] Hafting, T., Fyhn, M., Molden, S., Moser, M.-B., & Moser, E. 2005, Microstructure of a spatial map in the entorhinal cortex, *Nature*, Vol. 436, pp. 801–806.

[107] The regular, square pattern of a chessboard or floor tiles is used for simplicity, but this is not entirely accurate. A grid of squares has diagonals at 45°. The grid created in the brain has diagonals closer to 30°. The resulting pattern consists of interweaved hexagons, as shown in Figure 7-4.

[108] Pavlides, C. & Winson, J. 1989, Influence of hippocampal place cell firing in the awake state on the activity of these cells during subsequent sleep episodes, *The Journal of Neuroscience*, Vol. 9(8), pp. 2907–2918; Wilson, M. A. & McNaughton, B. L. 1994, Reactivation of hippocampal ensemble memories during sleep, *Nature*, Vol. 265, pp. 676–679.

[109] Pfeiffer, B. & Foster, D. J. 2013, Hippocampal place-cell sequences depict future paths to remembered goals, *Nature*, Vol. 497, pp. 74–79.

[110] Barry, C., Ginzberg, L. L., O'Keefe, J., & Burgess, N. 2012, Grid cell firing patterns signal environmental novelty by expansion, *Proc. Nat. Acad. Sci.*, Vol. 109 (43), pp. 17687–17692.

[111] DeLong, A. J. 1981, Phenomenological space-time: Toward an experiential relativity, *Science*, Vol. 213, pp. 681–683.

[112] In experiments with rats using rectangular enclosures with moveable walls, researchers found that grid cell spacing decreased in a smaller enclosure size, but only by 48% of the change in enclosure scale; Barry, C., Hayman, R., Burgess, N. & Jeffery, K. J. 2007, Experience-dependent rescaling of entorhinal grids, *Nature Neuroscience*, Vol. 10 (6), pp. 682–684.

[113] Recent experiments support my hypothesis that other forms of knowledge, not just spatial, have a neural representation similar to the EC grid (Constantinescu, A. O., O'Reilly, J. X. & Behrens, T. E. J. 2016, Organizing conceptual knowledge in humans with a gridlike code, *Science*, Vol. 352, pp. 1464–1468.)

[114] Raichle, M. E., MacLeod, A. M., Snyder, A. Z., et al. 2001, A default mode of brain function, *Proc. Nat. Acad. Sci.*, Vol. 98, pp. 676–682.

[115] Swallow, K. M, Zacks, J. M. & Abrams, R. A. 2009, Event boundaries in perception affect memory encoding and updating, *J. Exp. Psychol. Gen.*, Vol. 138(2), pp. 236–257; Horner, A. J., Bisby, J. A., Wang, A., Bogus, K. & Burgess, N. 2016, The role of spatial boundaries in shaping long-term event representations, *Cognition*, Vol. 154, pp. 151–164.

[116] So, if one is trying to be a professional psychic where you see one customer every 30 minutes, it would be fairly important for the psychic to leave the room and perhaps go to the bathroom before every customer arrives, just for the sake of flushing working memory of the previous customer.

[117] Mayes, A. R., Isaac, C. L., Holdstock, J. S., et al. 2001, Memory for single items, word pairs, and temporal order of different kinds in a patient with selective hippocampal lesions, *Cognitive Neuropsychology*, Vol. 18(2), pp. 97–123; Fortin, N. J., Agster, K. L. & Eichenbaum, H. B. 2002, Critical role of the hippocampus in memory for sequences of events, *Nature Neuroscience*, Vol. 5(5), pp. 458–462.

[118] MacDonald, C. J., Carrow, S., Place, R., Eichenbaum, H. 2013, Distinct hippocampal time cell sequences represent odor memories in immobilized rats, *J. Neurosci.*, Vol. 33(36), pp. 14607–14616.

[119] Eichenbaum, H. 2013, Time cells in the hippocampus: a new dimension for mapping memories, *Nature Reviews Neuroscience*, Vol. 15, pp. 732–744.

[120] Skaggs, W. E. & McNaughton, B. L. 1996, Replay of neuronal firing sequences in rat hippocampus during sleep following spatial experience, *Science*, Vol. 271, pp. 1870–1873.

[121] Fernandez, F., Lu, D., Ha, P. et al. 2014, Dysrhythmia in the suprachiasmatic nucleus inhibits memory processing, *Science*, Vol. 346, pp. 854–857.

[122] Theta is a Greek letter that looks like a zero with a horizontal line in the middle; you can find one in the first sentence of my Preface.

[123] Vanderwolf, C. H. 1969, Hippocampal electrical activity and voluntary movement in the rat, *Electroencephalography and Clinical Neurophysiology*, Vol. 26, pp. 407–418; O'Keefe, J. & Recce, M. L. 1993, Phase relationship between hippocampal place units and the EEG theta rhythm, *Hippocampus*, Vol. 3(3) pp. 317–330; Colgin, L. L. 2013, Mechanisms and functions of theta rhythms, *Annu. Rev. Neurosci*, Vol. 36, pp. 295–312.

[124] Seidenbecher, T., Laxmi, T. R., Stork, O. & Pape, H.-C. 2003, Amygdalar and hippocampal theta rhythm synchronization during fear memory retrieval, *Science*, Vol. 301, pp. 846–850.

[125] Burgess, N., Barry, C. & O'Keefe, J. 2007, An oscillatory interference model of grid cell firing, *Hippocampus*, Vol. 17, pp. 801–812.

[126] Jezek, K., Henriksen, E. J., Treves, A., Moser, E. I. & Moser, M.-B. 2011, Theta-paced flickering between place-cell maps in the hippocampus, *Nature*, Vol. 478, pp. 246–249.

[127] "Survival" is the common usage term, but "reproduction" would be more accurate. The set of traits that maximizes how many offspring you can produce within the environment is the critical end game in the context of natural selection.

[128] Noor, E. & Milo, R. 2012, Efficiency in evolutionary trade-offs, *Science*, Vol. 336, pp. 1114–1115.

[129] Let's not give too much credit to the mammalian brain. Recall that other animals, such as the octopus, not only change their brain states, but can consciously manipulate the properties of their skin to accomplish various functions, such as protection from predators, attraction of mates and capture of prey.

[130] Alan S. Brown (2004) compiled at least 50 different explanations for déjà vu that have appeared in the literature.

[131] Loftus, E. F. 1993, The reality of repressed memories, *Am. Psychol.*, Vol. 48, pp. 518-537.

[132] Pat Conroy speaking at *An Evening with Pat Conroy*, Herbst Theater, San Francisco, City Arts & Lectures, February 16, 1993.

[133] Barry, C. et al. and Yartsev, M. M. et al. 2012, Models of grid cells and theta oscillations, *Nature*, Vol. 488, pp. E1-E3.

[134] Ratman's Angels is based on presentations given by my colleague at UC Berkeley, Professor Michael Yartsev, and his published work, Yartsev, M. M. & Ulanovsky, N. 2013, Representation of three-dimensional space in the hippocampus of flying bats, *Science*, Vol. 340, pp. 367-372, and references therein. In 2014 the Rat Doctors (E. Moser, M.-B. Moser & J. O'Keefe) won the Nobel Prize in Physiology or Medicine.

[135] Berdahl, A., Torney, C. J., Ioannou, C. C., Faria, J. J. & Couzin, I. D. 2013, Emergent sensing of complex environments by mobile animal groups, *Science*, Vol. 339, pp. 574-576.

[136] I once swam above a school of fish for about a kilometer and noticed that instead of seeking pockets of darkness for protection, their behavior maximized the goal of finding sparse food sources along the sea floor.

[137] I would call these the "zombie rules." This is any pair of rules that involve social cohesion and a simple response to a stimulus. After all, zombies also follow two rules: they attack quickly only when a non-zombie is detected, otherwise they are slow, and they stick together at all times. Thus the threat that emerges from a horde of zombies is much greater than that of any one zombie.

[138] Kong, Q., Allen, R. M., Schreier, L. & Kwon, Y.-W. 2016, MyShake: A smartphone seismic network for earthquake early warning and beyond, *Science Advances*, Vol. 2 (2), 8 pp.

[139] Horikawa, T., Tamaki, M., Miyawaki, Y. & Kamitani, Y. 2013, Neural decoding of visual imagery during sleep, *Science*, Vol. 340, pp. 639-642.

[140] Kay, K. N., Naselaris, T., Prenger, R. J. & Gallant, J. L. 2008, Identifying natural images from human brain activity, *Nature*, Vol. 452, pp. 352–355.

[141] *Bruce Lee: A Warrior's Journey*, 2000, Warner Home Video.

[142] Dream games have already started showing up. For example, "DreamThrower" attempts to influence your dream content by external stimuli, and then you can send the stimuli to other participants, who then see if their resulting dreams match your dreams (Kamal, N. H., Hajri, A. A. & Fels, S. 2012, DreamThrower: An audio/visual display for influencing dreams, *Entertainment Computing*, Vol. 3, pp. 121–128.)

[143] Koch, C. & Reid, R. C. 2012, Observatories of the mind, *Nature*, Vol. 483, pp. 397–398.

[144] http://www.alleninstitute.org/

[145] http://www.braininitiative.org

[146] *The Human Brain Project—A report to the European Commission*, 2012, HPB-PS Consortium, Lausanne.

[147] Modern experiments are summarized in Mossbridge, J. A. & Radin, D. 2018, Precognition as a form of introspection: A review of the evidence, *Psychology of Consciousness: Theory, Research, and Practice*, Vol. 5, pp. 78–93. For an autobiographical study by a psychology professor, see: Carlyle T. Smith, *Heads-Up Dreaming* (San Francisco: Turning Stone Press, 2014).

[148] Villeda, S. A., Plambeck, K. E., Middeldorp, J. et al. 2014, Young blood reverses age-related impairments in cognitive function and synaptic plasticity in mice, *Nature Medicine*, Vol. 20(6), pp. 659–663.

[149] Weber, F., Chung, S., Beier, K., Xu, M., Luo, L. & Dan, Y. 2015, Control of REM sleep by ventral medulla GABAergic neurons, *Nature*, Vol. 526, pp. 435–438.

[150] Anguera, J. A., Boccanfuso, J., Rintoul, J. L., et al. 2013, Video game training enhances cognitive control in older adults, *Nature*, Vol. 501, pp. 97–100.

[151] Ranganath, C. & Rainer, G. 2003, Neural mechanisms for detecting and remembering novel events, *Nature Reviews Neuroscience*, Vol. 4, pp. 192–202.

[152] Parris, K. "Video games could be the prescription drug of the future," *Tom's Hardware*, March 31, 2014.

[153] https://thedragonflywoman.com/2012/04/06/fabulous-salties/

[154] Harland, D. P. & Jackson, R. R. 2000, 'Eight-legged cats' and how they see—a review of recent research on jumping spiders (Araneae: Salticidae), *Cimbebasia*, Vol. 16, pp. 231–240.

[155] Tarsitano, M. S. & Jackson, R. R. 1997, Araneophagic jumping spiders discriminate between detour routes that do and do not lead to prey, *Anim. Behav.*, Vol. 53, pp. 257–266.

[156] Nestler, E. J. 2014, Epigenetic mechanisms of depression, *JAMA Psychiatry*, Vol. 71 (4), pp. 454–456.

[157] Wong, M. H., Giraldo, J. P., Kwak, S.-Y., et al. 2016, Nitroaromatic detection and infrared communication from wild-type plants using plant nanobionics, *Nature Materials*, Advance Online Publication, October 31, 2016.

[158] Students of physics may recognize this conundrum as Maxwell's demon—a hypothetical being can decrease entropy in a closed chamber by allowing only high entropy (warm) gas to leave the chamber, thus violating the second law of thermodynamics. Hungarian physicist Leo Szilard suggested that the overall cost for the demon to execute this task would in fact result in a net increase in entropy instead of a decrease.

[159] Andrews, T. M. "Facebook's Mark Zuckerberg apologizes for 'tone deaf' virtual trip to Puerto Rico," *The Washington Post*, October 11, 2017.

[160] Jonsson, K. I., Rabbow, E., Schill, R. O., Harms-Ringdahl, M. & Rettberg, P. 2008, Tardigrades survive exposure to space in low Earth orbit, *Current Biology*, Vol. 18 (17), R729–R731.

[161] Tsujimoto, M., Imura, S. & Kanda, H. 2016, Recovery and reproduction of an Antarctic tardigrade retrieved from a moss sample frozen for over 30 years, *Cryobiology*, Vol. 72, pp. 78–81.

[162] Legendre, M., Baroli, J., Shmakova, L., et al. 2013, Thirty-thousand-year-old distant relative of giant icosahedral DNA viruses with a pandoravirus morphology, *Proc. Nat. Acad. Sci.*, Vol. 111 (11) pp. 4274–4279.

163 Jonkers, H. M. 2011, Bacteria-based self-healing concrete, *Heron*, Vol. 56 (1), pp. 1–12.

164 Jared Diamond, *Guns, Germs and Steel: The Fates of Human Societies* (New York: W.W. Norton, 1997).

165 "Episode 3—Into the Tropics" *Guns, Germs, and Steel,* produced by Lion Television, broadcast on PBS, 2005.

166 Relatively speaking. Dr. Manyando said the following: "To be frank with you, Jared, I wouldn't say I'm used to this, because I don't think there's anyone who can be used to sickness and eventually death, especially of people that you love so very much and are a part of you."

167 For example, in the classic *Star Trek* episode "The Tholian Web," a rift in spacetime can make two worlds or universes interact (termed "interphase"). Unfortunately this rift also causes the human brain to malfunction and everyone murders each other.

168 https://archive.org/

169 Soltas, E. & Stephens-Davidowitz, S., The Rise of Hate Search, *The New York Times*, December 12, 2015.

170 Moyer, C. "How Google's AlphaGo beat a Go world champion," *The Atlantic*, March 28, 2016. Amazingly, the chief scientist in the 1973 science fiction film *Westworld* would also say, "In some cases they [the robots] have been designed by other computers. We don't know exactly how they work." By 2016, these statements were being made under real-world circumstances.

171 George Orwell, *Nineteen Eighty-four* (New York: New American Library, 1949), 26.

172 Rule 402, Federal Rules of Evidence (https://www.law.cornell.edu/rules/fre)

173 Holpuch, A., McDonald, H. & Mayton, J. "Six people killed and seven injured in balcony collapse at party in California," *The Guardian*, June 17, 2015.

174 Marc Goodman, *Future Crimes* (New York: Anchor Books, 2015), 222.

[175] I adopted the metaphor of a black hole because I think there is a genuine scientific question if information can escape a real black hole if the oneironaut phenomenon is real. If in the future an oneironaut is stuck within a black hole, can the oneironaut dream about the experience now when they are outside of it, or is the osignal trapped within a black hole just like everything else?

[176] Hu, Y.-F., Dawkins, J. F., Cho, H. C., Marban, E. & Cinolani, E. 2014, Biological pacemaker created by minimally invasive somatic reprogramming in pigs with complete heart block, *Science Translational Medicine*, Vol. 6 (245), pp. 1–10.

[177] Vierbuchen, T., Ostermeir, A., Pang, Z. P., Kokubu, Y., Suchof, T. C. & Wernig, M. 2010, Direct conversion of fibroblasts to functional neurons by defined factors, *Nature*, Vol. 463, pp. 1035–1041.

[178] Robinson, A. 2018, Did Einstein really say that? *Nature*, Vol. 557, pp. 30.

[179] Steven Johnson, *How we got to now: Six innovations that made the modern world* (New York: Riverhead Books, 2014).

[180] Indeed, in *The Summa Theologica*, St. Thomas Aquinas argued that God couldn't have a name because names are given to the corporeal things that God created and which we have the capacity to perceive. We do not have the capacity to fully perceive God, and therefore a name is inadequate.

INDEX

24-hour déjà vu, 114, 200

alien, 151, 202, 257, 269, 285
Allen Institute for Brain Science, 238
allocentric, 37–38, 187, 243
AlphaGo, 264
Ammon's horn, 180
anterograde amnesia, 182, 183
Apollo 11, 239
Apostle Paul, 283
Aristotle, 24, 36–37, 245, 315, 318, 324
arrow of time, 162

Bargain Universe, 28, 33, 35, 39, 225, 251, 253, 265
beholder's share, 71–77, 108, 147, 167, 211, 217, 258, 289
beta Pic, 58
Big Knife, 153
black hole, 162, 163, 275
Bohr, Niels, 167
Boston Marathon bombing, 118, 249, 260
BRAIN Initiative, 238
brazen head, 94, 219, 267
Brown, Alan, 117, 132, 133
bubblebrain, 279, 287

Captain Clock, 151–152, 167, 175, 254, 267, 275
causation, 154, 203
cell reprogramming, 278
chronoengineering, 221
Cicero, 198
circadian rhythm, 122, 153, 202
Clampin, Mark, 48, 52, 55
cognitive blunder, 8, 44, 69, 118, 145
cognitive map, 34–35, 189, 191, 219, 309
compensating theory, 110–111
confirmation bias, 44, 57, 61
confusion matrix, 144
consolidation, 114, 183, 184, 185, 186, 241
counterfactual definiteness, 134
counterfactual déjà vu, 134
counterfactual experience, 135, 233, 237, 246, 251, 254, 274, 282
counterfactual history, 257–258

counterfactual responder, 248
cryptobiosis, 251–253
cryptomnesia, 9, 43, 138, 228

Dali, Salvador, 10
day residue, 58–59, 62, 64, 74–75, 138, 223, 228
default mode network, 199
déjà rêvé, 2, 98
déjà vu, 2
destiny, 5, 19, 28, 40–41, 82, 316, 321, 323
Disney, 73, 115–116, 288
dopamine, 91, 106
Dostoevsky, 99, 182, 288, 322
double-slit experiment, 165
dream diary, 102
dream function, 148
Dreamnet, 216–248, 263–280
duality, 163

Earth, 46, 95, 119, 176, 202, 284
EEG, 121
egocentric, 36–38, 180, 187, 217, 243
Einstein, Albert, ii, 46, 157, 160, 165–167, 175, 187, 282, 288
entanglement, 171, 173, 175, 207, 245, 312
entorhinal cortex, 181
entropy, 139, 147, 148–149, 247, 334, 342
Epimenides, 283
episodic memory, 78–79, 287
event boundaries, 199
Everett, Hugh, 169
explicit memory, 7, 78–79, 142, 182
extinction, 255

fabrication, 65, 66
false memories, 118, 211
false negative, 142–143, 224
false positive, 50, 51, 65, 138, 142–145
falsification, 65, 66
fate, 5, 10, 12–23, 29, 34, 40–41, 83, 308, 316–317, 323
Feynman, Richard, 8, 20, 167, 170
fingerprint, 240, 272
Fomalhaut, 43, 55, 63–65, 75–88, 102–107, 114, 118–124, 130, 138–142, 199, 210–212, 221, 235, 240, 242, 283, 287–292, 304, 310, 325, 330
free will, 5, 17, 40, 82
Freud, Sigmund, 58

Gallant, Jack, 222
global oneironaut, 247
God, 262, 281
Graham, James, 48, 55, 60, 74–77, 210
Great Ambiguity, 206
grid cells, 190
Gulliver's Travels, 152, 195

Haycart, 2–12, 25, 63, 105–116, 122, 124, 130, 138–141, 177, 198
heartbeat sleep, 122
Heidelberg, 28
hippocampus, 179
hive mind, 219
hope, 5, 23, 40, 316–324
Hubble Space Telescope, 4, 28, 47, 66, 83, 88, 159, 238, 290, 310, 325
Human Brain Project, 239

IAPO, 229
identity, 79, 85, 89, 254, 284
illusion, 2–10, 14, 23, 41, 72, 180, 195, 199, 210, 258, 307, 319, 323
impersonal déjà vu, 114
implicit memory, 78, 182
individualization, 240, 272
instinct, 34
intuition, 35, 186, 235

jamais vu, 100, 211
Janus, 20, 70, 79, 179, 210, 271, 289
Jesus toast, 44, 62–63, 105
Jewitt, David, 48, 55, 56, 59, 70, 74–77, 108, 289
Joyce, James, 80

Koch, Christof, 238

Lao-Tzu, 7
learning, 20, 23, 36, 87, 104, 120, 132, 135, 179, 184, 187, 268
Leonardo da Vinci, 67–68, 72
local oneironaut, 230
Loewi, Otto, 91–92
lucid dreamer, 122

machine déjà vu, 266
machine oneironaut, 230, 270
many worlds, 14, 16, 21, 89, 169, 245, 252, 288

many-worlds voyeur, 231, 269
Mars, 40, 88, 119, 190, 250–251, 257, 268
matched filter, 143
Metamindnet, 216, 230, 268–271
Milky Way, 45
Molaison, Henry Gustav, 182
Museum of Counterfactual History, 257
myelination, 104

NASA, 48, 52, 54, 83, 292, 325
National Air and Space Museum, 54
neural correlate, 189, 193, 199, 201, 241
neural entertainment, 243
neuron, 8, 16–19, 75–77, 114, 184, 201
neurotransmitter, 91, 104, 105
Newton, Isaac, 68, 164
Nostradamus, 137, 291
novelty, 87, 117–118, 131, 139–141, 146, 193, 210, 226, 232, 240, 242

ocode, 217, 232
odating, 236
omoney, 234
oneironaut phenomenon, 4, 15
oneironauts, 4
oproducer, 248
osignal, 18, 70, 120, 139, 140–143, 216–218, 234–235, 247, 267–268
owar, 236

paradox, 7, 16, 35, 80, 166
paradoxical sleep, 121
pareidolia, 43–44, 62, 71, 105
Pareto efficiency, 207
Pareto front, 208, 247, 262
Pavlov's dogs, 184
photosynthesis, 176
place cells, 129, 189
polio vaccine, 90
Poultry Matrix, 85–87, 204, 240
predictable, 148
priming, 107, 111
protoDreamnet, 222
pseudodivine knowledge, 89
purpose, 17, 85, 89, 254, 279, 281, 284

quantum mechanics, 134, 167–178, 213, 298
quantum mind, 172

Radnoti, Miklos, 24, 315, 319
Ramon y Cajal, Santiago, 90
real-time déjà vu, 113, 200
reflex, 101, 111, 129
REFO branch, 237
reinforcing theory, 110
relativity, 157
REM, 122, 241
retrograde amnesia, 183
Rubik's Cube, 17–18

Sacks, Oliver, 53
Sagan, Carl, 27, 65, 117
scientific method, i, ii, 69, 89, 318
Scrooge effect, 120
second law of thermodynamics, 147
self, 79, 205
self-fulfilling prophecy, 17, 28, 30, 133, 142, 223
semantic memory, 78, 79, 287
Shakespeare, William, 80, 315, 316
Shroud of Turin, 113, 119, 223
signal-to-noise ratio, 141–142, 146
Simonides, 198
skepticism, ii, 3, 7, 53, 66, 69, 92, 105, 118, 199, 212
sleep, 120, 148, 183, 192, 203, 205, 209, 241
Socrates, i, ii, 292
Stage 1 sleep, 121
Stage 2 sleep, 121
Stage 3 sleep, 122
suprachiasmatic nucleus, 153
Svalbard Global Seed Vault, 255
synaptic plasticity, 185, 341
synthetic god, 152, 282
synthetic human, 247, 278

tall poppy syndrome, 12, 53
temporal lobe epilepsy, 99
The Great Ambiguity, 10–14, 36, 261
theta oscillation, 203, 207, 214
thigmotaxis, 127
thrallphobia, 262
time cells, 201
time dilation, 154, 162
time machine, 18, 101, 163, 179, 205
time settlers, 253

timeshot, 251–255
Tolman, Edward, 187–191, 245, 292, 309
Trifid Nebula, 5–25, 44–46, 63, 80–82, 89, 100, 113, 135, 170–171, 245, 308
true negative, 143
true positive, 138, 142–145, 224

ultradian rhythm, 122

virtual déjà vu, 135

wave function, 168–171
working memory, 200
World Trade Center, 2, 4, 25, 47, 64, 307

zero-sum, 207–209, 262

www.ingramcontent.com/pod-product-compliance
Lightning Source LLC
Chambersburg PA
CBHW052010070526
44584CB00016B/1693